VILLAINS, SCOUNDRELS, AND ROGUES

VILLAINS, SCOUNDRELS, AND ROGUES

Incredible True Tales of
MISCHIEF *And* MAYHEM

Paul Martin

Prometheus Books

59 John Glenn Drive
Amherst, New York 14228

Published 2014 by Prometheus Books

The Internet addresses listed in the text were accurate at the time of publication. The inclusion of a website does not indicate an endorsement by the author(s) or by Prometheus Books, and Prometheus Books does not guarantee the accuracy of the information presented at these sites.

Prometheus Books recognizes the following registered trademarks mentioned within the text: Amazon.com®, Avon®, Chevrolet®, Greatest Vitamin in the World®, Golden Globe®, Ivory Soap®, Orange Glo®, Oscar®, OxiClean®, Pocket Fisherman®, Rolls-Royce®, YouTube®

An abridged version of the chapter titled "Lincoln's Missing Bodyguard" was originally published by the Smithsonian Institution.

Cover image © 2014 Media Bakery
Cover design by Nicole Sommer-Lecht

Inquiries should be addressed to
Prometheus Books
59 John Glenn Drive
Amherst, New York 14228
VOICE: 716–691–0133
FAX: 716–691–0137
WWW.PROMETHEUSBOOKS.COM

18 17 16 15 14   5 4 3 2 1

Library of Congress Cataloging-in-Publication Data

Martin, Paul, 1946 June 6-
    Villains, scoundrels, and rogues : incredible true tales of mischief and mayhem / by Paul Martin.
        pages cm
    Includes bibliographical references and index.
    ISBN 978-1-61614-927-7 (paperback) — ISBN 978-1-61614-928-4 (ebook)
    1. Criminals—United States—Case studies. 2. Rogues and vagabonds—United States—Case studies. 3. Outlaws—United States—Case studies. 4. Immorality—Case studies. 5. United States—Civilization. I. Title.

HV6785.M37 2014
364.1092′273—dc23
                                                                                    2013037712

Printed in the United States of America

*For Donald George Romero, mentor, friend,
and a colorful rogue in his own right*

CONTENTS

Acknowledgments   9

Introduction   11

VILLAINS

1. Merchant of Misery—James DeWolf   15
2. The Cutthroat Captain of Cave-In-Rock—Samuel Mason   23
3. Architect of a Tragedy—John Chivington   29
4. The Late, Unlamented Little Pete—Fong Ching   37
5. The Killer They Called Hell's Belle—Belle Sorensen Gunness   45
6. Partners in Perfidy—Isaac Harris and Max Blanck   53
7. Chicago's Florist-Mobster—Dean O'Banion   61
8. A Huckster's Rise and Fall—John Brinkley   69
9. Hitchcock's Hideous Inspiration—Ed Gein   77

SCOUNDRELS

10. Salem's Rabid Witch-Hunter—William Stoughton   85
11. Uncle Daniel the "Speckerlator"—Daniel Drew   93
12. Unleashing the James-Younger Gang—James Lane   101
13. Lincoln's Missing Bodyguard—John Parker   107
14. Squirrel Tooth Alice—Libby Thompson   113
15. The Lawman Who Went Bad—Burt Alvord   121
16. The Very Mellow Yellow Kid—Joseph Weil   129
17. You Bet Your Life—Alvin Thomas   137
18. Keeper of the Immaculate Sperm—Charles Davenport   143
19. The Silken Voice of Treachery—Mildred Gillars   153

ROGUES

20. Who's That Rapping on My Floor?—Maggie and Kate Fox   163
21. The Witch of Wall Street—Hetty Green   171
22. King of the Cannibal Islands—David O'Keefe   179
23. Master Salesman of a Dubious Legend—Herbert Bridgman   187
24. The Consummate Gold Digger—Peggy Hopkins Joyce   195
25. The Mad, Sad Poet of Greenwich Village—Maxwell Bodenheim   203
26. The Bifurcated Congressman—Samuel Dickstein   211
27. The Frugal Counterfeiter—Emerich Juettner   219
28. Imperfect Pitch—Don Lapre   227

Notes   235

Bibliography   277

Illustration Credits   287

Index   289

ACKNOWLEDGMENTS

I would like to thank these individuals and organizations for helping me ferret out some of the characters included here: William Convery and Barbara Dey, History Colorado; Allison DePrey, Indiana Historical Society; Kate Reeve and Jim Turner, Arizona Historical Society; Marilyn Terrell, National Geographic Society.

Thanks to the following people for assisting me in my photo research: Jaime Bourassa, Missouri History Museum Library and Research Center; Heather Bourk, Art and Archives, US House of Representatives; Clare Clark, Cold Spring Harbor Laboratory Archives; Isabella Donadio, Harvard Art Museums; Coi E. Drummond-Gehrig, Denver Public Library; Don Evans, O'Keefe's Waterfront Inn; Mary French, the Explorers Club; Jessica M. Herrick, California State Archives; Melissa Holland, Kheel Center, Cornell University; Mary K. Huelsbeck, Wisconsin Center for Film and Theater Research; Debra Kaufman, California Historical Society; Lisa Keys, Kansas State Historical Society; Heather Moore, US Senate Historical Office; Angela Moore-Swafford, Southern Illinois University Press; Chris Reid, Pinal County Historical Society; Susie Richter, La Porte County Historical Society Museum; Angela Troisi, *New York Daily News;* and Erin Renee Wahl, Arizona Historical Society.

I'd also like to thank the always-helpful staff at the Library of Congress as well as the many friends who aided and encouraged me in this project. Many thanks to my wife, Janice, for her eagle-eyed proofing of the manuscript. And finally, thanks to the fine editors, designers, and other staff members at Prometheus Books who helped make this volume a reality.

INTRODUCTION

We're all fascinated by the lives and deeds of famous Americans, but minor historical figures can be even more intriguing. Like my previous collection of biographies—*Secret Heroes: Everyday Americans Who Shaped Our World*—this book is about the lives and deeds of a remarkable group of lesser-known Americans, all of whom had a perceptible impact on their world. But while the subjects of *Secret Heroes* had a lasting positive influence on history, the characters in *Villains, Scoundrels, and Rogues* each left behind some indelible negative legacy. Several were lifelong hardened criminals, others perfectly normal men and women who simply jumped the rails at some point in their lives, if only momentarily.

Although many of these people were famous in their own time, they've largely slipped into the shadows for most modern readers. In a few cases—such as World War II propagandist "Axis Sally," the *Psycho*-inspiring ghoul Ed Gein, and shrieking pitchman Don Lapre—their names may still be familiar but the general public knows little about who they really were. What makes these figures worthy of note is that their life stories all read like fiction. These were no run-of-the-mill miscreants. They're some of the most incredible ne'er-do-wells in American history.

As the three components of my title suggest, I've organized my subjects according to their relative "badness." The villains are the worst of the lot—habitual or heinous wrongdoers. The scoundrels are a shade less onerous, although they're still people guilty of a serious crime or significant misconduct. The members of my third category—the rogues—are wayward souls who committed lesser offenses, made personal mistakes of consequence, or possessed some destructive character flaw. To turn an old Clint Eastwood movie title on its head, you might think of these folks as The Ugly, The Bad, and The Not Always Good.

One trait all these varied individuals share is their ability to stir strong emotions. It's impossible to read about these scalawags and schemers without feeling anger, revulsion, curiosity, or astonishment. Each of them leaves us shaking our head and asking ourselves, "Why on earth would they *do* something like that?"

As with *Secret Heroes,* the people profiled here come from all periods in our nation's history and represent a wide variety of occupations. The characters include Washington cop John Parker, a drunken wastrel who abandoned his post at Ford's Theatre, allowing assassin John Wilkes Booth unchallenged access to President Lincoln's box. Other subjects range from the rabid, homicidal judge who presided over the Salem witch trials to one of America's most audacious medical charlatans, from a Civil War guerrilla leader whose murderous deeds influenced events for decades to a US congressman who doubled as a Russian spy.

There's a pair of early-day financial virtuosos who lived up to the worst images of Wall Street greed, along with a respected journalist whose infatuation with polar explorer Robert Peary led him to perpetrate one of the most effective cases of media manipulation ever—in effect dictating history. Whether con man, killer, or quirky counterfeiter, these over-the-top figures are all undeniably memorable.

Many of these antiheroes provide cautionary tales that enlighten and instruct (as English poet John Milton pointed out, it's easier to recognize good by knowing evil). However, the urge to assemble a catalog of morality lessons wasn't the reason I chose to write about these thirty individuals. The truth is that learning about this extraordinary group was just plain fun. As more than one armchair philosopher has argued, evil can sometimes be more interesting than good—which explains why most actors love to play the bad guy.

There's one final similarity between this book and *Secret Heroes.* In the introduction to *Secret Heroes* I noted that as I went about investigating the lives of the Americans included in that work, I felt as if I'd dropped in on a lively celebration, one at which every guest had a riveting tale to tell, with each of their stories offering a fresh perspective on America's past. The same was true with the characters featured here. So allow me to welcome you to *their* party—a fascinating get-together, even if it does take place on the shady side of the street.

—Paul Martin

VILLAINS

CHAPTER 1

MERCHANT OF MISERY

James DeWolf

O n a soft, greening afternoon in late April 1807, forty-three-year-old mer-chant James DeWolf stood at the window of his brick and clapboard counting house on the busy waterfront of Bristol, Rhode Island. In his elegant colonial-era garb—stockings and breeches, long dress coat, silk vest and high-collared white shirt—the tall, gray-haired businessman presented an imperious figure. DeWolf gazed contentedly at the harbor below, where many of the ships loading or unloading their cargos were his own. This was a favorite time of year for DeWolf. For the first time in weeks there had been no need to light a fire in his office fireplace. On his morning carriage ride from home, he'd noticed some daffodils poking into the sunshine. After a long, dreary winter, the sight had cheered the normally taciturn New Englander.

DeWolf turned from the window, thinking of his beloved wife, Nancy, who, at this moment, was probably hovering over their servants as they prepared for this evening's guests. There would be a light supper—a chowder of local seafood no doubt, perhaps a warm apple crumble. Some of Bristol's best musicians were scheduled to provide the entertainment. The sounds of violin, flute, and harpsichord would fill the house, with candles and whale oil lamps providing a warm glow as family and friends relaxed with a glass of fine port in hand. DeWolf was just sorry that his grand new three-story mansion hadn't been finished by now. He'd already selected a name for the estate: The Mount. It had a solid, prosperous ring—entirely fitting for the home of Bristol's wealthiest and most influential citizen.[1]

DeWolf returned to his desk and resumed the examination of his ledgers. He had so much to keep track of—ship manifests, the records of his Caribbean plantations, the family distilleries. Fortunately, he had an eye for detail. It was that attention to the smallest matter—along with his willingness to take chances and a streak of ruthlessness—that had carried DeWolf to success. He'd certainly come a long way since acquiring his first merchant ship less than twenty years earlier. The people hereabouts had even elected him to the state legislature. Yes, life was undeniably good for the Honorable James DeWolf. He seemed to be one of those rare individuals that fortune smiles on at every turn.

Several hundred miles to the south, the Bristol-based merchantman *Seminarius* leaned heavily on a port tack as it pounded through the Atlantic chop on its way to Charleston, South Carolina. Above the usual noises of a large sailing ship—the ceaseless rumble of breaking waves, the creak of planking, the rattle of wind-whipped lines, and the snap of taut canvas—a medley of unearthly sounds could be heard, a low moaning pierced now and then by wailing and shouts in strange foreign tongues. They were the sounds of human misery, a chorus of anguish raised by some of the unluckiest souls ever to walk the earth.

In a fetid, four-foot-high crawl space between the ship's main deck and cargo hold, 162 African slaves were chained fast to the wooden planking.[2] Each slave was allotted a space roughly twenty inches wide. Unable to stand, the slaves could only sit or recline with their heads shoved between the legs of the next person in the tightly packed line of sweating bodies, forcing them at times to lie in each other's waste. No prison dreamed up by the Devil himself could have been worse than this dark, jostling hellhole, with its overpowering stench, oppressive heat, and claustrophobic crowding. Some of the captives went mad— or jumped into the ocean if given the chance, death being preferable to the conditions they were subjected to.

Up on the main deck of the *Seminarius,* Captain Charles Slocum sniffed the bracing salt air as he scanned the horizon. After months at sea, he could finally smell land once more. It had been a challenging voyage. Nineteen of the 181 Negroes he'd purchased from a slave trader's dungeon on the west coast of Africa had perished during the rough Atlantic crossing.[3] And Slocum had been obliged to discipline a few of the more unruly males. As usual, iron muzzles and the lash had tamed them well enough. Fortunately, there had been no epidemics of smallpox, typhoid, or yellow fever, which might have necessitated tossing the sick over the side to prevent other valuable slaves from becoming infected.

The long, arduous voyage of the *Seminarius* was typical of vessels involved in New England's Triangle Trade—the slave-based commerce between North America and western Africa that flourished from the early 1700s to the early 1800s. During that period, Rhode Island merchants, who dominated the New England slave trade, underwrote nearly a thousand trips to Africa and transported more than one hundred thousand slaves to North America, chiefly to the Caribbean islands and America's southeastern ports.[4] Although that number was tiny compared to the millions of Africans brought to the New World by European slave traders, dealing in human chattel earned immense fortunes for many prominent Northern families, a heritage that's unfamiliar to most Americans, who generally associate slavery solely with the South and equate New England with the noble cause of abolitionism.

The truth, however, is that it was New Englanders who owned America's largest slave-trading fleet at this time.[5] Nearly every major New England port engaged in slave trafficking to some degree, although two towns—Newport and Bristol, Rhode Island—accounted for most of the voyages. Newport led the trade for much of the 1700s, with Bristol becoming the main port after 1790. For close to a century, tiny Rhode Island controlled 60 to 90 percent of America's slave-trading activities and may have been responsible for up to half of all slaving voyages originating in North America.[6] (Between the 1820s and 1860, merchants outside New England led the final surge of American slave trafficking.)

The highly profitable Triangle Trade was woven into just about every part of the New England economy. It helped finance colonial governments and employed thousands of seamen, shipbuilders, merchants, craftsmen, and farmers. Local townspeople even bought shares in slaving voyages. Part of the vast proceeds from the traffic in human beings was used to fund venerable New England public institutions, some of which continue to wrestle with the stigma of their founding.

For the *Seminarius,* the first leg of the Triangle had begun in Bristol, where the ship's hold was filled with the hogsheads of extra potent rum that were traded for slaves in Africa. The return transatlantic crossing—the infamous Middle Passage—constituted the second leg of the Triangle. When the *Seminarius* reached Charleston, Captain Slocum would sell the ship's cargo of slaves and use the proceeds to buy commodities such as cotton, indigo, or rice. Such staples would be transported back to New England on the Triangle's final leg.

The majority of the slaving fleet, however, delivered cargos not to American ports but to the West Indies, the main source of the North's most vital import—molasses. Northern distilleries turned that molasses into rum, and the ugly cycle began once more, each time fattening the purses of the Yankee merchants who financed the slave-trading voyages. In the case of the *Seminarius,* the beneficiary of this commerce in human degradation was none other than respected businessman and civic leader James DeWolf. DeWolf bears the inglorious distinction of being the leading figure in the most active slave-importing family in American history, an elite Rhode Island clan whose members enjoyed lives of extreme luxury paid for by the suffering of others. As one historian unequivocally states, the DeWolf family fortune "was built on the backs of slaves."[7]

The DeWolfs' slave-trading activities lasted half a century, from 1769 to 1820. The family owned four dozen other slave ships besides the *Seminarius.* The DeWolfs took part in some 60 percent of the Bristol Triangle Trade, either by themselves or with partners. During the busy years from 1784 to 1807, the family underwrote eighty-eight slave-trading voyages. The next two major Bristol competitors launched nineteen voyages *combined* during that period.[8] James DeWolf became one of the wealthiest men in the country, so rich that he could afford to loan money to the United States government.

The accumulation of James DeWolf's fabulous wealth is a paradoxical tale of ambition and business acumen coupled with moral blindness. Born in Bristol in 1764, DeWolf was the son of Mark Anthony DeWolf, a seagoing man who struggled to earn a living through the slave trade and privateering. The senior DeWolf sired fifteen children, eight sons and seven daughters. Five of Mark Anthony DeWolf's sons—Charles, John, William, James, and Levi—along with Charles's son George, would become partners in a hugely successful business empire, one that used profits from the slave trade to expand into agriculture, manufacturing, and finance (to his credit, son Levi soon soured on slave trading and quit to pursue a religious life). Among the DeWolfs, James was always the leading man.

If not for the manner in which he made his fortune, James DeWolf might be remembered as a swashbuckling American hero. He went to sea as a boy, serving aboard a privately owned combat vessel during the Revolutionary War. Captured twice by the British, he endured harsh conditions as a prisoner in Bermuda, which apparently turned him into a hard case. After the war, he followed his father into the slave trade. In 1786, at the age of twenty-two, he led a voyage to Africa aboard a ship owned by Providence slaver John Brown, a member of the wealthy family whose generosity to Rhode Island College prompted the school to change its name to Brown University. (The first Rhode Islander tried under the 1794 federal Slave Trade Act, John Brown footed half the bill for the college's original library, and his family provided slave labor to build the school's University Hall).[9]

In 1788, James DeWolf purchased his first slave ship, the *Polly*. It didn't take long for him to show his attitude toward his living cargo. On the return leg of a 1790 trip to Africa, one of the females among the 122 slaves DeWolf was transporting to Cuba fell ill.[10] Fearing that the woman had smallpox, DeWolf had her hoisted high onto the *Polly*'s main mast in an attempt to prevent her from infecting others. When the slave's condition failed to improve, DeWolf ordered his crew to lash the woman to a chair. He then personally lowered her over the side and dropped her into the ocean. According to witnesses, DeWolf's only regret was the loss of the chair.[11] The following year, a Rhode Island grand jury indicted DeWolf for murder, but he was never arrested and the charge was eventually dropped.

DeWolf quickly accumulated a sizeable fortune through slave trading, and he augmented his wealth in other ways. In 1790, he married the daughter of former Rhode Island deputy governor William Bradford, adding Nancy Bradford's dowry to his coffers. When the War of 1812 came along, DeWolf entered his own warships into the fight. His eighteen-gun brig *Yankee* became one of the conflict's most successful privateers, capturing forty British vessels and netting at least a million dollars in prize money—equivalent to $12.6 million today.[12] (DeWolf later tried to save face by claiming that he made more money from privateering than from the slave trade.)

Along with their fleet of slave ships, the DeWolfs owned a Bristol bank, an insurance company, and at least three distilleries, all extensions of the slave trade. James DeWolf started a Rhode Island cotton mill, and family members bought five sugar and coffee plantations in Cuba—again, all intimately linked to slavery. As the money poured in, the DeWolfs built themselves showplace mansions in their hometown. (One of their palatial estates still stands, George DeWolf's Linden Place; located near the Bristol waterfront, it's now open as a museum and is a popular stop on walking tours. James DeWolf's home, The Mount, burned in 1904.)

Paralleling his financial accomplishments, James DeWolf's political career hit one high point after another. Beginning in 1797, he served several terms in the Rhode Island legislature, including periods as speaker of the house. In 1820, he won a seat in the US Senate, where he served until 1825, resigning because of his aversion to life in Washington and business pressures at home. One biographer claimed that he quit because he was bored.[13] That's easy to believe. For a man of action such as DeWolf, the endless debates in Congress must have been grating. There's little doubt he would have felt certain that his own convictions were correct. Honoring opposing views must have struck him as a waste of time.

At least that's the impression he gave in his business affairs. When Rhode Island outlawed slave trading in 1787 following a long campaign by Quaker abolitionists, DeWolf simply ignored the law.[14] After the US Congress tightened restrictions on slaving voyages in 1794, DeWolf helped orchestrate the appointment of his brother-in-law, Charles Collins, as customs inspector for Bristol. A slave trader himself, Collins looked the other way while one ship after another departed Bristol on the way to Africa.

After 1807, when the federal government banned all importation of slaves, the DeWolfs shifted the center of their slaving activities to Cuba. They did, it seems, begin to slow their involvement in the trade, although apparently they didn't abandon it completely until 1820, after Congress passed a law that redefined slave trading as an act of piracy punishable by death. Even then, the DeWolfs continued to import cotton, molasses, and other slave-produced commodities for use in their Rhode Island factories.

The unbroken record of financial success enjoyed by the DeWolf family ended in 1825 when George DeWolf's Cuban sugar crop failed, causing him to default on several loans. In addition to pushing a number of banks to the brink of collapse, George DeWolf's difficulties rippled throughout Bristol, affecting everyone from farmers to tradesmen, along with members of his own family. The situation became so bad that George DeWolf stole away from his mansion in the dead of night, taking his wife and six children to his Cuban estate. When his creditors discovered that he'd left town, they broke into Linden Place and made off with everything they could find, right down to the chandeliers.

Although James DeWolf suffered a setback because of his nephew's bankruptcy (probably a major factor in his decision to leave Washington and return to Bristol), he wasn't wiped out. When he died in December 1837 at the age of seventy-three, he was still a millionaire, having long ago diversified his fortune into real estate and manufacturing.[15] On the whole, however, the DeWolfs struggled financially for decades, although they retained their elite social status. Members of the family continued to hold positions of respect—as legislators, Episcopal ministers, writers, scholars, artists, and architects. They clung proudly to their heritage, sometimes glossing over the clan's deep involvement in the slave trade.[16]

One contemporary DeWolf ancestor who chose not to continue looking the other way is Katrina Browne. A former social worker and seminarian, Browne has produced a moving documentary that closely examines her family's past (called *Traces of the Trade: A Story from the Deep North,* the film aired on PBS in 2008). In the film, Browne and nine other DeWolf descendants make a spiritual pilgrimage that re-creates the route of the notorious Triangle Trade. The group journeys from Bristol to a former slave dungeon in Ghana to the ruins of a DeWolf sugar plantation in Cuba. Browne and her relatives find themselves wrestling with a combination of guilt and uncertainty about what they and other white Americans could, or should, do to help heal the emotional scars left behind by America's involvement in slavery.

A member of the group, Thomas Norman DeWolf, published a book in 2008 that attempts to address that quandary. In *Inheriting the Trade: A Northern Family Confronts Its Legacy as the Largest Slave-Trading Dynasty in U.S. History,* DeWolf admits that "there are no simple answers." But by confronting the issue, "we will finally break through the scars to clean the living wound properly and begin the healing." DeWolf offers this advice: "People really need to examine their own lives and see the ways in which we perpetuate inequality."[17]

That's a thoughtful recommendation. It's too easy to overlook our own biases, to think of ourselves as open-minded even as we slight others, though the offense may only take place in the privacy of our own minds. Still, a baffling question remains: How could thousands of Americans in the eighteenth and nineteenth centuries have supported the existence of slavery—something so evil, so obviously wrong—in the first place? Many people in James DeWolf's day regarded attempts to end the trade as government oppression, an infringement of their rights. Slavery was essential to the American economy, they proclaimed—the same argument raised by every powerful interest group that puts profit above principle.

Just as puzzling is the suggestion that people of subsequent generations shouldn't judge slave traders and slave owners too harshly, since those activities were widely accepted at the time they occurred. "Let us not hold our ancestors responsible for deeds which in their day were not regarded as sinful," wrote Bristol historian Wilfred H. Munro in 1880.[18] Sorry, but that's impossible to do: there truly are unforgivable crimes, and growing obscenely rich as a merchant of misery is among them. Besides, if slavers didn't believe that what they were doing was sinful, which seems preposterous, that's an even greater reason to condemn them.

Some people have clearly never absolved James DeWolf—a man who reputedly wallowed in a pile of gold on the floor of his mansion in a sordid display of his worship of wealth.[19] DeWolf's body now lies in an unmarked plot in the family's private cemetery in Bristol. His grave was vandalized so often that his relatives were forced to remove his tombstone to conceal his whereabouts.[20]

CHAPTER 2

THE CUTTHROAT CAPTAIN OF CAVE-IN-ROCK

Samuel Mason

Pirate Samuel Mason's Illinois hideout Cave-In-Rock

A few miles upstream from its confluence with the Mississippi, the powerful Ohio River wriggled like a broad brown serpent between the shores of southern Illinois and western Kentucky. In the early 1800s, dense virgin woodlands still lined the banks of the Ohio, a busy watercourse that carried a picturesque assortment of river craft, from chuffing paddle wheelers and graceful sailboats to utilitarian keelboats, flatboats, barges, canoes, and even crude log rafts. Among the thousands of travelers on the Ohio, many were bound for St. Louis, Missouri, the gateway to the West during America's great nineteenth-century expansion.

On this bright summer afternoon, bearded, boisterous Zebulon Prescott and his wife and children drifted down the Ohio aboard the raft they'd launched somewhere below the river's Pittsburgh, Pennsylvania, headwaters. Like countless other families, the Prescotts had sold their farm back east and were headed to "the promised land" to forge a new life.

A short distance ahead, on the Illinois bank of the Ohio, a hand-painted banner heralded a makeshift store set up near a large cave. Zebulon Prescott steered his raft toward the trading post. After several days on the river, the family needed fresh supplies. The Prescotts eased their craft up to the riverbank and scrambled ashore. The trading post's jovial proprietor, Col. Jeb Hawkins, gave them a cheerful welcome—perhaps a little too cheerful.

As the Prescotts examined the store's offerings, a gang of ruffians suddenly appeared from the nearby woods, guns in hand. The unsuspecting travelers were shocked to realize that they'd been lured into a trap by river pirates. Fortunately for the Prescotts, a wiry, drawling mountain man named Linus Rawlings would come to their rescue. That's the way things played out in the 1962 movie *How the West Was Won,* an epic account of the settling of the American West. In real life, the outcome of such a riverside encounter might not have been so favorable.

During the frontier era depicted in this early scene in *How the West Was Won,* pirates did in fact rob and murder pioneer families, at times burning or scuttling their boats and tossing their bodies in the river.[1] The movie cutthroats who waylaid the Prescotts were based on an actual outlaw gang, one that operated from an Ohio River hideout known as Cave-In-Rock, a limestone cavern situated at the base of a high bluff some seventy miles northeast of present-day Cairo, Illinois. A perfect criminal sanctum, the cave presented sweeping views of the river and all the vessels that passed up and down it. (Located in Hardin County near the tiny town of Cave-In-Rock, the site is now a state park.)

From about 1790 to the early 1830s, Cave-In-Rock harbored a parade of counterfeiters, gamblers, prostitutes, and other riffraff. The fictional thief Col. Jeb Hawkins, played with oily malevolence by actor Walter Brennan, was patterned on one of Cave-in-Rock's most notorious denizens—Capt. Samuel Mason, a cunning brigand who conducted a reign of terror along the Ohio and Mississippi Rivers and the Natchez Trace at the turn of the nineteenth century, a time of general lawlessness throughout this sparsely populated region. From 1797 to 1799, Mason and his gang preyed on passing river traffic from Cave-In-Rock. Among the pirates and highwaymen of his day, Mason has been called "the worst of the worst," a relentless predator whose widespread marauding made the dangers of frontier travel even greater.[2]

Historians believe that Mason was born in Norfolk, Virginia, in 1739 and grew up near present-day Charles Town, West Virginia (an area that was then part of the huge Virginia Colony). Mason's family was evidently respectable. He had a brother who became a prominent Pennsylvania tradesman and a sister who married a Methodist minister. Despite a decent upbringing and rudimentary education, Samuel Mason had little use for honest work or religious niceties. He certainly didn't adhere to the Eighth Commandment: "Thou shalt not steal." As a young man, he helped himself to someone else's horses in Frederick County, Virginia, the first record of his criminal tendencies.[3]

The Revolutionary War temporarily diverted Mason's attention. During the war, Mason served as a captain in a Virginia militia. Assigned to Fort Henry, in present-day Wheeling, West Virginia, he fought against Native American allies of the British, surviving an ambush in which he was wounded and most of his men were killed. (To keep his pilfering skills sharp, he found time to steal supplies from Fort Henry.)[4] After his service, Mason settled in Washington County, Pennsylvania. Somehow, he fooled enough people to win an appointment as an associate judge. Not surprisingly, his flirtation with upholding the law didn't last long. By the mid-1780s, he'd run up a thumping debt in Pennsylvania and decamped to Tennessee, where he quickly earned a reputation for thievery.[5]

By the early 1790s, Mason had migrated to the Ohio River settlement of Red Banks, in western Kentucky (site of the present-day city of Henderson). From Red Banks, Mason launched his career as a river pirate, assisted by his sons and a gang of "worthless louts," as his cronies were described by a contemporary observer.[6] Mason himself didn't look anything like a storybook pirate. There was no eye patch, no parrot on his shoulder, no Jolly Roger fluttering overhead. Tall and heavyset, dressed in a frock coat, vest, and string tie, he looked more like a shopkeeper or gentleman farmer. But Mason had the instincts of a buccaneer: at Red Banks, he graduated from theft to murder, which became his hallmark ever after. (When Mason was finally captured, he had twenty human scalps in his possession.)[7]

In 1797, Mason fled Red Banks after a series of killings, moving his gang downriver to Cave-In-Rock. At their new hideout, the pirates used a variety of tricks to lure travelers within striking distance. Mason sometimes had a lone man or woman call out to passing boats from the riverbank, pretending that they were stranded. When a boat pulled ashore to offer assistance, the pirates attacked. Mason reportedly gave able-bodied male travelers the chance to join his gang. Refusing his offer wasn't a wise choice.

Mason capitalized on the dangerous water conditions along the lower Ohio by having some of his men pose as local river pilots. The pirates intercepted vessels traveling downriver and offered to guide them through the tricky channel below Cave-In-Rock, which was filled with snags, sandbars, and other obstructions. When a boat hired one of the fake pilots, the pirate would intentionally ground the vessel at Cave-In-Rock or some other rendezvous point so Mason's gang could swarm aboard.

Another ruse the pirates used was the one shown in *How the West Was Won*—enticing travelers ashore with a large banner. Mason put up a sign advertising Cave-In-Rock as "Wilson's Liquor Vault and House for Entertainment."[8] Much of the river traffic at the time consisted of flatboats carrying trade goods to New Orleans. The rowdy crews aboard these boats were highly susceptible to the offer of a good time. While a crew was busy gambling and swilling rotgut inside the cave, Mason's men leisurely inspected their cargo. If the goods were worth stealing, the pirates pounced on the drunken boatmen. Mason then replaced the crew with his own men, who sailed the vessel to New Orleans and sold the cargo themselves.

Among the collection of thugs who passed through Cave-In-Rock, the two most vicious by far were Micajah and Wiley Harpe, better known, respectively, as Big Harpe and Little Harpe. Thought to be brothers from North Carolina, the Harpes were even more bloodthirsty than Mason, having murdered perhaps dozens of people just for the hell of it.[9] The two psychopaths were known to disembowel their victims, fill their bodies with stones, and sink them in the nearest waterway. They killed women, children, and infants without remorse, sneaking up on lonely cabins, slaughtering everyone inside, and setting the dwellings ablaze. They ambushed travelers gathered around a campfire at night, mutilating their bodies with tomahawks and knives. Their victims probably fainted away when these buckskin-clad ogres emerged from the woods, firelight flickering on their swarthy faces as they announced themselves with the chilling proclamation, "We are the Harpes!"[10]

The outrages perpetrated by the Cave-In-Rock pirates naturally alarmed decent people living in the region. In 1799, a group of regulators launched a series of attacks on outlaws in western Kentucky and southern Illinois. On the frontier, volunteer militias and vigilante groups were often the only semblance of law and order. The raids prompted Mason to move his base of operations to Wolf Island in the Mississippi River, a few miles below the mouth of the Ohio. A short time later, he moved downriver to New Madrid, then part of the Spanish-occupied Louisiana Territory and the largest river settlement between St. Louis and Natchez, in the American-held Mississippi Territory. (Now a quiet Missouri town, New Madrid is famous for a series of powerful earthquakes that occurred there in late 1811 and early 1812. The tremors affected an area ten times larger than the famous 1906 San Francisco earthquake, shaking buildings as far away as New York City and Washington, DC.)[11]

From his sanctuary in Spanish Louisiana, Mason continued to plunder river traffic, and he widened his pillaging to the Natchez Trace, the five-hundred-mile-long wilderness trail linking southwestern Mississippi and Nashville, Tennessee. Flatboat crews returning to the Ohio Valley after delivering their cargoes to New Orleans routinely used the Natchez Trace, since they usually sold their boats for lumber at the end of each voyage (the clumsy, slow-moving craft were difficult to sail upriver). With the profits from their trip bulging in their pockets, the boat crews made tempting targets for highwaymen. Mason had a confederate in Natchez inform him when prosperous travelers were setting out along this lonely footpath so that he could lie in wait and swoop down on them. It's said that he carved the message "Done by Mason of the Woods" into a tree at the scene of his crimes, or wrote his name in his victims' blood.[12]

Mason's renown eventually led to his downfall. When a previous victim recognized the pirate leader in Mississippi in 1802, the territorial governor put a price on Mason's head. To avoid capture, Mason and his family slipped back into Spanish Louisiana. They hid out in an abandoned house at Little Prairie, south of New Madrid, passing themselves off as farmers. Suspicious of the new arrivals, neighbors alerted Spanish authorities. In January 1803, a militia troop raided the home, capturing Mason along with Wiley Harpe, who was then hiding under an assumed name. (Little Harpe had barely avoided capture by a Kentucky posse just three years before. Micajah Harpe had been killed by the posse, his severed head placed in the fork of a tree as a warning to other lawbreakers.)

The Spaniards took the suspects to New Madrid for a preliminary hearing. Mason kept up the pretense that he was a simple farmer, in spite of a glaring discrepancy in his story: the militiamen had confiscated his belongings, which included more than $7,000 in cash and those twenty human scalps—not exactly the possessions of an average farmer.[13] The commandant at New Madrid transferred the captives to New Orleans for final disposition. After determining that no crimes had taken place in Spanish territory, the governor general of Louisiana decided to hand over the outlaws to American authorities in Mississippi.

While Mason and Harpe were being transported upriver to Natchez, they managed to escape. That's when Little Harpe's character shone through once more. Hoping to earn the hefty reward that the governor of Mississippi had offered for Mason's recapture, Harpe and a fellow bandit named James May murdered the outlaw captain and cut off his head, which they delivered to Natchez to claim the bounty. Predictably, the two men were recognized, arrested, and tried. Little Harpe and his accomplice received a slightly different payoff than what they'd hoped for, one they thoroughly deserved: both men were convicted of piracy and hanged. Like Big Harpe, Little Harpe suffered the indignity of having his head lopped off and put on public display.

The death of Samuel Mason brought a brutal chapter in the history of the frontier to a close. Afterward, large-scale, organized piracy withered away along the lower Ohio and the Mississippi. Although brigands continued to plague travelers for several more years, the later gangs were smaller and more localized than Mason's roving band. Following the Louisiana Purchase in 1803—the same year that Mason died—the region's steadily growing population gradually produced more effective law enforcement. After 1820, the rapid increase in the number of steamboats on the rivers meant that fewer flatboats—the pirates' main target—were used to carry passengers and trade goods. The steamboats were too large and too fast for pirates to attack. By around 1830, river piracy had all but disappeared.[14]

In his forty years of thieving and decade of killing, Mason forged a deservedly fearsome reputation, although the mellowing effect of time might lead some people today to look back on him as a colorful rogue, like the seafaring pirates who've inspired so many fictionalized accounts in books and movies. But there was nothing romantic or swashbuckling about Samuel Mason. He was no Jack Sparrow, sashaying his way through rollicking adventures. Mason was an unregenerate troglodyte—a cave-dwelling miscreant who contributed little to the human race besides misery.

Mason enjoyed a surprisingly long life given his calling and the period in which he lived. It's ironic that he perished at the hands of fellow murderer Wiley Harpe, a man whose heart was as black as his own. Of course, there could have been no more fitting end for the cutthroat captain of Cave-In-Rock than to die by the sword by which he'd lived.

CHAPTER 3

ARCHITECT OF A TRAGEDY

John Chivington

Winter locked the windswept plains of the Colorado Territory in icy silence. On this frigid morning of November 29, 1864, more than a hundred Cheyenne and Arapaho teepees stood among the bare willows and cottonwoods along Sand Creek, a stretch of dry streambed fringed with bluffs and ridges. The Indians still slept soundly beneath their buffalo robes as the first faint traces of dawn reddened the horizon.

Just weeks before, the leader of the Indians, renowned Cheyenne war chief Black Kettle, had agreed to surrender to the US Army. The peace talks had taken place outside Denver and at Fort Lyon in southeastern Colorado. In return for the Indians' pledge to end hostilities against white settlers, Fort

Lyon's commanding officer, Maj. Edward Wynkoop, had given permission for Black Kettle's band of several hundred Cheyenne, along with a small number of Arapaho, to camp in peace here at Sand Creek, a day's ride north of the fort. Two banners hung from Black Kettle's lodge pole to show that the band was under army protection, the US flag and a white flag of surrender.

Once a fierce warrior, Black Kettle was now an old man of seventy summers. He'd grown tired of the struggles between his people and the endless waves of settlers. Other Plains Indians, mostly younger warriors, still fought against the miners, ranchers, and townspeople encroaching on their homeland. During the previous year, bands of Cheyenne, Arapaho, Sioux, and Kiowa had raided settlements all over the Colorado Territory. Tales of ambushes, murders, and scalpings kept white people on edge, whetting fears and hatreds that made coexistence seem impossible. For many settlers, the only solution was to eliminate every Indian from the territory.[1]

Inside his lodge, Chief Black Kettle awoke with a start. Women were shouting at what they thought were the hoof beats of an approaching herd of buffalo—a blessing that would mean fresh meat and additional hides to keep their people warm. The first warriors to emerge from their teepees gazed in the direction the sounds were coming from. What they saw weren't buffalo. In the distance, some seven hundred mounted soldiers advanced on the sleeping encampment.[2] The approaching troops resembled an apparition from hell. Bundled in thick coats, the men seemed to be frozen into their saddles, their beards rimed with frost. The majority of the troops belonged to the Third Colorado Cavalry, a ragtag group of short-term volunteers gathered from Denver's barrooms and mines. Swords, knives, and axes glinted at the volunteers' waists, and they carried a mismatched assortment of rifles, shotguns, and pistols. The rest of the soldiers were smart-looking troops of the First Colorado Cavalry assigned to Fort Lyon.

The men were led by Col. John Milton Chivington, a red-bearded giant who'd won acclaim two years earlier by helping to beat back a Confederate incursion in New Mexico, one of the few reminders in this region of the Civil War that was raging in the eastern part of the country. For some time, Chivington had held hopes that his military exploits would be a stepping-stone to public office. An ordained Methodist-Episcopal minister, he was nicknamed the "Fighting Parson," and he intended to deliver righteous retribution on the Indians camped at Sand Creek—an achievement that wouldn't go unnoticed by the voting public.[3]

Born on the Ohio frontier in 1821, Chivington was named after English poet John Milton. He learned to read from a copy of Milton's *Paradise Lost,* along with the Bible and Book of Common Prayer. After studying to become a minister, Chivington served for a short time as a missionary to the Wyandot Indians in the Kansas Territory. In the 1850s, he took up the abolitionist cause. By 1860 he'd moved to the Colorado Territory, where his fervent preaching was mingled with antisecessionist screeds. When the Civil War erupted, Chivington won a commission as a major in the Colorado Volunteers. Though he was undisciplined and a relentless self-promoter, he proved to be an effective soldier.[4] Following the victory in New Mexico, he was assigned to protect a large chunk of the Colorado Territory. With little threat remaining from Confederate forces, Chivington took the fight to a different enemy—the Plains Indians who'd been attacking settlers.

Chivington didn't make much distinction between hostile and peaceful bands. By this point in his life, he seemed to think that all Indians were murderous savages who deserved to die. "It simply is not possible for Indians to obey or even understand any treaty," he told a group of Denver church deacons. "I am fully satisfied ... that to kill them is the only way we will ever have peace and quiet in Colorado."[5] The army's regional commander, Gen. Samuel Curtis, was just as bellicose as the Fighting Parson. As far as Black Kettle was concerned, General Curtis felt that there was no binding peace agreement with the chief, despite the arrangement Major Wynkoop had made. Curtis assumed that Black Kettle would return to the warpath come spring.[6] It was shaky justification for an attack on the encampment at Sand Creek, but it was all Colonel Chivington needed.

From Denver, Chivington and his volunteers had ridden through two hundred fifty miles of snowy countryside to reach Fort Lyon, showing up unannounced on November 28. The colonel immediately informed the officers at the fort that he was ordering the First Colorado Cavalry to join his fight against Black Kettle. Two of the fort's officers, Capt. Silas Soule and Lt. Joseph Cramer, objected to the plan, telling Chivington that an attack on Sand Creek would be equivalent to murder, since the Indians there were technically prisoners of war. Chivington reacted with fury. "Damn any man who is in sympathy with an Indian," he bellowed.[7]

Most of Chivington's troops supported the venture wholeheartedly, especially the untested volunteers of the so-called "Bloodless Third." They were eager to get a taste of killing. On this bleak winter morning, as his men huddled in the subzero temperatures near the Indian encampment, Chivington announced that no prisoners were to be taken. When the burly colonel gave the order to attack, the troopers charged into the village, which had been shocked into wakefulness by an opening salvo from a battery of field guns. Chief Black Kettle's American flag would offer his people no protection this day.

The startled Indians darted about in terror and confusion. Some of the women and children sought shelter along the banks of the dry streambed. The cavalrymen rode among them, whooping and shouting, hacking wildly with their sabers. Mothers with babies in their arms were cut down, tottering old men and women shot or impaled, little children crushed beneath the soldiers' horses. As the killing frenzy heightened, the soldiers dismounted and began scalping and disemboweling their victims. It was a scene of such wanton slaughter that even battle-tested troopers were sickened.[8]

Relatively few of the village's inhabitants were able-bodied men. Most of the warriors had left camp on hunting forays. The men that remained at Sand Creek put up a faltering resistance before herding the survivors to safety and fleeing toward a larger Cheyenne encampment at Smoky Hill River, some sixty miles to the north. When the fighting ended after several hours, an estimated one hundred fifty Indians lay dead on the frozen ground—most of them women, children, and the elderly. Many of the dead had been mutilated by soldiers gathering grisly souvenirs.[9]

Although Chief Black Kettle managed to escape, Colonel Chivington put the best possible spin on the attack. He dashed off a letter to General Curtis, claiming that his men had defeated a village "from nine hundred to one thousand warriors strong," and that they had killed "between four and five hundred"— both gross overestimates.[10] The one-sided nature of the fight was underscored by Chivington's losses—only nine soldiers were killed. The colonel added that his men had performed "nobly."[11]

Chivington, however, had no praise for the First Colorado Cavalry's Company D, the unit led by Capt. Silas Soule. Captain Soule had held his men back, refusing to take part in the slaughter—an act of conscience that would have far-reaching consequences. After Soule returned to Fort Lyon, he documented the atrocities perpetrated by Chivington's men in a letter to Major Wynkoop, who'd been transferred to Fort Riley, Kansas, in punishment for establishing peace with Black Kettle without General Curtis's approval. "Hundreds of women and children were coming toward us and getting on their knees for mercy," Soule wrote. "It was hard to see little children . . . have their brains beat out by men professing to be civilized."[12] Lt. Joseph Cramer also described the horrors he witnessed to Wynkoop: "Women and children were scalped, fingers cut off to get the rings on them . . . a squaw ripped open and a child taken from her."[13]

Chivington called Soule a coward for disobeying his orders, but the young army veteran had proven his bravery many times over while fighting alongside Kansas abolitionists before the Civil War.[14] Soule had also fought the

Confederates in New Mexico—at the same battle in which John Chivington, then a major, earned his burst of fame. Any respect Soule had for Chivington evaporated the moment the colonel announced his plans to attack the Indian encampment at Sand Creek. "I knew it was being undertaken because of Chivington's lust for glory," Soule wrote to his fiancée in Denver.[15]

If that truly was Chivington's motivation, he got his wish. Following the events at Sand Creek, Chivington was hailed as a hero. The *Rocky Mountain News* held nothing back in celebrating Chivington's deeds: "Great Battle with Indians! The Savages Dispersed! 500 Indians Killed," the newspaper trumpeted on the front page of its December 14, 1864, edition. Folks in Denver cheered and made speeches and got convincingly drunk—except for the citizens who doubted Chivington's motives. They were worried that the attack on Black Kettle would just make the Indians more determined than ever to kill white people—which is precisely what happened.[16] After Sand Creek, the Cheyenne, Arapaho, and Sioux joined forces and fought white settlers with renewed fury. The ensuing conflict would drag on for years, costing the country dearly in lives and treasure.

Major Wynkoop was especially critical of Chivington's actions at Sand Creek.[17] The letters Wynkoop received from Silas Soule and Joseph Cramer were searing indictments. Wynkoop urged authorities to investigate whether Chivington's men had committed atrocities against women and children. Opposing Chivington, however, came at a price. The colonel's admirers reviled anyone who found fault with the attack on Black Kettle's band, calling them "Indian lovers" and threatening to shoot them on sight.[18] The controversy came to a climax when both the army and the US Congress decided to look into the Sand Creek affair. Colonel Chivington resigned his commission in January 1865, putting him out of reach of a court-martial, but the investigations still went forward.

In February 1865, a military board convened in Denver to "obtain a true picture of what transpired at Sand Creek."[19] The first witness called was Silas Soule. Despite having had an anonymous death threat shoved under his hotel room door, Soule took the stand and recounted every last gory detail of the attack on Black Kettle's camp. Soule told Chivington to his face that his hands were "dripping with the blood of innocent people."[20] Other witnesses gave evidence, but Soule's was among the most damning.

After his testimony, Soule was shot at in Denver on two occasions, presumably by Chivington's supporters. Then on the evening of April 23, 1865, as the twenty-six-year-old officer walked home with his bride of three weeks, he heard shots ring out in the distance. A soldier rushed up and told him there was fight a few blocks away. Having recently been appointed provost marshal of Denver, Soule set off to investigate the altercation. Kissing his wife good-bye, he told her he'd see her at home. Minutes later, Soule was lying dead in the street, shot down by Charles Squires, a vocal supporter of Colonel Chivington. Squires fled to New Mexico but was captured by one of Soule's associates, Lt. James Cannon. Brought back to Denver to stand trial, Squires escaped and disappeared. Around that same time, Lieutenant Cannon was found dead, apparently poisoned.

Though Chivington's involvement couldn't be proved, Soule's friends were convinced that he was behind the crimes.[21] Chivington never faced criminal charges for anything connected with Sand Creek or its aftermath, but he paid a heavy price nonetheless. Censured by the investigations, he couldn't escape the public disgrace that followed. His attempt to parlay his notoriety into a seat in the US Congress went nowhere, and he was relieved of his position as a church elder. He scuffled around the country, struggling in various occupations and failing in a subsequent attempt to win public office. However, he never expressed any regret over his actions against the Cheyenne and Arapaho. "I stand by Sand Creek," he declared toward the end of his life.[22] Chivington died of stomach cancer in 1894, still muttering to anyone who'd listen that the killings he'd unleashed were sanctioned by God.

The Sand Creek Massacre, as it came to be called, claimed one other victim. The fallout from the attack ended the political career of Colorado's territorial governor, John Evans, who'd actually backed the protection of peaceful Indians at one time. As for Chief Black Kettle, the old warrior escaped Sand Creek only to die four years later in a virtual replay of Chivington's dawn assault. In November 1868, he was killed when Lt. Col. George Armstrong Custer's Seventh Cavalry raided a sleeping Cheyenne encampment along the Washita River in Oklahoma.

Books and articles continue to be published about Sand Creek, as writers struggle to discover the "truth" about one of the worst massacres of Native Americans in our country's history. Some people remain convinced that Colonel Chivington did nothing wrong, that Sand Creek was a legitimate victory and its instigator a victim of personal animosities and political skullduggery.[23] Even if it were true that Chivington's enemies piled on while he was down, it's still impossible to condone what took place at Sand Creek, where—according to multiple eyewitness accounts—scores of defenseless noncombatants were slaughtered indiscriminately. Moreover, to attack a group of Native Americans that had accepted terms of peace on the assumption that they might resume their hostile ways was an example of racial hatred overwhelming reason—one of history's saddest and most repetitious storylines.

The most shocking aspect of Chivington's behavior is the fact that he was an ordained minister. For a man of God, a dedicated Christian, to ignore the key tenets of his faith—virtually every dictum laid down by Jesus himself—baffles the mind. Chivington apparently felt no compassion toward the women and innocent children being gunned down and hacked apart. He had no remorse that the old and infirm were shown no mercy. He reveled in the day's bloody toll, hoping it would lead to a campaign to "rid the country" of Indians, a shockingly genocidal mindset.[24]

The glory of Sand Creek evaporated like morning mist when the true nature of the attack became apparent—exactly as it should have. Otherwise, we would all share in John Chivington's shame and guilt.

CHAPTER 4

THE LATE, UNLAMENTED LITTLE PETE

Fong Ching

All Fong Ching—also known as "Little Pete"—wanted was a shave. After finishing his dinner at around 9:00 p.m. on the night of January 23, 1897, the diminutive, baby-faced Chinese entrepreneur left his wife and three children in the family residence above their Washington Street shoe factory, located within the teeming confines of San Francisco's Chinatown. He was headed downstairs to his neighborhood barbershop. Dressed in an expensive, loose-fitting mandarin silk jacket and wearing the traditional Chinese queue, or pigtail, the thirty-two-year-old Little Pete looked every inch the respectable Asian merchant. The only indication that he was not your typical businessman was the presence of his hulking Anglo bodyguard, the capable Ed Murray.

Down on the street next door to his factory, Little Pete entered the establishment run by his fellow countryman Wong Chung. Little Pete sat down on a straight-backed wooden chair and settled in for his customary Saturday-night grooming. With the queue hairstyle, the front and sides of the head are shaved, while the hair on the back of the head is gathered into a long braid that's never cut. China's Manchurian-ruled Qing Dynasty (1644–1911) required the conquered Han Chinese to conform to the distinctive Manchu hairstyle as proof of submission, making the act of cutting off your queue punishable by death.[1] Many Chinese immigrants kept their long braids even in America.

As Wong Chung went about his work, Little Pete glanced at the newspapers lying around the barbershop. An avid horseracing fan, the wealthy manufacturer told his bodyguard to run out to the hotel down the street and pick up a broadsheet with the day's results. When Murray objected to leaving him unguarded, Little Pete laughed and told him he'd be all right.

Reluctantly, Murray did as he was instructed. Within seconds of Murray leaving the shop, two Chinese toughs walked in off the street and pumped three bullets into Little Pete, who was still seated in the barber's chair. One of the bullets struck Little Pete in the corner of his right eye, another pierced his forehead, and the third slug tore into his chest. The two assassins immediately fled into the Chinese quarter's warren of crowded streets. Hearing the shots, Ed Murray raced back to the barbershop, where he found his employer lying dead on the floor, a pool of blood spreading outward from beneath his head. The pint-size businessman had paid the price for letting his guard down.

Why someone would want to kill Little Pete was no mystery, and it had nothing to do with making shoes. In addition to running his family business, the man had his hand in every vice operation in the Chinese district, from gambling to prostitution to the protection racket. He'd grown rich from human trafficking and fixing horse races, and he protected his empire with hired cutthroats and liberal bribes handed out to city officials.[2] The combination of his legitimate and criminal successes earned him the title "King of Chinatown." Such prominence naturally stirred up a viper's nest of jealous foes—enemies who finally caught up with him during his momentary lapse in security.

In historical context, Little Pete was part of the diaspora of Chinese merchants, farmers, and laborers that took place in the second half of the nineteenth century, an exodus sparked by China's extreme poverty and the ongoing wars and rebellions against the hated Qing Dynasty. After the discovery of gold in

California in 1848, Chinese immigrants—nearly all of them men—poured into the state, which was promoted in China as the land of the "Mountain of Gold." (The majority of these newcomers intended to return to China once they'd made their fortunes.)[3] As the main point of entry, San Francisco became home to the country's first Chinatown, which is still the largest Chinese enclave outside Asia.

By 1852, around twenty thousand Chinese had arrived in California, most of them heading on to the gold fields. By the late 1860s, Chinese immigration to the United States had topped sixty thousand, including some twelve thousand laborers recruited to help build the transcontinental railroad. By the 1880s, over a hundred thousand Chinese had arrived in this country.[4] The rising tide of Asian immigration worried white Americans, who feared losing their jobs or having their wages undercut. Assimilation was all but impossible, and discrimination against the Chinese was particularly virulent. It peaked in 1882, when the federal government passed the Chinese Exclusion Act, prohibiting further immigration of Chinese laborers and preventing the Chinese from becoming naturalized citizens (the law remained on the books until 1943). For crooks such as Little Pete, however, the act simply created a new stream of income: smuggling illegal immigrants, including hundreds of Chinese "slave girls," or prostitutes.[5]

Except for the murder and mayhem he was responsible for, Little Pete could have been admired for his record of hard-won self-improvement. Born near Canton, China, in 1864, the boy known as Fong Ching immigrated to San Francisco with his father when he was ten years old. A bright child, he soon became proficient in English through his studies at grammar school and the Methodist Chinese Mission. By the age of sixteen, he was working as an errand boy in a Chinatown shoe factory and helping to support several relatives.

Always ambitious, Fong Ching saved and borrowed enough money to begin making shoes on his own. Eventually his business grew to encompass a factory employing more than forty workers, including his brother and an uncle.[6] To pass his shoes off as an American brand, he named his manufacturing operation F. C. [for Fong Ching] Peters & Company, which, combined with the man's small stature, is how he ended up with the nickname Little Pete. The company became the largest of its kind in Chinatown, shipping its products all over the state and earning its owner a substantial income. But for some reason, his legitimate business achievements didn't satisfy Little Pete. That's when he began branching out into seamier endeavors.

A big part of Little Pete's criminal success came from his understanding of the American legal system. He quickly learned that a few hundred dollars in the right pockets could do wonders in tipping things in his favor. It was something

he'd picked up while working for one of the Six Companies, the Chinese benevolent associations formed to assist immigrants in their new homeland. Each of
the Six Companies served people from a specific region of China.[7] While still
a teenager, Little Pete had become an interpreter for the Sam Yup Company,
which introduced him to the ways of the San Francisco police and courts—both
their prescribed functions and those that took place behind closed doors.

The Six Companies represented the most public of the countless Chinese
community organizations. There were also dozens of so-called secret societies,
or tongs, representing a tangled mix of political, geographical, and occupational
loyalties.[8] The tongs included mutual aid groups, social clubs, administrative
bodies, and—perhaps best known to white Americans—criminal gangs. (Such
gangs were smaller, localized versions of the much older Chinese Triads, anti-
Manchu political societies that grew into powerful international crime syndi-
cates.) The criminal tongs thrived on extortion, demanding tribute money from
honest merchants as well as the owners of gambling halls, brothels, and opium
dens. And the gangs fought furiously among themselves to protect their turf.

Like the Sharks and the Jets in *West Side Story*, the Chinese tong members
were defined by their allegiances. Regional loyalties fueled the first outbreak of
violence between the tongs.[9] Rival groups of gold miners settling in the town of
Weaverville, California, were soon at each other's throats. In 1854, open warfare
broke out, with miners from Canton and Hong Kong hacking on one another
with medieval pikes and swords that they'd paid local blacksmiths to craft. The
fighting soon spread to other parts of the state, establishing a predilection for
violence that became the hallmark of the criminal tongs.

In San Francisco, the powerful Chee Kung Tong—the mother of all
Chinese secret societies in this country—owned a three-story building housing
a large hall where initiation ceremonies were regularly held involving swords,
exposed necks, and blood oaths. The Chee Kung Tong's unifying purpose was
opposition to China's Manchu rulers. By the 1880s, the tong claimed forty-five
hundred members in San Francisco and a total of fifteen thousand members
throughout the United States.[10] There were also numerous splinter groups with
a few hundred members each. One of these, the Gi Sin Seer Tong, was founded
by Little Pete to help him protect his growing criminal empire.

To fill out the ranks of the Gi Sin Seer Tong, Little Pete recruited the worst of
the city's *boo how doy*, the killers known as "highbinders" by white Americans. The
highbinders were the foot soldiers in the constant warfare between Chinatown's
rival gangs, a competition that left stacks of mutilated corpses littering the district's back streets and alleyways. Old photographs of weapons confiscated from

the highbinders are enough to give you a chill—a fearsome collection of knives, swords, cleavers, clubs, hammers, and other implements designed for slicing, dicing, and tenderizing. Of these, the hatchet was the weapon of choice, a fact that gave the highbinders their other label: hatchet men. Whenever one tong angered another, the hatchet men were deployed to settle things in the accepted fashion: by waylaying a rival gang member in a dark alley and reducing him to a bloody lump of meat (and sometimes scalping him for good measure). Despite the gruesomeness of the crimes, white San Franciscans largely looked the other way, as long as the tongs kept their butchery among themselves.[11]

Little Pete was the instigator of many such gang slayings. By the late 1880s, his dominance of Chinatown was so complete that newspapers claimed there wasn't a lottery ticket sold, a shipment of opium smuggled, a trick turned in a backstreet bordello, or a game of fan-tan played without his taking a cut.[12] Death threats from rival tongs continually swirled around Little Pete. He responded by hiring the town's most lethal boo how doy—a feral character named Lee Chuck—as his personal bodyguard. Little Pete outfitted Lee Chuck and himself with chain-mail shirts, and he acquired a small arsenal of pistols for protection. The arrangement worked well until Lee Chuck got himself into trouble with the law.

In July 1886, Lee Chuck received a tip that a member of the rival Bo Sin Seer Tong—a thug name Yen Yuen—intended to kill him. Figuring that a vigorous offense was the best defense, Lee Chuck waylaid Yen Yuen in Chinatown's Spofford Alley and shot him five times, just to make certain he was sufficiently dead. Lee Chuck bolted from the scene but was quickly caught and brought to trial on murder charges. Hoping to free his henchman, Little Pete offered the arresting officer $400 to swear that Lee Chuck had acted in self-defense. The upshot was that Lee Chuck was convicted and sentenced to fifty years in prison, while Little Pete was charged with attempted bribery. Following three trials—during which it came out that the Chinatown boss had spent $75,000 over the years in bribing public officials and buying off jurors—Little Pete was convicted and sentenced to five years in Folsom State Prison.[13]

Little Pete served his term without incident and returned to Chinatown, where his criminal empire was still intact. After lording it over the other tongs for several more years, Little Pete finally made one enemy too many. One of his rivals—it was never proven just who it was—got fed up and offered a $3,000 reward to anyone who managed to kill Little Pete. The two men who caught Little Pete unawares as he sat in Wong Chung's barbershop may have claimed that reward, although that, too, is unknown. Two men were arrested after the shooting, but no one was ever convicted for the murder. Little Pete's wife even offered a $2,000 reward for the capture and conviction of her husband's assassins. In April 1898, a highbinder named Lem Sier was shot and killed in Sullivan Alley. Authorities announced that he was the man who had fired the bullets that ended Little Pete's reign as the King of Chinatown, but some speculated that the real killers had hopped a boat back to China immediately after the shooting.[14]

The petite crime boss who ruled the Chinese underworld for so many years provided one last spectacle following his death. Little Pete's funeral was said to have been the largest and gaudiest San Francisco has ever known.[15] The January 27, 1897, issue of the *San Francisco Chronicle* captured the gist of the surreal proceedings in its multideck headline: "Barbaric Pomp for Little Pete; Weird Mingling of Funeral Ceremonies; Beethoven and the Tomtom; Disorderly Crowds at the Cemetery; after a Splendid Pageant the Body Was Not Buried at All."[16]

More than thirty thousand Chinese attended the funeral—essentially all of Chinatown—split between those loyal to Little Pete and rivals who cheered his demise.[17] A large crowd of white San Franciscans, along with thousands of tourists, also showed up to see the "heathen rascal" to his grave. What they witnessed was a parade featuring splashy floral arrangements, fluttering fistfuls of fake money, and a writhing seventy-foot-long paper dragon. Colorfully robed priests chanted against a cacophony of wailing hired mourners, brass bands, clanging gongs, thumping drums, and exploding fireworks. Walking behind the hearse, which was pulled by six black horses, were members of the family and close friends, followed by nearly a hundred carriages filled with other attendees. A police escort led the procession through the packed streets on the way to the cemetery, where things quickly got out of hand thanks to an unruly crowd of Americans.

Reporter Frank Norris documented the "unspeakable shamelessness" of the white spectators that day. Wanting to glimpse Little Pete's face through the window in his casket, "a mob of red-faced, pushing women thronged about the coffin and interrupted everything that went on. There was confusion and cries in Cantonese and English."[18] After the flustered Chinese cut the ceremonies short and left the cemetery, a horde of Americans "descended upon the raised platform, where the funeral meats were placed—pigs and sheep roasted whole, and chickens and bowls of gin and rice. Four men seized a roast pig by either leg and made off with it. . . . Then the crowd found amusement in throwing bowlfuls of gin at each other. The roast chickens were hurled back and forth in the air. The women scrambled for the China bowls for souvenirs."[19]

Even for an unrepentant criminal, it was a disrespectful send-off, although Little Pete wasn't actually buried that day. His remains were carried back to the city, and the family eventually transported them to China for interment, a common practice among Chinese immigrants at that time. Following Little Pete's death, the warfare between the tongs continued, and other leaders rose up to claim the mantle of Chinatown's top crime lord. The last of the really big old-time tong chieftains was Wong Doo King, a man newspapers called "the most notorious highbinder in America" before he was ordered to leave the country in 1915.[20]

While smaller, less influential tongs continued to exist, the criminal gangs had lost their grip on San Francisco's Chinese community by the early 1920s. Several factors contributed to the decline of the city's fighting tongs. The great earthquake and fire of 1906 leveled Chinatown, destroying its rat's nest of whorehouses, opium dens, gambling parlors, and tong hangouts. As the city was rebuilt, those centers of crime weren't resurrected, and law enforcement in the district was stepped up dramatically.

Also, a new generation of American-born Chinese refused to cower in fear of the old criminal gangs. At the same time, tourism began to replace sin as the chief appeal of the Chinese quarter. After a rowdy half-century or more, the honest, decent, law-abiding citizens of Chinatown finally became masters of their own home. Gradually, the memory of Little Pete and his hatchet-wielding minions receded into the sepia-tinted realms of yesteryear. And no one with the slightest sense of decency lamented its passing.

(Note: While it's true the traditional fighting tongs faded away, it's also an ugly reality that Asian youth gangs have sprung up in many large cities since the mid-1960s, some of them linked to their big brothers, the Chinese Triads.[21] Crime marches on.)

CHAPTER 5

THE KILLER THEY CALLED HELL'S BELLE

Belle Sorensen Gunness

Gunness with children Philip, Myrtle, and Lucy

The little Norwegian girl swept her huge, marveling blue eyes over the glass candy case, a smile of anticipation lighting her pretty face. Clutching her penny tightly, the towheaded six year old carefully considered the tempting assortment of sweets on display—licorice drops, wild cherry lozenges, tiny root beer barrels, peppermint sticks in gay swirling colors. The girl's parents stood nearby, watching patiently as their daughter decided what to buy. For a Chicago immigrant family in 1896, a Saturday afternoon trip to the candy store was one of the few indulgences they could afford.

Behind the counter, a thickset matron awaited the girl's decision. A tight smile seemed to be all the woman could muster by way of cordiality. Thirty-six-year-old Belle Sorensen had little reason to smile. The confectionary shop she'd opened after her marriage wasn't doing too well, despite its location amid Chicago's thriving Norwegian community. For over half a century, working-class Norwegians had been immigrating to the Windy City in search of a better life. Sorensen herself had come to America from Norway, but she discovered that making a go of it in her new homeland was tougher than she'd expected. She was, however, a resourceful woman. Even as she scooped out a penny's worth of licorice drops for her angelic young customer, she was contemplating a new career, one destined to reward her handsomely. In a matter of months, the stolid shopkeeper would embark on a decade-long crime spree, a rampage of exceptional deviousness and nightmarish brutality.[1]

Between the late 1890s and 1908, Belle Sorensen Gunness (she married a second time in 1902) is believed to have slain over forty people, including her two husbands and all seven of her children, profiting repeatedly from fraudulent property and life insurance claims and other financial scams.[2] Her victims included a string of love-starved, cash-bearing suitors she lured to her farm in Indiana, where, instead of finding romance, the men found violent death. The so-called "Lady Bluebeard" had a streak of the pyromaniac in her. She apparently faked her own demise in a 1908 house fire and disappeared for good, leaving behind a blood-drenched legacy as one of the country's most notorious lonely hearts killers and our worst female serial killer ever.[3]

Sorensen's grim story began on the cold shores of Lake Selbusjoen in central Norway. She was born Brynhild Paulsdatter Storset in November 1859. Her impoverished family lived in a farming village in the municipality of Selbu, a region known today as the birthplace of the Norwegian wool sweater industry. Around 1881, Brynhild immigrated to the United States, where she adopted the name "Belle." In 1884, she married Mads Sorensen, a Chicago department store guard.

When the candy store she and Mads opened on Grand Avenue failed to prosper, the calculating Mrs. Sorensen found another way to turn a profit—fraud. Less than a year after the store was opened, a fire destroyed the well-insured shop. Sorensen was present when the blaze broke out. She raised the alarm, telling authorities that a kerosene lamp had exploded. The money Sorensen collected enabled her and Mads to buy a new house on the city's West Side. It also paved the way for Sorensen's occupational makeover, one that entailed far less hard work and a generous helping of mayhem.

The most shocking aspect of Sorensen's criminality was the ease with which she directed her violence at her own family. She and Mads claimed four children in a 1900 census. Two of their children, Caroline and Axel, died as infants. The official cause of death for both was listed as acute colitis—a malady whose symptoms parallel those of strychnine poisoning.[4] As with her store, Sorensen had insured her children and collected a payout on the two deaths. She still had little Myrtle and Lucy to look after, and there was an older girl in the household as well, a foster child named Jennie Olsen. None of the children would live to adulthood.

In addition to the deaths of Caroline and Axel, other mishaps befell the Sorensens around this time. Their new house in Chicago's Austin neighborhood was destroyed by fire, generating an additional insurance check that paid for yet another home. That was followed by the death of Mads Sorensen, who perished on July 30, 1900—the only day that his two life insurance policies overlapped, boosting his widow's payout significantly. Poor old Mads died of convulsions, which the family doctor attributed to his heart condition. Other observers noted that the deceased's symptoms closely resembled strychnine poisoning.[5]

The ostentatiously grief-stricken Mrs. Sorensen collected an insurance windfall of $8,500 (she pulled herself together long enough to apply for the money the day after the funeral). Along with the $5,000 she got for selling their home, Sorensen had amassed a tidy nest egg—equivalent to nearly $350,000 today.[6] With her newfound wealth, she packed up the surviving kids and made for the Indiana countryside northwest of La Porte, where, in November 1901, she purchased a hog farm with a two-story brick home. Sorensen was about to enter the most prosperous—and bloody—period of her murderous life.

In April 1902, Sorensen married a Norwegian man from La Porte named Peter Gunness. Their union was star-crossed from the outset. Just one week after the wedding, Peter Gunness's seven-month-old daughter from an earlier marriage died of unknown causes while she was alone in the house with her new stepmother. In December of the same year, tragedy struck again when a sausage grinder fell on Peter Gunness's head and did him in. His widow had to find solace in her husband's $3,000 life insurance policy.[7]

The locals were curious about two mysterious deaths occurring in the same family in such a short span of time, especially in light of a remark one of Belle's daughters made to a classmate: "My momma killed my poppa," the girl is said to have confided to a friend. "She hit him with a cleaver and he died."[8] The comment naturally caused an uproar, but the kindly people of La Porte took pity on the twice-widowed Mrs. Gunness when they learned that she was pregnant with her late husband's child (she would give birth to a son, Philip). The coroner's inquest looking into Peter Gunness's suspicious death dropped the matter and Bloody Belle went about her business.

Fresh out of husbands to clobber or poison, Gunness turned to the lonely hearts columns for a new stream of income. Not long after Husband Number Two was safely tucked away, she ran the following advertisement in several newspapers aimed at Scandinavian readers: "Personal—comely widow who owns a large farm in one of the finest districts in La Porte County, Indiana, desires to make the acquaintance of a gentleman equally well provided, with view of joining fortunes. No replies by letter considered unless sender is willing to follow answer with personal visit. Triflers need not apply."[9]

Soon after the ads appeared, a lengthy procession of suitors began calling. How Gunness attracted all those men speaks to the innate desperation of the male contingent of our species. Gunness was by no means an attractive woman. In her forties by this time, she bore a striking resemblance to grizzled baseball manager Leo Durocher. A newspaper article described her as "a coarse, fat, heavy-featured woman . . . with a big head covered with a mop of mud-colored hair, small eyes, huge hands and arms, and a gross body with difficulty supported on feet grotesquely small."[10] Another newspaper description said she had a "generally vicious appearance" and lacked "womanly characteristics."[11] Her personality wasn't all that winsome either. In a family portrait taken with Myrtle, Lucy, and baby Philip, she wore an expression of barely suppressed rage, as if she were itching to strangle the photographer. But then, owning a nice spread in prime farm country could make up for a few deficiencies.

One of the suitors who hauled up on Mrs. Gunness's doorstep was fifty-year-old John Moo of Elbow Lake, Minnesota. Moo brought along a thousand dollars to pay off Mrs. Gunness's mortgage (that was her standard ploy for wangling money out of her visitors). Mr. Moo disappeared less than a week after his arrival.

Widower Ole Budsberg of Iola, Wisconsin, also came a-courting. After mortgaging his farm and withdrawing a large sum at the La Porte Savings Bank, Ole vanished. When his sons wrote to determine their father's whereabouts, Gunness told them she had no idea where he was, but that she was still willing to marry him if he could be located.[12]

Herman Konitzberg of Chicago showed up with a hatful of cash, as did Henry Gurholdt of Scandinavia, Wisconsin; George Berry of Tuscola, Illinois; Bert

Chase of Mishawaka, Indiana; and Charles Ermond of New Castle, Pennsylvania. No one ever saw any of them again after their visits to the Gunness farm.

Andrew Helgelein, a farmer from Aberdeen, South Dakota, exchanged a series of letters with Gunness. Even though she hadn't met him in person, Gunness professed her love for Helgelein, writing, "I can tell from your letters that you are the man I want." She added prophetically, "Come prepared to stay forever."[13] Shortly after Helgelein showed up in La Porte and cashed a large check, he too disappeared.

The only suitor who met Belle Gunness face-to-face and lived to tell about it appears to have been George Anderson of Tarkio, Missouri. Anderson only managed to survive because he hadn't brought all his money with him. Gunness insisted that he send home for the rest of his savings. While waiting for the money to arrive, Anderson slept in the guest bedroom. On his last night there, he awoke to find Gunness leaning over him with a malevolent look in her eyes. Terrified, Anderson jumped up, grabbed his clothes, and dashed out of the house, to his good fortune.

Evidently, Gunness's favorite method of dispatching her victims was to drug or poison them at dinner and then brain while they slept.[14] At five foot eight and well over two hundred pounds, Gunness was a powerful woman, strong enough to butcher her own hogs, so manhandling a measly human would have been no great challenge for her, and the grounds of her farm provided a convenient place to get rid of the bodies.

Gunness's grisly moneymaking scheme continued until the early months of 1908. That's when she began having trouble with the hired help. After her second husband's death, Gunness had employed a local handyman, Ray Lamphere, to assist her in running the farm. Lamphere fell in love with Gunness, despite witnessing the parade of gentlemen callers she entertained. When Lamphere began pressing his attentions on his employer, she fired him. She then started building a public case against the man, complaining to the sheriff that he'd threatened her and telling county authorities that Lamphere was mentally unbalanced.

In truth, Lamphere wasn't her chief concern. She was more worried about the brother of Andrew Helgelein. Asle Helgelein had written Gunness to find out what had happened to his brother after he didn't return home from his trip to La Porte. Gunness replied that she didn't know where Andrew was, but that she would help search for him if Asle would "sell off everything he owns, get together as much of your own money as you can and come here."[15] Gunness may have sensed it was time to make one final score and move on. To set the stage for her escape, she called on a lawyer in La Porte to draw up her will, telling him that she needed the document because Ray Lamphere had threatened to murder her and her children and burn down their house.[16]

Early the next morning—April 28, 1908—Gunness's new hired man, Joe Maxson, was awakened by the smell of smoke. Stumbling out of his bedroom, he found the house on fire. After shouting to alert the sleeping Gunness family, Maxson escaped from the burning house and ran to get help, but by the time the La Porte firefighters finally made it out to the Gunness farm the house was destroyed. Looking through the smoldering ruins, the firemen found four bodies in the basement—the three Gunness children, Myrtle, Lucy, and Philip, along with an adult victim, presumed to be their mother, although, strangely, the head of the adult victim was missing.[17] Ray Lamphere was immediately arrested for murder and arson.

While searching the farm for the missing head of the adult victim, investigators made a shocking discovery. Buried out in the yard were several more bodies. Some had been hacked up and stuffed in gunnysacks. Asle Helgelein, who'd just arrived in town, identified the remains of his brother. Another body was identified as Jennie Olsen, Gunness's foster daughter, who'd been absent from the household for more than a year (Gunness had spread the story that she'd sent the girl to school in another state). Three other bodies were identified as those of missing suitors John Moo, Ole Budsberg, and Henry Gurholdt.

The remains of the four fire victims and Andrew Helgelein were examined and found to contain high levels of arsenic and strychnine. The situation grew more tangled when authorities found some of Belle Gunness's dental bridgework in the ashes of her home. At first, the teeth appeared to indicate that Gunness had died in the fire, although they'd miraculously survived the conflagration in excellent condition, a physical impossibility according to tests. It seemed likely the teeth were a plant, and there was other evidence that things were amiss. Just days before the fire, Gunness had purchased a large quantity of kerosene and withdrawn most of her money from local banks. Also, the bodies discovered in the basement were pinned beneath the family piano, which had fallen from the first-floor parlor. If the fire victims had died in their second-floor bedrooms, they couldn't have ended up underneath the piano.

Suddenly, newspapers that had been reporting sympathetically about the deaths of Mrs. Gunness and her children began running stories about the Indiana "House of Horrors," raising the question of whether Belle Gunness had faked her own death and pulled a vanishing act.[18] Doctors determined that the headless fire victim would have been about five feet three and around one hundred fifty pounds—a much smaller woman than Belle Gunness (the body may have been that of Mae O'Reilly, a domestic worker hired by Gunness who was never seen again after the fire).[19] Despite the confusion, Ray Lamphere was still prosecuted for the murders of Gunness and her children. Found innocent of the killings but guilty of arson, he died shortly after being sent to prison. Just before his death, he confided to a fellow inmate that he'd assisted Gunness in disposing of the bodies of her many victims and had helped her escape the day before the fire.[20] No one knows if what he said was true.

As for Belle Gunness, she quickly passed into myth. The same issue of the *New York Tribune* that announced the headless victim's body couldn't have been that of Mrs. Gunness because of its size also ran an article about the murderess being spotted on the streets of Chicago. The claims were highly unreliable though. The article stated that she'd "been seen in several parts of the city and on different streetcars at the same time."[21] Even a devil like Gunness couldn't have pulled that off. The *Tribune* reinforced the suspicion that Gunness had murdered her own children, noting that the foreheads of all three victims appeared to have been bashed in.

In the following years, Gunness sightings were reported all over the country, none of them ever substantiated. Exactly what became of the woman was never discovered, although someone matching her description was arrested in Los Angeles in 1931 for poisoning a rich businessman. The woman went by the name of Esther Carlson, but two former residents of La Porte who were then living in California identified her as Belle Gunness. The woman's friends insisted she was really a Swedish immigrant named Esther Johnson. Whoever the prisoner actually was, she died in jail before she could be brought to trial.

The legend of Belle Gunness, however, didn't end in a Los Angeles jail cell. It continued to grow, sometimes in curious ways. Magazine covers depicted her as a beautiful Gibson Girl or glamorous flapper. In 1955, Gold Medal Books published a biography called *The Truth about Belle Gunness*. The cover featured a gorgeous, chesty blonde in the tradition of bodice-ripping romance novels, with a provocative blurb proclaiming that "men swarmed like flies to her embrace and one by one were loved—and died."[22] Hokie poems and ballads were written about the bloodthirsty black widow ("Lay that cleaver down, Belle, Lay that cleaver down"). She also inspired the 2004 movie *Method*, with the beautiful Elizabeth Hurley slowly going nuts in the starring role.[23] And Gunness's lonely hearts murders even have contemporary relevance—as a warning about the dangers of searching for love long distance via the Internet.

Countless unanswered questions remain about this horrible woman, but this much has been established as fact: the bodies of at least ten victims were dug up on Gunness's Indiana "murder farm."[24] The death list doubles if you add in the four burned bodies found in the basement of the home, plus Gunness's two dead husbands, her two children who died in Chicago, and Peter Gunness's infant daughter. And the list doubles again if all the missing suitors whose bodies were never found are counted. Handyman Ray Lamphere said that Gunness killed forty-two men on her farm—by no means an unbelievable number.[25]

Judging from old newspaper articles, people of Gunness's time were fascinated with this perverted creature in the same way that we're drawn to storybook monsters. But Gunness wasn't some made-up bogeyman. She was disgustingly real, a woman bereft of human feelings or maternal instincts. Belle Gunness was obviously an irredeemable psychopath, a person whose bloodlust had to have been fueled by something deeper and darker than greed (even though her sister said she was "crazy for money").[26] Gunness could have lived in ease for the rest of her days with the proceeds from her Chicago crimes, but she was driven to continue luring victims to her Indiana lair when there was no compelling reason for her to do so other than for the thrill of getting away with murder—the most frightening motivation of all for taking a human life.

CHAPTER 6

PARTNERS IN PERFIDY

Isaac Harris and Max Blanck

Max Blanck (left) and Isaac Harris

T he afternoon of March 25, 1911, was a fine time to be out and about in Greenwich Village. On this bracing Saturday in early spring, New Yorkers with errands to run hurried along the streets with collars raised against the gusty winds, their pale winter faces knotted in concentration. Weekend idlers casually sized up the passing crowd from park benches or took their ease indoors—maybe reading a book in the old Astor Library over on Lafayette or nursing a drink in a cozy MacDougal Street café.

For the five hundred workers of the Triangle Shirtwaist Factory, however, it was just another workday. Occupying the top three floors of the Asch Building—a modern ten-story structure on the corner of Washington Place and Greene Street just off Washington Square—the Triangle factory produced the long-sleeved women's blouses known as shirtwaists . . . and lots of them, more than a thousand a day.[1] Modeled on men's shirts, the blouses were part of the Gibson Girl look and had become the unofficial uniform of working women everywhere.

The factory's seamstresses, mostly Eastern European and Italian immigrants, sat elbow-to-elbow at long rows of tables, hunched over their ceaselessly clattering sewing machines for hours on end six days a week. Even though the ten-year-old building's lofty ceilings and large windows were improvements over the typical cave-like sweatshops of early-twentieth-century America, the seamstresses still faced the usual problems of overcrowding, long hours, and abysmal pay. And the poorly ventilated factory lacked basic safety features such as sprinkler systems and reliable emergency exits. But then worker output was the main concern here, not creature comforts.

Late in 1909, the Triangle seamstresses had gone on strike to better their conditions. They were joined by other New York garment workers in the largest walkout of women employees in the country's history.[2] While the strike forced smaller factories to agree to raises, shorter hours, and improved working conditions, the owners of the Triangle factory refused to give in. Isaac Harris and Max Blanck—known as the "Shirtwaist Kings" for their domination of the industry—paid hooligans to beat up the women picketers.[3] But after three months, even the wealthy Harris and Blanck were ready to make a few token concessions. The men agreed to minimally higher wages and shorter hours, although they adamantly refused to recognize the garment workers' union. They also disregarded complaints about workplace safety.[4] On this brisk March afternoon, that last oversight would foster a national tragedy.

By 4:40 p.m., the workday was coming to a close inside the busy factory. Two of Triangle's seamstresses, dark-haired sisters Sara and Tessie Saracino, ages twenty-five and twenty respectively, were chatting happily as they put away their work. Tomorrow would be their day off. The siblings had come to this country from Italy two years earlier and were helping to support their family, which lived on East 119th Street.

Suddenly, cries of "Fire!" startled the sisters. Smoke began seeping into the ninth-floor workshop from a blaze on the floor below (a fire started by a carelessly discarded match or cigarette, it was later surmised). The two young women crossed themselves and uttered quick prayers as pandemonium broke out.

Everywhere, screaming employees dashed for the exits. They were startled to find the stairway leading down the Greene Street side of the building already blocked by fire. Across the room, workers struggled in vain to open the door to the Washington Place stairway. The door, it seemed, was locked. A number of employees managed to escape by elevator, and others scrambled up the Greene Street stairway and onto the roof, where they climbed to safety in a nearby building. Workers on the eighth floor were aware of the fire sooner, so they had more time to flee. But for scores of employees, especially those working on the ninth floor—who only learned of the fire when it was completely out of control—there would be no escape. They were caught in the quintessential firetrap.

Although the metal-and-stone Asch building was touted as being fireproof, the contents of the Triangle factory were anything but. The blaze quickly became an inferno, feeding on wooden tables, paper patterns, oily rags, and piles of fabric. Unbelievably, Isaac Harris and Max Blanck had never bothered to conduct fire drills to prepare their workers for an emergency.[5] The only precautions consisted of hoses in the stairwells and a few water buckets. Workers attempted to fight the fire with the hoses, but there was no water pressure. The single rickety fire escape clinging to the side of the building gave way under the weight of a knot of frightened women, plunging them to their deaths. The overloaded elevators soon gave out, leaving those trapped on the upper floors with a sickening choice: they could either burn to death or leap from the windows and find death on the cold sidewalks below.

United Press reporter William Shepherd witnessed the tragic outcome of that dilemma from the pavement on Washington Place. He looked up in horror as women and young girls stood in the eighth-floor windows high above, flames beating all around them. He turned away when the first girl jumped but watched a second girl leap to her death. At first, some of the onlookers thought the people above were throwing down bundles of cloth in order to save the material. They were quickly stunned by the sight of dozens of women leaping from the windows, forced to fling themselves into space by the raging heat behind them. Shepherd saw a young man help several girls make the deadly plunge, as if he were politely holding a door open for them. Finally, one of the girls hugged him tightly and the two kissed, then the girl plummeted to her death, followed immediately by the young man.

"I learned a new sound," Shepherd wrote in despair, "a more horrible sound than description can picture. It was the thud of a speeding, living body on a stone sidewalk. Thud-dead, thud-dead, thud-dead, thud-dead. Sixty-two thud-deads. I call them that because the sound and the thought of death came to me each time at the same instant. There was plenty of chance to watch them as they came down. The height was eighty feet."[6]

Shepherd witnessed the futile efforts of the New York City Fire Department, whose streams of water fell short of the blaze and whose longest ladder only reached to the sixth floor of the ten-story building. The reporter saw one of the girls jump from above and attempt to grab the ladder, but she missed and fell to her death. On the sidewalk, the firemen held safety nets to catch the jumpers. The falling bodies tore through the nets as if they were made of cobweb.

Hearing screams, Shepherd raced around the corner to Greene Street and beheld an even more terrifying sight. Up on the ninth floor, more girls were trapped by the flames, burning to death in plain sight of the shrieking onlookers below. When the windows finally gave way, bodies came tumbling down— "burning, smoking, flaming bodies, with disheveled hair trailing upward," Shepherd wrote. "The whole, sound, unharmed girls who had jumped on the other side of the building had tried to fall feet down. But these fire torches, suffering ones, fell inertly, only intent that death should come to them on the sidewalk instead of in the furnace behind them."[7]

In less than thirty minutes, the gut-wrenching spectacle was over. There were no more jumpers, no more screams—only the anguished wailing of survivors and witnesses. In that brief span of time, 146 lives had been destroyed. Most of the dead were women, and almost half of the victims were still in their teens, some as young as fourteen.[8] Among those killed were the Saracino sisters, whose plans for their Sunday off literally went up in smoke. Many of the survivors darted about the streets in hysteria, driven wild by the things they'd seen.

The scorched and broken bodies of the jumpers were lined up on the sidewalks outside the Asch Building. The police attached numbered tags to the victims' wrists. Inside the building, fireman found dozens of charred bodies, some clinging tightly to one another. More victims were discovered in the elevator and ventilation shafts. In their desperation, the trapped girls had sought any means of escape. (Elevator operator Joseph Zito reported hearing the tinkling of coins from the pay envelopes of the girls who crashed onto the top of his car.)[9] A temporary morgue was set up at Charities Pier on 26th Street to allow families to identify their loved ones. In time, all but six of the victims were identified (Greenwich Village researcher Michael Hirsch established the identities of the last six in 2011).[10]

Two of those who managed to escape the fire were Isaac Harris and Max Blanck. Triangle's owners received a warning telephone call and climbed to safety from the roof of the building. However, the men weren't able to escape the public outrage that followed the disaster—the worst industrial accident in the city's history. On April 5, more than a hundred thousand New Yorkers turned out in a steady downpour to march in a funeral parade honoring the fire victims, and over two hundred fifty thousand more looked on in respectful silence.[11] All of those grieving citizens had one question on their minds: Who was to blame for this needless tragedy?

Though some faulted the city's building inspectors for failing to require adequate emergency exits at the Triangle factory, most people blamed the disaster on the company's tightfisted owners. Harris and Blanck were reviled for their lack of concern for employee safety. When Fire Chief Edward Croker told reporters that one of the doors to the ninth-floor workspace appeared to have been locked, public anger spiked.[12] Two weeks after the fire, Harris and Blanck were indicted by a grand jury on manslaughter charges.

The trial of the Shirtwaist Kings began the first week of December 1911. Strolling toward the courtroom in their derby hats—with cries of "Murderers!" ringing in their ears from distraught onlookers—the slightly built Harris and the thickset Blanck looked like comedians Laurel and Hardy, although there was nothing funny about these two steely businessmen. Russian Jews who'd immigrated to America two decades earlier, the two had succeeded in the extremely competitive garment industry with the classic formula of high volume and cheap labor. Both men owned swank, servant-filled homes, and they traveled to work in chauffeured limousines. Besides their Greenwich Village factory, they owned several other manufacturing facilities. They had it made, and they intended to hang on to the good life. Sparing no expense, the men hired one of the city's top defense lawyers, Max Steuer. The prosecution was led by Assistant District Attorney Charles Bostwick.

The trial hinged on the issue of the locked door blocking the Washington Place exit of the ninth-floor workroom. Bostwick contended that although fire had blocked the stairs on the Greene Street side of the building, many of those trapped on the ninth floor could have escaped down the Washington Place stairs—just as workers on the eighth floor had done—if the door there hadn't been locked.[13] Given the tragic consequences of the fire, the rationale for bolting that door was monstrous.

It was common knowledge that Harris and Blanck were inordinately concerned about employee theft, especially Blanck.[14] To prevent pilfering, the owners had their shop foreman examine the seamstresses' belongings each day as they left work down the narrow Greene Street stairway. To keep anyone from sneaking goods down the Washington Place stairway, the door on that side of the workroom was kept locked, in direct violation of the city safety code. Besides being against the law, the security measure was out of proportion to the threat. In his testimony, Isaac Harris admitted that pilfering had little financial impact on their business. Less than $25 worth of goods had been stolen from the Triangle factory in all its years of operation.[15] The irrational fear of theft was simply the paranoia of the selfish.

During the trial, the prosecution produced the fire-scorched lock assembly from the Washington Place door, which clearly showed the deadbolt in the locked position. A parade of survivors testified that they'd been unable to open the door. It seemed irrefutable that the door had been fastened shut, despite testimony to the contrary. (Several employees who claimed the door wasn't locked admitted that they'd received pay hikes from Harris and Blanck shortly before the trial—a barefaced example of witness bribery that was a possible felony in its own right. And some of these witnesses apparently perjured themselves by contradicting previous statements.)[16]

In a strange turn of events, Judge Thomas Crain told the jurors that they not only had to be convinced that the door was locked on the day of the fire, but that they also had to be sure that Harris and Blanck were *aware* it was locked. The second stipulation was virtually impossible to prove, and it seemed unnecessary besides, considering that the obsessive, penny-pinching owners were the only ones with any interest in seeing that the door was kept bolted. However, defense attorney Steuer succeeded in planting doubt in the jurors' minds about his clients' knowledge. After three weeks of testimony, the jury deliberated for less than two hours before acquitting the Shirtwaist Kings. It was not a popular verdict. When the proceedings adjourned, an angry, screaming crowd waited in the streets for Harris and Blanck. Running like a couple of purse snatchers, the two powerful businessmen escaped by ducking into a subway station.

To compound the injustice of the trial's outcome, Harris and Blanck ended up making a fat profit from the insurance they collected on the fire damage. The men received over $60,000 more in compensation than their losses.[17] (Known as over-insurers, the two had profited repeatedly in the past for smaller fires, although no one had died in those.) Many of the families of the fire victims brought civil suits against the owners of the Asch Building and the Triangle Shirtwaist Company. After lengthy wrangling, the families received $75 in damages for each of the dead.[18] The settlement was no doubt less than the plaintiffs had spent in legal fees.

Not everything went the Shirtwaist Kings' way in the succeeding years. Although Harris and Blanck attempted to reestablish their place in the garment industry after the fire, their reputations tanked. (It didn't help when Blanck's limousine struck two children in two different mishaps on the same day in 1912.) Worst of all, the two men learned nothing from the tragedy they'd caused: a new factory they set up immediately after the fire was found to violate several safety codes. In 1913, Blanck was fined $20 for once again locking a factory door with workers inside.[19] (The judge apologized for having to levy the fine.) That same year, a factory inspection revealed multiple fire hazards, and the following year, the partners were caught attaching fake labels to their garments intended to certify that the clothing had been manufactured under safe working conditions. In 1918, the Triangle Shirtwaist Company went out of business. Two years later, the partnership was dissolved and Harris and Blanck faded into oblivion.

Some good actually came of the events of March 25, 1911. Public revulsion at the horrors of the Triangle disaster forced the government to get serious about protecting workers. In the three years following the fire, New York's state legislature passed thirty-six new laws regulating workplace safety.[20] Increasingly powerful unions played a significant role in bringing safety concerns to light, and reformers also began to address the festering issues of low wages, long hours, and child labor. The New York laws became models for other states, as well as for the federal labor legislation passed in the 1930s as part of the New Deal. President Franklin D. Roosevelt's secretary of labor, Frances Perkins, went so far as to say that March 25, 1911, was the first day of the New Deal.[21] (In one of history's odd twists, Perkins had witnessed the Triangle fire herself.)

The inhumane conditions of the Triangle Shirtwaist Factory were by no means unique. They existed in thousands of American companies before the advent of tough labor laws and strong unions. (When one New York factory owner of the time was told he should initiate fire drills to protect his workers, he said, "Let 'em burn. They're a lot of cattle, anyway.")[22] Blinded by avarice, the Shirtwaist Kings wrung every possible measure of productivity from their workers with little regard for their safety or welfare. And yet, this unscrupulous pair had the gall to claim that their factory was a model of good working conditions.

Harris and Blanck may have been regarded as hardheaded businessmen by some, but anyone inclined to admire them should ask themselves this: Was Sara Saracino's life worth just $75? Or her sister Tessie's? Or the lives of any of the other 144 Triangle employees who died such unimaginably horrible deaths? The most blasphemous aspect of the Triangle fire is the haunting realization that many of those people perished simply because two greedy men were afraid someone might steal a few scraps of cloth. Just as heartrending is the knowledge that, on that fateful March afternoon, the workday was almost over. In only a few more minutes, all the employees would have been safely out of the building, their weekly pay envelopes in hand.

The fact that the Shirtwaist Kings avoided any significant punishment for their deeds should serve as a reminder that the need to protect the interests of employees never ends. Today, the lessons of the Triangle tragedy seem lost on some people—witness the ongoing assaults on collective bargaining rights and the recurring complaints from industry about "burdensome" safety regulations. Sadly, the US Department of Labor confirms that clothing sweatshops are once again flourishing in this country, preying chiefly on recent immigrants and following the same old patterns of low wages and worker exploitation.[23]

In 1991, the site of the Triangle factory fire was declared a National Historic Landmark. New York University now uses the building for offices and classrooms. History, in that regard at least, has moved on. But this much remains unchanged: for callously sacrificing others to enrich themselves, Isaac Harris and Max Blanck have earned a prominent place on the list of infamous Americans. The blind spot in their characters was enormous and unforgivable. As New York Fire Chief Edward Croker angrily summarized in the wake of the Triangle disaster, "It comes right down to dollars and cents against human lives."[24]

CHAPTER 7

CHICAGO'S FLORIST-MOBSTER

Dean O'Banion

On a raw November morning in 1924, a lengthy funeral procession moved with stately dignity along Chicago's North Wells Street. People surged along the sidewalks and peered from rooftops, straining to catch a glimpse of the passing cortege. Inside the hearse, a $10,000 silver and bronze casket bore the remains of one of the city's most well-known and flamboyant individuals. During the three days the body had been available for viewing, some forty thousand visitors had filed through the Sbarbaro funeral home, which overflowed with twenty-six carloads of flowers. By the time the procession reached the

Mount Carmel Cemetery, in suburban Hillside, an estimated fifteen thousand people had assembled to witness the graveside service.[1]

From such impressive numbers, strangers to Chicago might have assumed that the deceased had been an honored member of society—a philanthropist, perhaps, or maybe a high-ranking member of the clergy or revered public servant. They would have been wrong.

The massive crowd of Chicagoans had turned out to mourn—or secretly gloat over—the death of Charles Dean O'Banion, a kingpin in the local underworld. Before mob boss Al Capone rose to power, the short, chubby Irish American known variously as Dean, Deanie, or Dion O'Banion held sway over criminal activities throughout the city's northeastern neighborhoods. His North Side Gang kept the illegal beer and whiskey flowing during the early years of Prohibition. A paradoxical figure, O'Banion was normally jovial and outgoing, yet he packed three "gats" in his expensive three-piece suits and was linked to the deaths of twenty-five men. The chief of police called him "Chicago's arch criminal."[2] (In the 1931 film *The Public Enemy,* the jaunty mobster was a model for the character played by James Cagney—the menacing Tom Powers, a sneering psycho who famously smashes a grapefruit in his girlfriend's face.)[3]

Like many a gangster, O'Banion possessed the potentially fatal traits of hubris and ambition. On November 10, 1924, he was gunned down after repeated run-ins with his rivals. His murder set off the brutal "beer wars" that plagued Chicago for the remainder of the 1920s, climaxing in the gory St. Valentine's Day Massacre in 1929, when Al Capone's gunsels brazenly executed seven men associated with the North Side Gang. Hundreds of Chicago mobsters died during those violent years, but Dean O'Banion stood out from all the other hoods who went down in a hail of bullets. An alcohol-shunning family man, he was known for aiding the poor and generously staking friends who were down on their luck. And he had a surprising outlook on one of the mob's more lucrative rackets: as a devout Catholic, he abhorred prostitution. ("I don't peddle flesh," he said, "and I never will.")[4]

Even more surprising was O'Banion's everyday occupation. When he wasn't rubbing out a rival, highjacking a beer truck, or stealing a warehouse full of liquor, O'Banion spent his time creating artistic bouquets at a flower shop across from the Holy Name Cathedral, the church in which he'd received his religious instruction as a boy and still attended mass. It's said that a particularly stunning floral arrangement could make O'Banion giddy, just as the sight of a child in distress could reduce him to tears.[5] Without a doubt, this softhearted lover of beauty was no ordinary rum-running killer.

O'Banion was born in July 1892 in Maroa, a postage-stamp village hidden among the cornfields of central Illinois. His life might have turned out differently had his mother not died of tuberculosis in 1901. Afterward, his father took O'Banion and his older brother to Chicago to live near their maternal grandparents. O'Banion's new home was in the North Side neighborhood called Little Hell, an aptly named mire of poverty, crime, and desperation. Before long, the former small-town kid was running wild with the Little Hellions, one of the city's numerous street gangs. While showing off to his buddies one day, he fell under a streetcar and nearly lost a leg. The injury left him with a lifelong limp.

O'Banion's Jekyll-and-Hyde personality revealed itself during his early years in Chicago. Besides rolling drunks with the Little Hellions, he attended the Holy Name Parochial School, sang in the church choir, and sold newspapers on the street. After quitting school at fourteen, he put his strong tenor voice to good use in one of his few legitimate jobs—as a singing waiter at McGovern's bar and brothel, a North Clark Street dive frequented by a rowdy mix of gamblers, thieves, and other lowlifes. Despite his limp and short stature, O'Banion was a tough little fireplug of a brawler, and he sometimes filled in as a bouncer at McGovern's.

One of the crooks who patronized McGovern's introduced O'Banion to the delicate art of safecracking. Like everything he did, O'Banion embraced this new activity with gusto, figuring that if a little nitroglycerin was effective for opening a safe, even more would be that much better. As a result, he occasionally set a charge that destroyed both the targeted safe and its contents. On one botched job, he placed the nitro in the wrong position and blew out the wall of the building he'd broken into, leaving its safe unopened. Still, it was a dandy explosion.

As he grew older, O'Banion joined the Bloody Market Streeters, a gang that peddled stolen merchandise on Chicago's black market. The gang members also worked as "sluggers" during the city's newspaper circulation wars of the 1910s. The job was simple: O'Banion and his pals visited neighborhood newsstands and advised the owners to sell no newspapers other than the one that was currently paying the gang for its services. If anyone failed to heed their advice, the Market Streeters beat the stuffing out of them—a more effective marketing technique than quoting advertising rates or reader demographics. The competition between newspapers was so intense that rival sluggers sometimes had Wild West shootouts in the streets.[6]

O'Banion scuffled along as a minor hood throughout his teens and early twenties, bumping up against the law from time to time. In 1909, he broke into a drugstore and was caught stealing postage stamps. In 1911, he was hauled in for beating a fellow hood with a blackjack and carrying concealed weapons. Both arrests resulted in short jail terms—the only time O'Banion ever spent behind bars.[7] (He'd be indicted several times in the early 1920s, but by then he was rich and powerful enough to avoid further convictions.)

O'Banion's big opportunity came in January 1920 with the introduction of Prohibition, the "noble experiment" that turned average citizens into law-breakers and made criminals rich. Surrounded by his own loyal and growing gang, O'Banion was well positioned to capitalize on the new law. His lieutenants included longtime friends Earl "Hymie" Weiss, Vincent "Schemer" Drucci, and George "Bugs" Moran. Buying booze in Canada or from clandestine local manufacturers, the gang began supplying the underground speakeasies that were popping up like dandelions. O'Banion was soon running all of the bootlegging activities in Chicago's northern lakefront neighborhoods, which took in the affluent Gold Coast. (The North Siders would also insinuate themselves into the area's politics, stuffing ballot boxes and bashing heads as needed.)

With the boldness of a buccaneer, O'Banion built up his liquor supply by robbing the delivery trucks and storage facilities of his rivals. He pulled off his initial hijacking on December 30, 1919—one of the first in Chicago—and he continued to make news with his audacious raids. In one theft, the North Side Gang snatched $100,000 worth of Canadian whiskey from a freight car sitting in a rail yard on the West Side. At the giant Sibley Warehouse at Sixteenth and Peoria, the gang carted off a fortune in bonded Kentucky whiskey. The influence of the bootleggers was on full display in the Sibley operation: a squad of cops on O'Banion's payroll escorted the thieves as they drove away with their horde of stolen booze.[8]

From their headquarters above the Schofield Company—the North State Street flower shop partly owned by O'Banion—the North Siders oversaw a bootlegging empire that raked in a million dollars a year (equivalent to more than $12 million today).[9] It was enough to keep O'Banion dressed in fine tailored suits and his cuddly young wife, Viola, swaddled in furs. The couple lived in a swank apartment on North Pine Grove and owned a fleet of expensive cars. Perhaps to compensate for his hardscrabble upbringing, O'Banion loved to put on a dinner jacket and squire his wife to the latest shows.

O'Banion seemed to get along with everyone, greeting strangers with a slap on the back and a cheery "Nice to meet ya, swell fellow" (while keeping one hand hovering close to his pistols).[10] The North Side boss even managed a temporary coexistence with the powerful South Side gangsters led by Johnny Torrio and his lieutenant Al Capone. At the start of Prohibition, the predominantly Italian South

Siders and the Irish-dominated North Siders agreed to stay within their respective territories, but thanks to the impetuous Dean O'Banion, that didn't last.

In 1924, the South Side Gang expanded into the neighboring town of Cicero, and O'Banion expected to get his share of the action there. Johnny Torrio ceded O'Banion some of the new territory and gave him an interest in a casino. O'Banion immediately persuaded a number of Chicago speakeasies to relocate to his part of Cicero, angering the Torrio forces. When the Sicilian Genna brothers started selling their rotgut in O'Banion's North Side territory, Torrio was in no mood to act as peacemaker. O'Banion inflamed the situation by hijacking a Genna liquor truck. The Gennas wanted to eliminate O'Banion, but the Sicilian Union, a powerful mob-connected fraternal organization headed locally by Mike Merlo, refused to sanction his murder.

Things might have cooled off if O'Banion hadn't kept poking the South Siders (who, some say, he lumped together as "them Sicilians" and derided as "spaghetti-benders" and worse).[11] O'Banion had already tried to frame Johnny Torrio and "Scarface" Capone for a murder that he'd committed. After that, he cheated Torrio by selling him his share of a Chicago brewery the two owned jointly—knowing that the police were about to close the brewery. Torrio lost $500,000 to O'Banion and ended up facing a jail sentence.[12] O'Banion's double-cross left Torrio siding with the Gennas. When Mike Merlo died of cancer on November 8, 1924, there was no one to block the mobsters who wanted O'Banion dead. They didn't wait long to act.

Just two days later, O'Banion was in his flower shop trimming some chrysanthemums for one of the dozens of arrangements ordered for Mike Merlo's funeral. Chicago's mobsters never stinted on flowers to honor the deceased—including rivals they'd bumped off—and O'Banion's shop received most of their business. While O'Banion was busy with his flowers, three men walked into his store. O'Banion stepped into the showroom to greet them, still holding his scissors in one hand. Apparently recognizing the men, O'Banion held out his hand in greeting. One of the men seized O'Banion's hand and pulled him off balance. The two other men drew their weapons and fired a fusillade into O'Banion's body. Two bullets struck O'Banion in the chest, two in his throat, and one in his face. One of the gunmen fired a sixth bullet into O'Banion's face after he fell to the floor. The florist-mobster was dead in seconds.

The police made a show of searching for O'Banion's killers, but no one was ever convicted of the murder. It's generally believed that the three assassins included a top New York hood and a pair of local gunmen.[13] O'Banion's death set off a wave of killings. The next five years were the bloodiest in Chicago's history, as rival bootleggers blasted away at each other with pistols, shotguns, hand grenades, and Thompson submachine guns. Hundreds of mobsters were retired "at the insistence of bullets," as the *Chicago Tribune* neatly phrased it.[14]

Most sources claim that O'Banion's friends Hymie Weiss, Schemer Drucci, and Bugs Moran murdered one of the six Genna brothers in May 1925.[15] Two more Gennas were killed within two months, and the three surviving brothers decided it was time to relocate. The North Siders definitely went after Johnny Torrio, gunning him down in front of his apartment building and leaving him for dead. Torrio survived, but the attempt on his life prompted him to hand over his organization to Al Capone and fade away into retirement. The North Siders made repeated attempts to kill Capone but only succeeded in shooting up his car and his Cicero headquarters.

In 1926, the Capone mob cut down Hymie Weiss in front of the Holy Name Cathedral. After the police killed Schemer Drucci in 1927, Bugs Moran took over what remained of O'Banion's empire. The slaughter in Chicago's streets peaked on February 14, 1929, when a Capone hit squad lined up six of Moran's men and an unlucky hanger-on in a North Clark Street garage and riddled their bodies with dozens of bullets.

The St. Valentine's Day Massacre heralded the imminent demise of the North Side Gang.[16] Like a bloated, cigar-chomping emperor, Capone now reigned supreme over Chicago's criminal world, and the bootlegging wars would sputter out. However, the horrific nature of the St. Valentine's Day killings outraged the public. Afterward, federal prosecutors stepped up their efforts to bring down Capone. In 1931, he was convicted of income tax fraud and sentenced to eleven years in prison. Released in 1939, he died a few years later, his physical and mental health ravaged by syphilis of the brain.

Prohibition finally ended in December 1933, rendering the enormous profits from illegal alcohol flatter than last night's beer. While it's true that Prohibition increased crime throughout the country, Chicago was the epicenter of bootlegging lawlessness.[17] Scarface Al Capone has gone down as the most infamous of the Chicago gangsters, but chubby, cheerful Deanie O'Banion was just as avaricious and violent. What set him apart was his dual personality. It seems impossible that a man who could find joy in arranging flowers could also hold a pistol to someone's head and pull the trigger without remorse—as he did in February 1924 when he executed gangster John Duffy, a troublemaker who killed his own wife and made the unforgivable mistake of threatening O'Banion.[18] It's well documented that O'Banion attended church regularly, although he no longer went to confession. How could he?

Just imagine what he'd have had to admit. ("Forgive me, Father, but I had to kill a mug last week.")

O'Banion's funeral was said to have been one of the most expensive Chicago has ever known, costing a staggering $100,000 by some estimates. His friends called it the "funeral of funerals, just what Dean wanted—simple but lavish."[19] The only thing it lacked was the blessing of the Catholic Church. Officials at the Holy Name Cathedral turned away O'Banion's body and refused to conduct a graveside service. "A person who refuses the ministrations of the church in life need not expect to have the ministrations of the church in death," a spokesman said.[20]

Even so, O'Banion's wife insisted he was "a good man" who "never left home without telling me where he was going."[21] She said he was never late for dinner and that his greatest pleasures were sitting at home listening to the radio or to his player piano. People always seem to take a few steps toward sainthood after they pass on, but at least some of Viola O'Banion's claims were true. Although her hubby may have brought about the deaths of more than a score of his fellow human beings, he was also a hardworking businessman with an occasional streak of compassion.

Bullets, bootlegging, and bouquets . . . those were the watchwords of Dean O'Banion's life—a contradictory combination for a wildly unconventional crook. As the *Chicago Tribune* noted after his death, "He really was one hard boiled florist."[22]

CHAPTER 8

A HUCKSTER'S RISE AND FALL

John Brinkley

The sun pressed down like a hot flatiron on the roof of John Brinkley's tiny medical office—a rented room in the back of a drugstore in the somnolent burg of Milford, Kansas. A listless wind barely stirred the dust in the town's unpaved streets. There weren't any traffic lights in Milford because there wasn't any traffic. In 1917, the town of fewer than two hundred souls lacked electricity as well as municipal water and sewer systems. The place was as quiet as the surrounding Flint Hills prairie. Even the bees seemed loud here.

Inside his office, Doc Brinkley listened to a patient, a local farmer. An older man, the farmer was complaining about being "all in, no pep, a flat tire." The flat tire the man referred to was his libido. He and his wife had been trying to have a second child, but without success.

Doc Brinkley started telling the farmer about his recent job at the Swift meatpacking company over in Kansas City, where the randy billy goats awaiting slaughter would keep on copulating right up to the moment they were led away to their doom. "You wouldn't have any trouble if you had a pair of those buck glands in you," said Brinkley.

"Well, why don't you put 'em in?" the farmer replied.[1]

That's just what Doc Brinkley did—using the testicles of the farmer's own goat.

A few weeks later, a townsman named William Stittsworth stopped by for the same procedure. Afterward, he brought in his wife, and Brinkley installed a nanny goat ovary in the woman. When the couple later had a child—a boy they appropriately named Billy—word got out about the doc's magical cure. And that was the humble beginning of John Brinkley's medical empire. At his peak, he was one of the most successful frauds ever to prey on Americans.[2]

It might seem odd that Brinkley didn't settle in a big city, where he'd have a bountiful supply of suckers, but he didn't need to. Even though Milford was just a flyspeck surrounded by miles of farmland, the world soon beat a path through the lonesome fields. Thousands of men and women traveled to Brinkley's clinic sixty-five miles west of Topeka, eager to subject themselves to an operation that seems laughably suspect today but which, in the early years of the twentieth century, struck many people as perfectly plausible. The goat gland doctor would earn vast sums of money through the Roaring Twenties and the decade of the Great Depression, but his good fortune eventually ran its course.[3]

Born a poor, illegitimate North Carolina hillbilly in 1885, Brinkley had grown up with dreams of becoming a doctor. After scraping by as a mail carrier and telegraph operator, he commenced his career in fakery at the age of twenty-one, when he and his new bride, former schoolmate Sally Wike, set off on a spree of low-rent charlatanism. Posing as Quaker doctors, the two traveled around to small towns hawking patent medicines, impressing locals with their patter full of "thees" and "thous." Toward the end of 1907, they settled in Chicago, where Sally gave birth to the first of their three daughters and Brinkley enrolled in the Bennett Medical College, a school that taught "eclectic," or herbal, medicine. To feed his family, Brinkley worked nights at Western Union.

Brinkley made it into his junior year of college, but the financial and emotional strains were heavy. Sally left him once, moved back, then left him again. The second time she left, Brinkley quit school and followed her home to North

Carolina. A year later, he tried to resume his medical studies in St. Louis, but he couldn't get Bennett Medical College to release his records, since he still owed three year's worth of tuition (students were allowed to pay for all four years of schooling in their senior year).

Desperate to practice medicine, Brinkley purchased a certificate from a St. Louis diploma mill. His wife, however, had long since soured on his dream. In 1913, Sally moved out again, and this time, her husband didn't come trailing after her. Instead, he partnered with a flimflam artist named James Crawford and opened a clinic in Greenville, South Carolina. For two months, the "Greenville Electro Medic Doctors" enjoyed a brisk trade, enhancing the sexual vigor of local males by injecting them with colored water for $25 a pop.[4] When the pair fled town, they left behind dozens of angry merchants and a trail of debts.

Brinkley and Crawford lit out for Memphis, where Crawford once lived. There, Crawford introduced Brinkley to a friend, twenty-one-year-old Minnie Jones. Days later, Brinkley and Jones got married, despite the pesky fact that Brinkley still had a wife and three little girls back in North Carolina. The newlyweds were enjoying their honeymoon when Brinkley was nabbed in Knoxville and hustled back to Greenville. Indicted for check kiting and practicing medicine without a license, Brinkley squared his shoulders and manfully told authorities it had all been Crawford's fault. Fortunately, Crawford and Brinkley's new father-in-law settled most of their debts, and Brinkley was able to return to Minnie.[5] After a bit of unpleasantness—Sally Brinkley showed up in Memphis and informed her replacement that she was married to a good-for-nothing bigamist—Brinkley and Minnie took off for greener pastures.

With his three years of schooling and phony medical certificate, Brinkley finagled a few jobs in Arkansas as an "undergraduate" physician. He earned enough to pay off his tuition at Bennett Medical College, which allowed him to enroll in Kansas City's Eclectic Medical University and complete his studies. In May 1915, just before he turned thirty, Brinkley finally received a medical degree of sorts, one that permitted him to practice in eight states.

The newly minted doctor did everything he could to project a professional demeanor. A small, sandy-haired man, he grew a beard—a goatee, no less—to lend gravity to his boyish face. He took to wearing owlish horn-rimmed glasses and conservative suits, usually with a clutch of pens in his breast pocket. He also tidied up his marital status by divorcing Sally, although in the proceedings he lied about his legal residence, where they were married, and where Sally was currently living.[6]

Just two years later, John R. Brinkley, MD, was sitting pretty in Milford,

Kansas, talking up the amazing properties of goat glands and pondering a gold-plated future. Brinkley's goat gland surgery wasn't an original con. European scientists had been experimenting with gland implants for years, claiming to have rejuvenated men using the testicles of dogs, guinea pigs, and monkeys. All these treatments relied on the willingness of people to believe in a fountain of youth—and to pay dearly for a swig. The placebo effect convinced some patients that the procedure actually worked. Brinkley increased his own odds of success by announcing that the surgery worked best for those who were intelligent.[7] Anyone claiming the treatment was ineffective was essentially admitting his own stupidity.

Brinkley promoted his procedure with direct mail advertising featuring testimonials by William Stittsworth, whose virility he'd reputedly restored. The more success Brinkley had, the more he inflated his claims. Before long, he was touting goat glands as a cure for everything from epilepsy to insanity. (Brinkley also learned that some goat breeds made better "donors" than others. At one point, he implanted Angora testicles in a few unsuspecting patients, which left them stinking like a rank goat on a hot summer day.)

Brinkley got a major shot of publicity after he operated on J. J. Tobias, chancellor of the University of Chicago Law School. Tobias was so thrilled with the results that he awarded Brinkley an honorary doctor of science degree. With his reputation growing, Brinkley built a new sixteen-room clinic in Milford. Opened in 1918, the Brinkley-Jones Hospital included a training school for nurses, the first graduate being none other than Brinkley's true love, Minnie—who, as vice president of the institution, signed her own diploma.[8]

In 1922, Brinkley accepted an invitation to California from Harry Chandler, owner of the *Los Angeles Times*. The doctor worked his billy goat trick on Chandler and some of his editors. When the operations were declared successful, Brinkley gained more publicity. Soon, fifty new patients a week were arriving in Milford—people from all over the world, from millionaire businessmen to Hollywood stars, each of them paying $750 for their surgery.[9] Brinkley splashed their money around in his new hometown. He built sidewalks and electrical, water, and sewage systems. He even sponsored a baseball team, the Brinkley Goats. When he outgrew his sixteen-room clinic, he built a new and larger hospital.

While out in California, Brinkley had toured Harry Chandler's new radio station, KHJ. Impressed, Brinkley vowed to build his own station. In 1923, station KFKB ("Kansas First, Kansas Best") went on the air, with Brinkley's nasal twang cajoling male listeners to take advantage of his rejuvenating treatment. ("Tired of feeling like a eunuch?" he asked.)[10] Entertainment included astrological predictions, language lessons, and live country music. Brinkley's masterstroke was the "Medical Question Box," a segment that's been called radio's first advice program. Brinkley read listeners' letters over the air and prescribed medicines for their ailments, dispensing his wisdom with a patina of Midwestern folksiness and religious fundamentalism. The beauty of the concept was that his prescriptions were only available at authorized pharmacies—specifically, ones that agreed to pay him kickbacks. Between his surgical procedures and pharmaceutical scam, Brinkley was raking in an estimated $2,000,000 a year by the end of the 1920s (over $25,000,000 in current value).[11]

Dr. Brinkley was on top of the world, but cracks were forming beneath his feet. His goat gland implants sometimes caused infections that led to serious complications. In his first dozen years of practice, forty-two patients died at his clinic, many of whom were perfectly healthy when they arrived.[12] For years, Brinkley had been accused of quackery by the editor of the *Journal of the American Medical Association,* Dr. Morris Fishbein. In the spring of 1930, the *Kansas City Star* added its voice with a series of critical articles. The Kansas Medical Board responded by revoking Brinkley's license to practice in the state. The Federal Radio Commission piled on by refusing to renew his broadcasting license.

Brinkley decided that the best way to strike back was to get himself elected governor and name his own men to the Kansas Medical Board. He ran a write-in campaign in the fall of 1930, and some say he would have won if the state attorney general hadn't issued a last-minute ruling that disallowed as many as fifty thousand votes.[13] Brinkley would campaign again in 1932 and '34, although he lost both times.

Miffed by his treatment, Brinkley sold his radio station and relocated to Del Rio, Texas, where he opened a new hospital, eventually closing his Milford clinic. He thumbed his nose at the Federal Radio Commission by erecting a monster transmitter just across the Rio Grande in Villa Acuña, Mexico. In October 1931, Station XER became one of the first Mexican "border blasters," broadcasting facilities powerful enough to drown out the weaker signals of US-based transmitters—and beyond the reach of US laws.[14] Along with Brinkley's promotional spiels, XER featured live musicians such as Hank Williams, Eddie Arnold, and Gene Autry. Advertisers paid dearly to flog a hodgepodge of kooky products, including genuine simulated diamonds and autographed pictures of Jesus. XER became a prototype for border blaster stations used by moneygrubbing evangelists and screaming DJs like Wolfman Jack.

Despite his many challenges, Brinkley continued to prosper through most of the 1930s. His new radio station brought in all the business he could handle—an estimated sixteen thousand patients in one four-year stretch.[15] He purchased a mansion in Del Rio for his family, which now included a son, the beloved Johnny Boy. He bought yachts and a fleet of Cadillacs. He imported exotic animals to wander the grounds of his sixteen-acre estate. He threw lavish parties and traveled the world like a grand pooh-bah.

Brinkley had outfoxed his detractors for so long that he must have considered himself invincible—which is when he made the biggest mistake of his career. Fed up with the ongoing criticism from Morris Fishbein, he sued the AMA editor for libel in 1938. Unfortunately for Brinkley, the trial provided just the forum Fishbein had been looking for. In addition to underscoring Brinkley's medical shortcomings, Fishbein's attorneys laid out every detail of his lifelong history of deception—including his marital escapades and his larcenous Greenville partnership with the slippery "Dr." James Crawford. The Texas jury sided with Fishbein, confirming that Brinkley was precisely what Fishbein had been calling him—a quack.[16]

The upshot of the trial was the rapid and total collapse of Brinkley's empire. Publicly exposed as a fraud, Brinkley saw his business implode. He was hit with numerous malpractice suits, which drained his finances. The IRS came after him for back taxes. The US Postal Service indicted him for mail fraud. In 1939, the Mexican government took over his radio station. In February 1941, he was forced to declare bankruptcy. Finally, his health gave out. He suffered from cancer and heart problems, and he had to have a leg amputated because of a blood clot. On May 26, 1942, at the age of fifty-six, he died of heart failure in a San Antonio hospital.

The enormous success that Brinkley enjoyed for so long—and the preposterous nature of his scam—have earned him a special place among the world's long parade of medical charlatans. Even today, his impact can be felt. The courtroom exposure of the ineffectiveness of his goat-gland treatment raised the profile of the AMA as a watchdog against quackery, a function the association still performs.[17] Brinkley also had a lasting influence on broadcasting. His radio promotions of his fraudulent surgical procedure and prescription drugs underscored the need for greater vigilance against false medical advertising. Today, the Federal Trade Commission remains alert for bogus claims of miracle cures.

John Brinkley left this world with his reputation in tatters, his life a testament to the destructiveness of unbridled greed. Brinkley prospered by preying on the fears of physical decay and failure that exist in all of us. As newspaper editor William Allen White pointed out, with a little different wiring, Brinkley might have been "a real leader of men."[18] Instead, he deceived and robbed his patients, and far too often he was the direct cause of their deaths. Brinkley has been called one of America's worst serial killers.[19] He may have been a monster, but he wasn't an aberration. He was simply another member of what may be the world's second oldest profession—the smooth-talking peddlers of the illusion of youth.

CHAPTER 9

HITCHCOCK'S HIDEOUS INSPIRATION

Ed Gein

Gein (foreground) after his arrest

In the midnight hours of a summer evening in 1952, a radiant full moon shone down on Plainfield, Wisconsin, a small, tranquil farming community in the central part of the state. It was a warm, slumberous night. Strands of cirrus clouds, like wisps of smoke, drifted slowly across the moon's bright surface. Crickets chirped in the surrounding fields, and the occasional night bird boomed its melancholy notes in the nearby woodlands.

On the outskirts of Plainfield, the moonlight lit the town cemetery with startling clarity. The loudest sound to be heard here was the *chick* of a shovel biting into the loose soil above the casket of a middle-age woman who'd been laid to rest earlier in the day. If any of the residents of Plainfield had happened upon this lonely spot, the scene they would have witnessed might have sent them fleeing for their lives—or screaming into insanity. Someone, or some*thing*, was digging up the freshly buried body.

Standing waist deep in the open grave was a short, gray-haired man of slender build. As he paused from his digging and listened for signs of intruders, a beam of moonlight illuminated his upturned face. It was a visage straight from hell. The man wore a leather mask made from the facial skin of a human being he'd previously exhumed and violated, stealing the head and genitals of the female corpse. This nightmare figure, this beast, was forty-five-year-old Ed Gein, a local handyman and loner whose twisted thoughts and horrid desires churned in his mind like a pot of writhing eels.

Edward Theodore Gein was a true original in the annals of American crime.[1] Starting in the late 1940s, this grave-robbing abomination perpetrated some of the most ghoulish outrages ever committed by a man—and all because he wanted to be a woman, a longing prompted by his abiding love and reverence for his deceased, domineering mother.[2] When finally revealed, Gein's perversions would shock the world, ignite a firestorm of media coverage in his bucolic hometown, and inspire a slew of Hollywood horror films, led off by Alfred Hitchcock's terrifying master-piece *Psycho*. The irony of Ed Gein's warped existence was that this fearsome necro-phile, transsexual, and murderer was the quintessential momma's boy.

Ed Gein was born in La Crosse, Wisconsin, in August 1906, the second son of George and Augusta Gein, an unhappily married German couple who endured one another's presence solely because of their strong Lutheran beliefs. An alcoholic failure, George Gein was ridiculed by his wife as an example of male ineptitude. The strong-willed Augusta Gein also tyrannized her two sons, constantly preaching to them about the evils of the world. She bombarded them with Old Testament stories of sin and damnation, urging them to beware of scheming female temptresses. This bitter, angry harridan clearly had no love for any members of the human race.

Augusta Gein felt compelled to take over the responsibility for her family's financial support from her ne'er-do-well husband.[3] Shortly after Ed was born, she opened a grocery store in La Crosse. In 1914, she moved the family to a farm outside rural Plainfield, hoping to isolate her sons from the temptations of city life. Other than venturing off the farm to attend school, Ed Gein and his older brother, Henry, were virtual prisoners, subjected to an endless round of hard physical labor and verbal abuse.

The young Ed Gein was an average student, although he creeped out his teachers and schoolmates with his peculiar ways, which included the disconcerting habit of laughing at inappropriate moments.[4] Effeminate and bashful, he had trouble making friends and was frequently attacked by bullies. Throughout Gein's formative years, his entire life revolved around his sainted mother, who he always tried to please despite her constant hectoring. It would have taken a much stronger psyche than Ed Gein possessed to have emerged from that cauldron of wrath and angst without a warped personality.

The restricted, lonely lives of Ed and Henry Gein continued into adulthood. After their father died in 1940, the two men began doing odd jobs around town to help support the family. Perhaps because of his identification with his mother and his latent femininity, Ed started babysitting for neighbors. He seemed to get along better with kids than with adults, although the townsfolk in Plainfield regarded both Gein brothers as hardworking and honest.[5] If only they'd known about those eels wriggling around inside Ed Gein's head.

Unlike his younger brother, Henry Gein appeared to be emotionally stable. He managed to withstand his mother's constant disapproval, and he didn't share her hatred of the outside world. On occasion, Henry criticized his mother in front of Ed, which alarmed the younger Gein. That may have prompted the first violent expression of Ed Gein's perverse nature.

One day in the spring of 1944, Henry and Ed set about burning off a marshy area on their farm. At the end of the afternoon, Ed was supposedly unable to locate Henry and reported him missing. However, when a search party arrived at the farm, Gein took the men directly to his brother's dead body, which showed bruising about the head. Although the police were suspicious, they didn't pursue the matter. The county coroner ruled that Henry had been asphyxiated by smoke from the fire. Henry's death left Ed and his mother alone together in their bizarre self-exile.

Whatever joy Ed may have felt at having no competition for his mother's attention was short-lived. Not long after Henry's death, Augusta Gein suffered a disabling stroke. Ed nursed her tenderly during her illness, even sharing her bed at times. Then in December 1945, Augusta was felled by a second stroke and died, leaving her distraught thirty-nine-year-old son adrift without his guiding light. Over the next decade, Ed Gein became ever more unhinged mentally and morally, descending into madness while continuing to lead the life of an innocuous, retiring handyman.[6] What the world saw and what went on in Gein's mind and on the lonely farm out on the edge of Plainfield could not have been further apart.

The first symptom of Gein's mental deterioration came immediately after his mother's death, when he closed off most of the rooms in the family home, preserving his mother's downstairs bedroom and parlor exactly as they were as shrines to her memory. Gein retreated to the kitchen and a small connecting room where he slept. Closeted away in those two rooms, Gein slipped into a macabre fantasy world. Ever since his school days, he'd enjoyed reading adventure stories. Now he began reading horror magazines and accounts of freakish Nazi medical experiments. He studied human anatomy, transfixed by the female body. Silently, the eels were slithering to and fro.

The residents of Plainfield didn't pay much attention to what went on out at the Gein place until late in 1957.[7] On November 16 of that year, Bernice Worden, the owner of a local hardware store, went missing. From her sales receipts, the police learned that the last thing Worden had sold before she disappeared was a half-gallon of antifreeze. Worden's son, Deputy Sheriff Frank Worden, recalled that Ed Gein had been in the store a short time before and had commented that he needed some antifreeze.

The police paid a visit to the Gein farm. Gein wasn't home, but the police proceeded to look for the missing woman. What they discovered traumatized some of the investigating officers.[8] Hanging in a shed attached to the rear of the house was the naked body of Bernice Worden—what was left of her. Worden had been decapitated and disemboweled, slit from crotch to throat like a dressed-out deer carcass. As the police officers entered Ed Gein's fetid, trash-filled farmhouse, their eyes fell on one horror after another.

The men found Bernice Worden's heart in a plastic bag by the kitchen stove, and her entrails were wrapped in newspaper (Gein later said that he intended to burn them). The police recoiled at the sight of lampshades and chairs covered with human skin, several masks fashioned from human faces, and skulls sitting atop the bedposts in Gein's room. They found bowls made from sawed-off skulls, a shoebox filled with female genitals, a belt made from nipples, and human lips dangling from a window shade drawstring. The gruesome array inside the farmhouse was almost more than the human mind could comprehend. And all of it was the handiwork of shy little Eddie Gein.

Bernice Worden's head was discovered in a burlap bag, and the preserved face and scalp of another victim—local tavern owner Mary Hogan, who'd been missing since 1954—was found in a paper sack. The police also uncovered a vest-like wrap made from a female torso, a "woman suit" that Gein would admit to having worn around his house, along with other female body parts.[9] At times, he even donned these "trophies" and danced about in his yard at night in a vile subhuman ritual.

Altogether, the police discovered the remains of at least ten bodies. Gein was arrested and eventually confessed to the murders of Bernice Worden and Mary Hogan, saying both victims reminded him of his mother. He maintained that the rest of the body parts had come from corpses he'd dug up in area cemeteries, which authorities were able to corroborate by opening some of the graves. Gein claimed that he'd never had sex with any of the bodies he exhumed or eaten human flesh. He told investigators that he had a different reason for gathering his sickening collection: after his mother died, he'd wanted to have a sex change operation, and he'd taken to adorning himself with the skin of women so he could feel what it would be like to be female.[10]

As word of Gein's horrific crimes spread, reporters from all over the country—and even a few from abroad—descended on sleepy Plainfield. Every local who would stand still long enough was interviewed and quoted. Most people characterized Gein as odd, though seemingly harmless.[11] A woman who said she'd gone out with Gein, Adeline Watkins, swore that he was "good and kind and sweet."[12] The *Chicago Tribune* ran so many gory features about the "Butcher Gein" and his "murder farm" that the editors felt compelled to apologize for their zeal, issuing a brief statement headlined "Enough of Gein" on November 22, 1957. "We take no pleasure in publishing stories of this kind," the editors declared, "and will be glad when the case is no longer in the news."[13]

During his interrogations, Gein never showed the slightest remorse for his actions, or any inkling of the monstrous nature of his crimes. He talked about his savage deeds with detachment, mentioning that he'd interrupted his dismembering of Bernice Worden to work on his car and play with the cash register he'd stolen from the hardware store. A photograph taken at the time shows Gein smiling like a minor celebrity, apparently oblivious to the fear and revulsion he stirred in onlookers. When grilled on the specifics of his murders and graverobbing episodes, Gein said that he couldn't recall the details, claiming that he'd gone into a "daze" each time.[14]

It was obvious that Gein was hopelessly deranged. Doctors found him mentally unfit to stand trial, and a circuit court judge committed him to a state hospital for the criminally insane. A few months after his commitment, the county put his farm up for sale, but before anyone could buy it, the farmhouse burned to the ground. The Plainfield fire department arrived too late to extinguish the blaze. Arson was the likely cause of the fire, although no one was ever held accountable. When told that his family home was gone, Gein replied, "Just as well."[15]

A decade after Gein's arrest, his doctors determined that he was competent to stand trial. In November 1968, Gein was found guilty of first-degree murder in the death of Bernice Worden. He was also judged to be legally insane at the time of the crime and was returned to a state psychiatric institute. He remained institutionalized until he died of cancer in 1984 at the age of seventy-seven. Gein's doctors remarked that he was an ideal patient, never violent and always cooperative.[16] The only sign of his psychosis was the frightening manner in which he stared at females—not a look to invite conversation.

It was inevitable that Gein's grisly crimes would attract the attention of the entertainment industry. In 1959, Robert Bloch, a horror and science fiction writer, published his Gein-inspired novel *Psycho*. The following year, Alfred Hitchcock turned Bloch's book into the chilling movie of the same name, featuring murderous momma's boy Norman Bates cavorting with his mummy's shriveled corpse. In 1974, the slasher franchise *The Texas Chainsaw Massacre* debuted, with the killer-cannibal Leatherface sporting a mask of human skin, a direct take-off on Gein.[17] And in 1991, the mind-warping movie *The Silence of the Lambs* introduced us to serial killer Buffalo Bill, a demented transsexual who slays and flays his female victims in order to make a garment of their skin, just like Ed Gein's woman suit.[18] Had Gein not committed his crimes, who knows, Hollywood scriptwriters might never have conceived of such ghastly characters.

That the real-life monster Ed Gein could reach such depths of depravity attests to the unknown boundaries of the evil that humans are capable of. The judge who presided over Gein's murder trial, Robert H. Gollmar, said, "I know of no person like him in the whole history of the world."[19] After his atrocities came to light, a number of sick jokes, songs, comic books, and even fan clubs grew up around Ed Gein—examples of psychological coping, false bravado, or shock-value exploitation. But the man was no pretend slasher that we can laugh about when the house lights come up. He was and is a dark feral specter, a night-roaming apparition that flutters at the edge of consciousness and sends shivers through your soul.

SCOUNDRELS

CHAPTER 10

SALEM'S RABID WITCH-HUNTER

William Stoughton

The mellow dawn light slanted low across the greening fields and dusty lanes of Salem Village, firing the scattered clapboard houses with a rosy glow. Despite the warmth of the late spring morning, something about the day chilled the soul. A sense of unease enveloped this tiny outpost of civilization, clinging precariously to the Atlantic coast on the edge of a forbidding wilderness. In Salem Village, a farming community of 550 inhabitants just inland from the busy seaport of Salem Town, everyone firmly believed that the Devil lurked nearby, waiting for the chance to work his malefactions. Six decades before, the

Puritans had come to the land along Massachusetts Bay in search of religious freedom, and they practiced their faith with stern devotion. To escape the snares of Satan, they followed God's word to the letter.

Beyond Salem Village, a two-wheeled wooden cart creaked up Gallows Hill, a lonely patch of ground overlooking Salem Town and the sea. Trailed by a crowd of somber onlookers, a well-dressed older woman stood alone in the cart. Her name was Bridget Bishop, and she was, as had recently been determined in a court of law, a witch. What else could explain the strange occurrences that townsfolk had experienced? One villager claimed to have seen Bishop's specter appear at the foot of his bed at midnight, and another reportedly saw the woman turn herself into a black cat. It was even said that she'd caused part of Salem Town's meetinghouse to fall down merely by glancing at it.[1] It hadn't taken her judges long to reach their verdict: the woman was to be hanged for consorting with the Evil One.

When the noose was slipped around her neck on the morning of June 10, 1692, Bridget Bishop became the first of nineteen women and men to be tried, convicted, and executed in the notorious Salem witch trials, an episode in our nation's past that still puzzles historians.[2] Was it religious zealotry that sparked the trials ... mass hysteria ... petty jealousies ... greed ... some mysterious illness? All have been offered as possible explanations.

One factor, though, is indisputable: the influence of William Stoughton, the chief judge of the court that conducted the Salem trials. Stoughton's determination to stamp out witchcraft led to the deaths of twenty-five people and the imprisonment of more than one hundred and fifty others.[3] In his courtroom, the accused were presumed guilty and any personal grievance or imagined supernatural occurrence was admitted as evidence. Stoughton discouraged innocent verdicts, and he never apologized for the excesses of his court even after the public—along with his fellow judges—had turned against the trials and the Massachusetts governor had repudiated the court's extreme methods.[4]

Stoughton may have been Salem's most rabid witch-hunter, but the entire community shared in the creation of this bizarre event. Curiously, it all began with a few girls at play.

In 1689, former West Indies merchant Samuel Parris moved to Salem Village to take up his duties as minister in the community's church, which had been formed a few years before so villagers wouldn't have to make the inconvenient journey to attend services in Salem Town (in the 1750s, Salem Village would achieve separate status as the town of Danvers). Parris's family included his wife, Elizabeth, their nine-year-old daughter, Betty, and an eleven-year-old niece, Abigail Williams. Reverend Parris also brought along two slaves he'd purchased in Barbados, a man they called Indian John and his mate, Tituba.

Tituba was reputed to be a fortune-teller. According to some accounts, she began teaching her skills to young Betty and Abigail, along with a few of their friends, during the harsh winter of 1691–92.[5] With the winter winds moaning outside and firelight flickering on the walls of the Parris kitchen, the Indian woman is said to have told the girls frightening stories about voodoo and witches. In an age when virtually everyone believed in witchcraft, Tituba's disturbing tales may have caused her young charges to take the next steps down Salem's road to calamity.

In the latter part of January 1692, Betty and Abigail began experiencing seizures, delirium, and the sensation that someone was pinching them. Soon, several other girls in the village exhibited the same symptoms. A local doctor examined the girls. Unable to find any physical cause for their ailments, he decided that they were bewitched. The townsfolk looked on in alarm as the girls had fits during Sunday church services, crying out that they saw ghostly forms floating in the air. Reverend Parris attempted to ease their symptoms with prayer. One concerned villager resorted to an old folk remedy, encouraging Tituba to identify the source of the afflictions by baking a rye "witch cake" containing the girls' urine and feeding it to a dog.

When Reverend Parris and others pressed the girls to reveal who was tormenting them, the girls accused three women of being witches—Tituba, a beggar named Sarah Good, and Sarah Osborn, an old woman with a poor record of church attendance. The women were arrested at the end of February and interrogated by local magistrates. Surprisingly, Tituba admitted to being a witch (she later said that Reverend Parris had beaten a confession out of her).[6] The Indian gave a vivid account of her activities as a sorceress, describing the Devil as a tall, white-haired man dressed in black who sometimes assumed the form of a hog or a large black dog. She said that Good and Osborn were witches, too, despite their denials. They'd all zoomed around together on broomsticks, Tituba claimed. And there were still more witches in town, according to the Indian woman.

Tituba's confession paved the way for the hysteria that followed. Over the next few weeks, the afflicted girls implicated several more suspected witches, mostly people living on the fringes of Salem Village or in surrounding communities. Adults started hurling accusations at each other as well (and probably influenced who the afflicted girls singled out). In short order, the jails in Salem and nearby towns were crammed with people who'd been denounced by their neighbors. The magistrates even arrested Sarah Good's four-year-old daughter, Dorcas, who was bound in chains and locked up with her mother, an experience that drove the girl mad.[7]

As the incriminations mounted, it became apparent that Salem needed some mechanism to deal with its plague of witches. On May 27, 1692, the new governor of the royal colony of Massachusetts, William Phips, formed a special body—the Court of Oyer and Terminer, meaning "to hear and determine"—to handle the witchcraft cases. (Some historians say the governor wasn't empowered to establish such a court. If true, the Salem trials were conducted without valid authority.)[8] Phips named his new lieutenant governor, William Stoughton, to head the court. By any measure, Stoughton was a strange choice to conduct a legal proceeding. Rigid and prideful, the sixty-year-old bachelor with the sober countenance and flowing gray hair had no training whatsoever in law. He'd been educated for the ministry.

It's believed that Stoughton was born in England in 1631 and immigrated to Massachusetts with his family as a boy. His father acquired a considerable amount of land in the colony and became a prominent political figure. In 1650, young Stoughton completed a degree in theology at the recently founded Harvard College. Not long afterward, he returned to England to continue his studies at Oxford. He earned a master's degree in 1653 and remained at Oxford for the next few years. In 1659, he became a minister in a Sussex parish. Three years later, he returned to Massachusetts. Dabbling at preaching and farming, Stoughton gradually became enmeshed in colonial politics.

A consummate opportunist, Stoughton zigzagged his way through the constantly shifting power structure of colonial rule for the next two decades.[9] If he had shown that same dexterity in the Salem trials, things might have turned out better. Abetted by Cotton Mather, the influential Puritan minister who had witches on the brain, Stoughton quickly demonstrated the ham-fisted tactics of a grand inquisitor.[10] Stoughton's most controversial decision was to permit the introduction of "spectral evidence"—the unprovable claims of witnesses that they'd been haunted by apparitions of the accused. He also allowed the use of the "touching test," which was based on the belief that an afflicted person's symptoms would disappear if the victim were touched by a witch.

Stoughton and his fellow judges aggressively interrogated the accused, as if they were prosecutors rather than impartial arbiters. They allowed witnesses and even members of the audience to introduce any bit of gossip or conjecture. The defendants, on the other hand, had no legal representation. Alone, frightened, and often confused, they had to fend for themselves as best they could.

Stoughton accepted what were obviously false confessions—a suspect's only means of escaping the death penalty. According to an up-is-down Puritan tradition, no one who confessed to sorcery was hanged; only those courageous enough to maintain their innocence went to the gallows. All in all, it was a kangaroo court on steroids.[11]

Artist T. H. Matteson envisioned the atmosphere of the Court of Oyer and Terminer in his 1853 painting *Examination of a Witch*. The painting shows a young woman stripped to the waist as three older women inspect her for "witch marks"—unusual moles or other skin blemishes. One of the inspectors points to the accused's back as if she's found an incriminating spot. A man writhes on the floor, overcome with emotion, and another young woman, either a friend of the accused or a second defendant, swoons into a bystander's arms. People stare accusingly, the judges scowl, and a magistrate holds back spectators trying to get in the door. In real life, the chaos would have included the shouts and screams of the accused, along with the theatrical convulsions and caterwauling of the afflicted girls—a scene of total bedlam.

Stoughton convened this circus in Salem Town's two-story courthouse, a building large enough to hold the crush of suspects, jailers, witnesses, and gawkers. The first trial—that of Bridget Bishop—began on June 2, 1692. Eight days later, the elderly woman was dangling from a rope on Gallows Hill. Over the next four months, Stoughton signed a flurry of death warrants, including those for two dogs, which were thought to be witches' "familiars," or supernatural assistants. Many of the accused were either paupers or outcasts, but a high social standing didn't guarantee immunity, as was demonstrated by the case of the Reverend George Burroughs, a former Salem minister.

Years before the trials began, Burroughs had argued over money with one of Salem Village's leading families, the Putnams. After the dust-up, Burroughs had moved to Maine. He'd obviously made other enemies in Massachusetts besides the Putnams, since a horde of villagers accused him of performing black magic. Arrested and hauled back to Salem, he listened with disbelief as teenager Mercy Lewis described how he had flown her to a mountaintop and promised her dominion over all she saw if she would sign the Devil's book. The imaginative Mercy proclaimed, "I would not writ if he had throwed me down on one hundred pitchforks."[12] On August 19, Reverend Burroughs was hanged on Gallows Hill, despite having recited the Lord's Prayer, which sorcerers were supposedly unable to do.

Another defendant confounded Stoughton by rejecting the court's authority. When brought before the dour judge, octogenarian Giles Corey expressed his contempt for the trials by refusing to speak—some say to avoid a conviction that might lead to the confiscation of his property.[13] The downside to his tactic was the punishment he faced because of his silence: he was subjected to a procedure called *peine forte et dure*—being crushed under a tremendous weight. Corey was covered with boards, and large rocks were piled on top, a few at a time. It took two days to crush the life out of him, but Corey never submitted to the court. The defiant old codger's last words were supposedly a curse on Salem and his torturers.[14]

Fourteen of the nineteen convicted witches that Stoughton hanged were women. Four more of the accused died in jail, where they faced deplorable conditions (a baby girl born to Sarah Good also died in custody).[15] Then suddenly, like a fever that had broken, the Salem trials came to an end. The last eight persons to be executed were hanged on September 22, 1692. In early October, Puritan minister Increase Mather, the father of Cotton Mather and president of Harvard College, argued that spectral evidence should not be allowed in a court of law. Governor Phips agreed, and he barred its use, along with the touching test.

At the end of October, the governor suspended the Court of Oyer and Terminer, prohibited additional arrests for witchcraft, and freed many of those being held. When Stoughton ordered the execution of women prisoners who'd been exempted from hanging because they were pregnant, Phips countermanded the decision, infuriating the implacable judge (Stoughton later vented his anger by undermining Phips politically). In May 1693, Governor Phips pardoned all of the accused who were still in jail.

In the aftermath of the trials, many citizens of Massachusetts expressed shame for what had taken place. Samuel Sewall, a judge on the Court of Oyer and Terminer, publicly apologized for wrongs inflicted on the innocent, as did Ann Putnam, one of the most vocal of the girls who'd denounced their fellow villagers. In 1711, the colonial government of Massachusetts absolved all but a few of the accused of any guilt and paid restitution to their heirs (it wasn't until 2001 that the last victims of the witchcraft hysteria were absolved).[16] The only person involved in the Salem trials who refused to accept any blame or admit to any wrongdoing was William Stoughton. For the rest of his life, Stoughton clung to his position like a hidebound zealot.

It's clear that Betty Parris, Abigail Williams, and their circle of friends started Salem's witchcraft hysteria with their fits and visions. Most historians seem to think the girls simply faked their afflictions to attract attention, but recently, another explanation for their behavior has been suggested: they could have been suffering from a condition caused by ergot, a parasitic fungus containing an alkaloid similar to that found in LSD.[17] The fungus grows on cereal grains such as rye, a common colonial-era food crop. Usually affecting women and children, ergot poisoning produces crawling sensations on the skin, vertigo, and convulsions, along with hallucinations and delirium—the same symptoms reported by the village girls.

While the young people of Salem initiated the witchcraft controversy, other factors contributed to the frenzy. Colonial Salem wasn't a tranquil place at the best of times. In addition to the constant fear of Indian attacks, there was the ongoing political tug-of-war between the farmers of Salem Village and the merchants of Salem Town. Arguments raged over land ownership, and two rival families, the Putnams and the Porters, fought for control of Salem Village and its church. Any of these factors could have prompted villagers to lash out at their neighbors by accusing them of sorcery.

The chief villain of the witchcraft trials remains William Stoughton. For some reason, though, Stoughton's dismal record at Salem didn't damage his reputation during his lifetime. In spite of having compromised every legal aspect of the trials, Stoughton was named chief justice of Massachusetts in December 1692. He retained the office of lieutenant governor until his death in July 1701. Near the end of his life, he was also named acting governor of Massachusetts, which, if nothing else, proves that being a misguided executioner has never been an impediment to higher office. Stoughton's contemporaries were impressed by his generosity, which included the funding of the hall at Harvard College that bears his name.

Later generations, however, have judged Stoughton more harshly. He wasn't the first or the last judge to send innocent people to their deaths, but in this country, his sentences certainly rank among the most egregious. Nineteenth-century biographer John Langdon Sibley said that Stoughton ran the Salem trials "with a bigoted zeal akin to animosity," and that his conduct was "heartless, unjust, atrocious."[18] Emory Washburn, governor of Massachusetts in the mid-1850s and author of a judicial history of the colony, passed one of the most devastating judgments ever on Stoughton, writing that he "prostituted the forms of justice to consummate a series of judicial murders that have no parallel in our history."[19]

Even if you grant that seventeenth-century trials were far different from modern legal proceedings—and that Salem's judges were simply trying to fight evil as it was generally perceived at the time—Stoughton's performance was still a travesty. Witch-hunting in all its forms is ingrained in human nature. In that regard, the primary responsibility of any judge is to save us from our own ignorance and prejudices. That was William Stoughton's greatest failing. Instead of quelling the superstitious fears that set neighbor against neighbor—as many judges and clergymen in his day were known to do—Stoughton chose to inflame them.

CHAPTER 11

UNCLE DANIEL THE "SPECKERLATOR"

Daniel Drew

The old saying "You can lead a horse to water but you can't make it drink" has the ring of folk wisdom, but it's completely untrue. To make a horse drink, all you have to do is deprive it of water for a day or so and lace its feed with salt, and presto, when you lead the critter to a trough it will stand there slurping until its belly is ready to pop.

Of course, there's no point in doing that to a horse, but with a cow it's a different matter. That's something Daniel Drew knew well. In the early 1800s, Drew ran a thriving livestock business in New York State. He bought cattle from farmers all over the northern part of the country, from New England to Illinois. Legend has it that when it came time to sell his livestock, Drew kept them away from water and fed them salt, then he let them drink all they wanted right before they went to market—where the animals were sold by weight.

Drew reputedly made a lot of extra money off his waterlogged cattle—whose last-minute gulping could easily pack on an extra fifty pounds each. The practice was fraudulent, but apparently Drew didn't mind. The man seemed to have larceny in his soul, which may explain why he ended up on Wall Street. From the 1840s to the 1870s, Drew was one of the big fish who gobbled up the little fish—a double-dealing speculator and banker who believed that nothing should stand in the way of his making a profit.[1] (Drew's cattle-selling trick earned him a lasting place in the history of finance. The practice of bloating cattle with water prior to sale resulted in the term "watered stocks," which refers to assets whose value has been artificially inflated. Despite modern laws against the practice, it still goes on. Enron shares, anyone?)

Drew remains a terrific role model for today's "greed is good" Wall Street sharpsters, although the old pirate has been eclipsed in the history books by robber barons with names like Astor, Carnegie, Morgan, Rockefeller, and Vanderbilt. That's a shame, since Drew was perhaps the most interesting of all the Victorian-era tycoons, largely because he was such a bundle of contradictions. Though financially cunning, Drew was poorly educated—a sort of Warren Buffett cum Archie Bunker. Despite his lack of business ethics, he was extremely devout (like other cutpurse capitalists, he tried to buy his way to respectability through philanthropy). The thing that makes Drew most compelling is that he ultimately got what he deserved. He lost his entire fortune near the end of his life, a big chunk of it due to his involvement with a pair of con men wilier than himself.

Drew was born in 1797 on a hardscrabble farm near Carmel, New York, a backwater hamlet fifty miles north of New York City. His father was sixty-five years old when Drew was born, which necessitated young Drew pitching in around the farm at an early age. There was little time for schooling, so Drew only attended sporadically. He could barely write, and his spelling and grammar were atrocious. His speech was filled with colloquialisms that must have sounded like dialogue from *The Beverly Hillbillies*. Mostly he learned about cattle and crops. Drew also "got religion" during his early years when an itinerant Methodist preacher convinced him that his heart was full of sin and he was on the road to hell. Drew admitted to some "backslidden'" now and again, but he remained a devout Methodist all his life.[2]

When Drew was fourteen, his father passed away, leaving him an inheritance of $80. For three years, he worked the family farm and hired out as a laborer on other nearby farms. At the age of seventeen, he joined the state militia to help defend New York City against the British in the War of 1812. Sailing down the Hudson River on his way to the city, Drew got his first glimpse of the world beyond his circumscribed environs—and he took a likin' to what he encountered. It was an instant case of "How you gonna keep 'em down on the farm?" Amid the hurly-burly of the big city, Drew made note of the lofty going price for beef. When he got home from his hitch in the militia, he told his mother that he wanted his inheritance money so he could become a drover. "I'm going to buy cattle and sell 'em in New York," he announced.[3] The budding businessman was about to launch himself into an unsuspecting world.

Drew began his business career by purchasing small herds of cattle and sheep and personally driving them into the city for sale. He seemed to possess the right combination of skills to make a go of it. He was a hard worker, knew livestock well, and was adept at haggling for the best prices. But no sooner had he started out on his own than he took a detour. On a whim, he joined the circus—one of those frivolous displays of levity that the puritanical Methodists abhorred. For three seasons, Drew traveled with the June, Titus, Angevine & Crane Circus between New York and Philadelphia. Besides taking care of the animals, Drew dressed as a clown and went into towns ahead of the circus to drum up business. Everything was roars and chuckles until one day the show rolled into a town where a revival was taking place. Drew attended the meeting and immediately climbed back on the religious wagon. Thoroughly chastened, he hung up his clown suit and returned to a life of eating dust behind a gaggle of lurching, bawling cows.

In 1820, Drew married a local country girl. The newlyweds set up housekeeping on the family farm, then being run by Drew's younger brother. A few years later, Drew bought land of his own nearby, but he couldn't keep his thoughts from straying to the bustle and excitement of New York City. That was where an enterprising young fellow could make real money. Before long, he had his opportunity. In 1830, he sold his farm and became the manager of New York's only cattle market, as well as the proprietor of the tavern where all the drovers stayed. Fortune was about to beam on this ambitious, semiliterate backwoods entrepreneur.

Drew expanded his cattle-buying business by employing purchasing agents. He made enough money to start casting around for other investments. In 1831, he bought an interest in a steamboat, the *Water Witch*, a venture that allowed Drew to cultivate his managerial talents. It was also his first opportunity to go up against someone who was well ahead of him in the race to riches—Commodore Cornelius Vanderbilt, the New York Dutchman who would become the wealthiest man in America by the time he died.

In the 1830s, Vanderbilt was operating a fleet of steamboats that plied the Hudson River and other routes in the New York region. Passenger traffic was heavy on the lower Hudson between Peekskill and New York City, and Drew dove into that market with a splash. The new rivals were an interesting contrast—the hardy, handsome, outgoing Vanderbilt and the slinking, Uriah Heep–like Drew, his dark, thin face framed by whiskers. The two competitors soon began a ruinous fare war. To entice passengers, Drew ran newspaper advertisements accusing Vanderbilt of trying to establish a monopoly that would result in skyrocketing rates.[4] The attack worked. Passengers spurned Vanderbilt's boat for the *Water Witch*.

Despite Drew's victory, the *Water Witch* lost money the first year. Some of the major stockholders wanted out, enabling Drew to increase his interest in the boat. Afterward, he approached Vanderbilt to cut a deal. Vanderbilt paid Drew to withdraw from competition on the Peekskill route. Loyal passengers and small stockholders in the *Water Witch* were outraged, but Drew made a killing—the first in a long string of financial shenanigans that would earn Drew a reputation for underhandedness.[5]

Drew wasn't on the sidelines for long. After helping Vanderbilt gain a foothold in the lucrative New York–Albany steamboat route, Drew headed up a group of men that bought one of the commodore's boats and formed a new company in 1835. After adding another boat, the partners named their new fleet the People's Line. Over the next decade, Drew made money coming and going—from routine operations as well as fare-rigging deals and payoffs from other owners to reduce the number of trips his boats made.[6] By 1843, the People's Line owned nine steamboats.

Drew had proven to be the shrewdest operator on the Hudson, although he hit a rough patch in 1849. Stockholders in the People's Line complained about the highly profitable company's lack of dividends. Drew argued that all the profits had gone into building new boats. Drew was hauled before the state supreme court and charged with exceeding his authority, failure to declare dividends, and systematic fraud. The court ruled in favor of the stockholders, declaring that the People's Line would be sold at auction and the proceeds divided among the stockholders. It appeared to be a nettlesome defeat, but Drew turned the situation to his advantage. The receiver charged with liquidating the company was an old friend of his. By the time the auction was over, Drew had scooped up nearly all the company's assets at a little over fifty cents on the dollar. It appeared that the Lord was taking care of someone who took care of himself.

Even while he was still heavily involved with cattle and steamboats, Drew had begun to expand his financial interests. In 1838, he'd become a junior partner in a Wall Street brokerage and banking house. The next year, he founded Drew, Robinson & Company, a partnership that lasted until 1852. By that time, "Uncle Daniel," as he'd become known on the street, had achieved millionaire status. "I got to be a millionaire afore I know'd it, hardly," he said.[7] After he grew rich, Drew began to pine for the country life. He and his wife had an older daughter and a young son, and Drew wanted the boy to grow up in the country like he had. Drew sold his house in New York and bought another farm close to his brother, where he spent Sundays with his family. The other six days found him in his office in the city, usually pursuing his latest passion—railroads.

Cattle and steamboats may have been the foundation of Drew's wealth, but it was railroads that pushed him into the ranks of the plutocrats. Drew's trading in railroad stocks made him one of the country's first big stock speculators. He was always looking to make a quick profit, legal or otherwise. (He was quoted as saying that "speckerlatin'" on Wall Street without insider knowledge was like "buying cows by candlelight.")[8] Drew's most notorious transactions occurred after he became a director of the New York & Erie Railroad in 1853. Over the next fifteen years, he reaped huge profits by secretly manipulating Erie stock.[9] Like most wheeler-dealers, Drew regarded investing as a game. Standing in front of his office one day, he looked out on a crowd of speculators who were gleefully antici-pating big profits after selling Erie's troubled stock short. "Happy creeturs," the old man muttered. "Wal, I guess I must pinch 'em."[10] With that, Drew manipulated the stock upward and reaped another windfall. I win. You lose. Ha, ha.

Without a qualm, Drew used his steamboat and railroad connections to scalp the public during the Civil War, sometimes in collusion with the infa-mous Boss Tweed, the corrupt New York politician who was eventually jailed for stealing millions of taxpayer dollars.[11] Drew had a lot of nice friends like that. In 1867, he joined forces with up-and-coming swindlers Jay Gould and James Fisk to battle his old associate/antagonist Cornelius Vanderbilt. (Gould and Fisk were another mismatched pair—Gould the wispy, introverted family man and Fisk the large, loud backslapper with a diamond stickpin and gold-headed cane.) Like Drew, Commodore Vanderbilt had moved into the railroad business. He already owned three railroads, but he wanted the Erie as well. He intended to buy a controlling interest—and then get rid of Daniel Drew. Uncle Daniel responded by flooding the market with overvalued shares of Erie stock and convertible bonds, all in direct violation of court orders. While Vanderbilt furiously bought Erie stock, Drew and his new pals sold short, raking in eight million dollars at Vanderbilt's expense.

The affair seemed to have been stage-managed by Gilbert and Sullivan, as it zigzagged between drama and farce. Fearing imminent arrest for their stock manipulations, Drew and other members of the Erie board gathered up all the company records, withdrew millions of dollars from New York City banks, and hopped a steamer for Jersey City, where they holed up in a room on the second floor of Taylor's Hotel. Gould and Fisk, who'd both stayed behind in New York, barely escaped arrest. They had to commandeer a small boat and row across the Hudson to the Jersey shore in the dark. When they finally showed up at Taylor's Hotel—after rowing in circles for an hour in the fog and nearly being run down by ferryboats—Uncle Daniel looked at the sodden pair and inquired, "You didn't have to swim over, did you?"[12]

The great escape to New Jersey led to a long, leisurely state of siege. The Erie directors filled their idle hours with quail and champagne banquets, although Drew, ever the party-shunning Methodist, refused to take part. Fisk kept up his spirits by sending for his girlfriend, an "actress" he'd met in a ritzy bordello. (Fisk's wife was safely stashed in Boston.) After a few days, a gang of toughs arrived from across the river and hinted that they'd been offered $50,000 to snatch Drew and haul him back to New York. "Fort Taylor" was soon bristling with guns and Erie "detectives," scruffy men chomping cigars and swilling down lashings of whiskey.

The threat against Drew, if there ever was one, never came to anything, but Uncle Daniel realized he had enemies other than Vanderbilt when Gould and Fisk confronted him about receiving their share of the profits. It was becoming clear that this Mutt and Jeff pair of grifters intended to tip the seventy-year-old Drew off his throne.[13] Gould left for Albany with a suitcase stuffed with cash, money he used to bribe state legislators into declaring the questionable Erie stock and bond activities perfectly legal. (Though less colorful than Fisk, Gould was the more dangerous schemer.) In a typically duplicitous move, Gould and Fisk made amends to Vanderbilt by compensating him for his losses. The two interlopers emerged in control of the Erie board while Drew got the boot. It was major setback for an old trader who'd grown used to besting every adversary, but at least Drew was still a wealthy man. Even that, however, was soon to change.

In 1869, Gould and Fisk drove up the price of Erie stock, costing Drew— who'd sold short—$1.5 million.[14] In 1873, a six-year-long nationwide depression began, sweeping away the rest of Drew's fortune. His financial firm failed, and, in 1876, he had to file for bankruptcy. His empire fluttered to the ground like a house of cards in a March breeze. Once worth an estimated $13 million (equivalent to $194 million today), Drew had to rely on his son for support for the last three years of his life. He died in 1879, right back where he'd started out, as poor as a teenage cattle drover. Drew left his entire estate to his children, a sum of $148.22.[15]

During the years when he was flush, Drew gave generously to Methodist causes. He paid over three-quarters of the cost to build a new church in his hometown of Carmel and also paid for the construction of the nearby Drew Female Seminary. He funded half the cost of a new church in Brewster, New York, and donated a significant amount toward the construction of St. Paul's Methodist Episcopal Church in New York City. He supported Wesleyan University and established the Drew Theological Seminary (now Drew University) with an endowment of half a million dollars. All those good deeds stood in stark contrast to his professional career.[16]

Such a colorful, contradictory life raises an interesting question: Since it's impossible to be both moral and unethical, how does a person of faith become a ruthless tycoon in the first place? The trick to pulling it off must lie in self-perception (or self-*de*ception)—being able to see yourself as a smart businessperson instead of a crook, as clever rather than dishonest. At least one historian has speculated that Drew simply compartmentalized his roles as a Sunday Christian and a weekday marauder.[17] Drew would never have robbed the person in the pew next to him, but from the privileged, insulated confines of Wall Street, it was easy for him to view people in general as nameless marks. However Drew rationalized his hypocritical dishonesty, it seems unlikely that he could have squeezed his way through the Pearly Gates, despite his piety and financial support of the Methodists. After all, like other philanthropists of his era, the old devil was mostly just returning stolen money.

It's been said that Drew was a product of his times, an age when striving upward by almost any means was acceptable—even admirable—behavior, no matter how many people were hurt along the way.[18] In the years after the Civil War, increasing industrialization led to an ever greater concentration of riches in the hands of a few, along with widespread impoverishment. An 1892 political document stated that the shameful excesses of the Gilded Age had produced a nation of "tramps and millionaires."[19] A little over a century later, history seems to be repeating itself, with our country increasingly divided into extremes of wealth and poverty. As usual, sitting atop the largest mountains of lucre are the wizards of financial sleight of hand—confirmation that the spirit of Daniel Drew is with us still.

CHAPTER 12

UNLEASHING THE JAMES-YOUNGER GANG

James Lane

Deep into September of 1861, summer still clung to the peaceful stretch of the Osage River Valley angling across Missouri's St. Clair County. The broad brown Osage glided past wooded hills here on the northern fringe of the Ozark Highlands, just east of the heartland prairies. Patches of morning mist floated above the river, where giant spoonbill catfish patrolled the muddy bottom. Leggy herons slowly stalked the shallows while smaller birds bickered in the tall oaks lining the banks.

The idyllic Indian summer morning would have been perfect except for the riders. In the dawn light, fifteen hundred mounted men converged on the prosperous river town of Osceola. The horsemen were Kansas Jayhawkers, volunteer guerrilla fighters allied with the abolitionist cause that had helped provoke the Civil War. Made up mostly of poor whites, freed slaves, and a scattering of Indians, the company showed little sign of discipline. One Union Army officer who'd observed the men pegged them as riffraff—"ragged, half-armed, diseased, mutinous rabble."[1] The pro-Southern *Argus* newspaper in Weston, Missouri, described them as "thieves, cut-throats, and midnight robbers."[2]

At the head of the irregulars rode James H. Lane, an intense, hatchet-faced man with a wild shock of black hair hidden under a battered white hat. A veteran of the Mexican-American War, Lane had organized the guerrilla band, which he'd loftily named the Kansas Brigade. Lane liked to think big. A fervent antislavery campaigner and political opportunist, he entertained visions of being elected president. He would have to settle for becoming the man Missourians despised above all others—a death-dealing zealot known as the Grim Chieftain.[3] The fierce hatreds ignited by Lane's fanaticism would linger long after the war, and they flicker still in a benign rivalry between the residents of Missouri and Kansas.

Lane had moved to Kansas in 1855 after representing Indiana for a term as a US congressman. In the late 1850s, he fought in the Missouri-Kansas border war, a murderous struggle over the issue of slavery in the Kansas Territory. In April 1861, he returned to Washington as one of the first senators from the new free state of Kansas, just days before the Confederate attack on Fort Sumter. At the outbreak of war, Lane was soon back home in Kansas, eager to renew the fight against the proslavery "border ruffians" of western Missouri. It didn't matter that nearly half the people living in the area were either firmly pro-Union or uncommitted to either side. When it came to Missourians, the Grim Chieftain didn't discriminate.

Lane found it easy to motivate the ragtag guerrilla group he'd put together. The promise of plunder always set their eyes to dancing. Lane worked his men into a frenzy with impassioned, long-winded speeches. One listener described these talks: "His oratory was voluble and incessant, without logic, learning, rhetoric, or grace ... his diction is a pudding of slang, profanity and solecism; and yet the electric shock of his extraordinary eloquence thrills like the blast of a trumpet."[4] Another declared: "He talked like none of the others. None of the rest had his husky rasping, blood-curdling whisper or that menacing forefinger, or could shriek 'Great God!' on the same day with him."[5]

Jim Lane was ready to shriek Great God this day. Just three weeks earlier, Sterling Price and the Missouri State Guard had defeated his forces in the Battle of Dry Wood Creek, a short distance to the west in Vernon County. Still smarting, Lane proclaimed that Osceola was to be "knocked into Herculaneum."[6] His men were on alert as they approached the town of three thousand. During the night, enemy troops had fired on them from the surrounding woods. However, when the Jayhawkers rode into Osceola they encountered no opposition. All the able-bodied men had fled, leaving mostly women, children, and the elderly. The defenseless town was Lane's for the taking. The guerrillas surged through the streets, breaking into stores and warehouses. Commandeering every wagon and team they could find, they began loading their plunder: tons of lead for shot, kegs of powder, three thousand sacks of flour, plus large quantities of sugar, molasses, coffee, bacon, and other goods. The Kansans rounded up three hundred fifty horses and mules and four hundred head of cattle. They also freed two hundred slaves and encouraged them to join their ranks.[7]

No home was spared, despite the fact that perhaps a third of the town's residents were loyal to the Union, with many locals off serving in the Northern army. Lane himself claimed a piano, a carriage, and several silk dresses for his wife. The Jayhawkers robbed the local bank of $8,000 and stripped the courthouse of its records before setting it on fire. In a hillside cellar, they discovered one hundred fifty barrels of liquor. Although the barrels were staved in to destroy the cache, the men filled their canteens and got staggering drunk. Nearly three hundred had to be hauled off in wagons.[8]

Somehow the spilled liquor caught fire, igniting nearby buildings. Other structures were intentionally torched. By the time the rampage was over, few buildings in the town still stood, and those survived only because the guerrillas fled after scouts erroneously reported that Confederate troops were marching toward town. The value of what was stolen or destroyed was estimated at a million dollars. "As the sun went down on Sunday night," wrote one witness, "Osceola was a heap of smoldering ruins."[9]

The most lasting damage from Lane's assault on Osceola wasn't the loss of property. In the course of the raid, Lane had convened a drumhead court-martial and sentenced nine local citizens to death. This act would seal the Grim Chieftain's reputation among Missourians. Two years later, "Remember Osceola!" would serve as the rallying cry when a band of Missouri bushwhackers—guerrilla fighters every bit as merciless as the Jayhawkers—sought revenge in Lawrence, Kansas, the town that Jim Lane called home.[10]

The Missouri raiders who swooped down on Lawrence in 1863 were led by slender, sandy-haired William Quantrill, an exceptional horseman and crack shot. Though Quantrill had just turned twenty-six, songs had already been written about his exploits as a Southern guerrilla. Riding with him were veteran bushwhackers Frank James and Cole Younger, two men who, along with their respective brothers, would also go down in Western lore.

Some of the members of Quantrill's band thought that a raid on Lawrence was suicidal. The Jayhawker stronghold was too far into Kansas, they argued, and too well protected. Quantrill won them over by pointing out that the town of three thousand held most of the plunder stolen from Missouri homes. He also told them he intended to capture Jim Lane, bring him back to Missouri, and publicly execute him.[11]

The heat of the prairie dawn was rising when Quantrill and his four hundred men reached the outskirts of Lawrence on August 21. Meeting little resistance, the guerrillas galloped into the center of town, pistols blazing. They cut down every man and teenage boy they saw—anyone they deemed old enough to take up arms against the South. A survivor described the grisly spectacle: "Men falling dead and wounded, and women and children, half-dressed, running and screaming—some trying to escape the danger and some rushing to the side of their murdered friends."[12]

During the four hours that the raid lasted, Quantrill's men stripped the town of valuables, looted the banks, and burned around two hundred homes and stores, causing some two million dollars in damage. When the shooting finally stopped, more than one hundred fifty men and teenage boys lay dead.[13] Quantrill's force suffered minimal casualties and headed back to Missouri laden with booty.

The hated Jim Lane, however, had eluded Quantrill. Displaying an uncanny knack for self-preservation, Lane bolted at the first sound of gunfire. Leaping from bed, the Jayhawker ripped the nameplate from his front door in hopes of saving his house, ran out the back door in his nightshirt, dashed through a nearby cornfield, and kept on running, leaving his wife alone to face the marauding Missourians. Quantrill had to content himself with burning down the Grim Chieftain's fine new home. Lane later made a show of bravado by setting off after Quantrill in a buggy, although—luckily for him—he didn't catch up with the fleeing Missourians.

The repercussions of the Lawrence massacre, as it came to be known, were immediate. Four days later—at the heated insistence of Jim Lane—Gen. Thomas Ewing, the commander of Union troops along the Missouri-Kansas border, issued Order No. 11, one of the harshest government edicts ever enacted against Americans.[14] The order called for the depopulation, within fifteen days, of rural lands in four Missouri counties along the Kansas border. Ewing wanted to ensure that no bushwhacker would ever again find food or shelter there.

Over twenty thousand people were swept from their homes, their crops confiscated or destroyed, their livestock stolen. Gangs of Jayhawkers and Union militias roamed the countryside, torching everything in their path, robbing and killing evacuees even as they attempted to obey Ewing's directive.[15] Like a stone tossed in a lake, the sacking of Osceola had sent its ripples in ever-widening circles. One of Missouri's richest agricultural regions was rendered a wasteland—the Burnt District, it came to be called.

Although fighting along the border slackened during the last years of the Civil War, Missouri's Burnt District still smoldered when the conflict ended in 1865. Southern landowners who returned home to piece their lives together fell victim to carpetbagging Northern bankers and Northern-owned railroads. Former bushwhackers who wanted to settle down and forget the war found it hard to do. Radical Republican policies barred them from voting or holding office. Many of them were shot or lynched by vigilantes, and they were all subject to arrest and trial for their wartime activities.[16]

Some of these men fought back, including the James brothers and the Youngers. Both of their families had been run off their farms during the war and faced continued persecution afterward. Fed up with their bleak postwar prospects, the James and Younger boys began using their wartime hit-and-run guerrilla tactics in new pursuits: robbing banks and trains owned by hated Northerners. Not surprisingly, Missourians who'd been exploited by those Yankee businesses cheered for the James-Younger gang. Warranted or not, the men became folk heroes, with tales of their exploits written up in newspapers and dime novels. For a decade and a half, the gang rode wild across the Midwest, their reputations growing ever larger—although they probably had nothing to do with a good many of the crimes attributed to them. Cole Younger complained that "every daylight robbery in any part of the country, from the Alleghenies to the Rockies, was laid at our doors."[17]

The era of the James-Younger gang began to fade in 1876, when Cole, Jim, and Bob Younger went to prison after being wounded in the botched Northfield, Minnesota, bank robbery. Bob Younger died of pneumonia in prison. Cole and Jim were finally released, although Jim committed suicide less than a year later at the age of fifty-four. In 1882, Jesse James, Frank's notorious younger brother, was shot dead in St. Joseph, Missouri. He was thirty-four. Frank surrendered to authorities that same year and somehow escaped any jail time.

Frank James and Cole Younger lived to be old men, cashing in on their reputations for a time in Wild West shows. While both men mellowed and became philosophical about the twists and turns life had shown them, it's unlikely they ever forgot their old enemy, the man who plundered Osceola. Jim Lane may not have turned the James and Younger boys into outlaws all by himself, but he was certainly the chief engineer on the train to hell. His destruction of Osceola was arguably the main provocation for the raid on Lawrence, which led directly to the suffering inflicted by Order No. 11—all formative experiences for the James and Younger clans. (A century later, the Jayhawkers' attacks on Missouri farmers would inspire the Forrest Carter novel *The Rebel Outlaw, Josey Wales,* on which Clint Eastwood based his 1976 film.)

Lane survived the war and was still a US senator when he died by his own hand in 1866. Despondent over his waning political influence, he shot himself in the head in Leavenworth, Kansas. It was a fittingly violent death for someone who'd unleashed so much violence in life. One newspaper reported that Lane had been haunted by memories of all the men he'd killed and the screams of women and children fleeing their burning homes in Osceola.[18] A fellow Kansan wrote: "No one can blame a person for wishing to hurry away from such a life as his."[19] It's possible, of course, to construe Lane's deeds as acts of war, although they seemed to reveal more about his personal obsessions than his loyalty to the Union cause.

The passions that Lane sparked survived into the present day in a thankfully milder form: the heated football and basketball competition between the Universities of Missouri and Kansas, which lasted for more than a century until the University of Missouri forsook tradition by moving from the Big 12 athletic conference to the Southeastern Conference in 2012. It's likely that most of the fans who sat in the stands in Columbia and Lawrence for all those years never gave much thought to the rivalry's bloody origins, but they always saved their loudest and most colorful invective for when their cross-border neighbors came to town. The rowdy animosity almost seemed inborn, as if such feelings are imprinted on the genes of Tiger and Jayhawk diehards. And who knows . . . maybe they are.

CHAPTER 13

LINCOLN'S MISSING BODYGUARD

John Parker

Ford's Theatre (left), scene of John Parker's disgrace

April 14, 1865, dawned balmy and bright in Washington, DC. It was Good Friday, and the sunny weather seemed to reflect the spirits of Washingtonians. Just days before, Richmond, the capital of the Confederacy, had fallen, followed quickly by the surrender of Robert E. Lee's Army of Northern Virginia to Gen. Ulysses S. Grant at Appomattox Court House. The Civil War was all but over.

The capital erupted in celebration at the news. After four years of conflict and doubt, it was finally time to whoop it up. All over town, the air shook with fireworks, cannon salutes, and wildly clanging church bells—startling horses, dogs, and the occasional meandering cow. Bands raced through "Yankee Doodle" and "Rally 'Round the Flag, Boys" again and again.

Cheering crowds surged through the dusty, unpaved streets. In makeshift hospitals around the city, smiles creased the haggard faces of wounded soldiers. Former slaves cavorted with joy, and drunken laughter spilled from the city's plentiful saloons and bordellos. "The entire population of Washington seemed to be abroad," wrote historian Margaret Leech, "shaking hands and embracing, throwing up their hats, shrieking and singing, like a carnival of lunatics."[1]

Even the president felt the urge to let off steam. Abraham Lincoln needed the break. The war had made an old man of him. He was gaunt and pale, and he complained that his hands and feet were always cold. He'd been haunted by a dream of himself lying in state in the East Room, cut down by an assassin. A night out would do him good, mentally and physically. Mrs. Lincoln suggested a play. *Our American Cousin,* a popular comedy about an awkward young Yankee and his aristocratic English kin, was ending its run at Ford's Theatre. That would be just the tonic the president needed.

Following Lee's surrender, General Grant returned to Washington. Lincoln knew it would be good for people to see their president and his victorious general enjoying an evening out, and he urged Grant and his wife to accompany him to the play. Grant halfheartedly accepted then later changed his mind, claiming he needed to leave Washington and get back home to New Jersey to see his children. The truth was that Grant had grown tired of all the public adulation. Besides, his wife couldn't stand Mrs. Lincoln, an unpredictable, short-tempered woman.[2] Mrs. Grant had witnessed the first lady's tantrums—and been a target of them on occasion. Spending over two hours cooped up with her in a tiny theater box would be torture.

When Grant turned him down, Lincoln was inclined to cancel the evening altogether, but newspapers had already announced he'd be attending the play, and Ford's Theatre had gone to the trouble of decorating the president's box with flags and a portrait of George Washington. To avoid disappointing anyone, Lincoln agreed to go ahead with the outing.

After Grant backed out, Lincoln invited Secretary of War Edwin Stanton. However, Stanton's wife also kept her distance from Mrs. Lincoln, and they begged off. At the last minute, Mrs. Lincoln invited a young couple to fill out the party, Maj. Henry Rathbone, a strapping soldier with impressive muttonchop whiskers, and his fiancée, Clara Harris, daughter of Senator Ira Harris of New York.

The Washington Metropolitan Police Force was to furnish an armed officer to accompany the group. While it's hard to believe that a single policeman would be the president's only protection, that wasn't unusual. Lincoln was cavalier about his personal safety—despite a near-miss attempt on his life in August 1864.[3] He'd often take in a play or go to church without guards, and he hated being encumbered by the military escort assigned to him. Sometimes he even walked alone at night between the White House and the War Department, a distance of around a quarter of a mile. But Lincoln's staff took the frequent threats against the president seriously. A bodyguard made sense, especially given the chaos in the capital at the end of the war. The man the police department assigned to the job was John Frederick Parker. If a committee had spent days pondering the matter, it couldn't have come up with a worse choice. Parker's staggering incompetence would lead directly to a national tragedy.

Born in Frederick County, Virginia, in 1830, John Parker moved to Washington as a young man. In 1855, he married Mary America Maus. The couple would have three children together. Originally a carpenter, Parker had become one of the capital's first one hundred fifty officers when the Metropolitan Police Force was organized in 1861.

Parker's record as a cop fell somewhere between pathetic and comical. He was hauled before the police board over a dozen times, facing a smorgasbord of charges that should have gotten him fired, but he received nothing more than an occasional reprimand.[4] His infractions included conduct unbecoming an officer, using intemperate language, and being drunk on duty. Charged with sleeping on a streetcar when he was supposed to be walking his beat, Parker declared that he'd heard ducks quacking on the streetcar and had climbed aboard to investigate.[5] The charge was dismissed. When he was brought before the board for frequenting a whorehouse, Parker argued that he'd only been there to protect the place—like a bank robber claiming he'd taken the money to safeguard it.[6] That he kept getting away with such behavior says as much about the police department of the period as it does about Parker.

In November 1864, the Metropolitan Police Force created a permanent detail to protect the president, made up of four officers. There must not have been any performance standards for the group, since John Parker was named to the detail. Parker was an unlikely candidate to protect anyone. He was the only officer with a spotty record, so it was a tragic coincidence that he drew the assignment to guard the president on the night of April 14.

As usual, Parker got off to a lousy start that fateful Friday. He was supposed to relieve Lincoln's previous bodyguard at four o'clock but was three hours late. When he finally showed up at the White House, Parker was ordered to report to Ford's Theatre and wait there for the president and his guests.

Lincoln's party arrived at the theater at around nine o'clock. The sparkling morning had given way to a foggy, chilly evening. The play had already started when the president and his companions entered their box directly above the right side of the stage. The flags put up in honor of the president's visit draped the front and sides of the box, a lively contrast to the somber crimson wallpaper that darkened the interior. The actors paused while the orchestra struck up "Hail to the Chief." Lincoln bowed to the applauding audience and took his seat in a comfortable upholstered rocking chair. Witnesses reported that relief and happiness seemed to soothe Lincoln's craggy, careworn face.[7]

Officer Parker was stationed in the narrow passageway outside the president's box, seated in a chair beside the door. Parker's irresponsibility soon revealed itself. From where he sat, Parker couldn't see the stage, so after Lincoln and his guests settled in, he abandoned his post and moved to the front of the first gallery to enjoy the play. Later, Parker committed an even greater folly: at intermission, he joined the footman and coachman of Lincoln's carriage for drinks in the Star Saloon next door to Ford's Theatre.[8]

John Wilkes Booth entered the theater sometime before ten o'clock. Ironically, he'd also been in the Star Saloon, working up some liquid courage. When Booth crept up to the door to Lincoln's box, Parker's chair was still empty, giving the assassin unfettered access to the president. Booth timed his attack to coincide with a scene in the play that always sparked loud laughter. Some of the audience may not have heard the fatal pistol shot, although inside the president's box it must have been deafening.

No one knows if John Parker ever returned to Ford's Theatre that night. When Booth struck, the vanishing policeman may have been sitting in his new seat with a nice view of the stage. Perhaps he stayed put in the Star Saloon. Just as likely, he could have been ensconced in the nearest cathouse—or leaning against a lamppost staring at the moon.

Even if Parker had remained at his post, it's not certain he would have stopped Booth. According to an interpreter at today's Ford's Theatre National Historic Site, "Booth was a well-known actor, a member of a famous theatrical family. They were like Hollywood stars today. Booth might have been allowed in to pay his respects. Lincoln knew of him. He'd seen him act in *The Marble Heart,* here in Ford's Theatre, in 1863."[9] However, had Parker been present to admit Booth to Lincoln's box, Booth would have lost the element of surprise and his attack might have been thwarted.

A fellow presidential bodyguard, William H. Crook, wouldn't accept any excuses for Parker. He held him directly responsible for Lincoln's death. "Had he done his duty, I believe President Lincoln would not have been murdered by Booth," wrote Crook. "Parker knew that he had failed in duty. He looked like a convicted criminal the next day. He was never the same man afterward."[10]

Nevertheless, Parker escaped punishment for his actions. Although he was charged with failing to protect the president, the complaint was dismissed. No local newspaper bothered to follow up on the issue of Parker's culpability, and he wasn't mentioned in the official report on Lincoln's death. Why he was let off so easily is baffling, although in the upheaval following the assassination, perhaps he seemed like too small a fish to bother with.

Incredibly, Parker remained on the White House security detail even after his pitiful performance. At least once, he was assigned to protect the grieving Mrs. Lincoln before she moved out of the presidential mansion and returned to Illinois. (Prior to the assassination, Mrs. Lincoln had written a letter on behalf of Parker exempting him from the draft, and some think she may even have been related to him on her mother's side.)[11] Mrs. Lincoln's dressmaker and confidante, former slave Elizabeth Keckley, recorded this outburst by the president's widow directed at Parker:

"So you are on guard tonight—on guard in the White House after helping to murder the President."

The shaken Parker made a feeble attempt to defend himself:

"I could never stoop to murder—much less to the murder of so good and great a man as the President. . . . I did wrong, I admit, and have bitterly repented. . . . I did not believe any one would try to kill so good a man in such a public place, and the belief made me careless."

Mrs. Lincoln snapped that she would always consider him guilty and ordered him from the room.[12]

Parker remained on the Metropolitan Police Force for three more years, but his shiftlessness finally did him in. He was fired on August 13, 1868, for once again sleeping on duty. Parker drifted back into work as a carpenter. He died in Washington in 1890, of pneumonia. Parker, his wife, and their three children are buried together in the capital's Glenwood Cemetery—on present-day Lincoln Road. Their graves are unmarked.

No photographs have ever been found of John Parker. Lincoln biographer Carl Sandburg wrote him off as a "muddle-headed wanderer . . . a weird and elusive Mr. Nobody-at-All—a player of a negation."[13] Parker remains a faceless character, a clown who fostered a tragedy. But what might have happened if Parker had done his duty and not abandoned his president?

Obviously, if Booth had been turned away, President Lincoln would have lived and would probably have served out his term in office. If that had happened, some of the acrimony of Reconstruction might have been avoided, and racial equality would surely have been advanced more forcefully, possibly improving race relations today. Whatever the outcome, we know that Lincoln would have applied the balm of forgiveness to the nation's wounds. That opportunity for Lincoln to at least attempt to forge a fairer, more *united* United States is really what the feckless John Frederick Parker stole from the country.

CHAPTER 14

SQUIRREL TOOTH ALICE

Libby Thompson

T he long golden days at the Sunbeam Rest Home were uniformly peaceful and quiet, like a dress rehearsal for the afterlife. For ninety-seven-year-old Libby Thompson, the Los Angeles care center offered a final snug harbor at the end of a tumultuous journey. Wizened to a wisp and kept alive for years on buttermilk and the occasional shot of whiskey, Thompson bore little resemblance to the pretty, petite woman she'd once been. Beyond her window spread a green lawn dotted with palm trees, although the frail little gray-haired lady with the flinty expression could no longer appreciate the view. Blind and failing, she'd sunk into the hazy realm of memory.

If Thompson had been aware of her surroundings, she probably would have spit in contempt. In the spring of 1953, all people seemed to be gabbing about was that new Superman TV show, or Patti Page's silly song about the doggie in the window (the one with the waggly tail). These days, people thought they had it tough swinging the payments on a new Chevy Bel Air, and they got all excited if they caught a glimpse of a second-rate movie star down on Hollywood Boulevard. Folks sure were different now.

Libby Thompson knew the kind of real problems life could fling at you. When she was a kid, Americans were still fighting the Civil War. Growing up in the wilds of Texas, Libby had to worry about Indian raids and drought and whether her family would make it to the next harvest. Of course, people today would think she was lying if she were to tell them about the old days—when she caroused with the likes of Wyatt Earp, Doc Holliday, and Bat Masterson.[1] She'd run her own dance hall and whorehouse back then. Her customers had known her as Squirrel Tooth Alice, one of the more colorful madams of the Old West. Yep, Libby Thompson had seen quite a lot in her century of life, and much of it would turn your face bright red. Her story captures some of the gritty truth about a time and place in American history that has been mythologized almost beyond recognition.[2]

Thompson's improbable adventure began in 1855 in the Brazos River Valley. She was born Mary Elizabeth Haley but was always known as Libby. Her father, James Haley, owned a dozen slaves and a good size farm south of Fort Worth. Though not rich, the family was better off than most. Libby and her two sisters grew up thinking of themselves as privileged, but the Civil War fixed that. With their slaves emancipated and much of their wealth gone, the family faced economic insecurity and physical danger. Their farm in Hood County lay on the edge of the frontier. As part of the prairie homeland of the Comanche, Kiowa, and Apache, that chunk of Texas came under frequent Indian attack. Sometime near the close of the Civil War, when Libby was around ten or eleven, a Comanche raiding party stole her away from her family, an event that set the course for her life.[3]

It's uncertain how long Libby remained a prisoner, perhaps up to three years. Her parents were finally able to get her back in exchange for some horses. As if she hadn't endured enough by then, once Libby returned home, she suffered from the worst sort of prejudice. On the assumption that her captors had sexually abused her, she was shunned by white society (Libby never spoke about her captivity). It was common for white females who'd been held captive by Indians to be regarded as spoiled, untouchables of a sort. Libby reacted to the injustice by thumbing her nose at those who looked down on her. When she was thirteen, she became the mistress of a considerably older man. She told people they were married, though that's doubtful.[4]

Nothing is known about Libby's lover, but the fellow must have been a more generous soul than most white people of the time. Unfortunately, James Haley didn't regard him as noble. Haley thought the man was taking advantage of a young girl. When Libby brought her beau home to meet her parents, her father shot him dead on the front porch.[5] It's not hard to guess how Libby must have felt. Captured by Indians, rejected by her own people, and now cut off from someone who'd offered her love and acceptance, she did the only thing that made sense to her—she ran away from home.

By 1869 or 1870, when she was about fifteen, Libby ended up in Abilene, Kansas, where she found work as a dance hall girl. Recently established as a rail-head, Abilene became the first great Kansas cattle town, the destination for herds of Texas longhorns driven up the Chisholm Trail after the Civil War.[6] When cowhands reached Abilene and collected their pay, they went looking for three things—whiskey, games of chance, and women. The town did its best to meet those needs, recruiting "entertainers" of all stripes. Abilene bulged with saloons, dance halls, and bordellos. Libby was part of an army of women who descended on Abilene with the intention of sharing in the prosperity, a phenomenon that would be repeated in cattle and mining towns all over the West.

As a dance hall girl, Libby played the lively hostess—chatting up customers, encouraging them to buy drinks, and, yes, even dancing with them, just like Miss Kitty on *Gunsmoke*. Her job, however, didn't require her to engage in sex.[7] That was left to the "fallen angels" who plied their trade in the local bordellos, which ranged from veritable mansions to shabby backstreet "crib houses." While prostitutes in the Old West were often forced into the trade by poverty, only a few made much money at it. The bulk of the profits went to the pimps, madams, and brothel owners. The "soiled doves" usually ended up with nothing other than a venereal disease and an addiction to alcohol or drugs. Many committed suicide. (Libby Haley also worked as a prostitute off and on, but she was lucky enough to survive, maybe because she'd been toughened by her earlier experiences.)[8]

Around the time that Libby left home, she met the man who would figure most prominently in her life, one "Texas Billy" Thompson, a hotheaded cowboy, gambler, and rustler who was at least ten years her senior. Libby and Texas Billy would share many an adventure over the next couple of decades. It was an unconventional relationship, but for the most part, it turned out to be as durable as a rawhide lariat.

Throughout their time together, Libby and Billy slipped back and forth between legitimate work and criminality with the nimbleness of a pair of otters sliding down a muddy creek bank. That wasn't so unusual in the rough-and-tumble frontier era, when people occasionally did desperate things to make ends meet. Single women had it especially tough. For them, honest jobs were few, and those that existed—cook, seamstress, laundress—paid starvation wages. As a result, prostitutes and dance hall girls far outnumbered "decent" women in cattle towns.[9] For men, jobs were often seasonal or boom and bust, leaving them to improvise at times. A hardworking drover, for instance, might be tempted to appropriate a few head of cattle to get through the winter. The challenging conditions made it difficult to tell a "hard" man from a "bad" one. In a strange sort of fellowship, even lawmen and known criminals drank and gambled together. Sometimes, the only difference between a peace officer and a desperado was a tin star (legendary marshal Wild Bill Hickok was just as likely to gun someone down over a game of cards as uphold the law).[10]

Libby and Texas Billy made a contrasting couple—she a pert little five-footer with dark curly hair and he a nearly six-foot beanpole with a handlebar mustache. The mismatched mavericks spent their first couple of years together on the Chisholm Trail. Libby came along when Billy was driving cattle north from Texas to the Kansas railheads. The pair frequently lived out of a covered wagon, or even in caves or crude shelters dug into a hillside. Whenever they hit a cattle town, Libby donned her ruffled skirts and slipped into her role as a dance hall gal, while Billy employed his card-playing skills. They had a series of more or less permanent homes in northern Texas, but they spent much of their time on the trail or bouncing between towns in Texas, Oklahoma, and Kansas.

It was in Kansas that Libby acquired the nickname she would use for the rest of her career: Squirrel Tooth Alice. In Abilene, she met a saloonkeeper with an unusual hobby—he loved to feed the prairie dogs that flourished on his property, and he had a lively trade in catching and selling them as pets. A type of ground squirrel, prairie dogs can make interesting companions. Libby Haley was taken by the cute little animals and soon had one of her own, which she kept on a leash like a toy poodle. Since Libby's front teeth were slightly prominent and had a noticeable gap between them, she adopted the name Squirrel Tooth Alice as her professional sobriquet. (Dance hall girls and prostitutes often went by a nickname, in some cases to hide their identity. The curious custom produced such fascinating handles as Big Nose Kate, Dutch Jake, Cotton Tail, Peg Leg Annie, Irish Queen, and Timberline.)[11]

By 1872, the railhead had moved west to Ellsworth, Kansas, and Libby and Billy followed. Like Abilene, Ellsworth was wide open, with saloons and bordellos lining the dusty streets. Drunken cowboys routinely charged through town, firing their pistols in the air. Libby and Billy got on well in Ellsworth. While Libby shook her booty in the dance halls, Billy haunted the local gambling dens. At the age of seventeen, Libby was a striking beauty, but she had no trouble fending off amorous cowboys. Everyone knew she was Texas Billy's girl, and Billy's reputation with a gun forestalled any untoward advances. Plus, the mere thought of angering Billy's older brother, Ben Thompson—the top gunfighter of his day, according to some—kept rowdies in check.[12]

In the spring of 1873, Libby and Billy again took to the Chisolm Trail. Libby rattled across the rolling grasslands in a covered wagon while Billy did his part to keep hundreds of cantankerous longhorns pointed north. In April, as they crossed the Oklahoma Territory, Libby gave birth to their first child, a boy they named Rance. The baby's arrival prompted the hard-living couple to turn conventional for a change. So their child would be legitimate, the two got married that July in Ellsworth. The couple's blissful stay in Ellsworth was interrupted when Billy got liquored up and shot the local sheriff, Chauncey Whitney.[13] To avoid arrest, Billy scooped up Libby and little Rance and fled westward. The family hid out in the mountains of Colorado for several months before returning to Texas.

By 1875, Billy was back on the cattle trails. Dodge City was then emerging as the newest railhead—and the wildest spot on the Kansas prairie. When Libby and Billy Thompson blew into Dodge, they resumed their usual trades. At the time, Billy's brother was a card dealer in Dodge City's famous Long Branch saloon. In the town's raucous bars and dance halls, the Thompsons rubbed elbows with future western legends Wyatt Earp and Doc Holliday.[14] Earp had been hired to bash a few heads and otherwise tone down the revelry that had regular citizens afraid to walk the streets. Libby became good friends with the marshal's mistress, Mattie Blaylock.

In the Kansas cow towns, Libby and Billy lived the sort of uninhibited lifestyle that would be exaggerated and glorified in dime novels and movies ever afterward, a brassy scenario played out to the sounds of tinkling pianos, drunken laughter, and the occasional explosion of six-guns. In truth, life in the frontier fast lane was a tawdry experience. Wild West "fun" was usually little more than the feral, liquor-fueled debauchery of lonely men who knew they were soon to return to lives of monotonous drudgery.[15] Like sailors on shore leave, hell-raising wranglers drank and whored and gambled with heedless urgency. A few days later, they rode out of town, broke and hung over and with a good chance of developing gonorrhea or syphilis as a reminder of their stay. No one was weaving memories to tell the grandkids about.

Toward the end of 1875, Libby and Billy moved to Sweetwater, Texas (a Panhandle town now known as Mobeetie). There they opened their own dance hall and bordello. Libby ran the girlie operation as the colorful Squirrel Tooth Alice while Billy spent his time at cards. The Thompsons befriended one of the town's faro dealers, Bat Masterson, who would later earn fame as a lawman and writer.[16] The Sweetwater property lent some stability to Libby and Billy's lives, although not for long. In 1876, a posse of Texas Rangers nabbed Billy for killing Sheriff Whitney. Hauled off to jail in Kansas, Billy spent nearly a year behind bars. When he finally stood trial, he was acquitted. By the time Billy was released, Libby had disposed of their Sweetwater holdings. In 1878, the two returned to Dodge City, but their nomadic life together was coming to an end.

The following year, Libby gave birth to her fourth child (her firstborn, Rance, had died as an infant). With a growing family to look after, Libby was becoming tired of all the moving around. From the early 1880s on, she remained in Texas, eventually settling in Palo Pinto, not far from where she'd grown up. A lifelong drifter, Billy found it impossible to stay in one place. He continued to pop in and out of Libby's life over the next several years. Whenever he did show up, Libby usually found herself pregnant a short time later. Gradually, however, Billy's appearances became less frequent, leaving Libby to get by on her own—or with whatever help she could find (although she continued to use the Thompson name, it's fairly certain that Libby had relationships with other men during Billy's absences, and she likely had children by them as well).[17]

In 1897, after a long absence from his wife, Texas Billy Thompson passed away. Libby was in her early forties then and had six kids to take care of, with another on the way. To provide for her family, she'd fallen back on prostitution. She may have even coaxed her two oldest daughters into the sad profession. Her sons kept up family traditions as well—all of them became criminals. The next quarter of a century was the most blatantly lawless period of Libby's life. She and her offspring ran wild, first in the Palo Pinto area, then later in Milford, and finally in the vicinity of Mountain View, Oklahoma. Besides prostitution and rustling, they had their hands in bootlegging, robberies, and, in later years, stealing cars—the modern replacement for horse theft.[18]

Unlike the prostitutes portrayed in romantic accounts of the Old West, Libby Thompson did not have a heart of gold—more like vinegar. As she got older, her desperate circumstances as a single mother with a large family to support made her as testy as a riled up rattlesnake. Her great-grandson and biographer, Laurence E. Gesell, said she was downright mean when he met her near the end of her life, especially toward other females. Her daughters, granddaughters, and great-granddaughters, he wrote, "came to know the meanness of the Old West every time Granny pinched them, pulled their hair, or hit them with her cane."[19]

In 1925, Libby Thompson left Oklahoma and moved to California. Settling in Burbank, the seventy-year-old former dance hall girl, drover's wife, prostitute, madam, and gang leader lived out her twilight years surrounded by her extended family (at least those who weren't dead or serving time). Squirrel Tooth Alice had finally come to rest in the brilliant sunshine of the Golden State. Not surprisingly, the tough old bird hung on for another twenty-eight years. She wasn't the kind to give up. By the time she passed away in April 1953, she had long outlived her era, a time when the West was still raw and the faint-of-heart fared best by staying safely at home.

Libby Thompson definitely added a splash of color to the lore of western America. And while she was no angel, who knows, perhaps she strengthened our gene pool just a bit, like a wild mustang breeding with a docile captive herd (in all, she had twelve children, thirty-seven grandchildren, and eighty-eight great-grandchildren).[20] As shockingly crude as her life might seem to us today, it was typical of a much larger percentage of the frontier population than we might care to admit. In the Old West, the greatest challenge was simple survival. And that was a game at which the profane, immoral, irascible Mrs. Thompson excelled.

CHAPTER 15

THE LAWMAN WHO WENT BAD

Burt Alvord

Burt Alvord

An errant breeze blowing down from the Huachuca Mountains brought a touch of coolness to the dusty streets of Tombstone on this late October afternoon in 1881. The sun glinted like a newly minted Mexican peso in the clear Sonoran Desert air. It was a good day to be alive—or to die, which is what Ike and

Billy Clanton had in mind for the Earp brothers, those three meddlesome do-gooders with their annoying ideas about law and order. The Clantons and their confederates the McLaurys did a little ranching and a little rustling, and when they felt like having a good time they didn't want anyone standing in their way. Tombstone had become one of the wildest boomtowns in the West after silver was discovered here in the southeastern corner of the Arizona Territory in 1877.[1] Then the Earp boys showed up and things began to quiet down. Earlier this day, Marshall Virgil Earp had arrested Ike Clanton for disorderly conduct after a long night of whiskey and cards. Disarmed and fined $25 before he was released, Clanton vowed revenge.

At the O. K. Corral, the Clantons met with Tom and Frank McLaury to plan what they were going to do about the hated lawmen. A few minutes later, they were confronted in a nearby vacant lot by Virgil, Morgan, and Wyatt Earp and their friend Doc Holliday. At around 3 p.m., after the Clantons and McLaurys refused Marshall Earp's order to give up their weapons, the most famous gunfight in the history of the American West erupted, a thirty-second melee in which some thirty shots were fired at close range.[2] Virgil and Morgan Earp and Doc Holliday were wounded in the shooting; Billy Clanton and Tom and Frank McLaury were killed. Not many townsfolk witnessed the shootout, although everyone had a chance to observe the outcome. Frontier justice was a public affair, with dead bodies displayed as a warning to would-be lawbreakers. Anyone who dropped by Ritter's undertaking parlor could gawk at the three dead men in their coffins—a bit shot up, but looking downright peaceful in their best laying-out clothes.

The ruckus in Tombstone that October day wasn't so unusual. In the 1880s, the Arizona Territory swarmed with men like the Clantons and McLaurys. The territory's silver and gold mines and the herds of cattle here and across the border in Mexico were all just waiting to be plundered. It was as if Hedley Lamarr, the glib conniver in *Blazing Saddles,* had assembled his personal army of deviants here. "Round up every vicious criminal and gunslinger in the West," Lamarr told his doofus factotum, played by the inimitable Slim Pickens. "I want rustlers, cutthroats, murderers, bounty hunters, desperadoes, mugs, pugs, thugs, nitwits, half-wits . . . vipers, snipers, con men, Indian agents, Mexican bandits, muggers . . . bushwhackers, hornswogglers, horse thieves . . . train robbers, bank robbers, ass-kickers. . . ."[3] Just sprinkle in your odd burglar, smuggler, arsonist, rapist, bigamist, claim jumper, cardsharp, hooker, and old-fashioned highwayman, and you had the Arizona criminal community down to a T.

Of course, there were plenty of law-abiding citizens as well. One of the most upstanding was Charles E. Alvord, a Tombstone justice of the peace and mining company employee who'd been a public servant in California for twenty years before moving to this rawboned desert town in 1880. Justice Alvord and his wife, Lucinda, had six children. One of them, their youngest son, fourteen-year-old Albert, or Burt, would one day follow in his father's footsteps. It's uncertain whether Burt witnessed the gunfight at the O. K. Corral, but a little over two years later, he saw another vivid example of the law in action when five members of the murderous Bisbee gang were publicly hanged in Tombstone amid a festive celebration. It was a harsh object lesson, and together with his father's long career in law enforcement, it should have kept Burt Alvord on the straight and narrow all his life. For some reason, though—despite the fact that he put in nearly fifteen years as a lawman himself—Alvord turned to crime. All but forgotten today, Alvord was notorious in his era, pursued by lawmen all over the West.[4] He remains a fascinating character study, since his life represents a classic example of a good man gone bad.

Growing up, Burt Alvord received a spotty education in California and Arizona schoolrooms, but he picked up plenty of other useful skills. He was an excellent tracker, and he knew horses well, working occasionally as a stable hand at the O. K. Corral. He learned much about the ways of the world from his father, whose experiences around the mines and in the courtroom made for lively conversation at the family home on Toughnut Street. And all Burt had to do was keep his eyes open to see the wild goings-on in Tombstone for himself. By his late teens, he was enjoying the uninhibited atmosphere of the town's many poolrooms and bars, where he developed a taste for boozing and brawling.[5] He'd matured into a tall, burly teenager who had an easy laugh—and who could just as easily knock your teeth out. He might not have had much formal education, but he had an advanced degree in how to survive on the Arizona frontier. Tombstone turned out one tough, cunning kid in Burt Alvord.

In 1886, Alvord began his career as a peace officer. At the age of nineteen he became a deputy to Cochise County's newly elected sheriff, John Slaughter, a pint-size rancher and former Texas Ranger with a stern view of the law. Criminals that Slaughter crossed paths with had a habit of simply disappearing. Though Slaughter knew of Alvord's fondness for a good time, he hired him anyway. Slaughter needed someone who wasn't afraid of a scrap. Also, Alvord was familiar with the local territory, having visited every corner of Cochise County on his father's rounds as a traveling justice of the peace. And Alvord was fluent in Spanish, which was useful when outlaws had to be pursued into Mexico. Alvord proved his worth with his fists and guns on many occasions—whether tracking rustlers, transporting prisoners, or taking part in shootouts with hombres the likes of multiple-murderer Augustine "The Hairy One" Chacon.[6]

After Sheriff Slaughter's four years in office, Alvord continued working intermittently as a lawman while trying his hand as a stagecoach driver, teamster, homesteader, and firewood dealer. In 1896, he served on a posse that rode after "Three-Fingered Jack" Dunlap following an attempted bank robbery in Nogales, Arizona. The posse never caught up with Dunlap, which Alvord may have filed away for future reference. (He would later recruit Three-Fingered Jack for his own gang.) By this date, Tombstone's silver mines had about played out. The latest frenzy was up north in Pearce, where recently discovered gold and silver deposits had set off another boom. Alvord had just gotten married, and he and his new wife, Lola, moved to Pearce. In March 1897, Alvord was appointed as the town's deputy constable.

Alvord's stay in Pearce didn't last long. In July 1897, he took over the job of constable in nearby Willcox, a town with a troublesome cowboy element. Alvord cleaned things up in short order. A few months after pinning on his badge, he shot and killed a young cowboy named Billy King over a bit of drunken horseplay. The following year, Alvord killed an inebriated Mexican who was making a nuisance of himself in the town's Headquarters Saloon.[7] It was clear that Constable Burt Alvord was no one to trifle with. The people of Willcox were pleased. Even the new sheriff of Cochise County, Scott White, took notice. In January 1899, White appointed Alvord as his deputy, meaning the tough lawman held two offices, extending his jurisdiction from Willcox to much of northern Cochise County.

Alvord was never one to let his police work interfere with his carousing. He still drank heavily, and he hung out with the same types of lowlifes he often had to arrest.[8] Alvord had always operated on the edge of the law. Once, while helping Sheriff John Slaughter track down and kill a gang of horse thieves, he relieved one of the dead bandits of his money belt, which contained $500 in gold coins, a stash Alvord kept for himself.[9] Then there were the rumors about his occasional appropriation of someone else's cattle. He was certainly wise to all the tricks of the criminal trade after years of chasing rustlers, bank robbers, and train robbers. He knew the roads, train routes, and mountain hideouts where a man could elude a posse. If he decided to become an outlaw, he'd be a formidable one. Just what pushed him over the line is hard to pin down, but it may have been nothing more complicated than the lust for easy money. With all the mining activity in southern Arizona, trains were loaded with treasure. In September 1899, Alvord gave in to the temptation. He and three friends robbed a train—the start of a brief but active criminal career that irrevocably ended the Alvord family's forty-year heritage of upholding the law.[10]

Alvord's gang included drinking buddies Billy Stiles, Matt Burts, and Bill Downing. Ironically, all three men had served as deputy constables under Alvord, meaning everyone involved in the robbery was making the leap from good guy to bad. Maybe they'd all been reading too many romanticized accounts of the James gang and other "Robin Hood" bandits who were glorified for sticking it to eastern-owned railroads and banks. And Alvord may have felt that he no longer had anyone to answer to, since his father had died the year before (his mother passed away in 1886). Whatever spurred them on, the gang waylaid a Southern Pacific train as it labored up a steep grade at the isolated town of Cochise ten miles outside of Willcox, making off with an estimated $2,500 in cash and jewelry.[11]

Besides doing the planning, Alvord arranged an alibi for the gang by wrapping himself around a glass of whiskey in a Willcox saloon while the robbery was taking place. When news of the holdup reached Constable Alvord, he was shocked—shocked. He immediately led a posse on a boisterous search for the perpetrators. Riding along in the posse were none other than messieurs Stiles and Downing, who'd returned to town and stashed the swag in a chicken coop at Alvord's place. When the sheriff of Cochise County showed up to look for the robbers, Alvord sent him on a wild goose chase in the Chiricahua Mountains. Despite everyone's best efforts, the robbers somehow got away. (The boys probably had a good laugh over a beer as they thought of Sheriff White blundering around in the hills.)

The success of the gang's first train robbery prompted Alvord and Stiles to plan another outing in February 1900. Burts and Downing had taken their cuts from the first job and bowed out, so some new gang members were recruited—five scruffy characters that included Three-Fingered Jack Dunlap and "Bravo Juan" Yoas. The gang's next target was the railway depot in the town of Fairbank. This time, both Alvord and Stiles would be elsewhere, establishing alibis. Led by Dunlap, the remaining gang members immediately ran into trouble. When they made their move, a guard opened fire with a shotgun, wounding Three-Fingered Jack and Bravo Juan. The thieves limped away with only $42.[12] They split up but were all eventually caught. Before he died from his wounds, Dunlap named Alvord and Stiles as the masterminds of the heist. To save himself, Stiles then fingered Alvord as the brains behind the Cochise robbery.

Alvord and the others were locked up in the Tombstone jail, with Stiles walking free as a government witness. Even though he'd evaded charges, Stiles decided to demonstrate his loyalty/bravery/stupidity by appearing at the jail with a gun, shooting a deputy sheriff in the leg, and springing Alvord and Bravo Juan. The three stole some horses and made for the Dragoon Mountains. Before long, the mercurial Stiles had grown tired of life on the run. He returned home and contacted the Cochise County sheriff's office, cutting another deal by providing information on the whereabouts of his partners, who'd headed for Mexico. Alvord hid out in Sonora for the next couple of years, living on money from the Cochise robbery.[13] (His wife gave up on him after his jailbreak; she got a divorce in 1901 and went back home to Nogales.)

In the summer of 1902, Arizona authorities offered Alvord a deal if he would assist in the capture of the elusive murderer Augustine Chacon. Alvord accepted, and after the Mexican killer was apprehended (with the help of the irrepressible Billy Stiles serving as an undercover Arizona Ranger), he gave himself up, expecting to be cleared of all charges. Alvord was free on bail for several months, but in July 1903, he found himself back in the Tombstone hoosgow, his "deal" forgotten. Billy Stiles ended up there, too, despite all his bobbing and weaving. Alvord saw the inevitability of his conviction and pleaded guilty to a single charge of stealing US mail. He received an extremely lenient two-year sentence. All other charges were dropped, including both train robberies. It was about as good an outcome as Alvord could have hoped for. But then the old magic kicked in between him and his on-again, off-again crony: he and Stiles hatched another jailbreak.

In December 1903, Alvord and Stiles acquired some tools and used them to saw through the bars of their cells and punch a hole in the jailhouse wall. Like a covey of quail, a dozen or so prisoners burst through the hole and scattered in every direction. Alvord and Stiles headed for Mexico. They eluded the Arizona Rangers and Mexican Rurales for several weeks, zigzagging all over Sonora and apparently supporting themselves with a string of robberies.[14] Some accounts say they faked their own deaths by shipping a pair of coffins to Tombstone with a message that they'd been killed, although the ruse failed when authorities looked inside the coffins and found two dead Mexicans.[15]

In February 1904, the Arizona Rangers and Cochise County's latest sheriff, Del Lewis, cornered Alvord and Stiles at a ranch near the town of Naco, Mexico. When the two fugitives drew their guns, the posse opened fire. The shootout was a farcical variation on the last stand of Butch Cassidy and the Sundance Kid. Alvord was hit in the ankle and thigh, while Stiles, with his usual dumb luck, got away. Alvord was hauled back to Tombstone and quickly transferred to the Yuma Territorial Prison. There would be no escaping this time. Inexplicably, his original sentence was not extended. For all his crimes, he got off with a piddling two-year term.

When Alvord's stretch at Yuma was over, he traveled to Los Angeles to visit his younger sister, Mary, announcing to the world, "I am out for good."[16] The tale of the lawman turned train robber might have ended there if he hadn't left so many hard feelings in his wake. Authorities in Arizona and Mexico still thought he had crimes to answer for. In October 1905, Los Angeles detectives showed up at his sister's house to serve extradition papers, but Alvord had disappeared. From then on, his life became a mystery. Stories cropped up about him living in Canada, in the Canal Zone, in Argentina, Brazil, Barbados, and Jamaica. In 1938, two of Alvord's nieces told the Arizona Historical Society that their uncle had died in 1910 on an island off the eastern coast of Panama.[17] Maybe he did, or maybe he hopped a slow boat to China or trekked to Timbuktu. With Alvord, nothing would be too outlandish to believe.

It's hard to fathom the life of Burt Alvord. Perhaps he spent so much time around criminals that the line between acceptable and unacceptable behavior became blurred for him. Criminals killed, and he killed. Criminals took what wasn't theirs, and he skimmed a little when he could. They were all men with guns, living violent lives. So what difference did it make if he robbed big time instead of just holding back a little recovered loot now and then? Or perhaps, like so many men in power, Alvord came to see himself as above the law. Most likely, he had the seed for lawlessness inside him from the beginning, and only his father's influence and the force of habit kept him on the up and up for those fifteen years he spent as a peacekeeper. Mix in alcohol and bad company, and you had the classic recipe for disaster.

Nonetheless, it's difficult to understand how a man who upheld the law with such vigor for so long could make the wrong turn. He wasn't desperate or down on his luck. He had a wife and home, a good job, a decent reputation. Why would someone with so much going for him throw it all away? At first, he probably thought he could avoid being caught, as most men do who dabble in larceny. Yet after his initial arrest, he wasn't contrite. He chose flight rather than doing his time and putting his mistake behind him, something you only expect from hardened offenders. Even stranger was his decision to escape a second time, when he knew he'd received little more than a slap on the wrist for two train robberies, a jailbreak, and assorted other transgressions. It seems by that point, Alvord just didn't give a damn, preferring to live for the moment.

Those who visit the old Cochise County Courthouse in Tombstone, now a state historic park, can still see the courtrooms where Justice Charles Alvord once sat in hearings and his wayward son later stood in the dock. It's sad to contemplate that juxtaposition. Of course, this isn't the only time a family has demonstrated such vivid contrasts in morality. It's virtually a cliché in the daily news, but it still seems shocking. The spectacle of a good person turning bad is one of the eternal mysteries of human behavior. The central question it raises just won't go away. *Why?* In the case of Burt Alvord, it whispers to us even after a hundred years, like an errant breeze blowing down from the Huachuca Mountains.

CHAPTER 16

THE VERY MELLOW YELLOW KID

Joseph Weil

"Yellow Kid" Weil
The Autobiography of America's Master Swindler

J.R. "Yellow Kid" Weil and W.T. Brannon

Judging by his exquisitely tailored suit, diamond stickpin, and aristocratic manner, the bearded, bespectacled Dr. James R. Warrington might have been a banker or a captain of industry. From the looks of his yellow vest and spats and the yellow gloves lying on the table beside his gray homburg and walking stick, he was also a man with a whimsical sense of style.

As a steady procession of cars and delivery trucks honked and jitterbugged down Chicago's Michigan Avenue, the red-haired Dr. Warrington leaned forward and confidentially mentioned to his companion that he'd recently acquired a $300,000 option on some oil lands that were worth millions. But, alas, Dr. Warrington had only been able to raise $262,000 toward the purchase of the property. It was frustrating for him to come so close to being able to profit from this fantastic opportunity. If he could just lay his hands on that last $38,000. Bargains like this didn't come along every day, even in the effervescent economic climate of 1924.

Seated across the table from Dr. Warrington, businessman H. L. Kutter of Hamilton, Ohio, stroked his chin and considered the situation. He hadn't known Dr. Warrington long, but he'd become convinced that the man was a savvy investor. Kutter had been impressed by Warrington's professional knowledge and his thriving place of business. As the dapper Dr. Warrington gazed thoughtfully into the middle distance, Mr. Kutter made up his mind. With a determined look, he announced that he wanted in on the deal.

A few hours later, Kutter delivered $38,000 in cash to Dr. Warrington, satisfied that his investment would pay him back with an immense windfall. Sadly for the Ohio executive, his new partner—along with his $38,000—disappeared forthwith. What's more, when Kutter returned to Warrington's office to make inquiries, he found it deserted, with a *For Rent* sign hanging on the door.[1]

Mr. H. L. Kutter had just become another victim of one of the slickest confidence men to ever ply his trade on American soil—the infamous Joseph "Yellow Kid" Weil, a colorful grifter with an uncanny talent for separating the gullible from their money while using a variety of assumed identities, this time as the elegant, sagacious Dr. Warrington. Over the years, the Yellow Kid passed himself off as a stockbroker, banker, physician, mining engineer, chemist, geologist, land developer, and international purchasing agent. His entire life was one elaborate game of make-believe. The *Chicago Tribune* dubbed him "the genius of things which are not as they seem to be."[2]

A natural-born actor and student of human nature, Weil knew how to take advantage of one of man's predominant traits: greed. With his old-school eloquence and distaste for violence—like most grifters, he declined to carry a gun—Weil was a sort of philosopher-hoodlum. He maintained that "you can't cheat an honest man."[3] He looked upon his crimes as opportunities to teach the avaricious a lesson. "Every victim of one of my schemes had larceny in his heart. An honest man would have had no part of any of my schemes. They all wanted something for nothing." Weil instead gave them "nothing for something."[4]

From the 1890s until 1942, when he retired after a stretch in the Atlanta federal penitentiary, Joseph Weil ran scams in and around Chicago and in other

US cities—inventing or perfecting many of the frauds that have become standards in the wildly creative repertoire of confidence men everywhere. Weil is credited with originating the phony bookie operation portrayed years later in the Paul Newman–Robert Redford movie *The Sting*, a "long con" that entailed setting up an ersatz betting parlor staffed by hired flimflammers pretending to be employees and gamblers. Weil himself was like a filmmaker. He had the ability to create a setting and assemble a cast of characters then orchestrate everything to the desired end. Only, "the actor has a script carefully prepared for him in advance," Weil said. "I made my own script as I went along."[5]

Weil was born in Chicago in 1875, the son of German immigrants who ran a neighborhood grocery store. Although he was a good student, Weil left school at seventeen and began working as a bill collector. The job didn't pay much, but Weil figured out a way to supplement his wages. Noticing that other employees were skimming from the collections, he informed them that he would keep quiet for a cut of the take, his first foray into crime. "I had seen how much more money was being made by skullduggery than by honest toil," he said.[6]

Two years later, Weil signed on as a shill in a traveling medicine show run by Chicago grifter Doc Meriwether, who would help educate Weil in the art of the con. Weil's role in the show was to pose as a member of the crowd and vouch for the curative powers of Meriwether's Elixir in order to encourage locals to buy a bottle of the potent concoction, a nasty-looking black liquid consisting of rainwater laced with alcohol and laxative.

During his time with Doc Meriwether, Weil honed his skills in a variety of "short cons"—simple scams that required little preparation, such as the shell game and three-card monte. After a couple of summers in the hinterlands, Weil returned to his hometown to take up his life's work as a big city con artist. He began to associate with other Chicago swindlers, including a man named Frank Hogan. The two became partners for a time, and they often hung out together at a bar owned by city alderman "Bathhouse John" Coughlin. It was Coughlin who gave Weil his nickname. The country's first successful newspaper comic strip, "Hogan's Alley," was popular at the time. The strip featured a goofy looking character named Mickey Dugan—also known as the Yellow Kid. Bathhouse John suggested that the sidekick of Frank Hogan should fittingly be known as the Yellow Kid, and the tag stuck.[7]

Chicago was particularly fertile ground for a grifter in the early 1900s, thanks to a local law that defined confidence schemes as activities that took "unfair advantage of an unwary stranger."[8] Yellow Kid Weil skirted the law by preying on Chicagoans who weren't exactly innocent. As usual, Weil knew how to find his victim's weak spots. He also knew where to flush out a pigeon, and the Chicago racetracks were some of the best places.

In one of his racetrack scams, Weil acquired a sleek, impressive-looking thoroughbred named Black Fonso. The animal turned out to be a "morning glory"—a horse with the curious trait of being fast in the morning but slow in the afternoon, which is when thoroughbred races take place. Nevertheless, Weil envisioned a way to make money with Black Fonso. He invited his marks to witness the horse's speed in a morning workout then told them that he owned a much slower look-alike horse he was running under the same name. Weil said that when the betting odds on the slow horse dropped far enough, he intended to substitute the fast Black Fonso in a race and clean up. The marks naturally wanted in on the action. Obviously, there never were two horses, just the one Black Fonso that always ran out of the money.

On the day of the race in which Weil supposedly substituted his speedier horse, he and his marks placed large bets on Black Fonso. The marks didn't realize they were handing over their money to one of Weil's pals who was posing as a betting agent. As usual, Black Fonso came in far back in the pack, and although no wagers were actually placed, the marks thought that they'd lost their money on a fair bet. But even if they'd suspected that Weil had ripped them off, they wouldn't have complained to the authorities, since they'd have had to admit that they'd bet on a horse they believed to be a ringer. Because of their willing participation in a shady deal, the victims were simultaneously fleeced and muzzled— the hallmark of most successful cons and the reason that relatively few swindlers are ever convicted.[9]

Weil always employed an exceptional level of detail in pulling off his scams, hewing as close to reality as possible. "I had a positive passion for fact," he said. "That's what made me such a good liar."[10] To set up his stock swindles, Weil would create a phony brokerage office that included scurrying messengers, a clattering ticker tape machine, and a functional stock index board. On other occasions, he simulated working bank offices, staffing them with cronies who passed themselves off as customers, tellers, and managers. He added touches of verisimilitude by setting out deposit slips swiped from a real bank and prominently displaying stacks of boodle—fake currency—and canvas bags filled with metal washers to look like sacks of coins. When the sting was over, Weil and his friends packed up their props and vamoosed.

To convince his marks that he was who he said he was, Weil fabricated magazine and newspaper articles describing the achievements of whatever character he was playing at the time, complete with photos of himself. He also inserted his photo in copies of books written by an eminent mining engineer he sometimes pretended to be. He printed phony business cards and stock certificates by the bushel. By writing to well-known companies and then copying the letterheads on the replies he received, he was able to forge seemingly real correspondence to dangle under the noses of his victims.

Another "long con" Weil took part in involved a mind-reading fortune-teller who preyed on wealthy women. With the aid of an accomplice concealed behind a curtain and a telephone headset hidden under his turban, the swami was able to "discover" secrets about his clients and offer them nuggets of wisdom. During one promising session, the bogus soothsayer dispensed this bit of bunkum to a rich spinster from Maryland: "I see a man coming into your life. This man wears a beard. I can't tell you when or under what circumstances you will meet him. Nor can I tell you what he will advise. But heed him! For the bearded one holds the key to your fortune."[11]

Shortly after the woman returned home, a bearded man appeared on her doorstep asking to use her telephone. The stranger's car had broken down as he was passing the woman's estate. It was the Yellow Kid, of course, posing as a well-to-do businessman on his way to Baltimore to close a sale on some valuable real estate. Ingratiating himself with his patter about his world travels, Weil accepted the woman's offer to stay in her home until his car could be repaired. By the time the Kid departed, he'd sold his hostess a parcel of "fabulously rich oil lands" in Texas for $180,000—property that had cost him $1,500 just days before.[12]

Weil delighted in inventing new ways to lighten his victims' wallets. He once published a financial newsletter touting the worthless Copper Queen mine in Colorado, whose stocks he'd acquired from a friend for a penny a share. After mailing his newsletter to a list of wealthy investors, he was able to unload thousands of Copper Queen shares for five dollars a pop. In another fit of inspiration, the artful grifter started a company that gave away free "dream vacation" lots. He then raked in exorbitant fees when the new owners registered their deeds. The lots, which had cost him a dollar an acre, were located in the middle of a Michigan wasteland.[13]

Weil also made a killing through a short-lived Ponzi scheme based on an "investment bank" that did nothing but bet on horse races, and in another imaginative ploy he conned a rich businessman into betting on a fixed boxing match in which one of the fighters spewed out copious amounts of chicken blood and pretended to die in the ring. In his most lucrative and long-running con, the Yellow Kid persuaded marks to invest in the nonexistent Verde-Grande Copper Mining Company, convincing them that the mammoth J. P. Morgan financial firm was secretly after the shares. He once touched an Omaha banker for $350,000 with this ruse, his biggest single score ever.[14] As with all his tricks, the moment Weil laid his hands on his victim's money, poof—he was gone.

Most of the suckers that Weil bamboozled with such schemes were wealthy businessmen, bankers, doctors, or lawyers. He seldom bothered with people who had little money. According to Weil, successful professionals were the most gullible marks of all because they felt that they were too smart to be hoodwinked. "They had plenty of money, but they fell for my schemes because they were greedy for more. In my time, I devised some ingenious plans to relieve these people of part of their wealth."[15]

This demi–Robin Hood stole from the rich all right, but he kept the proceeds for himself, although he didn't hold on to any of it for very long. He claimed to have raked in between eight and ten million dollars during his long career, and he blew it all on high living, freely indulging in his tastes for expensive clothes, fine food, and fancy cars. "People have often asked me what I did with all the money that came into my possession," he once wrote. "The cash melted away," he explained, noting that "we often entertained on a lavish scale."[16] That was an understatement. After laying out a small fortune in St. Louis for three days of champagne, showgirls, and a hired ten-piece band, he excused his excesses with a shrug. "We made money in large amounts and we spent it that way. We cared for money for only one reason—the fun and the things it would buy."[17]

Weil put his silver tongue to good use in Chicago's courtrooms, where he was a regular guest. A list of his larcenous activities in the October 26, 1918, edition of the *Chicago Tribune* ran nearly half a column—and that was early in his career. The *Tribune*'s September 19, 1925, edition reported that Weil had talked his way out of a year in jail and a thousand-dollar fine over a bad check charge. When the law caught up with him in the matter of the $38,000 swindle he'd pulled on H. L. Kutter, the Yellow Kid unleashed this flurry of oratory: "The dastardly fabrications of the metropolitan newspapers, the reprehensible conduct of journalists to surround me with a nimbus of guilt, is astonishing," he proclaimed. "It is what has led to this prosecution. I am an honest man now. I am innocent of the crime mentioned. There has been gross misrepresentation here."[18] Even though they had him dead to rights, you had to tip your hat to a crook who could come up with the phrase "nimbus of guilt."

For all of his many offenses, Weil paid a surprisingly small price. Though he was arrested repeatedly, he only served about a dozen years behind bars altogether, including stays in Joliet, Leavenworth, and Atlanta. He accepted his punishment with equanimity, saying his imprisonment gave him "time to relax, reflect, and catch up on my reading."[19]

Weil always announced that he was going straight after every jail term, and he gave it a try a few times, starting companies to sell chewing gum and coffee, working as a door-to-door salesman for the *Catholic Encyclopedia*, running a Chicago hotel, and even managing a circus. But each time he returned to the confidence game. However, in 1942, following his final two years in prison, Weil gave up his criminal career for good. In his late sixties, he retired to a quiet life in Chicago. Having blown through all the money he'd stolen over the years, he earned an honest living by making telephone solicitations for churches and charitable organizations.[20]

Weil also found time to write the story of his life, a collection of vivid, often humorous anecdotes filled with a Runyonesque cast of—in his own words— "pickpockets, thieves, safecrackers, and thugs of every degree," along with "card-sharps, swindlers, gamblers, policemen, and politicians."[21] Published in 1948, when Weil was in his early seventies, *"Yellow Kid" Weil: The Autobiography of America's Master Swindler* resoundingly confirmed the adage that there's a sucker born every minute.

Though the Kid had gone straight, the Chicago police continued to haul him in for questioning now and then, perhaps out of habit or just for old times' sake. The *Chicago Tribune*, which had generated a mountain of copy on Weil's escapades over the years, still followed him, running stories periodically as he grew older. It was a lengthy series, since Weil lived to be one hundred. In 1974, the paper interviewed the ninety-nine-year-old former grifter, who was then living in a convalescent center. Asked what he would change about his life if he could live it over again, the doddering fraudster, who once joked that he was writing a book called *Crime Does Not Pay—Enough*, was quick to reply: "I'd do it the same way again."[22]

In a previous interview, Weil had lamented that his line of criminal endeavor was fading away. "There are no good confidence men anymore," he said, "because they do not have the necessary knowledge of foreign affairs, domestic problems, and human nature."[23] Weil's comment reflected the tendency we all have to think that we've lived through some golden age. In truth, the confidence game is alive and well. Weil himself knew that the big con would never disappear. As he observed on his ninetieth birthday, "Just look at the gullibility of the American public today. I tell you there are vast sums of money to be made by a man with imagination."[24] That was one quality Yellow Kid Weil never lacked.

CHAPTER 17

YOU BET YOUR LIFE

Alvin Thomas

The fantastical tales about him abound, and if only a tenth of them are true, he must have possessed the conjuring skills of Merlin the Wizard, the wiles of Huck Finn, and the athletic prowess of Tiger Woods. His real name was Alvin Thomas, although the world came to know him better as the nattily dressed, viper-eyed gambler Titanic Thompson—a man who would wager on anything, from whether he could throw a walnut onto the roof of a five-story building (he could, but he substituted a nut filled with lead to pull it off) to whether his water spaniel could retrieve a marked stone from the bottom of a fishing hole (the dog managed it, although the sucker he bet against didn't know that the bottom of the fishing hole was covered with similar stones with identical markings).

In his glory days—from the 1920s to the 1940s—this tall, slender, dark-haired hustler from the Ozark hills fleeced cigar-chomping mobsters at poker and country club dandies at golf with equal ease. He even mastered bowling and horseshoes to round out his betting arsenal. Gambling was like breathing to the man they called Titanic. It was a passion he followed for all of his eighty-one years. Born in poverty, Thompson won millions, only to die broke in a Texas old folks' home. But it was a hell of a ride getting there—a tumultuous, not altogether savory trip in which he claimed five teenage brides, killed half a dozen men, and rubbed elbows with leading figures in crime, sports, and entertainment.[1]

If Titanic Thompson wasn't taking money from Al Capone with one of his inventive "proposition" bets (wagers on an individual's ability to accomplish some improbable feat) or beating champion golfers such as Byron Nelson at their own game, he was comparing card tricks with magician Harry Houdini or playing one-pocket pool with legendary shark Minnesota Fats. His flamboyant lifestyle even provided artistic inspiration: writer Damon Runyon based one of his short story creations on Thompson—the carousing gambler Sky Masterson, a character made famous in the hit Broadway musical *Guys and Dolls*. Pro golfer Paul Runyan summed up Thompson succinctly: "He was crooked and unscrupulous. He was also the most fascinating human being I ever met."[2]

For a man who won close to a million dollars in a long-running 1920s poker game in San Francisco (equivalent to more than $11 million today), Thompson wasn't obsessed with wealth. Money was simply his means of keeping score.[3] Like many a gambler, he was motivated by the exhilaration of scheming up some new wager and coming out on top. It's what prompted him to bet that he could hit a golf ball five hundred yards (he did it by hitting his ball onto a frozen lake) and to hone the improbable talent of flinging playing cards through an open transom window from across the room—just in case the opportunity ever came up to wager on it. Chances are, if someone had bet Titanic Thompson that he couldn't jump over the moon, he would have simply asked for odds.

Born in the fall of 1892, Alvin Clarence Thomas inherited the betting bug from his daddy, a gambler who abandoned his family when his son was just a few weeks old. Young Alvin grew up near Rogers, Arkansas, under the tutelage of his stepfather, grandfather, and six uncles. At the end of the workday, after they'd finished tending their pigs and chickens and maybe cutting a few railroad ties for cash, the menfolk taught Alvin how to play cards, checkers, and dominoes. "I didn't have much education," he said of himself, "but I had a natural head for mathematics," adding that he "worked out odds on just about everything you could put money on."[4] And put money on things he did. When he was sixteen, he blew the Arkansas dust off his shoes and headed for the bright lights of Missouri, after promising his mother he would never drink or smoke. He kept that promise, although he found plenty of other vices to fill his time.

Roaming from town to town, "Slim" Thomas, as he was called back then, polished his skills at cards, dice, and pool. For a few months, he worked as a trick shot artist with a traveling medicine show (an expert marksman before he was old enough to shave, he would later win the Arizona state trapshooting championship four years running). Around the time that he turned eighteen, the young gambler acquired a thirty-foot riverboat in a crap game. He didn't own the boat for long. During a cruise, a gambler named Jim Johnson accused him of cheating at dice and pulled a knife on him. Johnson then assaulted Thomas's girlfriend, trying to rip her clothes off. Thomas whacked Johnson on the head with a hammer and threw him overboard. Drunk, unable to swim, and probably unconscious, Johnson drowned.[5] Luckily for Thomas, the local sheriff was a crook. In exchange for the riverboat and a cash bribe, he let Thomas off.

In the spring of 1912—just after the British ocean liner *Titanic* went down in the North Atlantic—the young gambler found himself in Joplin, Missouri, where he won $500 shooting pool with a character named Snow Clark. In one of his typically offbeat wagers, Thomas bet Clark another $500 that he could jump over the pool table without touching it. He performed the stunt easily ("I could jump farther than a herd of bullfrogs in those days," he said).[6] As Thomas was pocketing his money, a bystander asked the name of the lean, leapin', pool-playin' stranger. "It must be Titanic," Clark said, because "he sinks everybody."[7] At that moment, Slim Thomas became Titanic Thomas. A few years later, he began calling himself Titanic Thompson after newspapers in New York got his last name wrong—which was fine with him, since he preferred to shroud his real identity.

Throughout the 1910s, the reputation of the hustler from the Arkansas sticks grew steadily among the checkered fraternity that traveled a mostly southern and Midwestern circuit in search of betting action (this was before Las Vegas and Atlantic City became gambling meccas). In addition to his proficiency at sports, games of chance, and inventive proposition bets, Thompson became known for his icy nerves. He said that he got "a very calm feeling" whenever "there was big trouble or big stakes," and he always carried a pistol in case anyone got frisky with him.[8]

In 1919, Thompson shot and killed two men in St. Louis when they tried to steal his winnings from a crap game, and he later gunned down another pair of robbers who were trying to hold up a poker game in St. Joseph, Missouri. Because all four victims were known criminals, no charges were filed. In 1932, Thompson shot and killed a masked man who tried to rob him at a Texas country club. The thief turned out to be the sixteen-year-old caddy who'd carried Thompson's clubs that day. Before the boy died, he confessed to police, and again no charges were filed. Thompson expressed remorse for the youngster's death, but not for the other four slayings. Of those killings, he said, "They needed it."[9]

By the Roaring Twenties, when jazz, gambling, and Prohibition-era booze were the country's main entertainments, Thompson had graduated to the status of high roller—someone who isn't afraid to lay down staggering wagers. Decked out like a Wall Street lawyer, he haunted swank hotel rooms and fancy clubs in New York, Chicago, San Francisco, and Los Angeles. Even the big-time games weren't always on the up and up, since gamblers at that level seemed to take pride in seeing who could cheat most effectively. Thompson himself could deal off the bottom of the deck or mark the cards in just a few hands, with no one the wiser.[10]

On the evening of September 8, 1928, Thompson took part in a historic marathon poker game in New York City. Among the shady characters seated around the table was mob boss Arnold Rothstein, reputed to be the man who fixed the 1919 World Series. Rothstein lost around $500,000 in the course of the game, according to Thompson, but instead of paying up, Rothstein handed out IOUs.[11] The players left holding his markers weren't too happy, even though they knew the game had been rigged. Several weeks went by and Rothstein still hadn't paid up. Then on the night of November 4, while Rothstein was in a third-floor room in the Park Central Hotel, someone shot him in the groin. Rothstein staggered down to the hotel service entrance and was rushed to the hospital. He died two days later.

The police arrested George McManus, a hulking "commission broker" (bookmaker) who'd gambled with Rothstein on September 8. Prosecutors contended that McManus held a grudge against the mob boss stemming from that evening. Titanic Thompson wasn't present at Rothstein's murder, but he was called as a witness in McManus's trial. Like the other participants in the September poker game, Thompson made McManus out to be a model citizen, and the bookie was acquitted. Privately, Thompson was sick over Rothstein's death. Half the money Rothstein had written IOUs for should have been his, and now he could never collect. Even more maddening, he was slapped with a $12,700 default judgment in favor of Rothstein's estate when the gangster's lawyers produced promissory notes Thompson had signed.[12]

Thompson just shrugged it off, knowing that bad luck was part of his trade—like the misfortune he routinely encountered at the racetrack. "I lost about $2 million fooling with the horses," he recalled.[13] In a race in Tijuana, he lost $150,000 on what he thought was a sure thing. He bet on a long shot named Nellie A after bribing the riders of the other horses to throw the race. To improve his odds, he let it be known that a sharpshooter was waiting to pick off any jockey who came in ahead of his horse. Things went according to plan, with Nellie A far ahead of the pack as the horses came toward home—until the poor animal fell down with a broken leg just short of the finish line. That may have been the only horse race in history in which every rider in the field struggled to avoid coming in first. Thompson would have pocketed more than a million dollars if Nellie A had made it a few more yards.[14]

Thompson fared better at horseshoes, largely because he manufactured his own "luck." When he took on world champion tosser Frank Jackson, Thompson tilted things in his favor by building a horseshoe court that was forty-one feet long. Regulation courts are forty feet long. After practicing on his rigged court, Thompson challenged Jackson to a match. At the end of the game—as Jackson paid out the $2,000 he'd lost—the champ expressed wonderment at why his tosses had kept coming up short.[15]

One sport Thompson didn't have to cheat at—at least not much—was golf. He didn't take up the sport until he was almost thirty years old, but he was a natural. In the first eighteen-hole match he ever played, he won $56,000. After that, he said, "I went purely crazy over golf. For the next 20 years I had a club in my hands nearly every day." People who saw how good he was encouraged him to turn pro, but he refused, saying he "couldn't afford the cut in pay." In the 1920s and '30s, "a top pro wouldn't win as much in a year as I would in a week," he said.[16]

Just to keep things interesting, Thompson pulled off some remarkable golf course scams. "No matter how good I was," he said, "I always liked to have an edge."[17] He once magnetized the putting green cup liners before a match and then played with golf balls with steel cores. Another time, he lifted the cups just enough to make his opponent's putts veer away from the hole if they weren't dead center. Since he could play equally well right- or left-handed, he used that ability to his advantage. After clipping some hotshot while playing right-handed, he would propose a rematch, offering to play left-handed to even things out. He knew it was a "lead-pipe cinch" that any dupe who accepted the offer would end up reaching for his wallet.[18]

Thompson was an equal-opportunity hustler. He beat professionals, fellow gamblers, and local duffers who thought they had game, but he always made sure that he only won by a stroke or two so he wouldn't frighten away prospects. Pro great Sam Snead called Thompson "golf's greatest hustler."[19] The legendary Ben Hogan said he was "the best shotmaker I ever saw."[20] Byron Nelson, who once won eleven consecutive tournaments—and lost a money match against Thompson in 1934—said Titanic would have done well on the professional tour, although by the time pro purses began to balloon, the gambler-golfer was well past his prime.[21]

Titanic Thompson's heyday occurred in an era when many people viewed itinerant gamblers as romantic characters, and Thompson was the most colorful of them all. Like a Hollywood leading man, he always surrounded himself with attractive women—the younger the better. He married his last wife, Jeannette, in 1954. He was sixty-one, she was eighteen. Jeannette stuck with her man until he grew too old to keep up his rambling ways. In 1973, she moved him into a nursing home in Euless, Texas. They divorced so that Thompson could qualify for government aid, and he died the following year.

A psychologist would say that Titanic Thompson had a debilitating addiction. "He didn't waste his time with anything that interfered with gambling," Jeannette Thomas admitted, "not food or sleep or love."[22]

Reflecting on his long career, Thompson wrote this self-appraisal in *Sports Illustrated* in 1972, two years before his death: "I was smart, which is better than lucky in some ways, and I was very cool and steady and a fine athlete, so I usually had the edge in most games. To be a winner a man has to feel good about himself and know he has some kind of skillful advantage going in. It's like what I told a judge one time when I was charged with operating a game of chance. 'Your Honor,' I said, 'this charge couldn't be right. There wasn't nobody in that room had a chance but me.'"[23]

Excelling at gambling might not be much to hang your hat on as a lifetime's accomplishment, but it was the hand that Titanic Thompson decided to play. And according to his wife Jeannette, this scheming, cheating, wayward child of the backwoods "enjoyed every minute he lived."[24]

CHAPTER 18

KEEPER OF THE IMMACULATE SPERM

Charles Davenport

Growing up in Charlottesville, Virginia, in the early 1900s, young Carrie Buck impressed those she met as serious and self-possessed, someone whose quiet demeanor hinted at a life filled with challenges. Of humble origins—her widowed mother had given her up to foster care as a child—the stocky, dark-haired girl didn't let her difficulties get her down. She enjoyed reading the newspaper, liked to fiddle with crossword puzzles, and always made herself useful around the house. She was a bit awkward in social situations, but otherwise she was a thoroughly average teenager. No one had any reason to think differently of her. Then something terrible occurred that changed Carrie's life forever.

In 1923, when she was seventeen, Carrie Buck was raped by a nephew of her foster parents. The girl became pregnant, and her foster parents—perhaps embarrassed by what their nephew had done—decided to hide the girl away by committing her to the Virginia Colony for the Epileptic and Feebleminded, a mental facility in the town of Lynchburg. Carrie's birth mother had previously been committed to the same institution, accused of being mentally deficient and promiscuous. The same reasons were given for Carrie's incarceration. It was a classic case of punishing the victim.

Carrie had her baby in the spring of 1924, the same year that Virginia passed a law permitting the involuntary sterilization of those judged to be mentally impaired.[1] The statute grew out of the early twentieth century's widely influential eugenics movement, a now discredited cousin of genetics that attempted to improve American society by "breeding out" a long list of undesirable traits ascribed to minorities, the poor, and certain immigrant populations. At the same time, eugenicists hoped to foster the increase of good breeding traits by encouraging "high-grade" citizens to go forth and multiply (the word eugenics means "well born").[2]

It's no surprise that complacently comfortable white folks conceived and promoted this scheme of biological discrimination. According to eugenicists, if you weren't of Nordic or Anglo-Saxon heritage, your genes were second rate. Even if you were white, if you happened to be epileptic, mentally ill, illegitimate, unemployed, homeless, a sexually active single woman, an alcoholic, a convicted criminal, or a prostitute—all signs of "feeblemindedness" or "hereditary degeneracy"—you were a threat to the purity of the nation's gene pool. Eugenicists advocated three ways of dealing with the perceived problem of bad genes: immigration restrictions, the prevention of "unfit" marriages, and involuntary sterilization of "defective" individuals in state care, chiefly mental patients and prison inmates.[3]

Carrie Buck had the misfortune of being the first Virginia resident chosen for compulsory sterilization. Her case became a test of the constitutionality of the state's new law, a challenge that went all the way to the US Supreme Court. With little justification beyond a family history of poverty and illegitimacy, Carrie and her birth mother were both portrayed as sexually deviant simpletons. Even Carrie's baby girl was said to be "not quite normal."[4] Years later, researchers determined that all three family members were of average intelligence, and that the arguments for Carrie's sterilization were based on faulty, biased testimony. "These people belong to the shiftless, ignorant and worthless class of anti-social whites of the South," one so-called expert declared—without ever having met Carrie Buck or her mother.[5]

Despite the flimsy testimony presented in the case, the Supreme Court upheld the Virginia law in 1927 by an eight-to-one margin, with justice Oliver Wendell Holmes Jr. issuing this shocking pronouncement: "It is better for all the world, if instead of waiting to execute degenerate offspring for crime, or to let them starve for their imbecility, society can prevent those who are manifestly unfit from continuing their kind. . . . Three generations of imbeciles are enough."[6] Shortly afterward, Carrie Buck, a perfectly normal citizen of the United States, was sterilized against her will. It was an outrage destined to be repeated many times over—mostly against poor, uneducated women—as the dark age of eugenics spread across the land in the 1920s, '30s, and '40s.

Thousands of activists had a hand in creating the conditions that permitted the abuse of Carrie Buck and others like her, but few bear a greater measure of responsibility than biologist Charles Davenport, a man who spent more than three decades leading the campaign for racial purity in the United States.[7] In essence, Davenport and his fellow eugenicists sought to create a master race of white Protestant Yankees, with all the frightening ramifications that implies. (Imagine the banality of an entire nation of Ward and June Cleavers.) Aside from being morally repulsive, their goal amounted to second-rate science, since biological strength lies in genetic diversity, not sameness.

Davenport's offenses went beyond the harm he caused here at home. His lengthy collaboration with eugenicists in Nazi Germany contributed to that country's brutal racial policies.[8] Today, we rightly reject what Davenport and others like him stood for as white supremacy gone berserk. In his own time, though, Davenport was hailed as a trailblazer, an honorable scientist who studied and taught at our nation's most prestigious institutions of higher learning. Davenport's chilling story demonstrates that when prejudice and public policy mix, the result can be a humanitarian nightmare.

A lanky, goatee-sporting man who favored all-white suits, Charles Benedict Davenport was the product of a puritanical upbringing. He was born in 1866 on his family's farm near Stamford, Connecticut. In his childhood and early teens, he spent the spring and summer months working on the farm. The rest of the year, he lived in Brooklyn, where his domineering father ran a successful real estate and insurance business. Davenport attended Brooklyn Polytechnic Institute, earning a bachelor of science in civil engineering in 1886. In 1889, he received a bachelor's degree from Harvard University, followed by a doctorate in zoology in 1892.

Even as a student, Davenport wrote prolifically, which he continued to do after being hired as an instructor at Harvard in 1893. A primary area of interest for the young scholar was the study of heredity and selective breeding in animals, a topic his years on the farm gave him practical insight into. His writing earned him a favorable reputation, and in 1899 the University of Chicago offered him an assistant professorship. In 1904, Davenport left Chicago to become the director of the new Station for Experimental Evolution at Cold Spring Harbor, New York, a genetics research center funded by the Carnegie Institution. It was the perfect place for Davenport to cultivate his interests in evolution, heredity, and eugenics.

In 1910, Davenport founded the Eugenics Record Office at Cold Spring Harbor, a facility that became the epicenter of the American eugenics movement.[9] By compiling detailed "pedigrees" on thousands of families, the office sought to document how desirable or undesirable traits are passed from one generation to the next. In addition to physical characteristics, Davenport and his staff considered a wide range of behavioral and cultural traits to be genetic in origin, including personality quirks such as a love of the sea, a fondness for songbirds, and a preference for city life.

As wacky as that sounds, many of the country's brightest leaders in education, politics, and business thought it was true. Moreover, those same people were convinced that some character traits are more prevalent in certain ethnic and socioeconomic groups than others. Specifically, they believed that good traits—intelligence, honesty, industriousness—are predominant in middle- and upper-class WASPs, and that bad traits—criminality, immorality, shiftlessness—tend to be found in just about everyone else, especially the poor and the disadvantaged.[10]

Englishman Francis Galton—a cousin of Charles Darwin—started this whole spurious exercise in 1883 when he came up with the concept of eugenics.[11] It was Galton who first suggested that society could be improved by encouraging intelligent, successful couples to marry and have children in order to perpetuate their superior qualities. Researchers in Britain and the United States quickly drew a link between Galton's idea and the genetic mechanisms of heredity outlined twenty years earlier by Augustinian monk Gregor Mendel. Suddenly, the advancement of society through science seemed possible.

Actually, Galton's concept of pairing individuals who might pass on desirable traits is practiced every day in cultures around the world. Whenever two bright, successful people get married, we look upon it as a "good match." Many early eugenicists emphasized this simple, positive goal. Where Charles Davenport and his cohorts went astray was to focus on the negative side of eugenics: attempting to eliminate "bad matches" by determining who, in their opinion, should not have children and doing all they could to prevent that from happening.

The negative approach to eugenics flourished in the United States thanks to the financial support of major philanthropic organizations such as the Rockefeller Foundation and the Carnegie Institution, as well as a pool of wealthy backers that included breakfast cereal tycoon John Kellogg and railroad fortune heiress Mary Harriman.[12] Respected public figures the likes of Teddy Roosevelt and Alexander Graham Bell supported the aims of the American eugenics movement, and courses in the subject were taught at Harvard, Yale, Princeton, Cornell, Columbia, and other top universities. (Many colleges adopted Charles Davenport's 1911 textbook *Heredity in Relation to Eugenics*, a book filled with inaccurate, oddball opinions about inherited traits within families.)[13]

What's indisputable about the eugenics movement in this country is that it was driven by racial and class prejudice. At the dawn of the twentieth century, white Protestant Americans feared being overrun by immigrants from southern and eastern Europe, people who traditionally had large families. Groups such as the Race Betterment Foundation and the American Eugenics Society stoked those fears by suggesting that the superior traits of industrious Anglo-Saxons were being undermined by the lazy, degenerate masses showing up on their shores.[14] Charles Davenport articulated the goal of encouraging white Americans to have more children and stemming the invasion of undesirables in his "eugenics creed":

> I believe in striving to raise the human race to the highest plane of social organization, of cooperative work and of effective endeavor.

> I believe that I am the trustee of the germ plasm that I carry; that this has been passed on to me through thousands of generations before me; and that I betray the trust if (that germ plasm being good) I so act as to jeopardize it, with its excellent possibilities, or, from motives of personal convenience, to unduly limit offspring.

> I believe that, having made our choice in marriage carefully, we, the married pair, should seek to have 4 to 6 children in order that our carefully selected germ plasm shall be reproduced in adequate degree and that this preferred stock shall not be swamped by that less carefully selected.

I believe in such a selection of immigrants as shall not tend to adulterate our national germ plasm with socially unfit traits.

I believe in repressing my instincts when to follow them would injure the next generation.[15]

Davenport's creepy doctrine was worthy of Jack D. Ripper, the mad general in *Dr. Strangelove* who raved about a communist conspiracy to pollute "our precious bodily fluids." From today's perspective, the call for racial purity and selective breeding smacks of Big Brotherism, but large numbers of Americans embraced it, a fact demonstrated in legislatures across the country. In 1907, the state of Indiana passed the nation's first eugenic sterilization law. By 1935, some thirty states had similar laws on the books, and around twenty thousand involuntary sterilizations had been performed, the majority of those in California and Virginia.[16]

By the time eugenic sterilizations were phased out (most of the laws had either been repealed or were no longer being enforced by the 1970s), between forty thousand and seventy thousand Americans had been sterilized against their will.[17] Roughly 40 percent of those sterilizations took place in California, where the eugenics movement had a cadre of rabid supporters, among them the first president of Stanford University and members of the University of California Board of Regents and the State Board of Charities and Corrections.[18]

In addition to lobbying for forced sterilizations and strict immigration laws (such as the highly prejudicial Immigration Act of 1924), the eugenics movement advocated legal restrictions on interracial marriages. "Race mixing" was a perceived threat to the genetic purity of white America. True to form, Charles Davenport did all he could to convince the world that mixed marriages produced inferior offspring. In 1929, he published a book called *Race Crossing in Jamaica*, a study of racial mixing and its supposedly negative effects. Now cited as a classic example of scientific racism—the attempt to prove racial superiority through pseudoscientific methods—the book drew numerous unfounded conclusions.[19]

Like some minstrel show jokester, Davenport reported that black people excelled at music but trailed whites in complex mental activities. "Browns," as he called his subjects of mixed parentage, represented "an exceptionally large befuddled class," a group with many members who "seem not to be able to utilize their native endowment."[20] Davenport loftily asserted that "the Blacks seemed inferior to the Whites in ability to criticize absurd statements."[21] (Obviously those blacks hadn't read Davenport's book or they'd have found plenty to criticize.) In the end, eugenicists' objections to interracial marriage produced the desired effect: new antimiscegenation laws were passed and old ones rewritten according to eugenic precepts.

As repugnant as their record was in the United States, American eugenicists hit absolute bottom through their support of Nazi Germany's infamous "racial hygiene" program. By touting the superiority of Northern European bloodlines, American eugenicists fed Adolf Hitler's delusion that Germans are members of a master race. Without a doubt, it was madness that drove Hitler to slaughter millions of Jews, Slavs, gypsies, homosexuals, and the mentally impaired, but the pseudoscientific claptrap of negative eugenics gave Hitler's quest for racial purity a veneer of scientific legitimacy, especially in the beginning, when the Nazis sterilized over a quarter of a million German citizens—the first step on the road to the Holocaust.

German scientists repeatedly looked to US race policies for inspiration. In fact, the Nazis based their 1933 law authorizing eugenic sterilizations on a model statute issued by the Eugenics Record Office.[22] At the outset of Germany's massive sterilization effort, American eugenicists bubbled over with praise, citing the "success" of the program as proof that the smaller numbers of eugenic sterilizations in the United States were inadequate.

Adolf Hitler himself had followed the eugenics movement in this country for years. In 1916, American attorney, conservationist, and arch-bigot Madison Grant published *The Passing of the Great Race, or The Racial Basis of European History*, a landmark work of scientific racism that exalted people of Nordic ancestry. Hitler called the book his "Bible," and he wrote Grant to tell him so. Hitler was also aware of the 1927 Supreme Court ruling that gave legal sanction to eugenic sterilizations (a ruling, by the way, that's never been overturned). Nazi leaders would later cite the Court's decision in their own defense at the Nuremberg war crimes tribunals.[23]

Charles Davenport's complicity with German eugenicists stretched throughout his tenure at the Eugenics Record Office. His affinity for biological fascism was coldly laid out in *Heredity in Relation to Eugenics*—a shocking set of principles not uncommon in America at the time: "The commonwealth is greater than any individual in it," Davenport wrote. "Hence the rights of society over the life, the reproduction, the behavior and the traits of the individuals that compose it are . . . limitless, and society may take life, may sterilize, may segregate so as to prevent marriage, may restrict liberty in a hundred ways."[24] Hitler couldn't have said it any better.

Davenport's Cold Spring Harbor facility functioned as the hub of international eugenics activities, and its influential journal *Eugenical News* enthusiastically endorsed the German movement at every opportunity. As president of the International Federation of Eugenics Organizations, Davenport worked with leading German eugenicists such as Ernst Rüdin, director of the Kaiser Wilhelm Institute for Psychiatry and a major architect of Hitler's heinous racial policies. Following his retirement from the Eugenics Record Office in 1934, Davenport continued to support German eugenicists—even as the Nazis began the systematic annihilation of millions of "inferior" Europeans, the darkest blot on Davenport's career.[25]

By the time the United States entered World War II, in 1941, most American eugenicists had finally distanced themselves from their German counterparts, but a growing number of scientists and members of the public were already turning against eugenics. The Eugenics Record Office had closed its doors in December 1939 in the face of criticism about its aims and methods. By the end of the war, as the Nazi concentration camps were liberated, every American was made sickeningly aware of the horror that had been wrought in the name of racial purity—a fatal blow to the eugenics movement in this country. The ugly spectacle of negative eugenics was finally recognized for what it truly is: racial and class prejudice, pure and simple.

Some outrageous scientific claims were made during the heyday of the eugenics movement. One of the notions the American Eugenics Society tried to plant in the public mind was the idea that "what you really *are* was all settled when your parents were born"—as if genetics alone determines our essential character.[26] The truth, of course, is that we're each molded through a complex interplay of inherited traits and environmental influences—the long-debated nature versus nurture equation. We also have the power to help shape ourselves through our own conscious efforts. The great promise of life is that any person of any background has the potential to succeed or fail, to soar intellectually or to remain a prisoner of ignorance. As Iowa-born politician and future US vice president Henry Wallace said when he spoke out against eugenics in 1939: "Superior ability is not the exclusive possession of any one race or any one class. It may arise anywhere, provided men are given the right opportunities."[27]

Charles Davenport died before the end of World War II (he passed away in February 1944), so he didn't live to see the final dismantling of his dream, as the discriminatory laws he'd supported were rolled back starting in the 1950s. In all honesty, the eugenics leader was a pitiable man. Nervous and completely lacking in empathy, he was so sensitive to criticism that he retreated into a shell of moody silence when anyone attacked his work. His habit of dressing in white as a symbol of racial purity was a disturbing characteristic. But the saddest thing about Charles Davenport is that such an intelligent human being would turn his mind to such an ignoble purpose. If Davenport hadn't become embroiled in the lunacy of eugenics, he would be remembered for his legitimate academic accomplishments. As it is, any good he did has been interred with his bones.

Today, the old-fashioned expression of positive eugenics—matchmaking— still flourishes, although now it's moved online. Meanwhile, more complicated issues regarding genetics—genetic engineering, cloning, biotechnology, gene therapy—have replaced eugenics as topics of public interest.[28] And while we can celebrate the fact that the bigoted, immoral pseudoscience of eugenics has been consigned to history's junk heap, regrettably the white supremacist attitude that shaped much of Charles Davenport's career lives on in the beliefs of diehard social Darwinists—an outlook as persistent as a noxious weed, a kudzu of the mind.

CHAPTER 19

THE SILKEN VOICE OF TREACHERY

Mildred Gillars

With her lilting speech and perfect diction, she sounded like an upper-crust British matron discussing her rose garden over tea. From 1942 to 1945, her breezy tones were beamed around the world from war-torn Europe in a series of carefully scripted shortwave radio broadcasts.[1] Although the woman seemed perfectly reasonable at first blush, anyone paying attention to what she was saying would have thought she'd lost her mind.

Broadcasting from the capital of Nazi Germany, propagandist Mildred Gillars—Axis Sally to millions of GIs—was trying to persuade Americans to give up their fight against Adolf Hitler. "Throw down those little old guns and toddle off home," she cooed.[2] Her honeyed words couldn't disguise the absurdity of her message, with its vile references to President Franklin D. Roosevelt and his "kike boyfriends."[3]

Defending Hitler—a psychopath that most of the world loathed—was barmy enough, but the most astonishing thing about Gillars's pro-German broadcasts was that she happened to be, as she described herself, a "100 percent American girl."[4] Mildred Gillars was siding with her country's enemy, the gravest of wartime sins.

As an employee of the RRG—the German state radio system—Gillars attempted to foment discontent among American servicemen stationed in Europe and North Africa. She told them they could never defeat the Third Reich, that their leaders were inept, and that they were certain to be killed or maimed. She tried to make soldiers homesick by suggesting that their wives and girlfriends were cheating on them while they were off fighting. She sought to undermine support for the war back home by telling American women that their loved ones were risking their lives for nothing. Cruelest of all were her interviews with POWs, in which she tried to make it appear that captured Americans were being treated well by the Nazis.[5]

No matter which tack she took, Gillars had little chance of persuading anyone that opposing Hitler was wrong. Since 1938, the world had seen too many examples of unprovoked Nazi aggression. By 1942, the truth was emerging about Hitler's systematic slaughter of Jews and other so-called inferior peoples. By supporting Hitler's madness, Gillars damned herself in the eyes of her fellow Americans, even though her broadcasts had little effect on morale. Soldiers laughed at her clumsy propaganda efforts and only tuned in because she played popular jazz and swing music between her monologues. Nevertheless, she would pay the price for her disloyalty after the war, when she was brought back to America to stand trial for treason.

Tall and slender, with long silver hair, Gillars was a striking woman—not beautiful, but stylish, and with a self-assurance some saw as arrogance. A photograph taken in 1946 shows her sitting on a cot after her arrest in Berlin. She seems perfectly at ease, holding a cigarette in one hand, her legs crossed in a slightly provocative pose. She is gazing at the camera with a pensive look, as if she were sizing up her captors and not the other way around. Gillars came by that aplomb through her theatrical training and her years as a struggling actress.

Her whole life, in fact, was a struggle, a prolonged effort to find happiness and success. Most of the time, she failed at both.

Born in Portland, Maine, in November 1900, Gillars had a turbulent childhood. When she was six, her mother left a violent, alcoholic husband, taking her daughter with her. In 1908, Gillars's mother remarried, and a few years later the family moved to Ohio. Gillars's stepfather turned out to be a drunkard as well and may have abused his stepdaughter.[6] Following high school, Gillars enrolled at Ohio Wesleyan University to study drama. She took classes in literature, oratory, and music, winning praise for her acting in student theatrical productions.

An indifferent student, Gillars failed to complete her degree. In 1923, she moved to New York City to pursue her dream of becoming an actress. Although she talked about lofty artistic goals, the best she could manage were a few parts with small-time touring companies and vaudeville revues. Her career settled into a pattern of frustration and mediocrity. At times, she was destitute and close to starvation. She was even taken into police custody for a publicity stunt related to an obscure movie.[7]

Hoping to improve her prospects, Gillars traveled to Paris at the age of twenty-eight. After a short stay, she returned to New York, only to find life even harder in the wake of the disastrous stock market crash of 1929. In 1933, she headed back across the Atlantic. She ended up in Algiers, working for a dressmaker for several months. By the summer of 1934, she was in Berlin, where she found employment as a translator and English instructor at the Berlitz Language School. She also did some freelance translating for a German film studio and wrote movie and theater reviews. Later, she served as an actress's personal assistant, a job she lost in 1939 following Germany's invasion of Poland, the catalyst for World War II.

During the early part of the war, Gillars made a decision that would set the course for the rest of her life: she accepted a job as an announcer with the RRG. She would offer several rationales for that decision during her postwar trial, although the real reason was obvious: her long-stymied desire for professional recognition.

Gillars's career as a Nazi broadcaster began in 1940. At first, she had no propaganda role. As an announcer, she earned 180 marks a month, at a time when the top American employed by German radio was being paid 2,500 marks.[8] After just a few months, however, Gillars had her own program. Going by the name Midge, she played music interspersed with cultural commentary. She also began appearing in radio dramas. In this cradle of evil, Gillars was finding the artistic outlet she craved.

In the spring of 1941, the American embassy in Berlin began encouraging US citizens to return home. Most of them did, although Mildred Gillars wasn't among them. She said later that an official at the American consulate had confiscated her passport, leaving her stranded in Germany. Another explanation she offered was that she'd fallen in love with naturalized German citizen Paul Karlson, who told her he wouldn't marry her unless she stayed in Germany.[9] The marriage never took place, though, since Karlson was soon killed in action.

America had yet to enter the war when Gillars decided to remain in Berlin. At the time, England was the main target of German propaganda. While turncoats such as William Joyce—popularly known as Lord Haw Haw—aimed their fascist, anti-Semitic rants at Britain, other radio propagandists spent their time trying to persuade America to stay out of the war. That all changed on December 7, 1941, when Japan, Germany's Axis ally, attacked the US fleet at Pearl Harbor.

Gillars later claimed that when she heard about the attack on Pearl Harbor, she broke down, criticizing Germany's alliance with Japan in front of her fellow employees. "I lost all discretion," she said.[10] Knowing that such comments could send her to prison, she allegedly signed a German loyalty oath in order to continue working, although no such document was ever found. Following that dramatic episode, her career headed in a new and sinister direction.

In 1942, Gillars began a close association with Max Otto Koischwitz, a naturalized American citizen who'd taught German literature at New York City's Hunter College before the war. The temperamental, pro-Nazi Koischwitz had left his teaching position in 1939 and returned to Germany. When he and Gillars met in Berlin, Koischwitz was a member of the German Foreign Office and a rising figure in Nazi radio operations.

Despite having a wife and three daughters, Koischwitz began an affair with the socially isolated Gillars. It was a symbiotic relationship. Gillars won steady promotion at the RRG, and Koischwitz reeled in a female propagandist with a smooth, sexy voice. Gillars's salary rose to 3,000 marks a month, making her Germany's highest paid broadcaster.[11] She convinced herself that everything she did from then on was because of her love for Koischwitz. "Of course I loved him," she would testify at her trial. "I consider Professor Koischwitz to have been my destiny."[12]

That destiny led her to partner with Koischwitz in the production of "Home Sweet Home," "Midge at the Mike," and other propaganda programs. Koischwitz wrote the scripts, and Gillars read them convincingly. Although she later claimed that Koischwitz had wielded mystical powers over her, her on-air delivery certainly made it sound like she agreed with what he'd written. If not, she was a much better actress than any of her former employers in American theater had given her credit for.

"Do the British love us?" Gillars asked American listeners in May 1943. "Well, I should say not! But we are fighting for them. We are shedding our good young blood for this 'kike' war, for this British war."[13] The words may have sprung from her anti-Semitic lover's demented mind, but Gillars spoke them, as she did in a July 1943 broadcast: "The Jews . . . have got us into this war. . . . The Jews are sending our men over to Europe to fight so that their money bags will get filled."[14] And this in October 1943: "This is no war between Germany and America . . . but a war between the Jews and the Gentiles."[15] It was hate-filled tripe, but Gillars spewed it out on cue.

Koischwitz's maddest creation was *Vision of Invasion,* a radio play that aired on May 11, 1944, shortly before Allied forces stormed the beaches of Normandy. Meant to demoralize Allied troops, the play graphically depicted the bloody horrors that awaited the invaders at the hands of the vaunted Germany army. Playing the distraught mother of an American soldier, Gillars lamented her son's death, which she could miraculously detect from afar. "The dead bells of Europe's bombed cathedrals are tolling the death knell of America's youth," she moaned.[16] As theater, the play was dreck, but as propaganda, it may have had some slight effect, if any of the anxious, frightened young soldiers preparing for the invasion chanced to hear it.

In August 1944, Koischwitz succumbed to tuberculosis and heart failure, knocking the props from beneath Mildred Gillars's tenuous stardom. The Third Reich was entering its death throes as well. Gillars continued broadcasting right up to the eve of Germany's surrender in May 1945. Afterward, she went into hiding. When American forces rolled into Berlin, they put up wanted posters bearing Gillars's photograph. On March 15, 1946, agents arrested the propagandist at a boardinghouse where she was living under an assumed name. She'd been selling off her few remaining possessions to get by, leaving a trail that authorities were able to follow.

Gillars spent more than two years under detention in Germany before she was flown back to the United States. Finally, on January 24, 1949, the forty-eight-year-old Gillars walked into the US District Court in Washington, DC, to stand trial for treason, a charge that carried a potential death penalty. In keeping with Gillars's background, the seven-week proceeding was pure theater. *Time* magazine gave a snarky description of her grand entrance: "Her silver-gray hair hung in a shoulder-length bob as she entered the Washington courtroom. She wore her unfashionably short dress with an ingenue air. There was a peacock blue scarf at her throat, her long, horse face was dazzlingly tan, her mouth and nails crimson."[17]

The prosecution produced a number of ex-employees of the Nazi radio service who identified Gillars as Axis Sally. Gillars's immediate supervisor, Adelbert Houben, swore that "no foreigner was forced to work" for the RRG.[18] Several former American POWs who'd been interviewed by Gillars said that she'd told them she was working for the Red Cross in order to gain their trust.[19] The jury listened to hours of taped propaganda programs, including the dreadful radio play *Vision of Invasion*. (After listening to Gillars's histrionics in that broadcast, one writer said that she deserved to be convicted if only to keep her from ever again appearing on radio.)[20]

When it came time for Gillars to testify, she threw out a number of defenses, embellished with tears and studied gestures. She claimed that she'd never been disloyal . . . that she didn't believe any of the propaganda she'd broadcast . . . that she was merely trying to entertain American troops . . . that she'd only cooperated with her Nazi bosses out of fear. ("You could not just go around saying, 'I don't want to do this' and 'I don't want to do that.'")[21] She grasped at the notion that she couldn't be prosecuted for treason because she was a German subject. She had no proof of that, but a similar defense had worked for another wartime propagandist, Italian-American Rita Zucca. (Zucca had legally renounced her US citizenship before she began broadcasting to American troops in Italy. Confusingly, Zucca was also referred to as Axis Sally.)

Gillars's flimsiest excuse was that she'd done it all for love. With a heaving breast, she said that her deep bond with Max Otto Koischwitz had led her to reluctantly submit to his pressure to engage in propaganda directed at Americans.[22] As she and her attorney framed it, the manipulative professor had taken an innocent radio hostess and forced her into becoming a mouthpiece for the Nazis. How could a weak, love-besotted woman have resisted, Gillars seemed to be saying. All she needed to do to complete the scene was to hold the back of her hand to her brow. (Gillars actually swooned at one point in the trial.)

Her testimony was entertaining—if at times delusional—but the jury wasn't buying Gillars's dramatic pretensions. Neither was the press. *Time* said that "she slipped into the role of a foolish gentlewoman as though it were a loose kimono, got a handkerchief within easy dabbing distance of her eyes, and set out to explain that she had been true to the red, white & blue all the time."[23] *New Yorker* columnist Richard H. Rovere wrote that, while she was "determined not to destroy the illusion of herself as a woman of mystery, glamour, and intrigue," she seemed more like "a woman who has been fighting an uphill battle to make a living from a dress shop in Queens."[24]

On March 10, 1949, the jury found Gillars guilty on a single count of treason in connection with her participation in the *Vision of Invasion* broadcast. On March 25, she received a sentence of ten to thirty years in prison and a $10,000 fine.[25] In August 1950, after losing her appeals, Gillars was incarcerated in West Virginia's Federal Reformatory for Women (the same facility in which Japanese-American Iva Toguri—also known as Tokyo Rose—was held following her conviction for wartime propaganda in the Pacific).

Gillars busied herself in prison with gardening and crafts, and she also led the Protestant and Catholic choirs. Though she wasn't raised a Catholic, Gillars had spent a short time in a convent as a child. While in prison, she converted to Catholicism, and after she was paroled in July 1961, she returned to Ohio to teach music, drama, and languages at a convent school. She eventually completed enough college credits to earn her undergraduate degree in speech from Ohio Wesleyan University. She spent her final years in seclusion, passing away in Columbus in June 1988 at the age of eighty-seven. She was interred, possibly at her own request, in an unmarked grave.

By any measure, Mildred Gillars led a sorrowful life, although hers was a lowercase tragedy. As author Nathaniel Weyl observed shortly after Gillars's conviction, "She was not a very important figure in the scheme of things. She drifted into treason rather than deliberately seeking it. She was not the sort of woman who cares passionately for ideas or who is capable of spirit-destroying hatred. She was merely greedy and her greed increased as her time ran short."[26]

Throughout her trial, Gillars posed as a worldly sophisticate despite her history as a serial failure. In her own country, she'd been a nobody, but in Nazi Germany she was a rarity—a well-spoken, theatrically trained American female who was willing to set aside her loyalty to her country for money and fame. When the prosecutor pressed her on why she didn't go home in 1941, Gillars left no doubt as to her reason for staying in Nazi Germany. "Go home to what?" she asked incredulously. "To poverty again?"[27]

Even if Gillars truly was reluctant to engage in propaganda, as she claimed, she'd still agreed to work for a monstrous regime. In the end, her turn as a radio star was a mirage, a desperate attempt to rise above a lifetime of commonness. This lonely, frustrated woman bargained away her honor for a pittance and paid for her moment of acclaim with lasting infamy.

ROGUES

CHAPTER 20

WHO'S THAT RAPPING ON MY FLOOR?

Maggie and Kate Fox

Maggie Fox (left) and Kate Fox

Icy blasts swirled around the tiny frame farmhouse on a bleak March evening in 1848. The weathered story-and-a-half dwelling sat in a snow-covered field in the hamlet of Hydesville, New York, a farming community just east of Rochester, midway between the Finger Lakes and Lake Ontario. Inside the home, the Fox family—John, Margaret, and their two daughters, Maggie and Kate, huddled in the dark beneath their blankets and quilts, shivering from the cold and, perhaps, from the desolate night sounds as well. The howling wind seemed to carry the voices of the dead as it probed the cracks and crevices of the old wooden house. If spirits were to walk abroad to meddle in the affairs of man, it would be on a night like this.

The family shared the same bedroom in the tiny home, with John and Margaret sleeping in one bed and Maggie, age fourteen, and Kate, eleven, in another. The two girls snuggled together for warmth, an easy camaraderie for the sisters, who were seldom far apart at any time. The dark-haired Fox girls were a fetching pair: Maggie, plump and pixie cute, and Kate, slender, solemn, and ethereal, with huge, soulful eyes. Maggie and Kate were the only Fox children remaining at home, their four older siblings having grown up and moved on. Perhaps that was why the sisters felt the loneliness of their isolated dwelling so keenly. It would have been nice to have more friends around to dispel the monotony. As the girls whispered beneath their blankets, they may have been discussing an ingenious way to add a bit of fun to their lives.

The Fox family had moved into their rented home the previous December, while awaiting the completion of their new house a short distance away. The winter was especially harsh that year, trapping the family indoors for much of the day, the long nights sending them to bed at an early hour. Those nights seemed to stretch forever, black and silent except for the ghostly voices carried on the wind. Maybe there were spirits hovering about the house—who could say? That question seemed to find an answer in the middle of March, when a new night sound startled the Fox family into alertness. Shortly after the four had retired, they heard distinct rapping noises, as if someone were knocking on the floor, walls, and ceiling of their bedroom.[1] Mrs. Fox implored her husband to investigate, although a search of the house revealed no possible source of the noises.

The rapping sounds continued every night for the next two weeks. On the night of March 31—the eve of April Fool's Day—Mrs. Fox sent her husband to ask a neighbor family to come witness the strange noises. Mr. Fox returned home with their neighbor Mary Redfield. Mrs. Redfield listened to the rapping sounds, which appeared on que. Mrs. Fox and her daughters had recently begun interacting with the rapping noises, convinced that they came from the spirit of a murdered peddler who'd been buried in their cellar (itinerant peddlers were often the focus of ghost stories in that period). Mrs. Fox asked the "spirit" a series of questions, to which it responded with a rap for "yes" and silence for "no." Other questions required the spirit to answer with a series of raps: How old is Maggie? *Fourteen raps.* How old is Kate? *Eleven raps.*[2]

The incredulous Mrs. Redfield immediately fetched her husband, who invited several other neighbors. Before the night was over, a crowd of villagers filled the Fox home. The next night, several hundred people stopped by to witness the spectacle, which Mrs. Fox attributed to her daughters' affinity with the spirit world, since the rapping only occurred in their presence. Maggie and Kate were delighted to play their parts, asking their resident shade numerous questions on behalf of their neighbors: Who was your murderer? *A former resident of the house named John Bell.* Is there a heaven? *Yes.* Are the spirits of our dead friends and loved ones around us? *Yes.*[3]

Before long, newspapers carried stories about the strange goings-on in Hydesville, some of them supporting the claim that Maggie and Kate Fox possessed the ability to communicate with the spirits of the departed.[4] The accounts signaled the start of lifelong careers for the two girls. In short order, they would become the most famous mediums in the country. The curious events at Hydesville in 1848 marked the birth of the phenomenon known as Spiritualism, an international movement based on the belief that the human spirit passes through many states and that the dead can speak to the living. In the heyday of Spiritualism, from the 1840s to the 1920s, vast numbers of adherents—some say millions—hung on the words of an army of self-professed mediums, those "gifted" individuals who could supposedly call forth the spirits of eminent historical figures and deceased loved ones.[5]

The belief that humans can communicate with the spirit world was nothing new. It's been a staple of religion and the occult for centuries, although the seers and oracles of old tended to do their spiritual communicating in private, hidden away in caves and other mystical hotspots. The new Spiritualism democratized the contact process, bringing it to theaters and into people's homes so the public could hear what the dead were saying firsthand. Mushrooming into a combination of entertainment industry and unorganized religion, the movement rewarded its most celebrated practitioners handsomely through their lectures and private séances.

Spiritualism appealed to people from every level of society, although the bulk of its supporters were from the middle and upper classes, many of them active in abolitionist and women's suffrage efforts.[6] Author Sir Arthur Conan Doyle, the creator of Sherlock Holmes, was an enthusiastic believer, as was noted British scientist Alfred Russel Wallace and First Lady Mary Todd Lincoln, who held séances in the White House to communicate with her dead son.

In addition to launching the modern Spiritualism movement, Maggie and Kate Fox symbolized its contradictions. The two sisters wore the mantle of fame for four decades—uneasily at times—then fell into disrepute after publicly confessing that they'd been perpetuating an elaborate hoax all along. Although Maggie later recanted and once again took up her role as a medium, the sisters ended their days in poverty.[7] Despite the frequent unmasking of fraudulent mediums, people continued to believe in Spiritualism, and many still do, as witnessed by the scattering of Spiritualist churches in the United States, Britain, and other countries.

The Fox sisters lived in a place and time of great cultural upheaval. Their home in western New York State was located in the Burned-Over District, a region named for its frequent fire-and-brimstone religious revivals. It was there that Joseph Smith claimed to have discovered the golden tablets that sparked the creation of Mormonism. The area was home to utopian groups and communities of Shakers and radical Quakers, the latter being among the strongest supporters of abolitionism and women's suffrage. In 1848, the Burned-Over District was the site of the first women's rights convention in America, held in Seneca Falls.[8]

Internationally, the second half of the 1800s saw seismic shifts in scientific thinking. In 1859, Charles Darwin published *On the Origin of Species*, the foundation of evolutionary biology. At the same time, geologists were proclaiming that our planet is many millions of years old (scientists have now determined that the earth is at least 4.5 billion years old). The mechanisms of evolution and the discovery that the earth is far older than formerly thought contradicted long-held religious views, igniting controversies that have never gone away.

In the early 1860s, the Civil War—the bloodiest conflict Americans have ever fought—added to the nation's ferment. The country seemed to come untethered as more than six hundred thousand soldiers perished. Spiritualism offered the prospect of communing with those lost loved ones. And the testament of departed souls that heaven was real and that the dead were waiting there for us gave comfort to the religious, whose beliefs seemed to be under assault.

It was the ideal moment for the Fox girls and Spiritualism to catch the public's fancy. Maggie and Kate's older sister Leah was quick to seize the opportunity. Following up on the notoriety of the first spirit rappings in Hydesville, Leah, a single mother living in nearby Rochester, took her younger sisters in tow and guided their careers as professional mediums. Leah moved her sisters to Rochester, where they continued to demonstrate their abilities at a series of private "spirit circles," or séances. Maggie and Kate summoned the spirit of the murdered peddler and also that of a local woman who'd been poisoned by her husband. Besides making the usual rapping noises, the spirits moved a heavy parlor table, tugged at guests' clothing, and played the piano. Even a skeptical visiting minister was convinced the girls' abilities were genuine.[9]

In Rochester, the girls perfected their routine, working out a system of communication with the spirit world in which rapping sounds could be linked to the letters of the alphabet. Despite continuing skepticism and occasional hostility—many Christians thought that communicating with spirits was akin to witchcraft—the sisters prepared to make the leap to public presentations. On the evening of November 14, 1849, four hundred people paid a twenty-five-cent admission fee to attend their inaugural appearance. Although Kate was away visiting friends, Maggie and Leah took their place on the stage of Corinthian Hall, Rochester's largest theater. After a windy lecture by their presenter, Maggie called up the spirits to answer questions from the audience. The performance stirred up the locals so much that they formed a committee of town residents to determine if the sisters were pulling off a hoax.[10]

At the end of three days of tests and observations, during which Maggie and Leah were subjected to a tearful strip search by Rochester matrons, the committee announced that the sisters had not used fraudulent means to create the rapping sounds. The decision did little to settle the issue. Skeptics still thought the sisters were tricking the public, while believers saw the decision as confirmation that the sisters could actually talk with spirits. It was an argument without the slightest chance of resolution. The only thing it accomplished was to publicize Spiritualism beyond western New York. Following their profitable four-night run in Rochester, the Fox sisters were unleashed upon the world, for better or for worse.

In the ensuing years, the Fox sisters inspired, baffled, and entertained audiences in the United States and Britain through their private séances and public appearances. Although Maggie and Kate were the stars, Leah eventually proclaimed her own powers as a medium.[11] People attended their demonstrations for a variety of reasons. Some hoped to catch the girls out, to see if they could spot how they pulled off their parlor tricks. Others came with open minds, willing to be amazed. The sisters' most ardent—and vulnerable—patrons were people grieving for departed loved ones. The entire Spiritualism movement leaned heavily on the supposition that the living could find comfort from the spirits of the dead. In that regard, the Fox sisters no doubt brought solace to many—as long as they plunked down the price of admission.

The notoriety the Fox sisters received naturally inspired imitators. Hundreds of people suddenly discovered that, lo and behold, they too possessed the talents of a spiritual medium. The gorgeous young Cora L. V. Scott, for example, produced a surge of interest in spiritual matters among men. A full-blown industry sprang up, complete with conventions and summer camps. Private home séances became immensely popular with women's groups—like metaphysical Avon parties. Publishers cranked out books and periodicals to serve the market, some emphasizing the religious aspects of Spiritualism and others promoting social reform.[12]

As Spiritualism gained in popularity, adepts competed to come up with showier types of spiritual manifestations. In addition to rapping noises and levitating furniture, mediums conjured up spirit lights and ghostly writing (predecessors of the Ouija board came into widespread use in the 1860s). Hypnotists claimed they could put their subjects into contact with spirits while they were in a trance, and stage performers such as the famous Davenport brothers created the illusion of visitations while tied up inside a "spirit cabinet," a sort of telephone booth to the beyond.[13] Spiritualism clearly offered as much chicanery as solace.

The pressure for mediums to spice up their demonstrations was intense, since they had to compete for public attention with the period's glut of theatrical presentations—everything from boxers, comedians, and Shakespearean actors to mesmerists, magicians, and ventriloquists. P. T. Barnum's circus and museum offered elephants, acrobats, and oddities. Traveling minstrel shows featured raucous troupes of singers and dancers. And public displays of scientific discoveries and technological innovations introduced such marvels as electric lights, the telegraph, and newly discovered dinosaur fossils.[14] The pre-television world had no shortage of entertainment.

For Maggie and Kate Fox, achieving success at a young age came at a high cost. Just two years after leaving the backwater of Hydesville, the girls were appearing in New York City before luminaries such as editor Horace Greeley, poet William Cullen Bryant, and novelist James Fenimore Cooper. By experiencing widespread fame while they were still teenagers, Maggie and Kate were thrown into an adult world before they'd matured. They received minimal supervision from their parents, and the guidance they received from their sister Leah, who was more than twenty years their senior, consisted mostly of manipulation.[15]

Maggie and Kate began drinking at an early age, and both ended up as alcoholics. Gradually, the excitement of public adulation began to pall. Maggie had a tragic love affair and ceased making public appearances for several years. Kate married but lost her husband early, leaving her with two young sons to support. In May 1888, New York City police arrested Kate in a drunken stupor and charged her with child neglect.[16]

By that point, Maggie and Kate both faced financial difficulties. They'd also fallen out with the leaders of Spiritualism—especially their older sister, who'd written a book portraying herself as the movement's guiding light. Maggie and Kate decided that the best way to lash out at their antagonists was to confess that their entire careers had been built on deceit. On October 21, 1888, Maggie appeared before an audience of two thousand at the New York Academy of Music and announced that the spirits of the dead did not speak to anyone. "I am here tonight as one of the founders of Spiritualism to denounce it as an absolute falsehood from beginning to end, as the flimsiest of superstitions, the most wicked blasphemy known to the world."[17]

With Kate seated nearby, Maggie explained that she and her sister had produced the mysterious rapping sounds by cracking their knuckles and toe joints, a trick they'd played on their skittish mother as a joke. They'd created other noises in their Hydesville farmhouse by tying an apple to a string and bouncing it on the floor of their bedroom.[18] Originating as a private prank, the rapping phenomenon had spiraled beyond their control as first their mother and then more and more people came to believe that the noises emanated from the spirits of the dead. For Maggie and Kate, Spiritualism became a runaway train on which they were trapped.

Nonbelievers gloried in Maggie's confession, calling it the "death-blow to Spiritualism," but their pronouncement turned out to be wrong.[19] Spiritualism had become too widespread and entrenched. A year later, Maggie retracted her confession, claiming she'd been unduly influenced by opponents of the movement and was under extreme financial pressure. Her flip-flop didn't have much impact either. Within five years, Maggie, Kate, and Leah were all dead—Maggie and Kate as destitute pariahs.[20]

The phenomenon the Fox sisters initiated, however, steamed ahead into the twentieth century, gaining fresh momentum from the slaughter that took place during World War I, when a new generation of mourners embraced the possibility of contacting the spirits of their loved ones. After the war, Spiritualism endured the derision of one of its harshest critics, the master magician Houdini, who exposed many of the gimmicks used by fraudulent mediums. Houdini called the movement "the result of deluded brains or those which were too actively and intensely willing to believe."[21]

Spiritualism has survived such ridicule into the twenty-first century, with two American towns—Lily Dale, New York, and Cassadaga, Florida—still supporting communities of Spiritualists.[22] Only the residents of those towns could tell you whether they actually believe their own claims about communicating with the spirits of the dead or simply enjoy the thrill of dabbling in mystical affairs.

Today, movies and television shows abound with psychics and ghosts, and New Age bookstores are crammed with works about the spirit world—demonstrating that the market for the paranormal is at least one thing that never dies.

Spiritualism has been labeled a total fraud, a form of theatrical entertainment, and its own form of religion. As with other contested beliefs, we're all free to decide for ourselves how we choose to perceive it. For Maggie and Kate Fox, Spiritualism brought a level of fame that proved more burden than blessing. They spent much of their youth and their entire adult lives living up to the expectations of others. They did fulfill a need for certain people, although tricking grieving families in exchange for cash doesn't seem in the least spiritual. Like so many mediums since, these sad, conflicted sisters were lost in the gray borderland between comforters and con artists.

CHAPTER 21

THE WITCH OF WALL STREET

Hetty Green

Alone and unprotected, the gray-haired lady in the shabby black dress and frowsy bonnet marched down the derelict-filled streets of New York City's Bowery district on a winter night in 1903. The woman seemed undaunted by the hodgepodge of saloons, brothels, tattoo parlors, and flophouses she passed along the way. Although the stern look on her face was enough to discourage most would-be muggers—she looked as if she could literally bite a nail in two—

the bedraggled figure carried a revolver in her handbag just in case. To ward off the biting cold, she wore men's long underwear. For extra insulation, she'd stuffed crumpled newspapers under her dress, a garment that hadn't seen soap and water in ages. Climbing the steps of a ramshackle boardinghouse, she shut the door behind her and prepared to face another frigid night. To save a few precious pennies, the woman declined to pay for fuel to heat her room. Her evening meal would be the plain fare common to a poorhouse.

Most people observing the elderly woman's hardscrabble existence would have been filled with pity. Unless, that is, they happened to know that this apparently poverty-stricken creature was, in reality, the richest woman in America. For sixty-eight-year-old Hetty Green, the first woman to earn a fortune on Wall Street, living like a pauper was a choice.[1] In addition to being fabulously wealthy—rich enough to bail out the City of New York and the government of Texas during financial downturns—the woman was miserly beyond imagining. She was so niggardly that she once dressed her son in rags in an attempt to receive free medical treatment. Hetty Green's financial success, coupled with her personal eccentricities, earned her an unflattering nickname: "The Witch of Wall Street." There may be room for debate about whether she was a good witch or a bad witch, but this much is certain: she was the quintessential example of the remarkably stunted life that human beings can lead when their only joys are making and hoarding money.

Born Henrietta Howland Robinson in November 1834 (some sources say 1835), the future financial whiz was the daughter of accomplished businessman Edward Mott Robinson and Abby Howland Robinson, a member of a wealthy Quaker family in New Bedford, Massachusetts. (The Howlands' Quaker belief in simplicity meant simply making money, vast sums of it.) When Hetty was not quite two, her mother gave birth to a son, although the boy soon died. Always a sickly woman, Abby Robinson was no longer able to care for her rambunctious daughter. The family sent Hetty to live with her maternal grandfather, Gideon Howland, and her maiden aunt, Sylvia Howland. Although Hetty stayed with her parents from time to time as she grew older, her relatives would play an important role in raising her and overseeing her education, which included time at a Quaker boarding school in Sandwich and a Boston finishing school.

Hetty heard the call of Wall Street as a young girl, thanks to her father and grandfather. After his marriage, Edward Robinson had become a partner with Gideon Howland in the Howland family's prosperous whaling company, which claimed a fleet of thirty ships. Because both men suffered from weak eyesight, Hetty read the financial pages to them each day at the company's headquarters on the New Bedford waterfront. By the time she was a teenager, Hetty knew as much about bulls and bears as most girls her age knew about cooking and sewing.

Hetty's father and grandfather stoked her love of money in other ways. The hardheaded businessmen took the girl with them to inspect the firm's ships when they were in port. Hetty learned how to check a cargo to insure that the company wasn't being shortchanged by as much as a single barrel of whale oil, the costly substance that lit America's lamps and lubricated its machinery before the birth of the petroleum industry. (Hetty acquired one other bit of knowledge on the waterfront: an impressive vocabulary of salty language. In the future, more than one antagonist would be startled to hear the grandmotherly old lady cuss like a sailor.)[2]

Hetty also picked up habits of stinginess from her father that she would later magnify to the point of absurdity. Worth a considerable amount in his own right, Edward Robinson chose to eat at a free dockside lunch counter rather than spend any money, and he only smoked the very cheapest cigars. As a way to cut expenses, he encouraged his daughter to wear her dresses until they were threadbare, a practice she followed for the rest of her life.[3]

When her grandfather died in 1847, Hetty looked forward to a hefty bequest as Gideon Howland's only grandchild. She was crushed to learn that the old sea captain had left her nothing from his estate of several hundred thousand dollars. Nearly everything went to Gideon's two daughters—prompting Hetty to turn her avaricious eye on dear Aunt Sylvia. As Sylvia's only niece, Hetty expected to inherit her share of the family fortune at some point. Consequently, she began lecturing her aunt about excessive household expenditures.[4] Hetty wanted to make sure that her inheritance would be the maximum amount possible. If that meant serving guests skimpy portions of food, then so be it. Hetty had clearly inherited the greed gene, and she meant to make sure no one squandered what she thought she had coming to her.

In 1860, the lust for money created a family rift when Hetty's mother died without a will. Even though she was an heir to one of New Bedford's preeminent whaling companies—which her husband had taken over after Gideon Howland died—Abby Robinson possessed a surprisingly modest estate of around $130,000 at the time of her death.[5] Edward Robinson had assumed control of the rest of her money, arousing Sylvia Howland's suspicions that her sister had married a fortune hunter. Sylvia argued that her sister's assets should go to Hetty, but Edward claimed everything except for a house worth $8,000.[6] The quarrel may have been one reason Edward decided to leave New Bedford (another being the decline of the whaling industry). In 1861, he moved to New York City and went to work for a shipping firm.

Hetty also began living in New York around this time, although she returned often to New Bedford to keep tabs on Aunt Sylvia and her money, an estate that eventually ballooned to around $2 million.[7] As she reached her late twenties, Hetty must have lain awake at night counting that money in her head—her money, she reasoned, if only her aunt didn't waste it on fripperies such as food and clothing. When Hetty's father died in June 1865, followed by her aunt just eighteen days later, Hetty expected to inherit a total of seven to eight million dollars (an amount equivalent to around $100 million today). As it turned out, she received about $1 million from her father plus a trust fund in excess of $4 million. Sylvia Howland bequeathed her a lifetime income from a trust fund of $1 million; the other half of her aunt's estate went to a variety of charities and other beneficiaries.[8] Reasonable people would have been ecstatic. Hetty, of course, was not.

The grasping young woman spent more than two years trying to overturn her aunt's final will, which had replaced an earlier will that would have given everything to Hetty free and clear. At first Hetty argued that her aunt was mentally and physically incapacitated when the new will was written. After that line of attack bogged down, Hetty miraculously discovered a codicil to the earlier will stating that its terms could not be changed by any later will. However, handwriting experts who examined Sylvia Howland's signatures on the two copies of the codicil felt certain they were forgeries.[9] Hetty had always been a clever girl.

In July 1867, in the midst of the protracted legal proceedings, Hetty married wealthy commodity trader Edward Green, a business associate of Hetty's father. The two made an unlikely pair. Whereas Hetty dressed like a charwoman and pinched every penny hard enough to leave her fingerprints in the metal, Edward Green reveled in luxury—enjoying lavish meals, fine wine, and elegant clothing. About all they had in common was their love of money. It's said that Hetty made her fiancé sign a prenuptial agreement, even though he was worth $1 million at the time of their marriage. The pact reportedly obligated Edward to pay for all household expenses and made him responsible for his own debts.[10] (Edward did pay for their living expenses, but that second stipulation would later be put to the test.)

Before the trial over her aunt's estate was settled, Hetty and Edward moved from New York to London. Some said the relocation was spurred by Hetty's fear of being indicted for fraud over the dubious codicil she'd come up with.[11] In London, the Greens took up residence in the grand new Langham Hotel. There, in November 1868, Hetty received the news that she'd lost the suit over her aunt's will. The judgment was a bitter disappointment, but at least Hetty would now receive the income from the million-dollar trust fund her aunt had established on her behalf.

As soon as she could, Hetty put that money to work, along with the funds she'd inherited from her father. While Edward Green enjoyed his London clubs, Hetty began investing in securities issued by the United States government after the Civil War. When the value of federal greenbacks fell to half their face value, Hetty snapped them up, confident that the notes would rebound, which they did. She invested heavily in government bonds, again turning huge profits. One year, she earned $1.25 million, and on one especially bountiful day, she made a profit of $200,000.[12] It was the beginning of a nearly fifty-year run of successful investing, all based on a simple principle: "I buy when things are low and no one wants them," Hetty told the *New York Times*. "I keep them . . . until they go up and people are anxious to buy."[13]

Hetty was never a borrower or a speculator. "More money is made in the end by an over-supply of caution than by indiscriminate recklessness," she wrote.[14] She relied on the conservative approach of value investing—buying the securities of companies that are trading for less than their intrinsic worth. It's a philosophy that calls for shrewd judgment in gauging a company's underlying value, which Hetty Green displayed to an uncanny degree. She excelled at sweeping up bargains during market crashes, when most investors were busy jumping out windows. The most unusual aspect of her success was that she achieved it essentially on her own: she had no partners, shunned financial advisors, hated the legal establishment, and was suspicious of most businessmen she dealt with.[15] As far as Hetty was concerned, it was herself against the world.

Around the end of 1873, the family—which now included two children, Ned and Sylvia—moved back to the United States, settling in Edward Green's hometown of Bellows Falls, Vermont. By then, Hetty had increased her net worth many times over. Back in the United States, she began to focus on railroad and real estate investments. No matter where Hetty put her money, she usually reaped huge profits. Her free-spending spouse, however, wasn't nearly as fortunate. Edward Green wasn't averse to leaping into a risky speculative deal. By 1885, he'd depleted his fortune and run up $700,000 in debt at the Wall Street financial firm of John J. Cisco and Son. Hetty kept her own money at Cisco and Son in a separate account. When the bank managers asked her to pay them what her husband owed, she refused, telling the firm that she wanted to withdraw all of her deposits—more than $25 million in cash and securities.[16]

Cisco's managers wouldn't allow Hetty to withdraw her assets until she'd settled her husband's debts. She finally relented and paid up. Afterward, she personally removed every greenback, mortgage, and stock and bond certificate she owned from the Cisco vaults. Loading her stash into a hansom cab, she drove over to the Chemical National Bank and deposited it all. The Cisco bank, already in financial difficulty, immediately went under. And that wasn't the only carnage. Hetty and Edward Green had recently been living apart, their marriage strained by disputes over money. After the Cisco bank incident, Hetty had no further use for her husband. "I wish I did not have him," she declared. "He is a burden to me."[17] Though they never divorced, they went their separate ways. (Hetty did help nurse Edward during his final illness; he died in 1902.)

After she shucked off Edward, Hetty continued to grow her fortune. During the financial panics of 1893 and 1907, she had sufficient cash reserves to provide high-interest loans to individuals, companies, and even governments. She acquired railroads in Texas and mines in California and other states. She accumulated a vast real estate empire worth tens of millions, with extensive holdings in New York, Boston, Chicago, and St. Louis. In Chicago alone, she collected more than $40,000 a month in income.[18] (Hetty dispatched her son Ned, who'd graduated from Fordham University in 1888, to act as her Chicago agent, paying him a salary of $3 a day. He could have earned more shining shoes.)

But even as Hetty increased her wealth, her personal behavior grew ever more eccentric. She began moving from one mean boardinghouse or apartment to another, partly to avoid the assassins she imagined were after her—which is why she went about armed with a revolver—but also to avoid establishing a permanent residence and being forced to pay taxes.[19] In her efforts to dodge the taxman, she hopscotched around the New York area like a fugitive on the run, bouncing from lower Manhattan to Brooklyn to Hoboken, New Jersey. Usually renting under assumed names, Hetty was completely at home in the rundown neighborhoods she inhabited. She always wore the same tatty black dress and bonnet (legend says that to save money she only had the bottom edges of her long dress and petticoats laundered). She quibbled over pennies at local shops and cafés, and she avoided the luxury of taking cabs if she could walk or ride a streetcar.

Hetty was just as cheap in conducting her business affairs. She never paid for office space, preferring to squat for free at the Chemical National Bank, whose managers were happy to oblige someone with her astronomical deposits.[20] Whenever she left town for any length of time, Hetty moved all her personal belongings to the bank so she wouldn't have to pay rent on an empty lodging. At one point, she even stashed a wagon and a buggy there. The bank's managers must have developed the skills of Broadway actors in order to hide their shock over their prize customer's persistent nuttiness.

Perhaps the most bizarre thing Hetty Green ever did was to attempt to cage free medical care for her son. (Hetty also made repeated attempts to obtain free treatment for herself.)[21] When he was a teenager, Ned hurt his knee sledding. At first, Hetty thought she could treat the injury, but when the problem lingered, she disguised Ned in ragged clothing and took him to a charity ward. To her chagrin, someone recognized her. The doctor insisted that she pay for Ned's treatment, which naturally infuriated her. She left and never returned. Although she took Ned to other doctors, his leg didn't heal properly. Years later, it had to be amputated. (Edward Green ended up paying for the operation.) For the rest of his life, Ned wore a prosthesis.

Decade after decade, the black-clad figure of Hetty Green haunted the streets of New York's financial district like a fierce old crow. Despite her incredible miserliness, she seems to have found her own sort of happiness. She had one or two close friends, and, surprisingly, a touch of wit (she sometimes rented rooms using her dog's name, C. Dewey). She obviously took delight in besting her rivals and amassing riches. She was just unable to find pleasure in spending money or sharing it with others. Aside from being female, what set her apart from her contemporary financial titans—the Rockefellers, Carnegies, Vanderbilts, and Morgans—was the fact that she never leavened her insatiable desire for money with any notable acts of philanthropy.[22] All her life, she hoarded her fortune like a storybook dragon sitting alone in its cave atop a pile of gold.

Hetty Green's historical stature is revealed by the lack of public memorials in her honor. Only one such monument exists, a building on the campus of Wellesley College, and that was paid for by Hetty's children. Were it not for her vast wealth and legendary stinginess, Hetty Green might be completely forgotten. At times, it almost seemed as if she suffered from savant syndrome, excelling at the single skill of making money but deficient in other realms of mental and emotional development. English writer Ladbroke Black called her "an artist among misers."[23] When she died in July 1916 at the age of eighty-one—from a series of strokes brought on by an argument with a friend's cook over some petty household expenses—she was worth at least $100 million, an amount equivalent to nearly $2 billion today. She's said to have been the world's richest woman at the time.[24]

Writers have praised Hetty Green for her financial acumen and her pioneering role on Wall Street. There's no denying her ability to make money, but that alone has never represented much of a case for a life well spent. And then there's the matter of her tax avoidance/evasion. Although Hetty Green came by her fortune without the outrageous manipulation of financial markets common to the robber barons of her day, that didn't stop her from becoming a member of that tiny subspecies of American: the super-rich tax dodger.

In her gyrations to elude tax collectors, Hetty Green skirted the law and likely broke it.[25] Her rolling stone lifestyle provided a boon to her heirs: New York and New Jersey both failed in their separate attempts to levy around $5 million in state inheritance taxes; Vermont, meanwhile, collected a paltry $58,000. New Jersey did collect $60,000 in transfer taxes on assets Hetty owned within the state, and another $1.5 million in transfer taxes were levied on her New York assets.[26] All told, the taxes on the mammoth estate were miniscule. A *New York Times* editorial fumed that Hetty had never paid her yearly taxes in any of the states in which she'd lived. The editorial implied that she was a free-loader, a deadbeat citizen—a charge Congressman William Jennings Bryan had leveled in his successful argument for the institution of a federal income tax in 1894.[27] (Hetty Green was in good company: most of the plutocrats of her day were adept at tangoing past the taxman—seemingly a genetically transmitted trait among the rich.)

Virtually all of Hetty Green's immense fortune was divided between her son and daughter. Ned, who took after his father, spent freely on every indul-gence that struck his fancy, although he did engage in some philanthropy and public-spirited projects as well. Still, he wasn't quite able to blow through the entire pile of loot his mother left him. When Ned died in 1936, his widowed, reclusive sister inherited more than $10 million from her brother's estate. When Sylvia passed away in 1951, her estate was worth roughly $100 million, which she lavished on a long list of charities, friends, former employees, and distant relatives (both she and Ned were childless).[28]

And so at last, Hetty Green's relentlessly accumulated, fiercely guarded fortune finally trickled out into the world to do some good. It just took someone other than the dour old Witch of Wall Street to make that happen.

There is one final memento of Hetty Green's life. Her lengthy record of tax avoidance helped spur the passage of a federal estate tax, enacted two months after her death.

CHAPTER 22

KING OF THE CANNIBAL ISLANDS

David O'Keefe

David Dean O'Keefe was not a man to run afoul of. The hulking Irishman had a temper as fiery as his shock of red hair and flowing mustache. After making his way to America in 1848 at the age of twenty-four, O'Keefe had migrated to Georgia, where he worked for a short time on a railroad gang, a backbreaking job he abandoned to become an apprentice seaman aboard a windjammer. In a few years, he earned his master's license and began skippering coastal steamers out of Savannah. Some said he was a blockade runner for the South during the Civil War, a story he tried to quash by claiming he wasn't old enough then to have been a captain, although that was clearly a lie, since now, in February 1866—not yet a year after the end of the war—he was the master of the schooner *Anna Sims.*[1]

On this mild winter's day, Captain O'Keefe was livid. One of his crewmen had failed to follow his orders. O'Keefe's face flushed crimson as he upbraided the sailor. Suddenly O'Keefe struck the man. The sailor retaliated, pummeling O'Keefe and knocking him to the deck. Such insubordination was more than O'Keefe could tolerate. He jumped up and ran to his cabin, reappearing moments later with a pistol. O'Keefe leveled the weapon and pulled the trigger. Nothing happened—a misfire. O'Keefe tried once more, but again the pistol misfired. With a roar, the seaman charged O'Keefe, just as—on the third try— the pistol went off. The bullet struck the sailor in the forehead, killing him instantly. When the police arrived, they escorted O'Keefe to the county jail. He spent the next eight months in custody, until he was tried and acquitted. The jury ruled that the killing had been in self-defense.[2]

O'Keefe was freed, but his reputation around Savannah suffered greatly, and his finances took a hit as well. Those setbacks didn't prevent him from marrying Catherine Masters in April 1869. The new Mrs. O'Keefe was almost two decades younger than her husband, who would have been around forty-five by then. Another O'Keefe quickly made an appearance, a baby girl named Louisa—little Lulu. David O'Keefe was now a family man, although his fortunes were still spiraling downward.

In 1871, O'Keefe tried to change his luck by signing on as first mate aboard the merchant ship *Belvidere.* The vessel took him to New York, Liverpool, and, finally, Manila. From there O'Keefe sailed for China on another ship. Fetching up in Hong Kong in September 1871, he sent word to his wife that he would be home before long. As it turned out, O'Keefe never returned to Savannah. He spent the next thirty years among the islands of the western Pacific—building a reputation as a wily trader and accumulating a horde of money, property, wives, and children. Along the way, someone decided he'd become, more or less, a king (O'Keefe may have helped plant this notion with his own fanciful yarns).[3] Whatever his status may have been, O'Keefe left an imprint on the islands that's still in evidence.

O'Keefe launched his adventures in paradise by going to work for a Hong Kong trading company. By the summer of 1872, he'd become the captain of a Chinese junk bound for the Caroline Islands in Micronesia. In a valedictory nod to his old life, he named the junk after his wife. Around the end of the year, O'Keefe reached Yap, an island complex twelve hundred miles southeast of Manila (some versions of the O'Keefe legend say he washed ashore there after a shipwreck).[4] Although Yap was a trading center for bêche-de-mer (the edible sea cucumber) and copra (dried coconut meat, used to produce cooking oil and animal feed), the eight thousand or so residents of the islands remained aloof from the foreign merchants.

Organized socially into several castes, the Yapese were ruled by village chiefs. They lived in huts, wore loincloths and grass skirts, and spent their time fishing and raising taro—just as they had for centuries. Their most striking trait was the use of large stone discs, called *rai,* for money. The discs, measuring up to twelve feet in diameter, took several men to carry. (The islanders still revere the ancient stones and continue to attach value to them. However, they don't cart this cumbersome cash about like pocket change. Since everyone knows who owns which stones, exchanges can take place without the money ever moving.)[5]

After working for various trading companies for a few years, O'Keefe started his own business. He quickly established himself as a wheeler-dealer. Focusing on the copra trade, he set up a network of trading stations on Yap and other islands, and he assembled a fleet of sailing ships to haul his cargoes to markets in the Philippines, Hong Kong, and Singapore. His trade on Yap flourished thanks to his understanding of the local culture. Earlier traders had never done well at motivating the islanders to expand their production of copra, since the Yapese had little interest in the manufactured goods they were offered in exchange. The islanders were content with their traditional way of life. O'Keefe, however, saw one area he could take advantage of—helping the Yapese obtain the stone they used to make their money, which they could only find on distant islands, chiefly Palau, over two hundred fifty miles to the southwest.

In exchange for copra, O'Keefe offered to provide metal tools for use in quarrying the heavy stones, and he also offered to haul the stones back to Yap aboard his ships. This seemed like a good idea to the Yapese. Previously, they'd had to make long ocean journeys in open canoes and transport the stones aboard rafts—a difficult and dangerous undertaking. Now the stones would be delivered right to their shores. By keeping the stones in his possession until the Yapese handed over the specified amount of copra, O'Keefe energized the laid-back islanders.[6]

One of O'Keefe's most productive ventures involved St. David's Island (now known as Mapia), a flyspeck atoll near the western fringe of the Carolines. O'Keefe leased the island for $50 a year and established a thriving, highly profitable coconut plantation there, bringing in laborers from Yap and other islands for six-month periods.

St. David's held natural resources beyond its bountiful copra crop. When he first visited the island, O'Keefe met an Englishman living there with his Micronesian wife and daughter. O'Keefe married the daughter, Charlotte, but instead of taking her back to Yap, he sequestered her on St. David's. O'Keefe's eye later fell on Charlotte's aunt, an island beauty named Dolibu. Apparently subscribing to the girl-in-every-port tradition of seafaring (some sources say O'Keefe had numerous paramours sprinkled around the islands), he whisked Dolibu back to Yap and married her as well. Though he only visited poor Charlotte a few times a year, O'Keefe gave her something to remember him by—three children. He also fathered five children with Dolibu. Along with his wife Catherine and daughter Lulu back in Savannah, O'Keefe had assembled a dynastic menagerie worthy of an Oriental potentate. Legal and moral issues aside, he did support all three families financially, which must have earned him a few crumbs of karma.[7]

O'Keefe's reputation grew as he tightened his control over the copra trade throughout the western Carolines. A number of trading companies—representing German, Spanish, and other interests—continued to do business in the islands, with Yap as their center of operations, but few of their managers were as capable as O'Keefe. The big Irishman's empathy with the Yapese and exclusive arrangement to provide them with stone for their money gave him a significant advantage—a kingly domination some said.

Besides his financial success and multiple wives, O'Keefe displayed other trappings of royalty. He flew his own flag, emblazoned with the initials "OK," over a private isle called Tarang, a tree-covered sliver of land in the channel between Yap's four main islands. There he built an impressive two-story brick home, workers' quarters, and shipping facilities. Tarang swarmed with men loading O'Keefe's ships or imbibing the rations of rum included in their pay. O'Keefe filled his house with fine furniture, a piano, and a library brimming with books, and he gave Dolibu a staff of servants to help with the cooking and cleaning. The genial master of Tarang entertained guests with elaborate dinners, music, and card games. It was a sweet life for someone who'd had to slink out of Savannah a beaten man just a few years before.[8]

Not surprisingly, O'Keefe's accomplishments didn't thrill his competitors. His chief nemesis was a fellow American with the toothsome name of Crayton Philo Holcomb. In 1883, Holcomb and other rival traders leveled several legal charges against O'Keefe. They said he'd cheated Holcomb out of twenty-five tons of copra, defrauded a former employee, and tortured islanders who worked for him. British authorities cleared O'Keefe of all the charges, accusing his rivals of acting out of jealousy and asserting that O'Keefe had always done well by the locals. But, just as in Savannah, while O'Keefe may have been acquitted of wrongdoing, his reputation still suffered. "He is at war with all the other whites on the Island," claimed one observer, "all of whom thoroughly detest him."[9]

O'Keefe didn't allow his antagonists to get him down. Even with ongoing trade wars, he continued to prosper. He also weathered the unstable political situation in the Caroline Islands, which was like a party with two petulant dandies—in this case, Germany and Spain—squabbling over who got to dance with the prettiest girl. Although Germany had set up the first permanent trading station on Yap, in 1869, Spain announced its sovereignty over the island five years later. Germany responded by dispatching a warship to guard its turf. In 1885, Spain attempted to cement its claim by building a governor's mansion on Yap, duly hauling in a collection of bureaucrats, priests, convict laborers, and water buffalo. Germany hurriedly hoisted its own flag over the island. It was a big kerfuffle for such a small place, but this was when Europe's colonizing powers grew apoplectic over every contested speck of land. The tug-of-war was settled in 1886 by Pope Leo XIII, who awarded Yap and the rest of the Caroline Islands to Spain but granted trading rights to Germany and other countries.[10] (Who knew the pope could do that sort of thing?)

Despite a few tussles with the Spanish colonial administration, O'Keefe made money up through the early 1890s. Then in 1895, a series of disasters occurred. First, the copra crop was devastated when leaf lice infested Yap's coconut palms. Next came two typhoons, one in 1895 and a second in 1899 (the year that Spain ended up selling Yap and its other Micronesian possessions to Germany following the Spanish-American War). In 1900, the islands suffered a severe drought. Those calamities forced O'Keefe to abandon the copra trade and put his ships to work hauling general cargo.

Around this same time, O'Keefe got religion. (When Spain took possession of the Carolines, one of the first things it did was to build several Catholic churches.) Perhaps the unrepentant bigamist and one-time taker of human life, now in his sixties, felt it was time to start hedging his bets. With Dolibu and the kids in tow, he began attending mass regularly. O'Keefe supported the church financially and sent two of his sons to the mission school on Yap. He also sent his two oldest daughters (one by Dolibu and one by lonely Charlotte back on St. David's Island) to a convent school in Hong Kong.[11]

In 1901, while returning from a trip to Hong Kong, O'Keefe's luck ran out altogether. On May 7, he and two of his sons sailed from Hong Kong harbor bound for Yap. They never made it home. O'Keefe's schooner, the *Santa Cruz,* is believed to have gone down in a storm. None of the passengers or crew were ever found. The estate O'Keefe left behind was a tangled mess. Estimates of its value ran as high as $10 million, although the actual amount was probably far less. O'Keefe's will provided for his families in the islands and his daughter Lulu in Savannah. However, he left nothing to his first wife, Catherine, who sent a lawyer to Yap to recover what she thought was hers. O'Keefe's heirs fought over the estate for years.[12]

Dolibu lived out her life on Tarang, and other family members stayed on the island until the Japanese pushed them out during World War II. In 1944, American planes bombed a Japanese munitions dump on Tarang. After the war, the Yapese removed the bricks from the shattered O'Keefe mansion, although a few ruins still stand to remind visitors of the mighty Captain O'Keefe.

It's easy to understand how people who witnessed O'Keefe's influence in the islands and his lavish lifestyle might have come to regard him as a virtual king. Historian Francis X. Hezel, who has written extensively about the Caroline and Marshall Islands and dispelled several O'Keefe myths, cites comments made by a Norwegian man who worked for the wealthy American. Writing to his parents, the man claimed that his boss owned a sizable chunk of Micronesian real estate and enjoyed "unlimited favour" as the "King of the Cannibal Islands."[13] After O'Keefe's death, American newspapers embellished this image. The *New York Daily Tribune* ran a story in 1903 headlined "An Irishman Who Became King." The story pushed the fantasy that O'Keefe reigned over thousands of islanders, who looked upon him as a white god à la Joseph Conrad's title character in *Lord Jim,* a novel that came out just before O'Keefe's death (although the story wasn't based on O'Keefe).[14]

What fixed the image of O'Keefe as an island ruler was the 1950 book *His Majesty O'Keefe,* a melodramatic biography by Lawrence Klingman and Gerald Green. Klingman and Green liberally mixed facts and conjecture, writing that O'Keefe held royal sway over the islands of Yap, Mapia, and Sonsorol.[15] Their book, in turn, inspired a massively hokey 1954 movie with the same title, starring Burt Lancaster. Grinning manically, the tousled, bare-chested Lancaster battles fractious islanders, lecherous slavers, and dastardly, monocled Germans as he goes about setting up his copra business and winning the affection of demure tropical hottie "Dalabo" (a character loosely based on O'Keefe's real-life spouse Dolibu). In the end, the islanders recognize O'Keefe's "wisdom" and anoint him king. The film highlights O'Keefe's role in helping the Yapese quarry and transport the large stones they used for money, and it touches on the actual outcome of that arrangement: the stones that O'Keefe provided eventually lost value in the eyes of the Yapese. They came to be referred to as "O'Keefe's Money," a kind of ersatz coinage, in that they lacked the heritage of sacrifice and toil associated with the older stones.[16]

Regardless of whether the real David O'Keefe held the power of a king or was just a highly influential trader, there's no doubt that he played a significant role in the history of Yap and the western Caroline Islands. What he was, it appears, was a benevolent rogue—a major league bigamist, ruthless competitor, spinner of self-promoting yarns, and, to his credit, a fair and generous boss. In all the legal proceedings he faced, no islander ever spoke out against him, most likely because he treated his employees with respect (he originally refused to sell the islanders liquor, only giving in when that stance put him at a competitive disadvantage with other traders).[17]

On the Pacific islands colonized by Western powers, new ways were often cavalierly imposed on the locals (chiefly the three "B's"—booze, Bibles, and breeches), but David O'Keefe represented a different mentality. He attempted to adapt to the Yapese culture. Admittedly, he exploited the culture to advance his business interests, but he wasn't some rapacious foreigner who swooped in and tricked the locals into giving away their treasures for a box of trinkets. Nevertheless, by providing iron tools and ships to mine and transport the Yapese stone currency, he unintentionally altered the islanders' way of life.

The stone rai produced during O'Keefe's heyday can still be seen around the island, standing here and there in the thick vegetation and weathering slowly in the tropical sun and rain. The pioneering trader's memory is also kept alive at two establishments located along Yap's harbor—O'Keefe's Kanteen, a historic store, and O'Keefe's Waterfront Inn, a colonial-style lodge.[18] Visitors who make their way to Yap, a celebrated diving mecca, can stop by the bar in O'Keefe's Inn and hoist a rum punch in memory of the American who, for thirty years, loomed over these islands like a colossus—one of the western Pacific's most memorable characters of the late nineteenth century.

CHAPTER 23

MASTER SALESMAN OF A DUBIOUS LEGEND

Herbert Bridgman

Herbert Bridgman's summer ocean voyage was no relaxing pleasure cruise. In 1894, the avuncular fifty-year-old Brooklyn newspaperman traded his bustling hometown for the bleak waters off western Greenland, a realm of ice and eerie silence. As Bridgman stood on the deck of the steamer *Falcon*, the only comforting sounds he heard were the vessel's constant creaks, groans, and hisses. Against the immensity of their surroundings, the *Falcon* was nothing more than a toy boat chugging bravely through an intimidating expanse of blue—a hostile seaway congested with icebergs as big as office buildings, Egyptian pyramids, glistening mountain peaks. In this otherworldly zone, it would come as no great shock to see a phantom long ship emerge from the mists with a crew of hollow-eyed Norsemen sitting at the oars. Bridgman watched a passing pod of bowhead whales with relief—life existed here after all.

As the *Falcon* eased its way up Davis Straight and across Baffin Bay—"Iceberg Alley" to generations of edgy seafarers—Bridgman and the others aboard the little steamship stayed on the alert. Only in these warmer months, when the normally frozen sea briefly opened up, could ships reach far northwestern Greenland. It was there that explorer Robert E. Peary had established a base camp at the southern end of Smith Sound—the channel separating Greenland and Canada's Ellesmere Island. Bridgman and Peary had become friends in 1892, just after the explorer's first major expedition to the Arctic, during which he attempted to prove that Greenland is an island. An ardent admirer of Peary, Bridgman began raising funds for the dashing naval officer's polar adventures. In appreciation, Peary would name a cape on the northern tip of Greenland after his friend.[1] Peary had returned to the Arctic in 1893, and now Bridgman was heading northward to resupply the explorer's party.

Bridgman's rendezvous with Peary took place as planned. The relief expedition delivered vital provisions to the beleaguered group, which included Peary's wife, Josephine, along with a tiny addition—the couple's infant daughter, Marie, who'd been born in the Arctic the previous September. Bridgman brought back Mrs. Peary and Marie when the *Falcon* returned home, while Peary and two companions remained in Greenland to investigate the Cape York meteorites, the mysterious source of iron from which the Inuit had been fashioning tools for centuries. (Three years after Peary found the massive chunks of iron, they were transported to the American Museum of Natural History, where they're still on display.)[2]

Bridgman's 1894 voyage turned out to be the first of three such trips he would mount on Peary's behalf over a period of seven years. Afterward, the journalist assisted his friend in an even more important way. In September 1909, Bridgman received a telegram from Labrador announcing Peary's claim that he had reached the North Pole in April of that year. Bridgman, who'd helped organize the expedition, became one of Peary's leading cheerleaders, championing him in newspaper and magazine articles over rival explorer Dr. Frederick A. Cook, who maintained that he'd reached the pole a year before Peary.

Bridgman's efforts were instrumental in convincing the public that Peary was the North Pole's true discoverer, an accomplishment many experts now question. In promoting Peary and casting Cook as a pretender, Bridgman went off the deep end as a journalist, becoming one of the twentieth century's early masters of media manipulation. His fanatical support for Peary's assertions helped lay the groundwork for a debate that still rages today.[3]

Bridgman had forged a respected career as a newsman before he took to shouting Peary's praises. Born in 1844 in Amherst, Massachusetts, he earned bachelor's and master's degrees from Amherst College, apprenticing on local newspapers while still a student. In 1866, he landed his first professional newspaper job, on the *Springfield Republican,* where he rose to be city editor. After stints with the Associated Press, *Frank Leslie's Illustrated Newspaper,* and the *New York Tribune,* Bridgman began the most enduring journalistic association of his life. In 1887, he became the business manager and part owner of the *Brooklyn Standard Union.* He would remain with that newspaper for the next thirty-seven years, a period in which he helped to establish the American Newspaper Publishers Association, serving as the group's president from 1914 to 1916. He also found time to head the geography department at the Brooklyn Institute of Arts and Sciences and to serve as a regent of the State University of New York.

Bridgman's senior management role on the *Brooklyn Standard Union* gave him the freedom to pursue his personal interests. A prominent member of the Explorers Club and other geographical organizations, he traveled the world and wrote extensively about his adventures. He rambled through the Balkans, sailed to Hawaii, climbed Mesa Encantada in New Mexico, and traced the source of the Nile in Africa, an experience that resulted in a book, *The Sudan: Africa from Sea to Center.* Throughout his nearly sixty-year journalism career, Bridgman never lost his boyish enthusiasm for visiting new places, which is undoubtedly why his connection with Robert Peary proved so strong. In 1898, Bridgman helped establish the Peary Arctic Club, a group dedicated to funding the explorer's quest to become the first man to reach the North Pole.[4] The following year, Bridgman again came to his friend's assistance, leading a second relief expedition to the Arctic.

Two years later, Bridgman led his third and final relief expedition in support of Peary. During that 1901 voyage, Bridgman engaged Brooklyn physician Frederick Cook as the expedition's surgeon. Cook had served on Peary's first expedition to northern Greenland in 1891 and afterward had earned a reputation as an explorer in his own right, twice performing acts of valor on polar voyages. In 1894, he crossed ninety miles of the Arctic Ocean in a small boat to find help after the ship he was serving on, the *Miranda,* hit an iceberg. Four years later, while taking part in a Belgian voyage to Antarctica, he led the successful effort to save the expedition's ship after it became trapped in the ice, earning him a knighthood from the king of Belgium. Shipmate Roald Amundsen—who later became the first man to reach the South Pole—described Cook as "the most honest and most dependable man I have ever known," a person of "unfailing hope and unfaltering courage."[5] Cook commanded sufficient respect to be elected president of the Explorers Club in 1906. All of which may have made it inevitable that Cook and the egocentric Robert Peary would never get along.

Peary was said to have regarded Cook as a potential rival as far back as their 1891 trip together.[6] Eventually their differences came to a head. Shortly after the 1901 relief expedition led by Bridgman, Cook refused to serve under Peary ever again. He occupied himself with two expeditions to Alaska's Mount McKinley (Denali), before the Arctic called once more. In 1907, Cook launched a two-year expedition to the North Pole, which he claimed to have reached on April 21, 1908. It took him over a year to make it back from the far north and publicize his exploit. In one of the great ironies of modern exploration, Cook wired the news that he had attained the pole just *five days* before Peary telegraphed his own similar announcement to Bridgman. Both explorers were feted for their achievements. Cook was honored by the Royal Geographical Society of Denmark, while Peary received recognition from America's National Geographic Society.

Naturally, the issue of who had really been first to reach the North Pole became a whopping controversy. Peary had the weight of the National Geographic Society on his side, although the organization was clearly biased, since it was one of the sponsors of the adventurer's final expedition. After a superficial look at the records of the trip, the society certified Peary's claim, a move that helped persuade Congress to issue a gold medal in the explorer's honor.[7] Cook, however, had plenty of supporters himself, some of whom insisted on a congressional investigation into the matter. No such hearings ever took place. That left the issue in the court of public opinion.

Peary and his allies responded with a relentless smear campaign against Cook. To cast doubt on his rival's claim of reaching the pole, Peary tried to show that Cook had lied about an earlier achievement. In 1906, Cook claimed to have become the first to reach the top of Mount McKinley. Peary funded an expedition to the Alaskan peak with the sole purpose of discrediting Cook. Peary ended up paying a member of Cook's climbing team $5,000 to swear that the team had never reached the summit. The skullduggery paid off, and Cook's claim of conquering North America's highest mountain came under a cloud.[8]

Herbert Bridgman played a leading role in swaying the public through a barrage of pro-Peary articles, letters, and public lectures. Bridgman helped convince Americans that the walrus-mustachioed navy man was an iconic hero. Writing in *Natural History* magazine, Bridgman made Peary out to be a saint, an outsize human of the noblest demeanor: "Ambition urged him on, but science and patriotism fed its flame."[9] As for Frederick Cook, Bridgman and his fellow propagandists took every opportunity to disparage the man. The criticisms of Cook ranged from the serious, such as the accusation that he never left sight of land on his North Pole expedition, to the ridiculous, including the nonsensical charge that he'd stolen a missionary's dictionary.[10]

Even Bridgman's wife, writer Helen Bartlett Bridgman, got into the act. In her book *Within My Horizon,* she described Peary as a "man of irreproachable standing" and called Frederick Cook "a rank charlatan."[11] Such characterizations eventually took hold. For decades, generations of school kids read about the exploits of the famous admiral. Who knows how many youngsters dreamed about their own exotic adventures as they stared at photographs of the grim-faced explorer in his impressive fur parka. What none of them realized was that Peary's major claim to fame may have been a soap bubble of wishful thinking.

Doubts existed from the first about Peary's achievement. The records relating to his attainment of the North Pole were like Swiss cheese—so full of holes that they were mostly air. His navigational calculations to determine his position in relation to the pole were shoddy and incomplete and included the failure to factor in ice drift and detours around obstacles. His chronometer was ten minutes fast, which would have thrown him off course. On several days, he reported covering impossible distances.[12]

Peary's records were turned over to the National Archives, where they were kept from the public for seventy-five years. After the records were released, a September 1988 article in *National Geographic* magazine sought to determine once and for all whether Peary had made it to the North Pole. Veteran British polar explorer Wally Herbert examined all of the evidence. His conclusion would have disappointed Herbert Bridgman: it's possible that Peary may have missed the pole by as much as sixty miles.[13] Though no one can say for sure, Frederick Cook could well have had a better claim to the pole than his more celebrated rival (although Cook's proofs were no more conclusive than Peary's; hard as it is to believe, Cook left most of the records of his polar trip in Greenland, where they were lost thanks to Peary's interference).[14]

Peary and his supporters never wavered in their belief that he had attained the pole. After all the time he'd spent in the effort—twenty-three years—Peary seemed to feel that he alone had the right to the honor of reaching the imaginary landmark first. He told Helen Bartlett Bridgman of his consuming desire to add his name to the list of history's immortals—giants such as Columbus, Washington, and Napoleon—and he unabashedly proclaimed this to his mother: "I want my fame *now*."[15] For over half of his naval career, Peary used political connections to help him avoid regular duty so he could pursue his personal quest for glory—acclaim he was reluctant to share with anyone. During a National Geographic dinner at which Alexander Graham Bell praised Frederick Cook as the first American to explore both the Arctic and Antarctic, Peary sat fuming like a jealous teenager.[16]

It's curious why the public embraced Robert Peary and rejected Frederick Cook. Perhaps, as a military man, Peary fit the heroic image better than the Brooklyn physician. There's no doubt that Peary was a demigod to Herbert Bridgman. When Bridgman died in September 1924, the *New York Times* commented on his intimate relationship with the explorer he'd promoted so unstintingly, observing that "as Secretary of the Peary Arctic Club [Bridgman] did more than any other one man to help as well as to encourage Peary."[17]

Over the decades, however, the reputation of Bridgman's paragon has shrunk like a melting iceberg. There's no doubt that Peary endured great hardship and accomplished legitimate feats of exploration—he's credited with the discovery of the northernmost point of land in the world, in Greenland—but there's also something off-putting about him. He seems to have been a vainglorious, spiteful man of wobbly integrity and elastic morals (he took a fourteen-year-old Inuit girl as his Arctic "wife" while his real wife was back home, and he stooped to hiring thugs to disrupt his rival's public lectures).[18] The words he recorded on his supposed attainment of the North Pole reveal much about his character: "Mine at last," he crowed, as if his longtime African-American assistant Matthew Henson and the Inuit members of the expedition did not exist.[19] Frederick Cook, in contrast, included his two Inuit companions in his ruminations about reaching the pole. "We were the only pulsating creatures in a dead world of ice," he wrote in his diary.[20] As Bridgman's idol, Peary certainly had feet of clay.

It's clear that Bridgman did a disservice to Frederick Cook—and to history—by contributing to the blatant character assassination that undermined Cook's claims. Bridgman's biased media campaign on Peary's behalf was more appropriate to politics than journalism. In the world of communications, the hard sell is the stock-in-trade of advertising and public relations. Journalism, on the other hand, is supposed to be impartial. At least that's what they used to teach in journalism schools, although it sometimes seems like that lofty standard is becoming about as rare as a polar bear on Madison Avenue.

It's a truism that the winners have always written history. In Bridgman's case, a writer spun history to try to determine a winner. In the tangled chronicles of Arctic exploration, the proselytizing of Herbert Bridgman and other diehard Peary boosters shaped public opinion for the better part of a century. The truth of whether Peary reached the North Pole, or if he was indeed the first to do so, may never be known. Those arguments continue, with nearly as much unalloyed partisanship on behalf of Frederick Cook as Herbert Bridgman displayed for Robert Peary.

CHAPTER 24

THE CONSUMMATE GOLD DIGGER

Peggy Hopkins Joyce

In the spring of 1920, twenty-six-year-old Peggy Hopkins Joyce—a slender, seductive beauty who could reduce most men to gibbering idiots with a single glance—sat fretting in her suite in New York City's luxurious St. Regis Hotel. The sometime theater and film actress and full-time socialite was about to depart for a Paris honeymoon with her new husband, millionaire Chicago lumberman Stanley Joyce. Lamentably, the new Mrs. Joyce felt totally unprepared for their European getaway.

"I will need a few things for the voyage," she informed Mr. Joyce.

"Well charge them," replied her distracted spouse, who was busy attending to some last-minute business affairs.

Taking her husband at his word, Mrs. Joyce went shopping. Her first stop was at Fifth Avenue jewelry store Black, Starr & Frost, where she bought a $200,000 diamond necklace. She followed that with the purchase of a $65,000 sable coat, a $30,000 chinchilla coat for knocking around in, and a new wardrobe of dresses. Oh, and there was also that attractive little $325,000 pearl necklace her husband had promised her.

Later, when her husband expressed his shock at her profligate spending, Mrs. Joyce rebuked him. "Well if a girl can't buy herself a few things when she is going to Paris without being questioned by her husband who is a millionaire, what is the use of being married to a millionaire or going to Paris?"

Mrs. Joyce then burst into tears and accused her husband of not loving her, since all he seemed to think about was money and she wasn't the least bit interested in money.

"No," her husband replied, "I see you are not."

This episode sounds like a drawing room scene from a Noel Coward comedy, but that was the way Peggy Hopkins Joyce described it in *Men, Marriage, and Me*, her frothy 1930 memoir.[1] By the time that book came out, the acquisitive actress had already divorced Stanley Joyce—her third husband—and married and divorced another man as well. She would wed six times in all. Her most celebrated marriages were commercial ventures, calculated liaisons with men of wealth or position that vaulted this woman of humble birth into high society. Her fortuitous marriages, coupled with one particularly lucrative, highly publicized divorce, established her as one of the great gold diggers of all time. It was a role she admitted to without apology. "It is better to be mercenary than miserable," she said. "I may be expensive, but I do deliver the goods."[2]

If that unvarnished self-appraisal makes Peggy Hopkins Joyce seem predatory and self-centered, it's because she was. She dedicated herself to gratifying her own hedonistic whims, and she wasn't above marketing the one bankable asset she'd been born with to make that happen. It was a vocation she clearly enjoyed. Besides her string of hubbies, she toted up an impressive number of rich and influential lovers, including Charlie Chaplin, automaker Walter Chrysler, producers Irving Thalberg and Lee Shubert, and a lengthy list of European playboys.[3] She was, in short, a courtesan, although one who sandwiched her sex-for-prosperity lifestyle around a middling theatrical career.

Despite her modest talent, Peggy Hopkins Joyce stayed in the public eye throughout the 1920s and early '30s. She did it by dazzling people with her good looks and outrageous behavior. Tabloid newspapers, eager for gossip, turned her into one of the country's first "famous for being famous" celebrities. During the height of her notoriety, reporters dogged Peggy Hopkins Joyce for the latest juicy tidbit about her private life, and she was always happy to oblige them, a willing partner in the creation of her own scandalous public image. She became the emblem of Jazz Age "gaiety," the drunken, sexed-up, go-for-broke frenzy that flourished under Prohibition, when forbidden fruit was the sweetest.

In her youth, Peggy Hopkins Joyce vowed not to lead a "Dull and Dreary" existence, and she succeeded.[4] It wasn't an admirable life, but no one could ever say it was boring. Born in 1893 near Norfolk, Virginia, Marguerite "Peggy" Upton was the daughter of an itinerant barber—ironic, given that she spent her whole life clipping men herself. When Peggy was ten, her mother abandoned the family. As Peggy grew older, she dreamed of escaping her conventional circumstances, convinced that she would one day be a "Great Star."[5] In 1909, at the age of sixteen, she joined a small vaudeville troupe in Richmond, Virginia. She traveled to Denver with the troupe, making her professional show business debut somewhere along the way.

In Denver, a twenty-two-year-old salesman named Everett Archibald Jr. spied the nubile young Peggy Upton onstage and decided she was for him. A few months later, the two were married. It was not a tranquil union. Whenever her husband traveled on business, Peggy whiled away her lonely nights by working her way through Denver's bachelor population. After Archibald walked in on her and a guest one evening, the blushing bride packed up and fled from Husband Number One. The profits from her initial foray into matrimony were small, just a few hundred bucks.[6] She would do better the next time.

Peggy took to the road after her fling in the Rockies, ending up on the East Coast. In Washington, DC, she struck a deal with a local dressmaker to show off his creations by wearing them around town. Gorgeous and fashionably dressed, Peggy caught the eye of the city's smart set. In addition to cloaking herself in someone else's clothes, she wrapped herself in a mantle of lies, telling people she was the daughter of a rakish Southern gentleman, and that she'd attended Chevy Chase College, an exclusive finishing school.[7] Swathed in this fantasy, she made the acquaintance of Sherburne P. Hopkins, the son of a powerful Washington attorney. "I have met a Millionaire!" Peggy wrote of their first encounter.[8] She didn't waste the opportunity. On September 1, 1913, at the age of twenty, Peggy Upton was a bride once more.

Firmly hitched to a fat bank account, Peggy dove into the luxurious life as if she were born to it, despite a frosty reception from her new in-laws. She squeezed her husband for an endless array of gifts—jewelry, clothes, an expensive new chauffeured limousine. She was the toast of Washington, a bright ornament on the arm of her husband at balls and receptions. In a remarkably short time, though, she began to find society in the capital confining. And Husband Number Two—no great wit—quickly bored her. In 1915, she escaped to New York City, armed with her new social standing and a taste for the high life. What she craved now was fame and excitement.

In Manhattan, Peggy met the owner of an exclusive dress salon, Madame Frances, who provided introductions to several influential New Yorkers. In short order, the young woman found herself in a vaudeville revue called the "Style Show," which was exactly that—a presentation of the latest fashions, with models swishing around the Palace Theatre stage to music. This was precisely the type of show that fit Peggy's "talent," which consisted of looking pretty. Newspapers hailed her "performance," noting that she "wears a gown the way some prima donnas sing a song."[9] Reporters seldom failed to mention that she'd left a millionaire husband and given up a life in Washington society to pursue her stage career, which enhanced Peggy's reputation as a captivating free spirit.

A surprise hit, the "Style Show" traveled across the country, affording Peggy the chance to strut her stuff as far away as Los Angeles. The exposure probably helped her land a role in a silent film in 1916. In *The Turmoil,* she had a small part as a cheating wife, a portrayal for which she would have needed no coaching. That same year she played another minor character in *Dimples,* a film as forgettable as her first. When Peggy's film career stalled, she returned to the New York stage in 1917, appearing in that season's *Ziegfeld Follies*. Once again, she was little more than a mannequin, with reviewers noting how nice she looked.[10]

Peggy's *Follies* performance and a second Ziegfeld production, *Miss 1917,* led to more movie offers. In 1918, she appeared in three films, none of which amounted to much, although they did enhance Peggy's status as a sex symbol. She next tried acting in Broadway plays and was drubbed by critics, one saying, "She is about as convincing as a doll hanging from the limb of a Christmas tree."[11] Even so, society reporters loved the stylish adventuress, and her photos started to pop up in the leading fashion magazines.

In 1919, Peggy went on the road with *A Sleepless Night,* a play in which her dramatic challenge was to loll about on a canopy bed in satin pajamas. During the play's run in Chicago, thirty-two-year-old lumberman James Stanley Joyce was taken with the willowy beauty. The fabulously wealthy Joyce wooed the young actress, asking her to stay in Chicago. To help her make up her mind,

Joyce bought her a large emerald. When she hesitated at his marriage proposal, he produced a very convincing diamond.

The courtship bounced from Chicago to New York to Palm Beach, with more ostentatious gifts appearing at each stop. At last, Peggy consented to the marriage, realizing that, even though she didn't love Joyce, and despite the fact that he was a mousy little man of no great physical or intellectual attraction, he apparently couldn't say no to her insatiable demand for baubles.[12] Her divorce from Husband Number Two came through on January 20, 1920. Three days later, Peggy married Husband Number Three. This time she'd hit the jackpot.

For roughly a year, Peggy did everything she could to spend her way through Joyce's fortune, acquiring a mansion in Miami and absurd amounts of clothes, furs, and jewelry. Her adoring husband could put up with all that, but he couldn't abide Peggy's other obsession: her ceaseless procession of lovers. During their extended European honeymoon—and even before—she fornicated like a nymphomaniac.[13] Joyce finally became fed up. He left his bride in Europe, saying that he had to get back home to attend to business. Peggy soon received a cable from her lawyer stating that her husband had filed for divorce on the grounds of infidelity.

Joyce had plenty of ammunition to back up his charge. Both Peggy's maid and her social secretary testified against her during the Chicago divorce trial, naming four New York gents—Barton French, Evan Spaulding, Ernest Hudson, and Joe Pani—that she'd canoodled with. French had even met Peggy in England while she was on her honeymoon and continued their affair. In Europe, she'd had liaisons with Paris newspaper publisher Henri Letellier, tango dancer Maurice Mouvet, Englishman Edgar James, Albania's Prince Noureddin Vlora, and the Spanish playboy the Duke of Durcal.[14]

Joyce shored up his argument that his wife was a faithless gold digger by providing a list of the jewelry he'd given her—some three dozen separate items that included multiple bracelets, necklaces, and rings set with diamonds, emeralds, or sapphires, along with a diamond tiara, a jade necklace and pendant, three pearl necklaces, several diamond watches and pins, and a gold cigarette case and jewel-encrusted cigarette holder. In their two-year courtship and marriage, Joyce said he had lavished close to a million dollars worth of jewelry on the woman. In all, he claimed to have spent $1.4 million for his wife's jewelry, clothes, and cars (about $17 million today).[15]

As her defense, Peggy claimed that her husband had been cruel to her, sometimes striking her in a jealous rage. That was true enough, although Peggy always gave as good as she got. Her maid said that she often clawed Joyce's face like a tigress. An out-of-court settlement in November 1921 left Peggy with most of her jewelry, two fur coats, a Rolls-Royce, and $80,000 in cash.[16] Although she received no alimony, she'd scored a million-dollar windfall in her brief marriage to the lumber king, who probably counted himself lucky to be rid of this avaricious slattern at any price.

After her divorce, Peggy continued to bounce around European and American high society. In 1923, she returned to the stage, headlining the first of producer-songwriter Earl Carroll's *Vanities,* a theatrical revue cum girlie show that had the men panting and newspapers snickering at its star ("She cannot sing, dance, or act," wrote a critic for the *New York Evening Post).*[17] Peggy's part consisted of little more than lending her scandalous reputation to the show and flouncing around onstage in a succession of provocative outfits and expensive jewelry. In other words, she was simply *there.* For this lightly taxing role, Earl Carroll reportedly paid her $5,000 a week, which also granted him visitation rights in Peggy's dressing room.

In 1924, Peggy wed Husband Number Four, a minor Swedish count named Gosta Morner. The marriage lasted barely two months. For that brief span, Peggy was a legitimate countess, which she tried to leverage by seeking exorbitant theatrical fees.[18]

In the years that followed, Peggy made intermittent appearances on stage and in film. Her last play was 1928's short-lived *The Lady of the Orchids,* in which she portrayed, appropriately enough, a courtesan. Her final movie and only talkie, *International House,* came out in 1933, with Peggy essentially playing herself, a character the entire country had become intimately familiar with. Because of her notoriety, she got top billing in the occasionally racy comedy, above W. C. Fields, Rudy Vallee, and Burns & Allen. That same year saw the publication of Peggy's lone—and universally panned—novel, *Transatlantic Wife,* a giddy depiction of the rich and lustful in the Jazz Age based on her own experiences.[19]

When Peggy's novel appeared, the heady times it described were already drawing to a close in the face of the Great Depression. Peggy's years in the spotlight were soon to end as well. She turned forty in 1933, and her looks were starting to go. She continued to be a part of the American and European social swirl, but she was becoming a sad figure, a boozy, bloated character that bore little resemblance to the lithe, glamorous creature she'd once been.

In 1945, Peggy wed California engineer Anthony Easton, a union that ran its course in six months. In 1956, she married retired New York bank clerk Andrew Meyer, a lonely lifelong bachelor more than twenty years her junior. It was her sixth excursion into marital bliss, a mundane anticlimax to her tumultuous wedded life.

The young Peggy Hopkins Joyce had been a woman of predictable ambition. All she desired was the best of everything—the most expensive jewels, furs, houses, clothes, cars—and then a just a bit more of it. "It is marvelous to be rich," she gushed shortly after marrying Stanley Joyce.[20] That may be true, but Peggy didn't do much that was laudable with her wealth. For as long as she could manage it, she simply wallowed in luxury, always anticipating her next acquisition. "Why be beautiful if you can't have what you want?" she babbled in her memoir, her vacuous self-absorption worthy of a ten year old.[21]

For Peggy, love came down to the sparkly things she could wear on her neck, wrists, and fingers. Her shameless gold digging is said to have inspired the character Lorelei Lee in Anita Loos's 1925 novel *Gentlemen Prefer Blondes*.[22] In 1949, the story was made into a musical of the same name. Four years later, the movie version featured Marilyn Monroe cooing her unforgettable rendition of "Diamonds Are a Girl's Best Friend," which could have been Peggy Hopkins Joyce's theme song (her most famous rock was the 127.01-carat Portuguese Diamond, which is now in the Smithsonian National Gem Collection).

In June 1957, Peggy died of throat cancer at the age of sixty-four. By then, she possessed less than half of the fortune she'd amassed through her earlier marriages, having been forced to sell off her worldly treasures one by one when the money stopped rolling in. She left the bulk of her estate to Andrew Meyer, but she also bequeathed $25,000 to her sister, $25,000 to a cousin, $10,000 to a friend, and $5,000 to her maid. That $65,000 was the same amount she'd paid for the sable coat she bought before her honeymoon with Stanley Joyce, an extravagance, she'd assured her Daddy Warbucks husband, that was "really quite cheap considering."[23]

For a moment in time, Peggy Hopkins Joyce blazed across the firmament like a skyrocket, an explosion of color and excitement that, inevitably, drifted back toward earth in a shower of fading sparkles. In her bawdy love life, she'd bedded more men than probably even she could recall. At least two of them were said to have committed suicide because of her.[24] Her serial marriages inspired several songs and countless jokes. Her seductive image appeared on magazine covers and in advertisements—the famous beauty who was . . . well, famous. For a decade or more, the public had stared at her in wonder, and when the show was over, they turned away and soon forgot her name.

CHAPTER 25

THE MAD, SAD POET OF GREENWICH VILLAGE

Maxwell Bodenheim

In the summer of 1925, a slender, sandy-haired man in a rumpled three-piece suit casually descends a stairway in a crowded house in New Rochelle, New York. Like a European nobleman about to make a grand entrance before his court, he pauses to gaze across the room with his uncommonly pale blue eyes, a sardonic smile on his lips. The people packed into the home of publisher Horace B. Liveright jabber in each other's faces, their conversation animated by their host's generous supply of bootleg hooch. A raucous jazz number blares from a radio, the frantic live-for-today yowl of Prohibition-era America. Maxwell Bodenheim—"Bogie" to his many friends and admirers—lights his ever-present corncob pipe and ambles on down the stairs. For Bodenheim, the party is a candy store, and all the bright young flappers enthusiastically laughing and tippling bathtub gin are so many bonbons. Bodenheim is smiling because he knows he can have his pick of these tasty treats. In his early thirties, the rakish Greenwich Village bohemian has several volumes of critically acclaimed poetry to his credit and a novel in the bookstores that everyone is talking about. As always, fame is a powerful aphrodisiac.

Flash forward two dozen years to a lonely side street in Greenwich Village. A middle-aged Maxwell Bodenheim sits by himself on a park bench. Attached to the wall behind him, scraps of paper flutter in the chilly breeze of a spring afternoon. The papers bear Bodenheim's latest poems, all of them for sale—for ten cents, a quarter, whatever anyone is willing to pay. Bodenheim huddles in a filthy overcoat, his once handsome face eroded to a fright mask by years of hard living. He clutches a pipe in his hand, filled with tobacco from cigarette butts scrounged from the gutter. Bodenheim's eyes are downcast, his expression blank. From the heights of literary success, Bodenheim has fallen to the depths of squalor. Still famous in the Village, he's become a figure of derision, a pathetic panhandler and peddler of doggerel, always desperate to collect enough change for his next shot of rotgut.[1]

Those two scenes bracket the career of one of America's most intriguing writers, a once immensely popular figure who began his ascent in the years just before World War I. During the 1920s, his most productive period, Bodenheim turned out a dozen books of poetry and prose, including a controversial best-selling novel, *Replenishing Jessica*. His decline sputtered across three decades, from the 1930s to the early '50s. It was triggered by the Great Depression, the national hangover that brought the gaiety of the Roaring Twenties to a sudden and painful end. For most of the 1930s, Bodenheim struggled to keep a roof over his head and food in his stomach. Although World War II pulled the country out of the Depression, Bodenheim never recovered. Mentally, he was ill equipped to handle either poverty or prosperity.[2] The story of this eccentric artist with a bent toward self-destruction encapsulates the highs and lows of the 1920s and '30s. It's also a reminder that fame is often written in erasable ink.

Bodenheim was born in Hermanville, Mississippi, in 1892, a first-generation American. Both his parents were from Alsace. (The family name was actually Bodenheimer, which Maxwell shortened to Bodenheim to downplay his Jewish heritage.) Maxwell's mother, Caroline, came from a well-to-do background, making his father's lack of business acumen a source of constant friction. Solomon Bodenheimer worked as a traveling whiskey salesman and clothing store clerk, both without success. The family relocated to Memphis, then Chicago, always hoping to find a prosperity that never came. Intense arguments poisoned the home, leaving young Maxwell disillusioned with family life. When he expressed an interest in poetry, his father berated him, pushing him toward the usual middle-class path to respectability. Maxwell ended up loathing all forms of tradition and authority, an attitude that stuck with him his entire life, coloring his personal relationships as well as his writing.[3]

When he was sixteen, Bodenheim either quit or was kicked out of high school. He fled his unhappy home and joined the army, an odd choice for a teenager who chafed at discipline. It may have been the first example of what would become a pattern of self-abuse. Bodenheim had an Eeyore personality—always expecting the worst and doing whatever was necessary to make sure it happened. Predictably, he hated everything about the military. He went AWOL, was arrested, and finished his tour of duty behind bars at Fort Leavenworth, Kansas. Years later, he spun fanciful stories about his time in the army, claiming to have fought against Pancho Villa and to have earned his dishonorable discharge by bashing an anti-Semitic officer over the head with a rifle.[4] After his time in the service, Bodenheim went on the bum for a couple of years, hopping freight trains, picking cotton, and mixing with migrant laborers, hobos, and petty criminals—a walk on the wild side that provided material for his future novels and kindled his sympathy for the underdog.

Late in 1912, Bodenheim returned to his parents' Chicago home, his suitcase stuffed with poems. He began to submit his work to Chicago literary magazines, earning a name for himself as a bright new voice. Luckily, he came along near the beginning of the Chicago Renaissance, the heady period between 1910 and the mid-1920s when Chicago was awash with talented writers and influential literary journals. Bodenheim was befriended by Harriet Monroe, founding editor of *Poetry* magazine, and Margaret Anderson, editor of *The Little Review*. The two women gushed over the young writer, Monroe calling him "a new genius in American poetry,"[5] and Anderson anointing him as "probably one of the greatest in America."[6] The two editors argued over who had discovered him and been the first to publish his work. Bodenheim seemed to have that effect on women. As he hit the coffeehouses and literary salons, the ladies swooned over his good looks and lyrical endearments. "Your face is an incense bowl from which a single name arises," he was heard to whisper in the ear of more than one admirer.[7]

Bodenheim came to know all the leading Chicago writers, including Carl Sandburg, Theodore Dreiser, Edgar Lee Masters, and Sherwood Anderson. His closest friend was Ben Hecht, then a budding newspaperman but destined to become a prolific screenwriter, playwright, and novelist. (The screenplays Hecht wrote or worked on include such Hollywood classics as *The Front Page, Stagecoach, Some Like It Hot, Gone with the Wind, Notorious, A Farewell to Arms,* and *Mutiny on the Bounty*.) Hecht and Bodenheim pulled off some interesting stunts. Frequent speakers at literary gatherings, the pair once scheduled a meeting on the following topic: "Resolved: that people who attend literary debates are imbeciles." Arguing the affirmative viewpoint, Hecht looked out over the crowded room and announced, "The affirmative rests." Bodenheim then stood up, surveyed the audience, and proclaimed, "You win."[8] In the heat of discussions, Bodenheim wielded ridicule and sarcasm with gleeful abandon. Hecht described him as "the ideal lunatic," one who "greets an adversary's replies with horrible parrot screams" and finishes his own thoughts with "ear-splitting guffaws."[9]

Despite his rise in the Chicago literary world, Bodenheim began to feel slighted by his friends. He decided it was time to move on. Early in 1915, he showed up at the home of New York poet and critic Alfred Kreymborg, who'd written to Bodenheim and praised his work. Kreymborg gave Bodenheim a place to stay and introduced him to the city's literary crowd. The older writer made Bodenheim an editor of *Others* magazine, bringing him in contact with leading poets such as William Carlos Williams and Conrad Aiken. Bodenheim continued to produce poetry of his own, and he tried his hand at writing plays, becoming friends with Eugene O'Neill. After a few years, Bodenheim had a falling out with Alfred Kreymborg, again over perceived slights. Bodenheim's friends found that sustaining a relationship with the touchy poet was like petting a porcupine.[10]

One of the few relationships that endured was Bodenheim's marriage to Minna Schein, a petite, attractive woman he met in 1918 in a Greenwich Village tearoom. They were wed for twenty years and had a son, although their marital arrangement was unusual. Bodenheim made attempts at supporting his wife and child, but he often acted as if he were still a swinging bachelor, living apart from his family and carrying on with other women. Despite her husband's very public reputation as a Don Juan, Minna didn't seek a divorce until 1938. Stranger still, the unfaithful Bodenheim wrote his wife passionate letters, assuring her of his love and telling her how much he missed her when he was away. His first book of poetry, *Minna and Myself,* published in 1918, contained tender love poems about her. Clearly, Bodenheim was a better husband on paper than in reality. Having an ordinary marriage would have made him too much like his parents.

By 1920, Bodenheim had become a fixture in Greenwich Village. The American equivalent of Paris's Left Bank, the Village provided the perfect bohemian setting—rents were cheap, and the speakeasies and cafeterias stayed open every night into the morning hours. It didn't take much income to sustain a life of doing precisely what you wanted, society's rules be damned. Following the approval of Prohibition in 1919, Greenwich Village became a sustained, over-the-top circus, and Bodenheim was one of its ringmasters. He presided at drunken all-night poetry slams in MacDougal Street bars, using a hammer for a gavel. Along with millionaire poet Robert Clairmont and other pals, he founded the Greta Garbo Social Club, whose chief aim was to seduce the New York working girls who flocked to Greenwich Village looking for excitement. Partygoers cavorted at artists' soirees such as the Blaze Ball, where the women were said to be—in a take-off on the old Ivory Soap advertising slogan—99 and 44/100ths percent naked.[11]

Like Greenwich Village—and the entire country—Bodenheim seemed to be riding a shooting star all through the 1920s. He turned out a prodigious stream of poetry and novels. He wrote literary criticism for top magazines such as the *New Yorker*, the *New Republic*, and *American Mercury*. He traveled to England and hung out with fellow poet T. S. Eliot. Among the avant-garde, he was the poster boy for Jazz Age cool. Bodenheim's 1925 novel *Replenishing Jessica* increased his notoriety after New York censors declared it obscene. Bodenheim's publisher, Horace Liveright, was prosecuted—and ultimately acquitted—in a farcical trial that involved reading the entire novel into the court record. Far from titillated, the jurors fell asleep as the prosecutor droned on for three days. The novel about a rich young woman who dabbled at painting and promiscuity was actually quite tame. Thanks to the newspaper coverage of the trial, it hit the bestseller list.[12] Bodenheim realized a cash windfall, but as he'd done all his life, he quickly burned through it.

The uproar over *Replenishing Jessica* had women throwing themselves at Bodenheim's feet. For two frenzied months in the summer of 1928, the clamoring turned tragic. First came Gladys Loeb, an eighteen-year-old aspiring poet who sought Bodenheim's literary guidance. After a brief affair, Bodenheim callously dumped her, telling her that her poetry reeked. Brokenhearted, Loeb went home and put her head inside the oven while holding a photograph of her lover. Loeb was lucky. Her landlady smelled the gas and rescued her.[13] Next came twenty-two-year-old Virginia Drew, who followed Loeb's script except for the oven. Drew threw herself into the Hudson and drowned. The Drew suicide made front-page news: "Bodenheim Vanishes as Girl Takes Life," the *New York Times* blared.[14] Papers in London and Paris picked up the story, which was about to turn more bizarre.

Following Drew's suicide, another Bodenheim admirer decided she couldn't go on living. Like Gladys Loeb, Aimee Cortez stuck her head in the oven while clutching a photo of Bodenheim, an apparent copycat suicide. This time, no one was around to come to the rescue.[15] Finally, a girl with the felicitous name of Dorothy Dear presented herself to Bodenheim. The poet-libertine wrote her a series of love letters, which Dorothy kept in her purse. She had them with her the day she boarded a subway bound for Greenwich Village, a destination she never reached. Her train crashed at Times Square. Dear was killed, her treasured love letters scattered like leaves among the wreckage.[16] Bodenheim himself never suffered from any of these tragedies, although in retrospect they appear to be a harbinger of what was headed his way.

In the early 1930s, Bodenheim's shooting star finally fizzled out, leaving him tumbling back to earth, scorched and shaken. The stock market crash of 1929 had eviscerated the carefree bohemian life of Greenwich Village. By the end of 1930, unemployed men crowded New York's sidewalks, hawking apples for a nickel apiece. Bodenheim's 1928 novel *Georgie May* and 1930's *A Virtuous Girl* and *Naked on Roller Skates*—a sensationalist Jazz Age crime and sex tale— all sold well, but the spendthrift author had nothing to show for it. Book publishing suffered along with the rest of the economy. In May 1933, Bodenheim's longtime publisher, Liveright, Inc., went bust. His 1934 novel *Slow Vision,* a stark portrait of the human toll of the Great Depression, would be his last. Afterward, he simply fell apart, a personal decline as inexorable as death by quicksand. By the mid-1930s, he was homeless and on relief, a drunken wreck selling his poems on the street to buy liquor.

Bodenheim found a temporary reprieve when he was hired by the Federal Writers' Project, a program started in July 1935 as part of the Works Progress Administration, Franklin Roosevelt's New Deal effort to put Americans back to work. The Federal Writers' Project hired 6,600 writers, editors, researchers, and academics to produce a variety of publications, the most famous being the American Guide Series, detailed guidebooks to every state. For at least three years, Bodenheim worked on the Bibliographies and Indices Project, a position he lost in 1940 when he was purged along with other writers suspected of having ties to the Communist Party. Support for the labor movement and left-wing causes flourished during the Depression years, and though Bodenheim flirted with radical politics, he was more bleeding-heart liberal than Marxist.

Ben Hecht described him as one of the "daft knights with no other program than to battle for the disinherited."[17]

Once the United States entered World War II in 1941, the economy began to rebound as arms production revived the nation's industry. Bodenheim never shared in the growing prosperity. He continued his downward trajectory throughout the forties, now with a new companion. After his first wife divorced him, Bodenheim married Grace Finan, a widow with a meager income. The couple evidently achieved a bit of happiness now and then. Grace helped Bodenheim prepare his last book of poetry, published in 1942. Shortly before she died from cancer in 1950, Bodenheim showed up at Ben Hecht's New York home, filthy and drunk but still his old sarcastic self. Before he left, Bodenheim turned serious. "Honestly, Ben, I am sick of the whole thing," he said. "I'd commit suicide tonight except that I am in love with my wife. She is very sick and full of suffering. And she needs me."[18]

After Grace's death, Bodenheim married Ruth Fagan, a mentally unstable woman nearly thirty years his junior. At age fifty-nine, Bodenheim was about to sink to a new low. He now spent as much time in the Bowery as Greenwich Village. Reeling through life in a stupor, he became a bitter caricature of his old self, a ragbag of sullied dreams. When he couldn't raise enough money by begging (he sometimes hung a sign around his neck claiming he was blind) or selling his booze-addled verses to sympathetic passersby, he allowed Ruth to turn tricks.[19] The two fought constantly and lived in squalor. They often slept on park benches, but on a freezing February night in 1954, they went home with a twenty-five-year-old dishwasher named Harold Weinberg, a mildly retarded man with a $5-a-week cold-water room on the edge of the Bowery. Bodenheim fell asleep reading Rachel Carson's *The Sea Around Us*. He was awakened by the sounds of Weinberg attempting to have sex with his wife. When Bodenheim challenged Weinberg, the younger man shot him in the chest, killing him instantly. Weinberg then grabbed a knife and stabbed Ruth to death. He fled but was caught and committed to a mental institution.[20]

Bodenheim's murder seems like a caprice of fate. The turbulence of his life, however, was foreordained, given his rejection of society's conventions and constant rebellion against authority. His difficult personality and heavy drinking didn't help. In truth, he courted trouble, thrived on it. He very consciously made his bed as a cynic early in life and was content to sleep in it all his days. He had no faith in lasting happiness. Believing that things were going to hell anyway, he always gave them a nudge. Booze- or drug-fueled self-destruction has always been the melodramatic refuge of minor artists, but in Bodenheim's case, the compulsion to squander his abilities through a life of dissipation seems to have sprung from the core of his being. "I have a malady of the soul," he proclaimed.[21] He was one of those unlucky people with the knack for pricking their finger on misery's needle even when it's buried in a haystack of happiness.

Historically, Bodenheim was a barometer of his times—indulging in all the hedonistic excesses of the 1920s and suffering the dispiriting effects of poverty during the Great Depression. His writing reflected the opposite natures of those two periods, although not as effectively as F. Scott Fitzgerald's *The Great Gatsby* and John Steinbeck's *The Grapes of Wrath*. It would be surprising if Bodenheim's novels ever experience a renaissance. Critics have called them uneven, filled with energy and insight in places, tedious and unpolished in others.[22] Even Bodenheim regarded himself chiefly as a poet, and while his verse suffers from the same up and down quality as his novels, his earliest compositions often sparkle with subtle, original images that linger in the mind. *Minna and Myself* contains a short poem titled "Death." Reading the following lines, you get the faint chill that only first-rate poetry evokes—the feeling that something new, strange, and wonderful has entered the world.

> I shall walk down the road.
> I shall turn and feel upon my feet
> The kisses of Death, like scented rain.
> For Death is a black slave with little silver birds
> Perched in a sleeping wreath upon his head.
> He will tell me, his voice like jewels
> Dropped into a satin bag,
> How he has tiptoed after me down the road,
> His heart made a dark whirlpool with longing for me.
> Then he will graze me with his hands
> And I shall be one of the sleeping silver birds
> Between the cold waves of his hair as he tiptoes on.[23]

Bodenheim's first wife arranged for his burial in her family's plot in a cemetery near Oradell, New Jersey. In his memoirs, Ben Hecht pointed out that the mad, sad old poet never lost his swagger, no matter the circumstances. "Despite the continuing, unvarying defeats of his life, it is this strut I remember as Bogie's signature. Ignored, slapped around, reduced to beggary, Bodenheim's mocking grin remained flying in his private war like a tattered flag. God knows what he was mocking. Possibly, mankind."[24] In the end, it's clear that the most memorable character Bodenheim ever created was himself.

CHAPTER 26

THE BIFURCATED CONGRESSMAN

Samuel Dickstein

Th
he trim, distinguished-looking US congressman from New York strode pur-
posefully to the front of the House Chamber. Standing before the massive
marble rostrum in the Well of the House, Democrat Samuel Dickstein looked
out over the more than four hundred legislators assembled for the opening day
of the second session of the 73rd Congress—January 3, 1934. The forty-eight-
year-old representative had European affairs on his mind this day. A Jewish
immigrant from near Vilnius in present-day Lithuania, Dickstein was acutely
aware of the dangers posed by Adolf Hitler's recent ascent to power in Germany.

Nazism was a threat not only to European Jews and Dickstein's homeland, but also to the United States. It was a threat Dickstein intended to counter.

In a clear voice, Dickstein outlined the dangers of Nazi agitation in America. He proposed the formation of a special committee to investigate subversive activities. The Dickstein Resolution passed in March 1934, and the new committee was formed, with Massachusetts Democrat John McCormack as its chairman and Congressman Dickstein as vice chairman. (Dickstein turned down the chairmanship over concern that his Jewish background might prejudice the committee's work.) The group's formal title was a mouthful: the Special Committee on Un-American Activities Authorized to Investigate Nazi Propaganda and Certain Other Propaganda Activities. Usually referred to as the McCormack-Dickstein Committee, its mandate was simple—to prevent those advocating other forms of government from subverting the US Constitution.

To all appearances, Samuel Dickstein was an admirable man, a staunch defender of his adopted country. Thanks to his efforts, the House of Representatives kept a close watch on Nazi supporters in the United States in the years just prior to and during World War II. Though Dickstein was chiefly interested in thwarting fascism and anti-Semitism, his work led to the creation of the House Un-American Activities Committee (HUAC), an investigative body that focused almost exclusively on communist subversion during its nearly four-decade-long existence. In its fervor to root out communists inside and outside the government, HUAC routinely ran roughshod over individual rights. The excesses of HUAC became a blot on Dickstein's legacy. The other blemish on the congressman's career was the fact that, from 1937 to 1940, he was a Soviet spy, although not a very good one.[1]

Born in 1885, Dickstein arrived in this country at the age of two. His family settled on the Lower East Side of New York, where his rabbi father became cantor at the Orthodox Norfolk Street Synagogue. Dickstein was educated at public and private schools before going on to earn degrees at City College and New York Law School. After practicing law in the city for a short time, he began a career in public service that would last more than forty years. Dickstein was adept at politics, rising methodically through the ranks in municipal, state, and federal government. In 1911, he was appointed special deputy attorney general of the State of New York. In 1917, he won election to the New York City board of aldermen. In 1919, he was elected to the New York State Assembly, and in 1922, he won a seat in the US Congress, representing the New York City district where he grew up. He was reelected to Congress eleven times.

Being an immigrant himself—and representing a community with a large number of foreign-born residents—Dickstein was naturally interested in immigration and citizenship laws. He was appointed to the House Committee on Immigration and Naturalization, serving as chairman from 1931 through 1945. Among his accomplishments was the establishment of a nationality code, detailing the legalities of naturalized citizenship. His work on the committee introduced him to some unsettling trends. The rise of Nazism in Germany had been paralleled by an increase in anti-Semitism in the United States. Anti-Semitic literature was flooding the country. Waves of foreigners were entering the United States, both legally and illegally, and German groups such as the Friends of New Germany and the Silver Shirts of America attracted substantial support, some of them running youth camps to indoctrinate children with pro-Hitler views.[2]

It was this knowledge that prompted Dickstein to propose the formation of a committee to investigate subversive activities on American soil. Dickstein claimed that Hitler had spent $32 million on anti-Jewish propaganda in the United States by the mid-thirties, and that every German merchant ship arriving here carried spies and agitators who infiltrated the country.[3] Through much of 1934, the McCormack-Dickstein Committee conducted hearings in Washington, New York, Chicago, Los Angeles, and other cities, interviewing hundreds of witnesses. Dickstein's brainchild was responsible for two new laws, one requiring the registration of agents engaged in propaganda for a foreign power and another allowing congressional committees to subpoena witnesses for hearings outside the District of Columbia. Other than that, about all that came out of the investigation was a lot of talk. Dickstein himself did a fair share of the chin-wagging. He questioned witnesses with the theatrics of a ham actor. He tossed out sensational claims about the dangers the country faced, provoking scary headlines.[4] His methods may have been extreme, but his motives were sincere. Dickstein knew that millions of European Jews were in great peril. His anger and anguish were real.

After the short life of the McCormack-Dickstein Committee, another group was formed to carry on its work, again at Congressman Dickstein's urging. (Two similar committees had preceded McCormack-Dickstein: In 1918, the Overman Committee investigated communist influence in America following the Russian Revolution, and in 1930, the Fish Committee investigated suspected communist organizations, including the American Civil Liberties Union.) In May 1938, the first incarnation of the House Un-American Activities Committee took up the pursuit of subversives, led by conservative Democrat Martin Dies of Texas.

The Dies Committee investigated Nazi and communist agitators in the

United States and also sniffed around the edges of the Ku Klux Klan's activities. However, the committee devoted a large part of its time to booting suspected communists off the government payroll, specifically writers and actors employed by the Works Progress Administration's Federal Writers' Project and Federal Theatre Project, two of the federal government's Depression-era job creation programs that were favorite targets of critics. (When the Dies Committee grilled Hallie Flanagan, the head of the Federal Theatre Project, Alabama congressman Joe Starnes asked her if Elizabethan playwright Christopher Marlowe belonged to the Communist Party.)[5] For the conservatives who dominated the committee, the investigations were a handy way to whack their liberal opponents, buff their patriotism credentials, and get their own names in the newspapers—a trifecta of opportunism no politician could pass up.

Samuel Dickstein wasn't named to the Dies Committee, although initially he gave it his full support. He kept busy in other ways: shortly before the new investigative committee was established, Dickstein became a Soviet operative.[6] There may have been a certain logic to his decision. Dickstein hated Hitler, who was persecuting Jews; Soviet dictator Joseph Stalin also hated Germany's fascist leader—ergo, the enemy of my enemy is my friend. That doesn't excuse Dickstein's actions, but it would make his motivation understandable. On the other hand, Dickstein may have just been out to make a profit. Unlike most American spies of the era, he apparently wasn't motivated by communist ideology.[7]

The congressman's foray into espionage began in 1937 when he agreed to fix a Soviet secret agent's immigration papers for a fee of $3,000. He only realized $1,200 out of the deal, but it was easy money, so Dickstein approached the Soviet ambassador in Washington with an offer to sell information on pro-Nazi Russians operating in the United States. Although the Soviets agreed to the arrangement, Dickstein asked for $2,500 a month for his services, which the Russians thought was too high. They offered him $500. A compromise figure of $1,250 was reached, and the new secret agent set to work.[8]

Because of Dickstein's financial demands, the Soviets gave him the code name "Crook." The first "intelligence documents" he delivered contained information that was already common knowledge. The Russians were not pleased. They wanted inside information on Nazis, White Russians, Ukrainian nationalists, and other enemies of the Soviet state. Dickstein gave them the transcripts of the Dies Committee's investigations, along with lists of known fascists operating in America. As the Dies panel began to focus more on communists than Nazis, Dickstein attacked the committee publicly, even suggesting that it be disbanded. The Russians still didn't think they were getting their money's worth. "'Crook' is completely justifying his code name," wrote a high-ranking Soviet spook in America to his superiors in Moscow. "This is an unscrupulous type, greedy for money . . . a very cunning swindler."[9]

Dickstein continued to feed the Soviets dribs and drabs of information—sometimes culled from newspaper articles and public speeches—but when they asked him to penetrate American intelligence operations and provide them with information gathered on Soviet enemies, the congressman dithered. He finally said that he could obtain information from the FBI, but he'd need more money.[10] The Soviets were getting fed up. Early in 1940, they cut Dickstein loose. By then, they'd shelled out more than $12,000, an amount equivalent to nearly $200,000 today.[11] It was money poorly spent. Dickstein may even have been working both sides of the street in his low-grade "spying." A Soviet memo reported that he also sold information to the Poles and the British.[12] If Dickstein fed them the same type of material he gave the Soviets—"rubbish," his handlers called it—he truly was "a very cunning swindler."

Dickstein remained in Congress until December 1945, when he resigned and returned home to run for election to the New York State Supreme Court. He was elected and served on the court until his death in April 1954. The public didn't learn about his work for the Russians until 1999, when authors Allen Weinstein and Alexander Vassiliev, the latter a former KGB agent, published their book *The Haunted Wood: Soviet Espionage in America—the Stalin Era*. Weinstein and Vassiliev discovered Dickstein's secret life while combing through intelligence files in Moscow in the mid-nineties.

After Dickstein left Congress, the investigation of American subversives took a new turn. In 1945, the temporary Dies Committee gave way to a permanent House Un-American Activities Committee. The Nazis had been defeated, and in the aftermath of World War II, the now standing committee devoted its full attention to fighting communism. Over the next three decades, HUAC conducted ongoing hearings aimed at uncovering communist infiltration of the federal government, organized labor, and the entertainment industry.

In the frightening years of the Cold War, the Red Menace seemed very real, and the public supported the aggressive pursuit of communists. American spies actually were stealing secrets about nuclear weapons and other sensitive matters. A few famous cases grabbed national attention, notably those of Julius and Ethel Rosenberg, who were executed for espionage in 1953, and Alger Hiss, who served forty-four months in prison on a perjury conviction related to his testimony before the House Un-American Activities Committee. HUAC made its biggest splash when it investigated communist influence in Hollywood. As a result of the hearings, more than three hundred artists were blacklisted by the studios, some because of their ties to the American Communist Party and others simply because they supported liberal causes the enforcers of the blacklist found objectionable.

Despite legitimate successes in exposing spies, the HUAC hearings were often nothing more than witch-hunts, grand inquisitions conducted without regard for the rights of those under investigation.[13] The search for truth blurred into persecution as the committee members pursued anyone with the slightest connection to communism at any time in their life—which was considered automatic proof of disloyalty. Witnesses were subpoenaed and badgered into testifying against themselves and "naming names" of others. Those who refused to appear before Congress or declined to answer questions could be held in contempt and imprisoned, and they risked losing their jobs and being publicly branded as traitors. J. Edgar Hoover's FBI intimidated citizens who opposed the congressional investigations by tapping their phones, opening their mail, keeping them under surveillance, and even burglarizing their offices.[14] At its height, the anticommunist frenzy spawned the showboating demagoguery of Republican senator Joseph McCarthy, a publicity hound who made unsubstantiated claims about the number of communists in the federal government. McCarthy's reign was blessedly short. His police-state tactics of character assassination and guilt by association led to his censure by the Senate in 1954.

HUAC's investigations divided the country, with conservatives cheering them on and liberals arguing that they were a stain on our democratic heritage. In 1954, the committee published a fifty-page defense of its activities called *This Is YOUR House Committee on Un-American Activities*. While acknowledging that some of the criticism of HUAC came from "perfectly loyal American citizens," the authors thundered that much of the criticism came from "Communists and other enemies of the committee," along with "uninformed or misinformed individuals."[15] The pamphlet is a bizarre document, filled with self-justification and self-congratulations over the committee's goals and accomplishments.

Regardless of such PR offensives, by the late 1950s the public began to sour on Congress's endless red-baiting interrogations. In 1959, Harry Truman—who'd endorsed loyalty oaths for federal employees while he was president—called HUAC the "most un-American thing in the country today."[16] In the 1960s, the antics of renegades Jerry Rubin and Abbie Hoffman held the congressional investigations up to ridicule. Rubin once showed up dressed as a Revolutionary War soldier, and Hoffman appeared in a Santa Claus suit. Intellectuals blasted

HUAC—writer James Baldwin called it "one of the most sinister facts of the national life."[17] Like a papier-mâché bogeyman left out in the rain, the committee slowly disintegrated, its prestige and clout diminishing year by year. In 1975, HUAC was abolished.

To be sure, the McCormack-Dickstein Committee's pursuit of Nazi agitators and the search for communist spies by HUAC (dubbed "Dickstein's Monster" by writer Walter Goodman) were both legitimate exercises.[18] Exposing the criminal activity of subversive elements is critical to the country's survival, although it's a task best left to law enforcement. The trick in any case is to distinguish between subversion and the expression of differing but perfectly legal political views. The abuses of HUAC and Joseph McCarthy proved that "un-American" can mean whatever the gentleman pounding the gavel decides upon. Like "patriotism" and "disloyalty," the concept is very much in the eye of the beholder. Dickstein contemporary and opponent Maury Maverick, a Texas congressman, certainly felt that way. As he succinctly put it in 1938, "Un-American is simply something that somebody else does not agree to."[19]

Samuel Dickstein set out to do right in his career as a public servant, and in many ways he did. He demonstrated a genuine concern for the disadvantaged through his work. Without pay, he defended thousands of New York tenants who'd been hit with rent increases after World War I. He sponsored state legislation to improve housing conditions. He was one of the first and among the most persistent voices to warn the nation about the evils of Nazism and the threat of a second world war. He tried to persuade the federal government to allow unused refugee quotas to be given to Jews fleeing Hitler. And while he was unremittingly greedy during his brief turn as a spy, he apparently never gouged his constituents. When he died at the age of sixty-nine, his estate came to a paltry $2,500.[20]

After Dickstein's death, three hundred judges and attorneys attended a memorial service in his honor at the New York State Supreme Court building. Dickstein's *New York Times* obituary said that he'd "achieved a distinguished record as a legislator."[21] Expressing a far different opinion, a frustrated Soviet agent once called the congressman-spy "a complete racketeer and a black-mailer."[22] From all indications, there was probably a certain amount of truth in both assessments.

The residue of Dickstein's congressional career still influences the nation's political discourse. Every time a politician slings the un-American label at an adversary, the ghost of Samuel Dickstein is hovering nearby. Although Dickstein eventually realized he'd loosed a dangerous toxin in American society, by then it was too late. What was born of a legitimate concern over foreign subversives quickly mutated into a blunt-edged weapon used to attack domestic political enemies. If Dickstein's life teaches us anything, it's that the proper response to blustering superpatriots is always a healthy dose of skepticism.

CHAPTER 27

THE FRUGAL COUNTERFEITER

Emerich Juettner

T he mid-autumn weather had artfully daubed Central Park in luminous oranges and muted browns. These final days of October 1947 were crisp and bright, the nights pleasantly cool. It was the time of year that made you think of hot cider and pumpkin pie or of giggling young witches and goblins rustling through fallen leaves. Over on nearby West 96th Street, seventy-two-year-old Emerich Juettner paused to admire a pot of bright yellow mums making their final stand before the first hard freeze. A bald, blue-eyed elf—he topped five feet by just a couple of inches and weighed no more than 120 pounds—Juettner

wore a frayed army jacket over a sweater and vest, an old man's grab-bag arma-
ment against the morning chill. A handyman's ever-present screwdriver pro-
truded from his back pocket.

With his grandfatherly demeanor and ready, toothless grin, Juettner had
become a fixture in this part of Manhattan. The old fellow pushed a wooden cart
filled with an assortment of castoffs he'd scrounged from empty lots and along
the Hudson waterfront—a broken baby carriage, a battered lamp, a birdcage
that had seen better days. What other people threw away, Juettner collected.
With a bit of luck, he could repair and sell these oddments. It was how he'd
helped to support himself for several years. Truth be told, though, he was just as
likely to give his treasures away. And he was always willing to lend his neighbors
a hand with his Mr. Fix-It skills, like the time he'd revived a faulty electric train
set on Christmas Eve for a frantic mom.

A scruffy terrier mutt padded along next to the old man's feet, a faithful
friend of many seasons that, strangely, Juettner had never bothered to name.
Juettner looked down at his dog. "You hungry, boy?" he asked in his reedy voice,
which still carried traces of his native Austria. The terrier sat on its haunches and
stared up at its master, its head cocked as if it could actually understand what
Juettner was saying. The old man bent down and scratched the dog's ears. "Let's
see if we can find you a treat."[1]

Juettner parked his pushcart in front of a butcher shop and tied his dog to
one of the wheels. Stepping inside, the old man approached the glass display
case. He tugged at his scraggly white mustache as he eyed the selections—plump
roasts, thick-cut steaks, and an assortment of poultry, sausages, and chops. "Got
any scraps to sell?" he asked, tilting his head toward the door. "For my dog."
The butcher wiped his hands on his apron and glanced at the chopping block
behind him. "I can give you those trimmings for 15 cents." The old man nodded
and reached into his coat pocket, retrieving a crumpled dollar bill, which he
placed on the counter. The butcher wrapped the meat scraps and handed them
to Juettner, along with 85 cents in change.[2]

Juettner walked out of the butcher shop and dropped the package into his
cart. He winked at his dog as he rolled on down the sidewalk, knowing that he'd
just pulled off another successful caper, one that he'd executed more than five
thousand times in the past. You see, sweet old Emerich Juettner (he also used the
name Edward Mueller) was a counterfeiter—moreover, a record-setting counterfeiter. The kindly neighborhood junkman had run his scam—swapping phony
paper money for real change—for over nine years now, which was longer than any
other currency forger in the nation's history had operated before being caught.[3]

That wasn't the only thing that set Juettner apart. While most counterfeiters went for the big score—churning out a glut of ten-, twenty-, or hundred-dollar bills—Juettner was the only modern-day forger who produced nothing but $1 bills. And he did it at a snail's pace, printing just enough bogus bucks to supplement his meager junkman income and keep himself and his pooch housed and fed.[4] Indeed, Emerich Juettner was a singular man, possibly the world's first and only frugal money faker.

Juettner turned to counterfeiting late in life, and then only out of necessity. The Austrian immigrant had arrived in the United States in his early teens. For several years, he earned a living by gilding picture frames. He eventually married, and he and his wife had a son and a daughter. In 1932, after the children were grown, Juettner took a job as the superintendent of an apartment building at Broadway and 99th Street. In his spare time, he tinkered with a series of inventions, none of which ever came to anything.

In 1937, Juettner's wife passed away. At the age of sixty-two, the little handyman was no longer able to keep up with the duties of a building super. He and his dog moved to a two-room, top-floor apartment on West 96th. Shortly afterward, Juettner began gathering and selling junk. He struggled to make a go of it for several months, but the junk business just didn't bring in enough money. That's when he decided to call on a different set of skills to supplement his income.

Back in Austria, Juettner had studied photoengraving, a procedure that involves exposing a photographic image onto a sensitized metal plate, developing the plate, and then etching it in an acid bath so it can be used to print copies of the original image. Late in the summer of 1938, Juettner sat down at his kitchen table and photographed a $1 bill. After transferring the image to a sheet of sensitized copper, he processed the plate and fitted it onto a small manually operated printing press he set up next to his sink. Gingerly, the old man cranked out a few faux greenbacks. They were quite possibly the worst looking counterfeits ever.[5]

Unlike professional counterfeiters, who use high-quality paper similar to the cotton and linen stock used for real currency, Juettner printed his fakes on inexpensive bond paper. In addition, his photoengraving skills were rudimentary at best. Numbers and letters on the bills were crudely shaped, and George Washington came out looking downright comical: his left eye was a black blob, like a cartoon character's, and the right eye made the father of our country appear to be Asian. Later, while retouching the image of his phony dollar, Juettner would misspell Washington's name, making it "Wahsington."[6] This truly was funny money, but Juettner just smiled at his handiwork and set the damp bills aside to dry.

In reality, Juettner's counterfeits didn't need to be perfect, for some very simple reasons. For one thing, no one would be looking for fake $1 bills. After all, what self-respecting forger bothered with singles? Then there was Juettner's clever method of passing off his bogus currency. Usually, he sought out a busy place to make his exchanges, such as the subway at rush hour, where a harried ticket agent wouldn't have time to inspect a bill. By purchasing a five-cent fare, Juettner got back 95 cents in real money. It was a sweet, if extraordinarily small-time, deal. In keeping with his philosophy of subsistence-level crime, he passed no more than one or two bills a day, and he never victimized the same establishment twice. He wanted to make sure that no one lost too much money because of him.[7] Juettner was a strange character all right—a crook with scruples.

By never hitting the same location twice, Juettner inadvertently lessened his chances of being caught. From November 1938 on, the old man spread his kitchen currency all over the Upper West Side, as well as in other parts of Manhattan and in surrounding locales—at bars, newsstands, and small shops of all sorts. It wasn't long before someone noticed the bogus bills. The first was spotted when a cigar-store owner tried to deposit one of Juettner's notes at his bank. The teller recognized it as a crude fake and informed the Secret Service.[8]

Originally part of the Treasury Department but now under the Department of Homeland Security, the Secret Service has been responsible for nabbing counterfeiters since 1865 (three decades would pass before the service assumed the role of protecting the president). The federal agency gave Juettner's phony currency a thorough analysis at its Washington, DC, headquarters (there must have been a lot of chuckles and head-scratching involved). The unknown New York money faker was assigned a case number—880—and agents began pursuing the perpetrator. Even though Juettner's output was miniscule, the feds employed all the government's resources, interviewing the merchants who'd been victimized and giving out stacks of warning notices.

Most counterfeiters quickly end up behind bars, but Emerich Juettner frustrated the Secret Service like no other forger before him. The feds actually wondered if their elusive quarry was toying with them as they fruitlessly pressed their most prolonged manhunt ever.[9] No doubt the agents would have slapped their foreheads in disbelief if they'd known that the brilliant felon they were after was a scrawny junk collector with a furry, tail-wagging sidekick. To top it off, Juettner wasn't even trying to elude them. His lack of greed simply rendered him invisible.

Years went by, and there was still no clue as to the mystery moneymaker's identity. Like a national game of Where's Waldo?, Juettner's humble homemade dollar bills cropped up all over the country, passed along by unsuspecting individuals and banks. In time, the under-the-radar counterfeiter began to acquire the aura of a legend. "Old Mr. 880" lawmen started calling him. Merchants who discovered that they'd accepted Juettner bucks came to prize them as souvenirs—a rarity in the annals of counterfeiting.[10]

Traditionally, counterfeiting has been regarded as one of the gravest of crimes, with correspondingly harsh penalties. Money fakers during the time of the Roman Empire risked having their ears, nose, or even more sensitive body parts lopped off. In Renaissance Europe, currency forgers were subject to being drawn and quartered and burned at the stake. In colonial America, convicted counterfeiters faced the good old-fashioned hangman's noose.[11]

The first counterfeiters—who go back to the beginning of recorded history—produced fake coins by plating base metal with a thin coating of gold or silver. With the advent of paper currency—thought to have originated, like everything else, in China—artists and engravers got into the act. The United States issued its first national paper currency during the Civil War, replacing a hodgepodge of different currencies issued by state banks. Naturally, the federal notes quickly became a target for forgers and have been ever since. A fortune in counterfeit bills is in circulation in this country at any given time, although more sophisticated security measures are making it harder to produce quality fakes.[12]

The practice of counterfeiting isn't limited to individuals. A greater threat comes from bogus currency produced by governments, which can be used to disrupt an enemy nation's economy. During the American Revolution, Great Britain inundated the breakaway colonies with phony Continental dollars (which gave rise to the saying "not worth a Continental"). In the Civil War years, the North distributed wagonloads of counterfeit Confederate money, causing hyperinflation in the South. North Korea is now believed to be the source of the most realistic counterfeit American currency, the so-called "superdollars."[13]

By 1947, the Secret Service had amassed more than five thousand of Emerich Juettner's primitive bank notes in its files. However, at the end of that year a series of coincidences soured the elderly counterfeiter's uninterrupted streak of good luck. In early December, Juettner was awakened in the night by his dog. A fire had broken out in his junk-filled rooms. The old man escaped from the burning apartment, although his little dog didn't make it. Rendered temporarily homeless, Juettner went to live with his daughter in Queens until his apartment could be repaired. The old man was distraught over the death of his dog, but he would soon face a graver issue.

While battling the blaze, firemen had tossed some of Juettner's belongings onto a trash heap next to his apartment building. A heavy snow soon buried the discarded effects. After the snow melted, some neighborhood boys came across a collection of printing plates and dollar bills. Thinking the bills were stage money, the boys divvied them up to use when they played poker. The father of one of the boys noticed the odd-looking notes and became suspicious. He took the bills to the local police station, where they were identified as the handiwork of the city's long sought, will-o'-the-wisp counterfeiter.[14]

Secret Service agents immediately interviewed the boys to find out where the illegal money and printing plates had come from. The agents traced the evidence to the apartment in which the recent fire had taken place, and on January 14, 1948, they collared Emerich Juettner when he returned to his rooms.[15] Inside the apartment, the agents found Juettner's printing press, photographic negatives of currency, tubes of ink, and a small amount of bogus money. Notorious Old Mr. 880 was done for at last.

The *New York Times* trumpeted Juettner's arrest on page one, under a headline that read "Snow, Fire Turn Up Elusive Suspect in 15-Year Crop of Bogus $1 Bills" (the paper overstated the time span by six years).[16] The Secret Service agents were taken aback when the genial counterfeiter freely admitted to his illicit activities. With a childlike lack of guile and his habitual toothless grin, Juettner explained that his little sideline was his way of making ends meet. To their surprise, the agents interrogating the polite, garrulous duffer found themselves taking a shine to him.[17] They didn't even lock the old guy up. Instead, they allowed him to return to his daughter's house on his own recognizance.

When the diminutive lawbreaker finally stood trial, he pleaded guilty (for some odd reason, he invented an eleventh-hour tale about a mysterious accomplice, which the authorities rightly dismissed as fantasy). He was given an extraordinarily lenient sentence of a year and a day in jail. The judge took Juettner's age and the absence of any prior criminal record into consideration in his decision. Juettner also had to pay a fine of, fittingly, one dollar—and not one of his own creations, either. The old rogue served four months behind bars before being released.[18] He then went back to living quietly with his daughter.

That might have been the end of Old Mr. 880's tale if a staff writer for the *New Yorker* hadn't taken an interest in his case. In 1949, St. Clair McKelway wrote a three-part series of articles about Juettner and the history of counterfeiting. Hollywood picked up on the story and bought the film rights. In 1950,

Twentieth Century Fox released the movie *Mister 880*, starring Edmund Gwenn in the title role. The elderly British actor was the perfect choice to portray a likable eccentric such as Juettner. It was just the sort of character Gwenn had played before, most notably in his Oscar-winning role as Kris Kringle in the original (1947) version of *Miracle On 34th Street*. (Gwenn's only other Oscar nomination was for his role in *Mister 880*, which also won him a Golden Globe Award.)

In the end, Emerich Juettner made as much money from the movie about his life as he made in all his years of manufacturing those laughable dollar bills.[19] Before he was celebrated in film, Juettner announced that his criminal career was over. In July 1948, he told reporters he'd given up counterfeiting forever. Flashing his toothless grin, the old gent offered an explanation. "There isn't enough money in it," he said.[20]

CHAPTER 28

IMPERFECT PITCH

Don Lapre

He appeared on our television sets late at night, standing, for no apparent reason, on an isolated beach in front of the rolling surf. A clean-cut young man with short dark hair and an insistent, almost hysterical manner, he was shrieking repetitiously about how to make a fortune by placing "tiny classified ads" in thousands of newspapers.[1] With his boyish looks and overwrought sales pitch—which never once mentioned what those tiny classified ads were supposed to be selling—he seemed like an overcaffeinated high school kid trying to convince his best buddy that setting the principal's car on fire was a swell idea. ("Come on, man, let's do it!")

The name of this seaside Eddie Haskell was Don Lapre (pronounced la-pree), and his strident television ad promoting his "Making Money" self-help package (available for the nominal fee of $39.95—marked down from $149.95!) first appeared in the early 1990s. The frequently aired infomercial touted get-rich-quick schemes related to newspaper advertising, 1-900 phone numbers, and the Internet, all explained in an impressive bundle of books, tapes, and videos Lapre had produced. (Offering testimonials about the effectiveness of the "Making Money" package was a bizarre collection of sad sacks that Lapre must have recruited directly from their parole hearings.)

In twenty years of hustling television viewers, Lapre reached surprising heights of notoriety, so much so that he was parodied on *Saturday Night Live,* which was unnecessary, since Lapre's frenzied TV ads were a form of self-parody. As a businessman, Lapre was never hesitant to take chances. His record included failed companies and fortunes won and lost. Like most manic personalities, Lapre kept charging ahead. "I fail at more things than anyone I've ever met," he said. "But I try more things than anyone I've ever met. I'm a good loser."[2] That last statement held true until the day his career as a pitchman ended in shocking fashion. On October 2, 2011, the forty-seven-year-old father of two committed suicide in an Arizona jail after being indicted for fraud.

For years prior to his arrest, the news media had lambasted Lapre as a smarmy huckster peddling questionable products and services. His friends and family, not surprisingly, portrayed him as a whiz-bang entrepreneur, one whose "greatest love was doing for others."[3] The evidence tilts toward the first characterization, but either way, as a pitchman, Lapre was part of a long and colorful tradition in American history, one that parallels the growth of our country and takes in a wild assortment of product-pushers—from frontier medicine show barkers to radio, television, and Internet "personalities" hawking everything from salvation to salad choppers. When it comes to the pitch, Lapre was just one voice among thousands shouting to the masses, hoping to sell us something we probably don't need but can't live without. Just dial this number now! And hurry—supplies are limited!

Americans have always been intrigued by a good pitch—the promise of getting something new and wonderful at a bargain price—even though we tend to scoff at these frequently cheesy commercial appeals. But no one can laugh at the money pitchmen generate. Television direct-response advertising—from two-minute spots pushing Chia Pets or oldies CDs to extended infomercials trumpeting exercise equipment, jewelry, cosmetics, and who knows what else— rakes in more than $100 billion a year (about 80 percent of which comes from women over forty).[4] Some sources credit Ron Popeil with the creation of TV direct-response advertising, which he began using in the 1950s to flog his Pocket Fisherman, Smokeless Ashtray, and countless other gadgets.

Whatever their era or product, successful pitchmen have always had one trait in common: the ability to persuade an audience. Their ethics, on the other hand, are as flexible as a politician's spine. The very word "pitchman" carries a negative connotation. It's essentially a synonym for swindler, despite the fact that there are plenty of reputable pitchmen around. The late Billy Mays—the burly, squeaky-voiced spokesperson for OxiClean and Orange Glo—investigated products before he agreed to sell them, to make sure that they did what they claimed.[5] Unfortunately, there's no correlation between a pitchman's ethics and his marketing skills. The operative principle is that no matter how shoddy the product, there's always a pitchman willing to foist it off on the public.

The reputation for dodginess attached to America's pitchmen goes back to the early 1800s, when snake oil salesmen began traveling from town to town peddling home-brewed elixirs and patent medicines purported to cure everything from tapeworms to toothaches, but which were often nothing more than water mixed with coloring and flavoring agents and a hefty dose of alcohol to keep the customers happy. Pitch artists such as Brother Jonathan, Silk Hat Harry, and Princess Lotus Blossom sold imaginatively named nostrums the likes of Kickapoo Indian Sagwa and Hamlin's Wizard Oil—right into the early decades of the twentieth century.[6] The larger medicine shows featured vaudeville-style troupes of musicians, singers, dancers, and other performers. Couching their sales pitch amid entertainment, the medicine shows foreshadowed modern radio and television advertising.

Exactly when Don Lapre joined the pitchman fraternity is debatable. If his later years are any indication, he was probably one of those kids who can con their friends into covering their paper route for them for pocket change. Lapre himself says he got his start in junior high. According to a biographical video, that's when he began selling bubble gum, which must have taken up most of his time, since he never finished school. Born in Providence, Rhode Island, in 1964, Lapre moved to Phoenix in 1971. His father was a house painter, and his mother worked at a quickie mart. Quitting high school during his senior year, Lapre went to work at a Gemco department store, rising to assistant manager. He later worked for his father's painting company.

Throughout his twenties, Lapre dabbled in business ventures of his own. In 1988, he started a dating service. It went bust in two months. In 1990, he and his wife of two years opened a credit repair service, which was quickly shut down by the Arizona attorney general's office for misleading practices.[7] After that, as Lapre tells it, he discovered the power of newspaper classifieds. He advertised a booklet he'd written that described how to make money by helping people get a refund from the federal government after they'd paid off their home mortgage. The ad reportedly generated $1,100 a day in book sales.[8] Lapre then began churning out a flurry of self-help manuals, published by a company he started called New Strategies (search "Don Lapre" on Amazon.com and you'll find nearly a hundred items).

Lapre's thin paperback manuals are printed with ruled lines to look like school notebooks. The relentlessly upbeat texts contain a good deal of useful, commonsense information, although many of the tips are painfully obvious—surround yourself with positive friends, make a list of things to do each day, and so on. Some pointers appear to have been written after a couple of mighty pulls on a bong. In *Small Ads, Big Profits: How You Could Turn $30 into a Fortune,* Lapre offered this insight on the best things to advertise in classified ads: "Make sure you're selling something that most people might want!"[9]

In 1992, Lapre began marketing a package of books and tapes as his "Making Money" kit, which he promoted in a thirty-minute infomercial called "The Making Money Show with Don Lapre." Along with classified ads, Lapre recommended 1-900 numbers—those special-interest lines dispensing everything from phone sex to psychic readings—as a great moneymaking opportunity. He assured viewers that they could earn $50,000 or more a month with their own 900 lines.[10] The secrets were all in his book *Profit Per Minute: How to Get into the 900 Number Business.* Best of all, Lapre would help his customers set up and run their 900 lines.

People who bought the "Making Money" package or set up 900 numbers through Lapre's company instantly found themselves riding a merry-go-round of sales pitches. Lapre's staff pushed numerous add-on products and services that could easily run into thousands of dollars. (Lapre was following his own advice: "Up-selling can make your ads big winners!")[11] Even after paying extra fees for Lapre's assistance and supplemental products, most customers realized little or no income from their 900 lines. Before long, they were flooding the Phoenix Better Business Bureau with complaints. Lapre—who was milking his "Making Money" kit for millions of dollars a year—argued that he had far more satisfied customers than unhappy ones, although there was no way of proving that claim.[12]

The first pothole on Lapre's highway to success came in 1994, when the State of Arizona hit him for $45,000 in unpaid unemployment and withholding taxes. A bigger bump came in 1997. That year, the IRS issued a lien of close to a million dollars against Lapre and his wife for delinquent taxes. Two years later, Lapre filed for bankruptcy for himself and his companies, showing a gap of $3.5 million between his assets and liabilities. A new, ill-conceived Internet-based product, combined with a disastrous investment in a Mexican resort, precipitated the financial collapse. Prophetically, when Lapre broke the news to his staff that they were being laid off, he told them he felt like committing suicide.[13]

It wasn't long, though, before Lapre emerged from the flames of his bankruptcy with yet another business concept. He entered into a partnership with a dodgy character named Doug Grant, a self-styled expert on dietary supplements. Grant came up with a new vitamin product on which Lapre bestowed the grandiose brand name of the Greatest Vitamin in the World. In 2004, Lapre began offering television viewers a chance to share in the bountiful profits to be made from selling the miracle vitamin ("Nothing like this has ever been seen before in the history of the world!" Lapre screeched in his infomercial).[14] All viewers had to do was pay him a $35 fee to become independent distributors of the vitamin, which they would sell online. Naturally, Lapre would help them set up and run their websites. According to Lapre's pitch, the distributors would be paid handsomely for their Internet sales and for recruiting other agents.

More than 226,000 people signed up, only to discover that their initial investment was merely a ticket to the merry-go-round. As he did with his 900-number program, Lapre pestered his vitamin distributors to purchase costly marketing products that did little other than fatten the company's bottom line. Few distributors made money from the Greatest Vitamin in the World. Between 2004 and 2007, the company collected nearly $52 million in fees and other charges from its independent agents. For their sales and recruitment efforts, about five thousand distributors received a little over $6.3 million in commissions, an average of $1,260 per person. Lapre took home $2.27 million in that four-year span.[15]

All along, Lapre had been doing his best to convince the public that his product actually was the world's greatest vitamin, suggesting that it could prevent or cure cancer, heart disease, and a number of other serious illnesses. The Food and Drug Administration admonished him to stop making such outrageous, unsubstantiated statements.[16] The Greatest Vitamin in the World, analysts found, contained nothing that wasn't available in less expensive vitamins sold at any drugstore. Following a rash of complaints from Lapre's independent distributors, federal authorities forced Lapre to close his vitamin business in 2007. Four years later, a grand jury indicted the pitchman on charges related to the company's activities.

On June 22, 2011, Lapre was scheduled to appear before the US District Court in Arizona, where he was to be arraigned on forty-one counts of conspiracy, mail and wire fraud, and money laundering.[17] He failed to show up. A judge immediately issued a bench warrant for Lapre's arrest. The next day, US marshals apprehended Lapre outside a health club in Tempe. Considered a flight risk, he was held without bond at a federal facility in Florence, Arizona. On October 2, two days before the start of his trial, guards found Lapre's lifeless body in his cell. He had slit his throat and bled to death. (Before his arrest, Lapre had tried to sever a femoral artery in his groin.)

Lapre's mother stated that her son had been seriously depressed, and that prison officials had taken away his medications.[18] It's impossible to know if that's what led to his suicide, although the fact that he'd already tried to kill himself before he was arrested attests to a preexisting state of mental distress. The anxiety over his latest setback may have simply become too much for him to bear. More likely, it was the fear of what he faced in his trial that caused Lapre to take his own life. Each of the forty-one counts against him carried fines ranging from $250,000 to $500,000 and jail terms of five to twenty-five years. If he'd been convicted, he might have spent most or all of his remaining years in prison.

There's also the possibility that Lapre was racked with guilt over all the money he'd made by taking advantage of people through his infomercials, although that seems remote. It's a truism that pitchmen—the slippery ones anyway—have a low regard for the "yokels" who fall for their spiels. Such contempt is almost understandable, considering how gullible some folks can be. Even highly intelligent people occasionally overlook the fact that much of the merchandise pitched in direct-response advertising is comparable to the gimcrack you might win at a carnival. But then, if people weren't so credulous, infomercials couldn't pay for the cost of airtime.

As always, the best counsel for any shopper is the familiar adage, "If it sounds too good to be true, it probably is." Still, watching Don Lapre on YouTube, it's easy to see how someone could be swept up by his performance. Like any good pitchman, Lapre had charm—in his case, a boyish enthusiasm and relentless optimism that made you think his ideas could possibly work. It's clear he possessed a marvelously inventive mind. If only he'd used it to better purpose. But that would have been against his nature. More than one flimflammer has admitted that his biggest thrill comes from concocting some improbable scheme and pulling it off. "I just want to have fun creating ideas and selling them," Lapre once told a reporter.[19]

Like most wheeler-dealers, Lapre kept upping the wager with his businesses—taking bigger chances for greater rewards. If he'd stuck to publishing financial self-help books, it's probable that no taint would be attached to his name. He entered a different territory when he began pushing customers to buy an endless stream of 900-number add-ons and marketing online vitamin distributorships that cost more than they ever earned. Lapre frequently called himself the King of Infomercials. In truth, he was the king of up-selling and unfulfilled promises. For Lapre, inventiveness and ambition—those hallowed staples of capitalism—proved a volatile mixture.

The final years of Lapre's career bound him even more closely to the checkered saga of the American pitchman. By hawking his Greatest Vitamin in the World—whose very name was a lesson in excess—Lapre echoed the medicine show salesmen of old, with their shameless hyperbole. In a sense, Lapre's misfortune was to have been born a century too late. If he'd spent his career selling bottles of snake oil from the back of a wagon, nobody would have complained when the stuff didn't work as promised.

Lapre's death left the question about his essential nature open to debate. Was he guilty of fraud, or did he just tiptoe perilously close to it? Because he was never tried or convicted of a crime, his defenders can continue to argue that he was simply a wily businessman who was unfairly accused. "From what I've seen of Don, he doesn't appear to be a bad person," a former Lapre employee remarked in 2000.[20] That might have been true, but Lapre did seem to possess the one character flaw that separates an honorable pitchman from a trickster: a willingness to sell just about anything as long as it makes a profit.

NOTES

CHAPTER 1. MERCHANT OF MISERY—JAMES DEWOLF

1. Paul Davis, "Unrighteous Traffick—Living Off the Trade: Bristol and the DeWolfs," *Providence Journal*, March 17, 2006, p. A12. See also M. A. DeWolfe Howe, *Bristol, Rhode Island: A Town Biography* (Cambridge, MA: Harvard University Press, 1930), p. 68, and Calbraith B. Perry, "Descendants of Anthony De Wolf," reprinted from *Charles D'Wolf of Guadaloupe, His Ancestors and Descendants* (New York: Press of T. A. Wright, 1902), Gonzaga.edu, http://guweb2.gonzaga.edu/~dewolf/perry/chapter1.htm (accessed December 1, 2011).

2. *The African Slave Trade and the Middle Passage: Africans in America* [television series], PBS/WGBH Interactive, 1998, http://www.pbs.org/wgbh/aia/part1/1narr4.html (accessed November 28, 2011). See also Jay Coughtry, *The Notorious Triangle: Rhode Island and the African Slave Trade, 1700–1807* (Philadelphia: Temple University Press, 1981), p. 284.

3. Coughtry, *Notorious Triangle*, p. 284.

4. Ibid., p. 6. See also Paul Davis, "The DeWolf Family Burden," *Providence Journal*, February 3, 2008, http://www.c3.ucla.edu/newsstand/history-1/the-dewolf-family-burden (accessed October 31, 2011); Davis, "Unrighteous Traffick," p. A13; and "The DeWolf Family of Bristol, Rhode Island," Rhode Island Historical Society Postal History Collection, 2008, http://thesaltysailor.com/rhodeisland-philatelic/rhodeisland/stampless66.htm (accessed December 1, 2011).

5. Coughtry, *Notorious Triangle*, pp. 5–7. See also "DeWolf Family of Bristol," and "A Walking Tour through Bristol's African-American History," OnlineBristol.com, http://www.onlinebristol.com/walking-tours-of-bristol/a-walking-tour-through-bristols-african-american-history.html (accessed December 3, 2011).

6. Coughtry, *Notorious Triangle*, pp. 5–6. See also Davis, "DeWolf Family Burden"; "DeWolf Family of Bristol"; Thomas Norman DeWolf, *Inheriting the Trade: A Northern Family Confronts Its Legacy as the Largest Slave-Trading Dynasty in U.S. History* (Boston: Beacon Press, 2008), p. xii; Douglas Harper, "Northern Profits from Slavery," Slavery in the North, 2003, http://www.slavenorth.com/profits.htm (accessed October 30, 2011); and "Traces of the Trade: A Story from the Deep North; Background," PBS POV, June 24, 2008, http://www.pbs.org/pov/tracesofthetrade/background.php (accessed October 31, 2011).

7. "DeWolf Family of Bristol."

8. Coughtry, *Notorious Triangle*, p. 47. See also Davis, "DeWolf Family Burden"; Davis, "Unrighteous Traffick," p. A12; and "DeWolf Family of Bristol."

9. "Brown University Committee Examines Historical Ties to Slavery," Associated Press, March 5, 2004. See also, Harper, "Northern Profits from Slavery."

10. Coughtry, *Notorious Triangle,* p. 264. See also Davis, "Unrighteous Traffick," p. A12.

11. Coughtry, *Notorious Triangle,* p. 145. See also Davis, "Unrighteous Traffick," p. A12; and "DeWolf Family of Bristol."

12. Davis, "Unrighteous Traffick," p. A12. See also "DeWolf Family of Bristol," and Howe, *Bristol, Rhode Island,* p. 93.

13. Davis, "Unrighteous Traffick," p. A12.

14. Ibid. See also DeWolf, *Inheriting the Trade,* p. 45, and "Traces of the Trade: A Story from the Deep North; Background."

15. Davis, "Unrighteous Traffick," p. A12. See also DeWolf, *Inheriting the Trade,* p. 45, and "Traces of the Trade: A Story from the Deep North; Background."

16. Katrina Browne, *Traces of the Trade: A Story from the Deep North* [film], PBS POV, 2008. See also Davis, "DeWolf Family Burden"; Paul Davis, "Slave Traders in the Family: Probing a Dark Past," *Providence Journal,* March 17, 2006, p. A13; and DeWolf, *Inheriting the Trade,* p. 52.

17. Davis, "DeWolf Family Burden." See also DeWolf, *Inheriting the Trade,* pp. 250–51.

18. Perry, "Descendants of Anthony De Wolf."

19. Howe, *Bristol, Rhode Island,* pp. 94–95.

20. DeWolf, *Inheriting the Trade,* pp. 55–56.

CHAPTER 2. THE CUTTHROAT CAPTAIN OF CAVE-IN-ROCK—SAMUEL MASON

1. Marilyn Davis, "River Pirates," *Perspectives,* Southern Illinois University Carbondale, Fall 2006, http://perspect.siuc.edu/06_fall/river_pirates.html (accessed October 27, 2011). See also Edward L. Lach Jr., "Mason, Samuel," American National Biography Online, February 2000, http://www.anb.org/articles/20/20-00644.html (accessed November 22, 2011); Otto A. Rothert, *The Outlaws of Cave-In-Rock* (Freeport, NY: Books for Libraries Press, 1970), pp. 43–44, 175; and Russell K. Skowronek and Charles R. Ewen, eds., *X Marks the Spot: The Archaeology of Piracy* (Gainesville, FL: University Press of Florida, 2006), pp. 233, 237, 244–45.

2. Davis, "River Pirates." See also Lach, "Mason, Samuel," and Skowronek and Ewen, *X Marks the Spot,* pp. 230–34, 237.

3. Raymond M. Bell, "Samuel Mason," The Raymond M. Bell Anthology, August 1998, http://www.chartiers.com/raybell/1995-mason.html (accessed December 20, 2011). See also Lach, "Mason, Samuel."

4. Bell, "Samuel Mason."

5. Lach, "Mason, Samuel." See also Bell, "Samuel Mason," and Skowronek and Ewen, *X Marks the Spot,* p. 230.

6. Rothert, *Outlaws of Cave-In-Rock,* p. 164. See also Skowronek and Ewen, *X Marks the Spot,* p. 230.

7. Davis, "River Pirates." See also Skowronek and Ewen, *X Marks the Spot,* pp. 234, 243.

8. "River Pirates [television program]," *In Search of History*, Gary Foreman Productions, History Channel, 1999. See also Lach, "Mason, Samuel," and Rothert, *Outlaws of Cave-In-Rock*, pp. 47, 175.

9. James Hall, "Hall on Frontier Outlaws," *Sketches of History, Life and Manners in the West*, 1835, reprinted by Hardin Co., Illinois: Folklore, Genealogy, and History Site, 2000, http://www. rootsweb.ancestry.com/~ilhardi2/hallonoutlaws.html (accessed December 20, 2011). See also Jon Musgrave, "Frontier Serial Killers: The Harpes," *American Weekend*, October 23, 1998, reprinted by Jon's Southern Illinois History Page, 1998, http://www.illinoishistory.com/harpes.html (accessed December 20, 2011); Frank Richard Prassel, *The Great American Outlaw* (Norman: University of Oklahoma Press, 1993), pp. 65–66; and Rothert, *Outlaws of Cave-In-Rock*, pp. 55–61, 87, 90.

10. Robert M. Coates, *The Outlaw Years: The History of the Land Pirates of the Natchez Trace* (New York: Macaulay Co., 1930), pp. 23–25. See also Prassel, *Great American Outlaw*, pp. 65–66, and Rothert, *Outlaws of Cave-In-Rock*, p. 61.

11. "Historic Earthquakes," US Geological Survey Earthquake Hazards Program, May 24, 2011, http://earthquake.usgs.gov/earthquakes/states/events/1811-1812.php (accessed January 4, 2012).

12. Coates, *Outlaw Years*, p. 144. See also Prassel, *Great American Outlaw*, p. 65.

13. Davis, "River Pirates." See also Skowronek and Ewen, *X Marks the Spot*, pp. 234, 243.

14. Davis, "River Pirates." See also "River Pirates [television program]."

CHAPTER 3. ARCHITECT OF A TRAGEDY—JOHN CHIVINGTON

1. Bob Scott, *Blood at Sand Creek: The Massacre Revisited* (Caldwell, ID: Caxton Printers, 1994), pp. 40, 63, 128, 168. See also Irving Werstein, *Massacre at Sand Creek* (New York: Charles Scribner's Sons, 1963), pp. 18–19, 121.

2. William J. Convery, "John M. Chivington," in *Soldiers West: Biographies from the Military Frontier*, ed. Paul Andrew Hutton and Durwood Ball (Norman: University of Oklahoma Press, 2009), p. 162. See also Patrick M. Mendoza, *Song of Sorrow: Massacre at Sand Creek* (Denver: Willow Wind Publishing Co., 1993), p. 90; Scott, *Blood at Sand Creek*, p. 139; and Werstein, *Massacre at Sand Creek*, pp. 19–20.

3. Werstein, *Massacre at Sand Creek*, pp. 29, 106, 112.

4. Convery, *Soldiers West*, pp. 150, 152. See also Scott, *Blood at Sand Creek*, pp. 31–32, and Werstein, *Massacre at Sand Creek*, pp. 115, 124–25.

5. "John M. Chivington," *New Perspectives on the West*, PBS, 2001, http://www.pbs.org/ weta/thewest/people/a_c/chivington.htm (accessed April 14, 2011).

6. Scott, *Blood at Sand Creek*, p. 127. See also Werstein, *Massacre at Sand Creek*, pp. 32–33.

7. Convery, *Soldiers West*, p. 162. See also Scott, *Blood at Sand Creek*, p. 167, and Werstein, *Massacre at Sand Creek*, pp. 45–47.

8. "John M. Chivington." See also Mendoza, *Song of Sorrow*, p. 99; Scott, *Blood at Sand Creek*, pp. 180–81; and Werstein, *Massacre at Sand Creek*, pp. 52–53, 58–60.

9. Convery, *Soldiers West,* p. 163. See also Scott, *Blood at Sand Creek,* pp. 151–53, and Werstein, *Massacre at Sand Creek,* pp. 71, 128.

10. Convery, *Soldiers West,* p. 163. See also Scott, *Blood at Sand Creek,* pp. 151–53, and Werstein, *Massacre at Sand Creek,* p. 88.

11. Werstein, *Massacre at Sand Creek,* p. 89.

12. Deborah Frazier, "Sins of Sand Creek," *Denver Rocky Mountain News,* September 15, 2000, pp. 7A–8A. See also Louis Kraft, "Major Ned Wynkoop Listened to His Heart and Attempted to Bring Peace to Colorado Territory," *Wild West,* December 2003, p. 70, and "The Sand Creek Massacre—Captain Silas S. Soule Letter to Major Edward Wynkoop regarding the Massacre [December 14, 1864]," KcLonewolf.com, 2005, http://www.kclonewolf.com/History/SandCreek/sc-documents/sc-soule-to-wynkoop-12-14-64.html (accessed March 30, 2011).

13. Frazier, "Sins of Sand Creek," p. 7A. See also Kraft, "Major Ned Wynkoop Listened to His Heart," p. 70.

14. "John M. Chivington." See also Mendoza, *Song of Sorrow,* p. 99; Scott, *Blood at Sand Creek,* pp. 156–57; and Werstein, *Massacre at Sand Creek,* p. 111.

15. Werstein, *Massacre at Sand Creek,* pp. 78–79.

16. Mendoza, *Song of Sorrow,* pp. 110–11. See also Scott, *Blood at Sand Creek,* pp. 155–56, and Werstein, *Massacre at Sand Creek,* pp. 88–89.

17. Kraft, "Major Ned Wynkoop Listened to His Heart," pp. 18, 20, 70.

18. Werstein, *Massacre at Sand Creek,* pp. 130–31.

19. Ibid., p. 156.

20. Convery, *Soldiers West,* p. 165. See also Werstein, *Massacre at Sand Creek,* pp. 158–59.

21. Mendoza, *Song of Sorrow,* p. 123. See also Werstein, *Massacre at Sand Creek,* p. 164.

22. Convery, *Soldiers West,* p. 167. See also Werstein, *Massacre at Sand Creek,* pp. 168, 173.

23. Gregory F. Michno, "The Real Villains of Sand Creek," *Wild West,* December 2003, pp. 22–29, 71.

24. Convery, *Soldiers West,* pp. 149, 164, 168. See also "John M. Chivington"; Mendoza, *Song of Sorrow,* p. 127; Scott, *Blood at Sand Creek,* pp. 31, 180–83; and Werstein, *Massacre at Sand Creek,* pp. 38–39.

CHAPTER 4. THE LATE, UNLAMENTED LITTLE PETE—FONG CHING

1. "The Queue Order in Early Qing Dynasty," Cultural China, http://history.cultural-china.com/en/34History5603.html (accessed October 1, 2011).

2. Richard H. Dillon, *The Hatchet Men: The Story of the Tong Wars in San Francisco's Chinatown* (New York: Coward-McCann, 1962), pp. 21, 314. See also Thomas S. Duke, *Celebrated Criminal Cases of America* (San Francisco: James H. Barry Co., 1910), pp. 107, 109–10; William B. Secrest, *California Feuds: Vengeance, Vendettas & Violence on the Old West Coast* (Sanger, CA: Quill Driver Books/World Dancer Press, 2005), pp. 192, 195–96; and "Story of Little Pete's Life," *San Francisco Chronicle,* January 24, 1897, p. 27.

3. Secrest, *California Feuds*, p. 175.

4. "The Chinese Experience: Timeline," PBS, 2003, http://www.pbs.org/becoming american/ce_timeline2.html (accessed October 13, 2011). See also Dillon, *Hatchet Men*, p. 80; Secrest, *California Feuds*, p. 175; and "Workers of the Central Pacific Railroad," *American Experience*, PBS, http://www.pbs.org/wgbh/americanexperience/features/general-article/tcrr-cprr (accessed May 15, 2013).

5. Secrest, *California Feuds*, pp. 186, 192.

6. Dillon, *Hatchet Men*, pp. 306–307. See also Secrest, *California Feuds*, p. 192.

7. "Chinese Highbinders," *Harper's Weekly*, February 13, 1886, http://immigrants. harpweek.com/chineseamericans/Items/Item129.htm (accessed September 30, 2011). See also Dillon, *Hatchet Men*, pp. 74–76, and Secrest, *California Feuds*, p. 176.

8. "Chinese Highbinders." See also Dillon, *Hatchet Men*, pp. 177–78, and Secrest, *California Feuds*, p. 176.

9. Secrest, *California Feuds*, pp. 177–81.

10. "Chinese Highbinders." See also Dillon, *Hatchet Men*, pp. 177–78, 182–83, 192–93.

11. "Chinese Highbinders." See also Dillon, *Hatchet Men*, pp. 17–18, 243–45; Ko-lin Chin, *Chinatown Gangs: Extortion, Enterprise, and Ethnicity* (New York: Oxford University Press, 1996), pp. 5–6; and Secrest, *California Feuds*, p. 193.

12. "Story of Little Pete's Life," p. 27.

13. Dillon, *Hatchet Men*, pp. 199–200, 308–309, 314–16. See also Duke, *Celebrated Criminal Cases of America*, pp. 108–109, and Secrest, *California Feuds*, pp.194–95.

14. Dillon, *Hatchet Men*, pp. 326, 328–32. See also Duke, *Celebrated Criminal Cases of America*, pp. 111–12, and Secrest, *California Feuds*, p.198.

15. Dillon, *Hatchet Men*, p. 337.

16. "Barbaric Pomp for Little Pete," *San Francisco Chronicle*, January 27, 1897, p. 9.

17. Dillon, *Hatchet Men*, p. 337. See also Duke, *Celebrated Criminal Cases of America*, p. 112, and Secrest, *California Feuds*, p.199.

18. Dillon, *Hatchet Men*, pp. 337–39.

19. Ibid., p. 339.

20. "'Most Notorious Highbinder in America' Loses His Long Fight against Deportation," *San Francisco Chronicle*, October 3, 1915, p. 1.

21. C. N. Le, "Asian American Gangs," Asian-Nation, October 13, 2011, http://www.asian-nation.org/gangs.shtml (accessed October 28, 2011).

CHAPTER 5. THE KILLER THEY CALLED HELL'S BELLE— BELLE SORENSEN GUNNESS

1. Edward Baumann and John O'Brien, "Hell's Belle," *Chicago Tribune Magazine*, March 1, 1987, http://articles.chicagotribune.com/1987-03-01/features/8701170475_1_light-sleeper-aged-three-children (accessed September 15, 2010). See also Edward Baumann and John O'Brien,

Murder Next Door: How Police Tracked Down 18 Brutal Killers (Chicago: Bonus Books, 1991), pp. 293–313, and Joseph Geringer, "Belle Gunness," truTV, 2010, http://www.trutv.com/library/crime/serial_killers/history/gunness/index_1.html (accessed September 30, 2010).

2. Baumann and O'Brien, "Hell's Belle." See also Baumann and O'Brien, *Murder Next Door,* pp. 293–313; Jay Robert Nash, ed., *World Encyclopedia of 20th Century Murder* (New York: Paragon House, 1992), pp. 255–61; "Scenes at the Indiana Murder Farm," *Richmond Times-Dispatch,* June 1, 1908, p. 3; and Kerry Segrave, *Women Serial and Mass Murderers: A Worldwide Reference, 1580 through 1990* (Jefferson, NC: McFarland & Co., 1992), pp. 155–61.

3. Baumann and O'Brien, "Hell's Belle." See also Baumann and O'Brien, *Murder Next Door,* pp. 293–313; Geringer, "Belle Gunness"; Nash, *World Encyclopedia of 20th Century Murder,* pp. 255–61; and Segrave, *Women Serial and Mass Murderers,* pp. 155–61.

4. Baumann and O'Brien, "Hell's Belle." See also Baumann and O'Brien, *Murder Next Door,* p. 300; "The Legend of Belle Gunness," La Porte County Public Library, May 15, 2003, http://www.alco.org/libraries/lcpl/belle.html (accessed September 23, 2010); and Segrave, *Women Serial and Mass Murderers,* p. 156.

5. Baumann and O'Brien, "Hell's Belle." See also Baumann and O'Brien, *Murder Next Door,* p. 300; "The Legend of Belle Gunness"; and Segrave, *Women Serial and Mass Murderers,* p. 156.

6. Baumann and O'Brien, "Hell's Belle." See also Baumann and O'Brien, *Murder Next Door,* p. 298, and Nash, *World Encyclopedia of 20th Century Murder,* p. 255.

7. "The Legend of Belle Gunness."

8. Baumann and O'Brien, "Hell's Belle." See also Geringer, "Belle Gunness," and Nash, *World Encyclopedia of 20th Century Murder,* p. 255.

9. Nash, *World Encyclopedia of 20th Century Murder,* p. 255.

10. "Scenes at the Indiana Murder Farm," p. 3.

11. "Mrs. Gunness Alive," *New York Tribune,* May 10, 1908, p. 8.

12. Baumann and O'Brien, *Murder Next Door,* p. 297. See also Nash, *World Encyclopedia of 20th Century Murder,* p. 256.

13. Nash, *World Encyclopedia of 20th Century Murder,* p. 256.

14. Baumann and O'Brien, *Murder Next Door,* p. 307. See also Nash, *World Encyclopedia of 20th Century Murder,* p. 260.

15. Segrave, *Women Serial and Mass Murderers,* p. 159.

16. Nash, *World Encyclopedia of 20th Century Murder,* p. 258.

17. Baumann and O'Brien, "Hell's Belle." See also Nash, *World Encyclopedia of 20th Century Murder,* pp. 258, 260

18. "Mrs. Gunness Alive," p. 8. See also "Scenes around La Porte's 'House of Horrors,'" *Washington Times,* May 9, 1908, p. 2, and "Scenes at the Indiana Murder Farm," p. 3.

19. Baumann and O'Brien, "Hell's Belle." See also "The Legend of Belle Gunness."

20. "The Legend of Belle Gunness." See also Nash, *World Encyclopedia of 20th Century Murder,* p. 260.

21. "Mrs. Gunness Alive," p. 8.

22. Lillian De La Torre, *The Truth about Belle Gunness* (New York: Gold Medal Books, 1955), cover. See also "Gold Medal Books 487," flickr, http://www.flickr.com/photos/56781833@N06/5301109044 (accessed July 9, 2011).

23. Janet L. Langlois, *Belle Gunness: The Lady Bluebeard* (Bloomington, IN: Indiana University Press, 1985), p. 147.

24. Baumann and O'Brien, "Hell's Belle." See also "Scenes at the Indiana Murder Farm," p. 3.

25. Baumann and O'Brien, "Hell's Belle." See also Nash, *World Encyclopedia of 20th Century Murder*, p. 260.

26. "The Legend of Belle Gunness." See also Segrave, *Women Serial and Mass Murderers*, p. 156.

CHAPTER 6. PARTNERS IN PERFIDY—ISAAC HARRIS AND MAX BLANCK

1. "Biography: Harris and Blanck," *American Experience*, PBS, 2011, http://www.pbs.org/wgbh/americanexperience/features/biography/triangle-harris-blanck (accessed July 22, 2011).

2. "Introduction: Triangle Fire," *American Experience*, PBS, 2011, http://www.pbs.org/wgbh/americanexperience/features/introduction/triangle-intro (accessed July 22, 2011). See also "Triangle Shirtwaist Factory Building," National Park Service, March 30, 1998, http://www.nps.gov/history/nr/travel/pwwmh/ny30.htm (accessed July 15, 2011).

3. "Biography: Harris and Blanck." See also "Introduction: Triangle Fire," and Doug Linder, "The Triangle Shirtwaist Factory Fire Trial," University of Missouri-Kansas City School of Law, 2002, http://law2.umkc.edu/faculty/projects/ftrials/triangle/triangleaccount.html (accessed July 3, 2011).

4. "Introduction: Triangle Fire." See also "Triangle Shirtwaist Factory Building."

5. "Introduction: Triangle Fire." See also Leon Stein, *The Triangle Fire* (Philadelphia: J. B. Lippincott Co., 1962), p. 25, and David Von Drehle, *Triangle: The Fire That Changed America* (New York: Atlantic Monthly Press, 2003), p. 164.

6. "The Triangle Factory Fire," Cornell University, 2011, http://www.ilr.cornell.edu/trianglefire (accessed July 22, 2011).

7. Ibid.

8. "Biography: Harris and Blanck." See also Allan Chernoff, "Remembering the Triangle Fire 100 Years Later," CNNMoney.com, March 25, 2011, http://money.cnn.com/2011/03/24/news/Triangle_fire_centennial/index.htm?hpt=C1 (accessed July 15, 2011); "Introduction: Triangle Fire"; "Triangle Fire [television program]," *American Experience*, PBS Station WGBH, 2011; and "Triangle Shirtwaist Factory Building."

9. "141 Men and Girls Die in Waist Factory Fire; Trapped High up in Washington Place Building; Street Strewn with Bodies; Piles of Dead Inside," *New York Times*, March 26, 1911, p. 2. See also, Stein, *Triangle Fire*, pp. 61–66.

10. Joseph Berger, "100 Years Later, the Roll of the Dead in a Factory Fire Is Complete," *New York Times*, February 20, 2011, http://www.nytimes.com/2011/02/21/nyregion/21triangle.

html?_r=1 (accessed July 15, 2011). See also Jon Kalish, "A Somber Centennial for the Triangle Factory Fire," NPR, March 24, 2011, http://www.npr.org/2011/03/24/134766737/a-somber-centennial-for-the-triangle-factory-fire (accessed July 16, 2011).

11. Marcus Baram and Andrea Stone, "Triangle Shirtwaist Co. Factory Fire's Legacy under Threat," HuffingtonPost.com, May 25, 2011, http://www.huffingtonpost.com/2011/03/25/triangle-shirtwaist-co-factory-fire-legacy_n_840835.html (accessed July 21, 2011). See also "Introduction: Triangle Fire," and "Triangle Shirtwaist: The Birth of the New Deal," *Economist,* March 17, 2011, http://www.economist.com/node/18396085?story_id=18396085 (accessed July 23, 2011).

12. "Biography: Harris and Blanck." See also "Introduction: Triangle Fire," and Linder, "Triangle Shirtwaist Factory Fire Trial."

13. "Biography: Harris and Blanck." See also Linder, "Triangle Shirtwaist Factory Fire Trial."

14. "Biography: Harris and Blanck." See also "Introduction: Triangle Fire"; Linder, "Triangle Shirtwaist Factory Fire Trial"; and Von Drehle, *Triangle: The Fire That Changed America,* p. 164.

15. Linder, "Triangle Shirtwaist Factory Fire Trial." See also Stein, *Triangle Fire,* pp. 201–203.

16. Linder, "Triangle Shirtwaist Factory Fire Trial." See also "Triangle Witnesses Got Increased Pay," *New York Times,* December 22, 1911, p. 7.

17. "Biography: Harris and Blanck."

18. Linder, "Triangle Shirtwaist Factory Fire Trial."

19. Baram and Stone, "Triangle Shirtwaist Co. Factory Fire's Legacy under Threat." See also "Biography: Harris and Blanck."

20. "Introduction: Triangle Fire." See also Linder, "Triangle Shirtwaist Factory Fire Trial," and "Triangle Shirtwaist: The Birth of the New Deal."

21. "Triangle Shirtwaist: The Birth of the New Deal."

22. Stein, *Triangle Fire,* p. 28.

23. Baram and Stone, "Triangle Shirtwaist Co. Factory Fire's Legacy under Threat." See also Gina De Angelis, *The Triangle Shirtwaist Company Fire of 1911* (Philadelphia: Chelsea House Publishers, 2001), pp. 102–103, and Suzanne Lieurance, *The Triangle Shirtwaist Fire and Sweatshop Reform in American History* (Berkeley Heights, NJ: Enslow Publishers, 2003), pp. 104–109.

24. Stein, *Triangle Fire,* p. 141.

CHAPTER 7. CHICAGO'S FLORIST-MOBSTER—DEAN O'BANION

1. James Doherty, "The Shooting of Dion O'Banion," *Chicago Tribune,* February 25, 1951, p. B4. See also T. J. English, *Paddy Whacked: The Untold Story of the Irish American Gangster* (New York: HarperCollins, 2005), p. 148; John H. Lyle, "'Kill Dion O'Banion'—The Mob Says It with Flowers," *Chicago Tribune,* November 26, 1960, p. 9; and Maureen M'Kernan, "In $10,000 Casket Dean Lies in State," *Chicago Tribune,* November 13, 1924, p. 1.

2. James O'Donnell Bennett, "Gangland: The True Story of Chicago Crime," *Chicago Tribune*, February 3, 1929, p. 1. See also English, *Paddy Whacked*, p. 144, and "Girl an O'Banion Death Clue," *Chicago Tribune*, November 11, 1924, p. 1.

3. Tim Dirks, "Filmsite Movie Review: *The Public Enemy* (1931)," AMC Filmsite, http://www.filmsite.org/publ.html (accessed March 11, 2012). See also Rose Keefe, *Guns and Roses: The Untold Story of Dean O'Banion, Chicago's Big Shot before Al Capone* (Nashville, TN: Cumberland House, 2003), p. 278.

4. Laurence Bergreen, *Capone: The Man and the Era* (New York: Simon & Schuster, 1994), p. 129. See also English, *Paddy Whacked*, p. 140; Lyle, "'Kill Dion O'Banion,'" p. 9; and Jay Robert Nash, *Bloodletters and Badmen: A Narrative Encyclopedia of American Criminals from the Pilgrims to the Present* (New York: M. Evans and Co.: 1995), p. 473.

5. Herbert Asbury, *Gem of the Prairie: An Informal History of the Chicago Underworld* (DeKalb, IL: Northern Illinois University Press, 1986), pp. 344–45. See also "Dean O'Banion Online," DeanOBanion.com, http://www.deanobanion.com (accessed March 8, 2012); English, *Paddy Whacked*, p. 137; Keefe, *Guns and Roses*, pp. 126, 153–54; and Nash, *Bloodletters and Badmen*, p. 474.

6. Keefe, *Guns and Roses*, p. 72. See also Steve Mills, "Vending Violence in a '.38-caliber Circulation Drive,'" *Chicago Tribune*, June 8, 1997, http://articles.chicagotribune.com/1997-06-08/news/9706300093_1_walter-h-annenberg-circulation-william-randolph-hearst (accessed March 16, 2012).

7. English, *Paddy Whacked*, p. 144. See also Keefe, *Guns and Roses*, p. 32–34, and Robert J. Schoenberg, *Mr. Capone* (New York: William Morrow, 1992), p. 107.

8. Asbury, *Gem of the Prairie*, p. 344. See also English, *Paddy Whacked*, p. 144; "Indict O'Banion, Lieut. M. Grady in Rum Scandal," *Chicago Tribune*, May 30, 1924, p. 3; and Nash, *Bloodletters and Badmen*, p. 475.

9. Asbury, *Gem of the Prairie*, p. 344. See also Bergreen, *Capone*, p. 129, and "Chicago Remains to Be Seen: Dean O'Banion," Cemeteryguide.com, http://cemeteryguide.com/obanion.html (accessed March 8, 2012).

10. English, *Paddy Whacked*, p. 137. See also Schoenberg, *Mr. Capone*, pp. 104–105.

11. Nash, *Bloodletters and Badmen*, p. 476.

12. Asbury, *Gem of the Prairie*, pp. 348–49. See also English, *Paddy Whacked*, pp. 140–41, and Keefe, *Guns and Roses*, pp. xix, 181–83.

13. Nash, *Bloodletters and Badmen*, p. 477. See also Schoenberg, *Mr. Capone*, pp. 117–20.

14. "The Age of the Rum Runner Passes with Repeal," *Chicago Tribune*, June 17, 1934, p. G4. See also Associated Press, "Capone Dead at 48; Dry Era Gang Chief," On This Day: January 26, 1947, *New York Times*, 2011, http://www.nytimes.com/learning/general/onthisday/bday/0117.html (accessed March17, 2012), and "O'Banion Gang like Pirates of Olden Days," *Chicago Tribune*, November 11, 1924, p. 3.

15. "The Age of the Rum Runner Passes with Repeal," p. G4. See also William Helmer with Rick Mattix, *Public Enemies: America's Criminal Past, 1919–1940* (New York: Facts on File, 1998), pp. 88–89.

16. Mark H. Haller, "Capone, Al," American National Biography Online, February 2000, http://www.anb.org/articles/20/20-00146.html (accessed February 26, 2012). See also "38 Slain in Four Years of Inter-Gang Warfare," *Chicago Tribune,* February 15, 1929, p. 2.

17. "The Age of the Rum Runner Passes with Repeal," p. G4.

18. "Dean O'Banion Online." See also Keefe, *Guns and Roses,* pp. 3–4, 161–63, 168–69, and Schoenberg, *Mr. Capone,* p. 109.

19. James Doherty, "Thousands at Funeral," *Chicago Tribune,* November 15, 1924, p. 1.

20. Ibid.

21. English, *Paddy Whacked,* p. 137. See also M'Kernan, "In $10,000 Casket Dean Lies in State," p. 4, and Nash, *Bloodletters and Badmen,* p. 478.

22. "Girl an O'Banion Death Clue," p. 1.

CHAPTER 8. A HUCKSTER'S RISE AND FALL—JOHN BRINKLEY

1. Gene Fowler and Bill Crawford, *Border Radio: Quacks, Yodelers, Pitchmen, Psychics, and Other Amazing Broadcasters of the American Airwaves* (Austin: University of Texas Press, 2004), p. 20. See also Alton R. Lee, *The Bizarre Careers of John R. Brinkley* (Lexington: University Press of Kentucky, 2002), pp. 30–31.

2. Fowler and Crawford, *Border Radio,* pp. 16–18. See also Joe Schwarcz, *The Genie in the Bottle* (New York: Henry Holt & Co., 2001), pp. 282–86.

3. Fowler and Crawford, *Border Radio,* pp. 61–65. See also Lee, *Bizarre Careers of John R. Brinkley,* pp. xv, 218, 236.

4. Lee, *Bizarre Careers of John R. Brinkley,* p. 20.

5. Ibid.

6. Ibid., pp. 23–24.

7. Joe Schwarcz, "The Goat Gland Doctor: The Story of John R. Brinkley," Quackwatch, April 17, 2002, http://www.quackwatch.com/11Ind/brinkley.html (accessed October 19, 2009).

8. Lee, *Bizarre Careers of John R. Brinkley,* pp. 35–36.

9. Fowler and Crawford, *Border Radio,* p. 24. See also Steve Fry, "'Goat Gland Doctor' Memorialized," *Topeka Capital-Journal,* September 16, 2002, http://findarticles.com/p/articles/mi_qn4179/is_20020916/ai_n11787293 (accessed October 19, 2009); Lee, *Bizarre Careers of John R. Brinkley,* p. 46; and Schwarcz, "Goat Gland Doctor."

10. Fry, "'Goat Gland Doctor' Memorialized."

11. Ibid. See also Lee, *Bizarre Careers of John R. Brinkley,* pp. 76–77, 80, and Schwarcz, "Goat Gland Doctor."

12. Pope Brock, *Charlatan: America's Most Dangerous Huckster, the Man Who Pursued Him, and the Age of Flimflam* (New York: Three River Press, 2008), p. 274.

13. Fowler and Crawford, *Border Radio,* pp. 27–28. See also Lee, *Bizarre Careers of John R. Brinkley,* pp. 127–31.

14. Fowler and Crawford, *Border Radio,* pp. 17–18, 28. See also Lee, *Bizarre Careers of John R. Brinkley,* pp. 155, 158.

15. Lee, *Bizarre Careers of John R. Brinkley,* p. 187.

16. Fowler and Crawford, *Border Radio,* pp. 61–65. See also Lee, *Bizarre Careers of John R. Brinkley,* p. 218.

17. Brock, *Charlatan,* p. 274. See also Lee, *Bizarre Careers of John R. Brinkley,* p. 218.

18. Lee, *Bizarre Careers of John R. Brinkley,* pp. 243–44.

19. Brock, *Charlatan,* p. 274.

CHAPTER 9. HITCHCOCK'S HIDEOUS INSPIRATION—ED GEIN

1. Robert Enstad, "Judge Digs up the Ed Gein Case," *Chicago Tribune,* January 27, 1982, p. B1. See also Robert H. Gollmar, *Edward Gein: America's Most Bizarre Murderer* (Delavan, WI: Chas. Hallberg & Co., 1981), pp. vii, xv, and Harold Schechter, *Deviant: The Shocking True Story of Ed Gein, the Original "Psycho"* (New York: Pocket Books, 1998), p. 134.

2. George Bliss, "Tell Gein's Crime Motive," *Chicago Tribune,* November 21, 1957, p. 1. See also Enstad, "Judge Digs Up the Ed Gein Case," p. B1; Gollmar, *Edward Gein,* pp. vii, xv; and Schechter, *Deviant,* pp. xii, 132–34.

3. Rachael Bell and Marilyn Bardsley, "Ed Gein: The Inspiration for Buffalo Bill and Psycho," truTV Crime Library, http://www.trutv.com/library/crime/serial_killers/notorious/gein/bill_1.html (accessed November 8, 2011). See also Schechter, *Deviant,* pp. 10–13, 17.

4. Schechter, *Deviant,* pp. 19–20.

5. Ibid., pp. 25–26, 37.

6. Bell and Bardsley, "Ed Gein." See also Schechter, *Deviant,* pp. 31, 36–39, 43–46.

7. Schechter, *Deviant,* pp. 36–37, 66–67.

8. Gollmar, *Edward Gein,* pp. 30, 34. See also Schechter, *Deviant,* pp. 76–82.

9. Joe Adonis and Jim Jones, *American Villains,* vol. 1 (Pasadena, CA: Salem Press, 2008), pp. 217–18. See also Bliss, "Tell Gein's Crime Motive," p. 1; Gollmar, *Edward Gein,* pp. 34, 53–56; and Schechter, *Deviant,* pp. 79–80, 123–24, 133.

10. Bell and Bardsley, "Ed Gein." See also Bliss, "Tell Gein's Crime Motive," p. 1; Gollmar, *Edward Gein,* pp. 52–53; Joseph McNamara, *The Justice Story: True Tales of Murder, Mystery, Mayhem* (New York: Bannon Multimedia Group, 2000), p. 40; and Schechter, *Deviant,* p. 133.

11. Bell and Bardsley, "Ed Gein." See also, Thomas Powers, "Hogan Slaying Re-Enacted by 'Butcher' Gein," *Chicago Tribune,* November 24, 1957, p. 37.

12. "Ed Gein Sweet to Woman He Asked to Wed," *Chicago Tribune,* November 21, 1957, p. 3.

13. "Bare Boyhood Obsession of 'Butcher Gein,'" *Chicago Tribune,* November 19, 1957, p. 8. See also "Enough of Gein," *Chicago Tribune,* November 22, 1957, p. 14, and "5 Slain on Murder Farm," *Chicago Tribune,* November 18, 1957, p. 1.

14. Bell and Bardsley, "Ed Gein." See also Gollmar, *Edward Gein,* p. 49, and Schechter, *Deviant,* p. 97.

15. Bell and Bardsley, "Ed Gein."

16. Ibid. See also Schechter, *Deviant,* p. 224.

17. Adonis and Jones, *American Villains,* p. 218. See also Bell and Bardsley, "Ed Gein"; Schechter, *Deviant,* pp. 237–38; and Joseph W. Smith III, *The Psycho File: A Comprehensive Guide to Hitchcock's Classic Shocker* (Jefferson, NC: McFarland & Co., 2009), p. 12.

18. Adonis and Jones, *American Villains,* p. 218. See also Bell and Bardsley, "Ed Gein," and Smith, *Psycho File,* p. 12.

19. Enstad, "Judge Digs Up the Ed Gein Case," p. B1.

CHAPTER 10. SALEM'S RABID WITCH-HUNTER—WILLIAM STOUGHTON

1. Douglas O. Linder, "The Witchcraft Trials in Salem: A Commentary," University of Missouri-Kansas City School of Law, September 2009, http://law2.umkc.edu/faculty/projects/ftrials/salem/SAL_ACCT.HTM (accessed October 27, 2011). See also Marion L. Starkey, *The Devil in Massachusetts: A Modern Inquiry into the Salem Witch Trials* (Alexandria, VA: Time-Life Books, 1982), p. 155, and Sarah-Nell Walsh, "Bridget Bishop," Salem Witch Trials, University of Virginia, 2001, http://salem.lib.virginia.edu/people?group.num=all&mbio.num=mb1 (accessed February 16, 2012).

2. "Important Persons in the Salem Court Records: Executed," Salem Witch Trials, University of Virginia, 2002, http://salem.lib.virginia.edu/people?group.num=G01 (accessed February 16, 2012). See also Linder, "Witchcraft Trials in Salem"; Starkey, *Devil in Massachusetts,* p. 158; Charles W. Upham, *Salem Witchcraft, with an Account of Salem Village and a History of Opinions on Witchcraft and Kindred Subjects* (Mineola, NY: Dover Publications, 2000, reprint of 1867 edition), p. vii; and Walsh, "Bridget Bishop."

3. "Important Persons in the Salem Court Records: Died in Jail," Salem Witch Trials, University of Virginia, 2002, http://salem.lib.virginia.edu/people?group.num=G02 (accessed February 16, 2012). See also "Important Persons in the Salem Court Records: Executed"; Linder, "Witchcraft Trials in Salem"; Upham, *Salem Witchcraft,* pp. vii, 556–57; and Julie Zeveloff, "William Stoughton: Chief Justice of the Court of Oyer and Terminer," Cornell University, 2006, http://salem.lib.virginia.edu/people?group.num=all&mbio.num=mb40 (accessed February 9, 2012).

4. Richard R. Johnson, "Stoughton, William," American National Biography Online, February 2000, http://www.anb.org/articles/01/01-00863.html (accessed November 22, 2011). See also Linder, "Witchcraft Trials in Salem"; "William Stoughton, Lieutenant-Governor of Massachusetts," *The New-England Historical and Genealogical Register (1874–1905),* vol. 50 (Boston: New England Historic Genealogical Society, 1896), p. 11; Upham, *Salem Witchcraft,* pp. 556–57; Laurel Van der Linde, *The Devil in Salem Village: The Story of the Salem Witchcraft Trials* (Brookfield, CT: Millbrook Press, 1992), pp. 62–63; and Zeveloff, "William Stoughton."

5. Alyssa Barillari, "Tituba," Salem Witch Trials, University of Virginia, 2001, http://salem.lib.virginia.edu/people?group.num=all&mbio.num=mb29 (accessed February 16, 2012). See also Linder, "Witchcraft Trials in Salem," and Starkey, *Devil in Massachusetts,* pp. 8, 13.

6. Barillari, "Tituba." See also Linder, "Witchcraft Trials in Salem," and Starkey, *Devil in Massachusetts,* pp. 31, 41–43.

7. Linder, "Witchcraft Trials in Salem."

8. Peter Charles Hoffer, *The Salem Witchcraft Trials: A Legal History* (Lawrence: University Press of Kansas, 1997), p. 71. See also "Sir William Phips," University of Missouri-Kansas City School of Law, September 2009, http://law2.umkc.edu/faculty/projects/ftrials/salem/SAL_BPHI.HTM (accessed October 27, 2011), and Upham, *Salem Witchcraft,* pp. 483–84.

9. Hoffer, *Salem Witchcraft Trials,* p. 72. See also Johnson, "Stoughton, William"; "William Stoughton, Lieutenant-Governor of Massachusetts," pp. 10–11; and Zeveloff, "William Stoughton."

10. Douglas O. Linder, "Cotton Mather," University of Missouri-Kansas City School of Law, September 2009, http://law2.umkc.edu/faculty/projects/ftrials/salem/SAL_BMAT.HTM (accessed October 27, 2011). See also Linder, "Witchcraft Trials in Salem"; "William Stoughton, Lieutenant-Governor of Massachusetts," p. 11; Upham, *Salem Witchcraft,* pp. 556–57; Rachel Walker, "Cotton Mather," Salem Witch Trials, University of Virginia, 2001, http://salem.lib.virginia.edu/people?group.num=all&mbio.num=mb5 (accessed February 16, 2012); and Zeveloff, "William Stoughton."

11. "Giles Cory and the Salem Witch Craft Trials," Cory Family Society, 2010, http://coryfamsoc.com/resources/articles/witch.htm (accessed February 9, 2012). See also Linder, "Witchcraft Trials in Salem"; Starkey, *Devil in Massachusetts,* pp. 196–97; "William Stoughton," University of Missouri-Kansas City School of Law, September 2009, http://law2.umkc.edu/faculty/projects/ftrials/salem/SAL_BSTO.HTM (accessed October 27, 2011); Upham, *Salem Witchcraft,* pp. viii, 553, 556–57; and Van der Linde, *Devil in Salem Village,* pp. 11–12.

12. Linder, "Witchcraft Trials in Salem." See also Amy Nichols and Elizabeth Whelan, "Rev. George Burroughs," Salem Witch Trials, University of Virginia, 2002, http://salem.lib.virginia.edu/people?group.num=all&mbio.num=mb3 (accessed February 16, 2012).

13. "Giles Cory and the Salem Witch Craft Trials." See also Linder, "Witchcraft Trials in Salem"; Heather Snyder, "Giles Cory," Salem Witch Trials, University of Virginia, 2001, http://salem.lib.virginia.edu/people?group.num=all&mbio.num=mb6 (accessed February 16, 2012); and Starkey, *Devil in Massachusetts,* p. 217.

14. "Giles Cory and the Salem Witch Craft Trials." See also Linder, "Witchcraft Trials in Salem."

15. "Important Persons in the Salem Court Records: Died in Jail." See also "Important Persons in the Salem Court Records: Executed"; Linder, "Witchcraft Trials in Salem"; and Upham, *Salem Witchcraft,* p. vii.

16. Linder, "Witchcraft Trials in Salem." See also "Pardoning of Witches," State Library of Massachusetts, April 29, 2010, http://mastatelibrary.blogspot.com/2010/04/pardoning-of-witches.html (accessed February 23, 2012), and Van der Linde, *Devil in Salem Village,* p. 63.

17. Linnda R. Caporael, "Ergotism: The Satan Loosed in Salem?" *Science,* April 2, 1976, http://web.utk.edu/~kstclair/221/ergotism.html (accessed February 9, 2012). See also Linder, "Witchcraft Trials in Salem."

18. John Langdon Sibley, *Biographical Sketches of Graduates of Harvard University,* vol. 1 (Cambridge, MA: Charles William Sever, 1873), pp. 200–201.

19. "William Stoughton, Lieutenant-Governor of Massachusetts," p. 11. See also Emory Washburn, *Sketches of the Judicial History of Massachusetts from 1630 to the Revolution in 1775* (Boston: Charles C. Little and James Brown, 1840) p. 245.

CHAPTER 11. UNCLE DANIEL THE "SPECKERLATOR"—DANIEL DREW

1. Clifford Browder, *The Money Game in Old New York: Daniel Drew and His Times* (Lexington: University Press of Kentucky, 1986), pp. 2, 275. See also Peter C. Holloran, "Drew, Daniel," American National Biography Online, February 2000, http://www.anb.org/articles/10/10-00454.html (accessed February 13, 2010); Maury Klein, *The Life and Legend of Jay Gould* (Baltimore: Johns Hopkins University Press, 1986), p. 77; and Bouck White, *The Book of Daniel Drew: A Glimpse of the Fisk-Gould-Tweed Régime from the Inside* (Larchmont, NY: American Research Council, 1910), p. vii.

2. Browder, *Money Game in Old New York,* pp. 8–9.

3. Ibid., p. 12.

4. Ibid., pp. 35–37.

5. Ibid., pp. 37–39. See also Holloran, "Drew, Daniel," and Klein, *Life and Legend of Jay Gould,* p. 77.

6. Browder, *Money Game in Old New York,* pp. 40–44.

7. Ibid., p. 57.

8. White, *Book of Daniel Drew,* p. viii.

9. Holloran, "Drew, Daniel." See also Klein, *Life and Legend of Jay Gould,* p. 78, and W. A. Swanberg, *Jim Fisk: The Career of an Improbable Rascal* (New York: Charles Scribner's Sons, 1959), p. 30.

10. Browder, *Money Game in Old New York,* p. 1.

11. Tyler Anbinder, "Tweed, William Magear," American National Biography Online, February 2000, http://www.anb.org/articles/04/04-01002.html?a=1&n=William%20Tweed &d=10&ss=0&q=1 (accessed March 31, 2010). See also, Holloran, "Drew, Daniel."

12. White, *Book of Daniel Drew,* p. v.

13. Holloran, "Drew, Daniel." See also Klein, *Life and Legend of Jay Gould,* pp. 90–91, and Swanberg, *Jim Fisk,* p. 73.

14. Holloran, "Drew, Daniel." See also Klein, *Life and Legend of Jay Gould,* pp. 90–91, and Swanberg, *Jim Fisk,* pp. 75–79.

15. Browder, *Money Game in Old New York,* p. 274.

16. "About the University," University Information, Drew University, http://www.drew.edu/university.aspx (accessed April 1, 2010). See also Browder, *Money Game in Old New York,* pp. 1, 92, 120, 134; "Daniel Drew," All Biographies, http://all-biographies.com/business/daniel_drew.htm (accessed February 20, 2010); and Holloran, "Drew, Daniel."

17. Browder, *Money Game in Old New York,* pp. 275–76. See also Klein, *Life and Legend of Jay Gould,* p. 77.

18. Browder, *Money Game in Old New York,* pp. 38–39, 275. See also Ginny Jones, "Tramps & Millionaires," New Spirits, October 28, 2005, http://alfred.vassar.edu:8180/newspirits/tramps_millionaires (accessed March 3, 2010).

19. Jones, "Tramps & Millionaires."

CHAPTER 12. UNLEASHING THE JAMES-YOUNGER GANG—JAMES LANE

1. Albert Castel, "Kansas Jayhawking Raids into Western Missouri in 1861," *Missouri Historical Review,* October 1959, reprinted by Civil War St. Louis, November 15, 2003, http://www.civilwarstlouis.com/History2/casteljayhawking.htm (accessed July 30, 2009). See also Thomas Goodrich, *Black Flag: Guerrilla Warfare on the Western Border, 1861–1865* (Bloomington: Indiana University Press, 1999), p. 7; Edward E. Leslie, *The Devil Knows How to Ride: The True Story of William Clarke Quantrill and His Confederate Raiders* (New York: De Capo Press, 1998), p. 93; and Jay Monaghan, *Civil War on the Western Border, 1854–1865* (Lincoln: University of Nebraska Press, 1984), pp. 195–97.

2. Goodrich, *Black Flag,* p. 16.

3. Castel, "Kansas Jayhawking Raids." See also Goodrich, *Black Flag,* pp. 16, 24–26; "James Henry Lane (1814–1866)," West Film Project, PBS Station WETA, 2001, http://www.pbs.org/weta/thewest/people/i_r/lane.htm (accessed August 4, 2009); Leslie, *Devil Knows How to Ride,* pp. 11–12, 210; Monaghan, *Civil War on the Western Border,* p. 197; and "Obituary: James H. Lane, United States Senator from Kansas," *New York Times,* July 4, 1866.

4. Goodrich, *Black Flag,* pp. 16, 23. See also Monaghan, *Civil War on the Western Border,* p. 197.

5. Leslie, *Devil Knows How to Ride,* p. 11.

6. Castel, "Kansas Jayhawking Raids." See also "Dry Wood Creek," Battle Summary, National Park Service, http://www.nps.gov/history/hps/abpp/battles/mo005.htm (accessed July 31, 2009), and Monaghan, *Civil War on the Western Border,* p. 196.

7. Castel, "Kansas Jayhawking Raids." See also, Goodrich, *Black Flag,* pp. 17–18; Leslie, *Devil Knows How to Ride,* p. 92; and Monaghan, *Civil War on the Western Border,* p. 196.

8. Castel, "Kansas Jayhawking Raids." See also Goodrich, *Black Flag,* p. 18, and Leslie, *Devil Knows How to Ride,* pp. 92–93.

9. Goodrich, *Black Flag,* p. 18. See also Leslie, *Devil Knows How to Ride,* pp. 92–93, and Monaghan, *Civil War on the Western Border,* p. 196.

10. Marley Brandt, *The Outlaw Youngers: A Confederate Brotherhood* (Lanham, MD: Madison Books, 1992), pp. 3, 44. See also Albert Castel and Thomas Goodrich, *Bloody Bill Anderson: The Short, Savage Life of a Civil War Guerrilla* (Mechanicsburg, PA: Stackpole Books, 1998), p. 28; Goodrich, *Black Flag,* pp. 26–28; Leslie, *Devil Knows How to Ride,* pp. 93, 194; and Monaghan, *Civil War on the Western Border,* p. 196.

11. Brandt, *Outlaw Youngers,* p. 45. See also Castel and Goodrich, *Bloody Bill Anderson,* p. 28, and Leslie, *Devil Knows How to Ride,* pp. 193, 210.

12. Castel and Goodrich, *Bloody Bill Anderson,* pp. 28–29. See also Goodrich, *Black Flag,* pp. 77–79, and Leslie, *Devil Knows How to Ride,* pp. 201–203, 209.

13. Castel and Goodrich, *Bloody Bill Anderson,* p. 29. See also Goodrich, *Black Flag,* pp. 94–95, and Monaghan, *Civil War on the Western Border,* p. 286.

14. Brandt, *Outlaw Youngers,* pp. 49–50. See also A. Loyd Collins and Georgia I. Collins, *Hero Stories from Missouri History* (Kansas City, MO: Burton Publishing Co., 1956), pp. 121–22, 124; Robert L. Dyer, *Jesse James and the Civil War in Missouri* (Columbia: University of Missouri Press, 1994), pp. 37–38; Goodrich, *Black Flag,* p. 100; and Leslie, *Devil Knows How to Ride,* pp. 174–75, 257–58.

15. Collins and Collins, *Hero Stories from Missouri History,* pp. 124–25. See also Dyer, *Jesse James and the Civil War in Missouri,* pp. 37–38; Goodrich, *Black Flag,* pp. 97–98; and Leslie, *Devil Knows How to Ride,* pp. 258, 260–62.

16. Brandt, *Outlaw Youngers,* pp. 62–63. See also Dyer, *Jesse James and the Civil War in Missouri,* pp. 3, 50; Goodrich, *Black Flag,* pp. 135, 163–64; Leslie, *Devil Knows How to Ride,* pp. 378–79; and Phillip W. Steele and Steve Cottrell, *Civil War in the Ozarks* (Gretna, LA: Pelican Publishing Co., 1993), p. 109.

17. Brandt, *Outlaw Youngers,* pp. 4, 50–52, 65, 72–73, 167. See also Dyer, *Jesse James and the Civil War in Missouri,* pp. 1, 3, 50–51; Leslie, *Devil Knows How to Ride,* p. 379; and Steele and Cottrell, *Civil War in the Ozarks,* pp. 121–23.

18. Leslie, *Devil Knows How to Ride,* pp. 381–82. See also Monaghan, *Civil War on the Western Border,* p. 351, and "Obituary: James H. Lane."

19. Leslie, *Devil Knows How to Ride,* pp. 381–82.

CHAPTER 13.   LINCOLN'S MISSING BODYGUARD—JOHN PARKER

1. Margaret Leech, *Reveille in Washington* (New York: Harper & Brothers, 1941), pp. 378–80. See also Carl Sandburg, *Abraham Lincoln: The War Years,* vol. 4 (New York: Harcourt, Brace & Co., 1939), p. 257.

2. Leech, *Reveille in Washington,* pp. 387–88. See also Eric Martin, interpreter presentation, Ford's Theatre, National Park Service, July 2009, and Sandburg, *Abraham Lincoln: The War Years,* pp. 261–62.

3. Leech, *Reveille in Washington,* pp. 391–92. See also Sandburg, *Abraham Lincoln: The War Years,* p. 262; "Security," Mr. Lincoln's White House, Lincoln Institute, 1999, http://www.mrlincolnswhitehouse.org/content_inside.asp?ID=78&subjectID=3 (accessed July 12, 2009); and "Soldiers' Home," Mr. Lincoln's White House, Lincoln Institute, 1999, http://www.mrlincolnswhitehouse.org/content_inside.asp?ID=119&subjectID=3 (accessed March 15, 2010).

4. R. J. Norton, "John F. Parker: The Guard Who Abandoned His Post," Abraham Lincoln Research Site, December 29, 1996. http://home.att.net/~rjnorton/Lincoln61.html (accessed

June 15, 2009). See also "John Parker," Mr. Lincoln's White House, Lincoln Institute, 2002, http://www.mrlincolnswhitehouse.org/inside.asp?ID=63&subjectID=2 (accessed June 18, 2009); Emerson Reck, *Abraham Lincoln: His Last 24 Hours* (Jefferson, NC: McFarland & Co., 1987), p. 163; and Sandburg, *Abraham Lincoln: The War Years,* pp. 272–73.

5. Norton, "John F. Parker." See also Reck, *Abraham Lincoln: His Last 24 Hours,* p. 163.

6. Sandburg, *Abraham Lincoln: The War Years,* pp. 272–73.

7. Leech, *Reveille in Washington,* p. 382. See also Sandburg, *Abraham Lincoln: The War Years,* p. 257.

8. Martin, interpreter presentation. See also Norton, "John F. Parker," and Sandburg, *Abraham Lincoln: The War Years,* pp. 278–79.

9. "Ford's Theater," Mr. Lincoln's White House, Lincoln Institute, 1999, http://www.mrlincolnswhitehouse.org/inside.asp?ID=188&subjectID=4 (accessed July 8, 2009). See also Leech, *Reveille in Washington,* p. 278, and Martin, interpreter presentation.

10. William H. Crook, *Through Five Administrations: Reminiscences of Colonel William H. Crook, Body-Guard to President Lincoln* (New York: Harper & Brothers, 1910), pp. 72, 74.

11. Reck, *Abraham Lincoln: His Last 24 Hours,* p. 164. See also Sandburg, *Abraham Lincoln: The War Years,* p. 273.

12. Becky Rutberg, *Mary Lincoln's Dressmaker: Elizabeth Keckley's Remarkable Rise from Slave to White House Confidante* (New York: Walker, 1995), pp. 110–11.

13. Sandburg, *Abraham Lincoln: The War Years,* p. 273.

CHAPTER 14. SQUIRREL TOOTH ALICE—LIBBY THOMPSON

1. Laurence E. Gesell, *Saddle the Wild Wind: The Saga of Squirrel Tooth Alice and Texas Billy Thompson* (Chandler, AZ: Coast Aire Publications, 2001), p. 10.

2. Gesell, *Saddle the Wild Wind,* pp. 10, 199–200, 440. See also David H. Murdoch, *The American West: The Invention of a Myth* (Reno: University of Nevada Press, 2001), pp. ix–xii, 1–2, 10–11.

3. Gesell, *Saddle the Wild Wind,* pp. 20–22. See also Kathy Weiser, "Texas Madam Squirrel Tooth Alice," Legends of America, March 2008, http://www.legendsofamerica.com/we-squirreltooth.html (accessed June 12, 2011).

4. Gesell, *Saddle the Wild Wind,* pp. 21–24, 269. See also Weiser, "Texas Madam Squirrel Tooth Alice."

5. Gesell, *Saddle the Wild Wind,* p. 24. See also Weiser, "Texas Madam Squirrel Tooth Alice."

6. "Along the Chisholm Trail," TheChisholmTrail.com, http://www.thechisholmtrail.com/cont.htm (accessed August 5, 2011). See also "The Beginning of the Chisholm Trail," Chisholm Trail Heritage Center, 2009, http://www.onthechisholmtrail.com/trail-info (accessed August 4, 2011); Gesell, *Saddle the Wild Wind,* pp. 24–25; Jim Gray, "Abilene, Kansas," *Kansas Cowboy,* http://www.kansascattletowns.org/abilene/abilene_history.html (accessed August 4, 2011); and Weiser, "Texas Madam Squirrel Tooth Alice."

7. Gesell, *Saddle the Wild Wind*, p. 233. See also Kathy Weiser, "Painted Ladies of the Old West," Legends of America, January 2010, http://www.legendsofamerica.com/we-paintedlady. html (accessed August 4, 2011).

8. Gesell, *Saddle the Wild Wind*, pp. 220, 225, 236, 242–46, 269–70. See also Cy Martin, *Whiskey and Wild Women: An Amusing Account of the Saloons and Bawds of the Old West* (New York: Hart Publishing, 1974), pp. 22, 24; Michael Rutter, *Upstairs Girls: Prostitution in the American West* (Helena, MT: Farcountry Press, 2005), pp. 1, 18–24; Weiser, "Painted Ladies of the Old West"; and Weiser, "Texas Madam Squirrel Tooth Alice."

9. Gesell, *Saddle the Wild Wind*, pp. 207, 458. See also Rutter, *Upstairs Girls*, p. x, and Weiser, "Painted Ladies of the Old West."

10. Gesell, *Saddle the Wild Wind*, pp. 169–70, 272–73. See also Murdoch, *American West*, p. 1, and Kathy Weiser, "Wild Bill Hickok & the Deadman's Hand," Legends of America, January 2010, http://www.legendsofamerica.com/we-billhickok.html (accessed August 4, 2011).

11. Gesell, *Saddle the Wild Wind*, pp. 11, 84–86, 237. See also Martin, *Whiskey and Wild Women*, pp. 9–10, 162–63, 213.

12. Gesell, *Saddle the Wild Wind*, pp. 12, 25, 39–41, 50. See also Gray, "Abilene, Kansas"; W. R. (Bat) Masterson, "Ben Thompson and Other Noted Gunmen," reprinted by Legends of America, February 2010, http://www.legendsofamerica.com/we-benthompson.html (accessed August 4, 2011); Weiser, "Texas Madam Squirrel Tooth Alice"; and Kathy Weiser, "Wyatt Earp—Frontier Lawman," Legends of America, February 2010. http://www.legendsofamerica.com/we-wyattearp.html (accessed August 4, 2011).

13. Gesell, *Saddle the Wild Wind*, pp. 11, 226. See also Weiser, "Texas Madam Squirrel Tooth Alice," and Weiser, "Wyatt Earp—Frontier Lawman."

14. "Dodge City History," KansasCattleTowns.org, http://www.kansascattletowns.org/dodge_city/dodgecity_history.html (accessed August 7, 2011). See also Gesell, *Saddle the Wild Wind*, pp. 10–11, 25, 327–28, 338–39, 346, and Weiser, "Wyatt Earp—Frontier Lawman."

15. Gesell, *Saddle the Wild Wind*, pp. 12, 199–200, 440–41.

16. Ibid., pp. 10, 25, 328–29. See also Alfred Henry Lewis, "Bat Masterson—King of the Gunplayers," reprinted by Legends of America, December 2012, http://www.legendsofamerica.com/we-batmasterson.html (accessed January 11, 2013), and Weiser, "Texas Madam Squirrel Tooth Alice."

17. Gesell, *Saddle the Wild Wind*, pp. 325–26, 400, 411. See also Weiser, "Texas Madam Squirrel Tooth Alice."

18. Gesell, *Saddle the Wild Wind*, pp. 236, 400, 406–14. See also Weiser, "Texas Madam Squirrel Tooth Alice."

19. Gesell, *Saddle the Wild Wind*, pp. 433, 435, 440.

20. Ibid., pp. 432–33.

CHAPTER 15. THE LAWMAN WHO WENT BAD—BURT ALVORD

1. "Cochise County's Legendary Past Sprang from Three R's: Riches, Railroads, and 'Roughs,'" Cochise Pressroom, Cochise County, Arizona, http://www.explorecochise.com/press.php (accessed June 12, 2010). See also Douglas O. Linder, "The Earp-Holliday Trial," University of Missouri-Kansas City School of Law, 2005, http://www.law.umkc.edu/faculty/projects/ftrials/earp/earpaccount.html (accessed June 9, 2010); "Tombstone, Arizona," City of Tombstone, 2009, http://www.cityoftombstone.com (accessed June 11, 2010); and "Tombstone Courthouse State Historic Park," Arizona State Parks, http://azstateparks.com/parks/TOCO/index.html (accessed June 15, 2010).

2. Linder, "Earp-Holliday Trial." See also "Yesterday's Tragedy: Three Men Hurled into Eternity in the Duration of a Moment," *Tombstone Daily Epitaph,* October 27, 1881, reprinted by University of Missouri-Kansas City School of Law, http://www.law.umkc.edu/faculty/projects/ftrials/earp/epitaph.html (accessed June 9, 2010).

3. "Blazing Saddles (1974), Quotes," IMDb, http://www.imdb.com/title/tt0071230/quotes (accessed June 10, 2010).

4. Don Chaput, *The Odyssey of Burt Alvord: Lawman, Train Robber, Fugitive* (Tucson: Westernlore Press, 2000), p. 11, back cover. See also Carl Sifakis, *The Encyclopedia of American Crime,* vol. 1 (New York: Facts On File, Inc., 2001), p. 23.

5. Chaput, *Odyssey of Burt Alvord,* pp. 25, 29–30. See also Kathy Weiser, "Burt Alvord—Lawman Turned Outlaw," Old West Legends, Legends of America, November 2009, http://www.legendsofamerica.com/WE-BurtonAlvord.html (accessed June 14, 2010).

6. Chaput, *Odyssey of Burt Alvord,* pp. 33–34, 38–39. See also Sifakis, *Encyclopedia of American Crime,* p. 23, and Weiser, "Burt Alvord—Lawman Turned Outlaw."

7. Chaput, *Odyssey of Burt Alvord,* pp. 50, 52–53. See also Sifakis, *Encyclopedia of American Crime,* p. 23.

8. Weiser, "Burt Alvord—Lawman Turned Outlaw."

9. Chaput, *Odyssey of Burt Alvord,* pp. 37–38.

10. Ibid., pp. 62–65, back cover. See also James Harvey McClintock, "The Cochise Train Robbery," from *Arizona: The Youngest State* (Chicago: S.J. Clarke Publishing Co., 1916), reprinted by Legends of America, November 2009, http://www.legendsofamerica.com/az-cochiserobbery.html (accessed June 15, 2010); Sifakis, *Encyclopedia of American Crime,* p. 23; and Weiser, "Burt Alvord—Lawman Turned Outlaw."

11. Chaput, *Odyssey of Burt Alvord,* pp. 62–65. See also McClintock, "Cochise Train Robbery," and Sifakis, *Encyclopedia of American Crime,* p. 23.

12. Chaput, *Odyssey of Burt Alvord,* pp. 69–72. See also McClintock, "Cochise Train Robbery."

13. Chaput, *Odyssey of Burt Alvord,* pp. 81–86. See also Weiser, "Burt Alvord—Lawman Turned Outlaw."

14. Chaput, *Odyssey of Burt Alvord,* pp. 107–109, 116. See also McClintock, "Cochise Train Robbery"; Sifakis, *Encyclopedia of American Crime,* p. 23; and Weiser, "Burt Alvord—Lawman Turned Outlaw."

15. Sifakis, *Encyclopedia of American Crime*, p. 23. See also Weiser, "Burt Alvord—Lawman Turned Outlaw."

16. Chaput, *Odyssey of Burt Alvord*, p. 120.

17. Ibid., pp. 131–32. See also McClintock, "Cochise Train Robbery"; Sifakis, *Encyclopedia of American Crime*, p. 23; and Weiser, "Burt Alvord—Lawman Turned Outlaw."

CHAPTER 16. THE VERY MELLOW YELLOW KID—JOSEPH WEIL

1. W. T. Brannon, "The Wiles of the Yellow Kid," *Chicago Tribune*, December 12, 1948, pp. B5, 14. See also J. R. "Yellow Kid" Weil and W. T. Brannon, *"Yellow Kid" Weil: The Autobiography of America's Master Swindler* (Oakland, CA: AK Press/Nabat, 2011, reprint of 1948 edition), pp. 100, 293, and "Weil Loses His Sangfroid as Accuser Glares," *Chicago Tribune*, December 31, 1924, p. 9.

2. "Kid Weil Picks Bosom of Law as a Hideaway," *Chicago Tribune*, August 6, 1937, p. 1. See also Joseph McNamara, *The Justice Story: True Tales of Murder, Mystery, Mayhem* (Champaign, IL: Bannon Multimedia Group, 2000), p. 195; Mr. Weil's Art," *Chicago Tribune*, January 24, 1931, p. 10; and Weil and Brannon, *"Yellow Kid" Weil*, p. 293.

3. "Hustle: Con Jargon," BBC, April 2007, http://www.bbc.co.uk/drama/hustle/con_jargon.shtml (accessed November 5, 2011). See also Weil and Brannon, *"Yellow Kid" Weil*, pp. 288–89; "'Yellow Kid' out again, but the Law Is Waiting," *Chicago Tribune*, May 15, 1942, p. 2; and "Yellow Kid Says He'd Do It Again," *Chicago Tribune*, June 24, 1974, p. 7.

4. Brannon, "The Wiles of the Yellow Kid," p. B5. See also "'Yellow Kid' out again, but the Law Is Waiting," p. 2.

5. Brannon, "The Wiles of the Yellow Kid," p. B5. See also "Hustle: Con Jargon"; Patricia Leeds, "Yellow Kid Is Active—But Honest—at 91," *Chicago Tribune*, June 30, 1966, p. B10; Thomas Streissguth, *Hoaxers & Hustlers* (Minneapolis: Oliver Press, 1994), pp. 50, 57–58; Weil and Brannon, *"Yellow Kid" Weil*, pp. 22–30, 268, 293; and "Yellow Kid Says He'd Do It Again," p. 7.

6. Weil and Brannon, *"Yellow Kid" Weil*, pp. 3–4.

7. "Hustle: Con Jargon." See also Weil and Brannon, *"Yellow Kid" Weil*, pp. 18–20; "The Yellow Kid [comic strip]," Ohio State University Libraries, http://cartoons.osu.edu/yellowkid/index.htm (accessed November 3, 2011), and "'Yellow Kid,' Master Swindler Who Made Millions, Dies at 100," *Chicago Tribune*, February 27, 1976, p. 3.

8. Streissguth, *Hoaxers & Hustlers*, p. 58. See also Weil and Brannon, *"Yellow Kid" Weil*, p. 42.

9. Brannon, "The Wiles of the Yellow Kid," p. B5. See also "Hustle: Con Jargon," and Weil and Brannon, *"Yellow Kid" Weil*, pp. 62–67.

10. "Yellow Kid, 90, Has New Pitch," *Chicago Tribune*, July 1, 1965, p. A1.

11. Brannon, "Wiles of the Yellow Kid," pp. B5, 14. See also Weil and Brannon, *"Yellow Kid" Weil*, pp. 162–65.

12. Brannon, "The Wiles of the Yellow Kid," pp. B5, 14. See also Weil and Brannon, *"Yellow Kid" Weil,* pp. 165–73.

13. McNamara, *Justice Story,* pp. 196–97. See also Streissguth, *Hoaxers & Hustlers,* pp. 59–61, and Weil and Brannon, *"Yellow Kid" Weil,* pp. 78–83, 100–104.

14. Brannon, "Wiles of the Yellow Kid," p. B14. See also Weil and Brannon, *"Yellow Kid" Weil,* pp. 87–91, 119–26, 201–203, 283–84.

15. Brannon, "Wiles of the Yellow Kid," p. B5. See also McNamara, *Justice Story,* p. 198, and Weil and Brannon, *"Yellow Kid" Weil,* pp. 292, 295.

16. Streissguth, *Hoaxers & Hustlers,* p. 67. See also Weil and Brannon, *"Yellow Kid" Weil,* pp. 196, 288, 290; "'Yellow Kid,' Master Swindler Who Made Millions, Dies at 100," p. 3; and "Yellow Kid, 90, Has New Pitch," p. A1.

17. Weil and Brannon, *"Yellow Kid" Weil,* pp. 198, 288.

18. "Weil Loses His Sangfroid as Accuser Glares," p. 9. See also "Weil's Record," *Chicago Tribune,* October 26, 1918, p. 15, and "Yellow Kid Weil Wins Probation, but May Lose It," *Chicago Tribune,* Sept 19, 1925, p. 4.

19. McNamara, *Justice Story,* p. 197. See also "'Yellow Kid,' Master Swindler Who Made Millions, Dies at 100," p. 3; and Weil and Brannon, *"Yellow Kid" Weil,* p. 295.

20. Brannon, "Wiles of the Yellow Kid," pp. B5, 23. See also "Mr. Weil Voices a Yearning for Public Esteem," *Chicago Tribune,* February 27, 1930, p. 2; Streissguth, *Hoaxers & Hustlers,* pp. 69–70; Weil and Brannon, *"Yellow Kid" Weil,* pp. 268, 291; and "'Yellow Kid,' Master Swindler Who Made Millions, Dies at 100," p. 3.

21. Weil and Brannon, *"Yellow Kid" Weil,* p. 21.

22. Brannon, "Wiles of the Yellow Kid," p. B23. See also Patricia Leeds, "Crime Doesn't Pay Enough—Yellow Kid," *Chicago Tribune,* June 30, 1963, p. D24; "The Yellow Kid Goes to Court without Fear," *Chicago Tribune,* December 1, 1946, p. 39; and "Yellow Kid Says He'd Do It Again," p. 7.

23. "'Yellow Kid,' Master Swindler Who Made Millions, Dies at 100," p. 3.

24. "Yellow Kid, 90, Has New Pitch," p. A1.

CHAPTER 17. YOU BET YOUR LIFE—ALVIN THOMAS

1. Kevin Cook, "Golf's Greatest Hustler," *Golf Magazine,* January 2011, pp. 70–74. See also Kevin Cook, *Titanic Thompson: The Man Who Bet on Everything* (New York: W. W. Norton, 2011), pp. 1–2; Barry Horn, "He Could Sure Do the Hustle," *Dallas Morning News,* August 26, 2001, http://howtobeattheodds.com/SportsDay.html (accessed February 25, 2012); Dave Kindred, "The Myths of Titanic," *Golf Digest,* May 1996, p. 132; Carlton Stowers, *The Unsinkable Titanic Thompson: A Good Ole Boy Who Became a World Super Star Gambler and Hustler* (Burnet, TX: Eakin Press, 1982), pp. 105, 144–47, 164–65, 231; and A. C. Thomas with Edwin Shrake, "Soundings from Titanic," *Sports Illustrated,* October 9, 1972, pp. 96–112.

2. Tom Buckley, "Runyon Legend Makes a 'Guys and Dolls' Tale," *New York Times,*

October 4, 1980, p. 27. See also Cook, *Titanic Thompson,* pp. 1–2, 78; Horn, "He Could Sure Do the Hustle"; Kindred, "Myths of Titanic"; and Stowers, *Unsinkable Titanic Thompson,* pp. 106–107, 194–95.

3. Stowers, *Unsinkable Titanic Thompson,* p. 3. See also, Thomas with Shrake, "Soundings from Titanic," pp. 98, 112.

4. Thomas with Shrake, "Soundings from Titanic," p. 98.

5. Cook, *Titanic Thompson,* pp. 14–18. See also Kindred, "Myths of Titanic"; Stowers, *Unsinkable Titanic Thompson,* pp. 50–52; and Thomas with Shrake, "Soundings from Titanic," pp. 98–99.

6. Kindred, "Myths of Titanic." See also Thomas with Shrake, "Soundings from Titanic," p. 100.

7. Cook, *Titanic Thompson,* pp. 2–3. See also Horn, "He Could Sure Do the Hustle"; Kindred, "Myths of Titanic"; and Thomas with Shrake, "Soundings from Titanic," p. 100.

8. Thomas with Shrake, "Soundings from Titanic," p. 100.

9. Cook, *Titanic Thompson,* pp. 58–60, 71, 138–39. See also Kindred, "Myths of Titanic"; Stowers, *Unsinkable Titanic Thompson,* pp. 82–83, 86–87, 184–86; and Thomas with Shrake, "Soundings from Titanic," pp. 98, 102.

10. Horn, "He Could Sure Do the Hustle." See also Kindred, "Myths of Titanic," and Stowers, *Unsinkable Titanic Thompson,* p. 212.

11. Cook, *Titanic Thompson,* p. 117. See also Stowers, *Unsinkable Titanic Thompson,* pp. 15–16, and Thomas with Shrake, "Soundings from Titanic," pp. 111–12.

12. Cook, *Titanic Thompson,* p. 117. See also "Gamblers Testify to Rothstein Loss in Big Poker Game," *New York Times,* November 22, 1929, p. 1; Horn, "He Could Sure Do the Hustle"; Kindred, "Myths of Titanic"; "Rothstein Estate Wins $12,700 Suit," *New York Times,* December 31, 1929, p. 10; Stowers, *Unsinkable Titanic Thompson,* pp. 16, 34; and Thomas with Shrake, "Soundings from Titanic," p. 112.

13. Thomas with Shrake, "Soundings from Titanic," p. 97.

14. Cook, *Titanic Thompson,* pp. 145–46. See also Horn, "He Could Sure Do the Hustle"; Stowers, *Unsinkable Titanic Thompson,* pp. 128–31; and Thomas with Shrake, "Soundings from Titanic," p. 106.

15. Cook, *Titanic Thompson,* pp. 67–69. See also Stowers, *Unsinkable Titanic Thompson,* pp. 93–95, and Thomas with Shrake, "Soundings from Titanic," p. 102.

16. Cook, *Titanic Thompson,* pp. 70, 82, 151. See also Tom LeCompte, "The 18-Hole Hustle," *American Heritage,* August/September 2005, http://www.americanheritage.com/content/18-hole-hustle (accessed February 25, 2012), and Thomas with Shrake, "Soundings from Titanic," pp. 106, 111.

17. Thomas with Shrake, "Soundings from Titanic," p. 112.

18. Cook, "Golf's Greatest Hustler," pp. 72–73. See also Cook, *Titanic Thompson,* pp. 82–83, 151–52; Horn, "He Could Sure Do the Hustle"; LeCompte, "18-Hole Hustle"; and Stowers, *Unsinkable Titanic Thompson,* p. 225.

19. Cook, "Golf's Greatest Hustler," p. 72. See also Cook, *Titanic Thompson,* p. 151.

20. Cook, "Golf's Greatest Hustler," p. 70. See also Cook, *Titanic Thompson,* p. 151.

21. Cook, "Golf's Greatest Hustler," p. 72. See also Cook, *Titanic Thompson,* pp. 87–88, 150–51, and Horn, "He Could Sure Do the Hustle."

22. Kindred, "Myths of Titanic."

23. Thomas with Shrake, "Soundings from Titanic," p. 97.

24. Kindred, "Myths of Titanic."

CHAPTER 18. KEEPER OF THE IMMACULATE SPERM—CHARLES DAVENPORT

1. "Eugenics: Three Generations, No Imbeciles: Virginia, Eugenics & *Buck v. Bell*," Claude Moore Health Sciences Library, University of Virginia Health System, 2004, http://www.hsl .virginia.edu/historical/eugenics/index.cfm (accessed September 15, 2011). See also Stephen Jay Gould, "Carrie Buck's Daughter," *Natural History,* July 1984, pp. 14–18.

2. Edwin Black, "The Horrifying American Roots of Nazi Eugenics," George Mason University's History News Network, November 25, 2003, http://hnn.us/articles/1796.html (accessed August 30, 2011). See also Vince Carducci, "Heart of Darkness," PopMatters.com, September 17, 2003, www.waragainsttheweak.com/offSiteArchive/popmatters (accessed August 12, 2011); "Eugenics: Three Generations, No Imbeciles"; and Gould, "Carrie Buck's Daughter," pp. 14–18.

3. Black, "Horrifying American Roots of Nazi Eugenics." See also "Eugenics: Three Generations, No Imbeciles"; Gould, "Carrie Buck's Daughter," pp. 14–18; Daniel J. Kevles, "Eugenics," American National Biography Online, *The Oxford Companion to United States History,* 2001, http://www.anb.org/articles/cush/e0491.html (accessed August 30, 2011); and Tony Platt, "The Frightening Agenda of the American Eugenics Movement," George Mason University's History News Network, July 7, 2003, http://hnn.us/articles/1551.html (accessed August 30, 2011).

4. "Eugenics: Three Generations, No Imbeciles." See also Gould, "Carrie Buck's Daughter," pp. 14–18.

5. "Eugenics: Three Generations, No Imbeciles." See also Gould, "Carrie Buck's Daughter," pp. 14–18.

6. Black, "Horrifying American Roots of Nazi Eugenics." See also "Eugenics: Three Generations, No Imbeciles," and Gould, "Carrie Buck's Daughter," pp. 14–18.

7. Edwin Black, *War against the Weak: Eugenics and America's Campaign to Create a Master Race* (New York: Four Walls Eight Windows, 2003), p. 32. See also Carducci, "Heart of Darkness"; "Dr. C. B. Davenport, a Noted Geneticist," *New York Times,* February 19, 1944, p. 13; Stephen S. Hall, "Genetics and Genetic Engineering," American National Biography Online, *The Oxford Companion to United States History,* 2001, http://www.anb.org/articles/cush/e0601.html (accessed August 30, 2011); and Kevles, "Eugenics."

8. Black, "Horrifying American Roots of Nazi Eugenics." See also Black, *War against the Weak,* pp. 258–60, and *Race and Membership in American History: The Eugenics Movement*

(Brookline, MA: Facing History and Ourselves, 2002), pp. 245–47, http://www.traces.org/Teachers/Chapter_8_TheNaziConnection.pdf (accessed August 30, 2011).

9. Black, "Horrifying American Roots of Nazi Eugenics." See also "Dr. C. B. Davenport, a Noted Geneticist," p. 13; Hall, "Genetics and Genetic Engineering"; Oscar Riddle, *Biographical Memoir of Charles Benedict Davenport, 1866–1944* (Washington, DC: National Academy of Sciences, 1949), pp. 82–83; and "Topic: International Eugenics," Dolan DNA Learning Center, Cold Spring Harbor Laboratory, http://www.eugenicsarchive.org/eugenics/topics_fs.pl?theme=25&search=&matches= (accessed August 30, 2011).

10. Black, "Horrifying American Roots of Nazi Eugenics." See also Gould, "Carrie Buck's Daughter," pp. 14–18; Kevles, "Eugenics"; Platt, "Frightening Agenda of the American Eugenics Movement"; and Jan A. Witkowski and John R. Inglis, eds., *Davenport's Dream: 21st Century Reflections on Heredity and Eugenics* (Cold Spring Harbor, NY: Cold Spring Harbor Laboratory Press, 2008) p. 10.

11. Black, "Horrifying American Roots of Nazi Eugenics." See also Carducci, "Heart of Darkness," and "Eugenics: Three Generations, No Imbeciles."

12. Black, "Horrifying American Roots of Nazi Eugenics." See also Carducci, "Heart of Darkness"; Daniel J. Kevles, *In the Name of Eugenics: Genetics and the Uses of Human Heredity* (New York: Alfred A. Knopf, 1985), p. 59; and Jonathan Peter Spiro, *Defending the Master Race: Conservation, Eugenics, and the Legacy of Madison Grant* (Burlington, VT: University of Vermont Press, 2009), p. 181.

13. Carducci, "Heart of Darkness." See also Witkowski and Inglis, *Davenport's Dream*, p. 7.

14. Black, "Horrifying American Roots of Nazi Eugenics." See also Hall, "Genetics and Genetic Engineering"; Kevles, "Eugenics"; Kevles, *In the Name of Eugenic*, p. 59; and Platt, "Frightening Agenda of the American Eugenics Movement."

15. Riddle, *Biographical Memoir of Charles Benedict Davenport*, pp. 84–85.

16. Black, "Horrifying American Roots of Nazi Eugenics." See also "Eugenics: Three Generations, No Imbeciles"; Gould, "Carrie Buck's Daughter," pp. 14–18; and "Topic: International Eugenics."

17. Black, "Horrifying American Roots of Nazi Eugenics." See also "Eugenics: Three Generations, No Imbeciles."

18. Black, "Horrifying American Roots of Nazi Eugenics." See also Platt, "Frightening Agenda of the American Eugenics Movement."

19. C. B. Davenport and Morris Steggerda, *Race Crossing in Jamaica* (Washington, DC: Carnegie Institution of Washington, 1929), pp. 468–77.

20. Davenport and Steggerda, *Race Crossing in Jamaica,* pp. 468, 475, 477.

21. Davenport and Steggerda, *Race Crossing in Jamaica,* p. 469.

22. Black, "Horrifying American Roots of Nazi Eugenics." See also Black, *War against the Weak,* pp. 258–60; "Eugenics: Three Generations, No Imbeciles"; Gould, "Carrie Buck's Daughter," pp. 14–18; and "Topic: International Eugenics."

23. Black, "Horrifying American Roots of Nazi Eugenics." See also Black, *War against the Weak,* p. 259; Carducci, "Heart of Darkness"; and "Eugenics: Three Generations, No Imbeciles."

24. Black, "Horrifying American Roots of Nazi Eugenics." See also Black, *War against the Weak*, p. 258, and Charles Benedict Davenport, *Heredity in Relation to Eugenics* (New York: Henry Holt and Company, 1911), p. 267.

25. Black, *War against the Weak*, pp. 344, 414. See also Carducci, "Heart of Darkness"; Stefan Kühl, *The Nazi Connection: Eugenics, American Racism, and German National Socialism* (New York: Oxford University Press, 1994), pp. 68–69; and *Race and Membership in American History*, pp. 251–53.

26. Rich Remsburg, "Found in the Archives: America's Unsettling Early Eugenics Movement, *The Picture Show*, NPR, June 1, 2001, www.npr.org/blogs/pictureshow/2011/06/01/136849387/found-in-the-archives-americas-unsettling-early-eugenics-movement (accessed June 3, 2011).

27. Kevles, "Eugenics." See also *Race and Membership in American History*, p. 285.

28. Hall, "Genetics and Genetic Engineering." See also Kevles, "Eugenics."

CHAPTER 19.   THE SILKEN VOICE OF TREACHERY—MILDRED GILLARS

1. "Axis Sally (Mildred Gillars)—Home Sweet Home 18-05-1943 [radio broadcast]," YouTube, http://www.youtube.com/watch?v=4INW7fgSqXQ (accessed January 27, 2012). See also Richard Lucas, "Axis Sally: The Americans behind That Alluring Voice," HistoryNet.com, November 23, 2009, http://www.historynet.com/axis-sally.htm/1 (accessed November 23, 2011), and Richard Lucas, *Axis Sally: The American Voice of Nazi Germany* (Havertown, PA: Casemate Publishers, 2010), p. 73.

2. Lucas, *Axis Sally*, p. 74. See also Anna Macías, "Gillars, Mildred Elizabeth," American National Biography Online, February 2000, http://www.anb.org/articles/07/07-00518.html (accessed November 22, 2011), and "'Treason: Big Role," *Time*, February 7, 1949, p. 15.

3. "Axis Sally (Mildred Gillars)—Home Sweet Home." See also "'Axis Sally' Voice Heard in Playback," *New York Times*, January 28, 1949, p. 18; Howard L. Dutkin, "Love for Mystic Professor Led Her to 'Destiny,' Sally Says," *Washington Post*, February 25, 1949, p. 10; Lucas, *Axis Sally*, p. 78; and "Treason: Big Role," p. 15.

4. "Axis Sally (Mildred Gillars)—Home Sweet Home." See also "'Axis Sally' Voice Heard in Playback," p. 18, and Lucas, *Axis Sally*, p. 77.

5. "Axis Sally (Mildred Gillars)—Home Sweet Home." See also Lucas, "Axis Sally: The Americans behind That Alluring Voice"; Macías, "Gillars, Mildred Elizabeth"; "Tricked by 'Sally,' War Captive Says," *New York Times*, February 16, 1949, p. 15; "2 More Ex-GI's Tell of 'Axis Sally' Ruse," *New York Times*, February 8, 1949, p. 5; and Nathaniel Weyl, *Treason: The Story of Disloyalty and Betrayal in American History* (Washington, DC: Public Affairs Press, 1950), pp. 380–81.

6. Lucas, *Axis Sally*, pp. 12–13, 15–17.

7. Ibid., pp. 5–11. See also Weyl, *Treason*, pp. 377–78.

8. Weyl, *Treason*, p. 378.

9. "'Axis Sally' Denies She Betrayed U.S.," *New York Times*, February 24, 1949, p. 5. See

also Lucas, "Axis Sally: The Americans behind That Alluring Voice"; Macías, "Gillars, Mildred Elizabeth"; "Treason: True to the Red, White & Blue," *Time,* March 7, 1949, p. 27; and Weyl, *Treason,* p. 379.

10. "'Axis Sally' Denies She Betrayed U.S.," p. 5. See also Lucas, "Axis Sally: The Americans behind That Alluring Voice," and Lucas, *Axis Sally,* pp. 69, 192.

11. "'Axis Sally' Portrayed as Dupe of Former Teacher at Hunter," *New York Times,* January 26, 1949, p. 16. See also Susan Heller Anderson, "Mildred Gillars, 87, of Nazi Radio, Axis Sally to an Allied Audience," *New York Times,* July 2, 1988, http://www.nytimes.com/1988/07/02/obituaries/midred-gillars-87-of-nazi-radio-axis-sally-to-an-allied-audience.html (accessed January 26, 2012); Macías, "Gillars, Mildred Elizabeth," and Weyl, *Treason,* p. 379.

12. Dutkin, "Love for Mystic Professor," p. 1. See also "Washington AKA One Minute News [film clip]," British Pathé, 1949, http://www.britishpathe.com/video/washington-aka-one-minute-news-1 (accessed January 27, 2012); "Treason: True to the Red, White & Blue," p. 27; and Weyl, *Treason,* p. 380.

13. "Axis Sally (Mildred Gillars)—Home Sweet Home." See also Lucas, *Axis Sally,* p. 78.

14. Lucas, *Axis Sally,* pp. 263–64.

15. Ibid., p. 265.

16. Ibid., pp. 178–79.

17. "Treason: Big Role," p. 15.

18. "'Axis Sally' Trial Hears Her Ex-Boss," *New York Times,* February 1, 1949, p. 5. See also "Germans Identify 'Axis Sally's' Voice," *New York Times,* January 27, 1949, p. 6.

19. "Ex-PW Discloses 'Axis Sally' Ruse," *New York Times,* February 4, 1949, p. 10. See also "2 More Ex-GI's Tell of 'Axis Sally' Ruse," p. 5.

20. Lucas, *Axis Sally,* pp. 179–80.

21. "'Axis Sally' Portrayed as Dupe of Former Teacher," p. 16. See also Lucas, "Axis Sally: The Americans behind That Alluring Voice."

22. "'Axis Sally' Portrayed as Dupe of Former Teacher," p. 16. See also Dutkin, "Love for Mystic Professor," p. 10; "Treason: True to the Red, White & Blue," p. 27; and "Washington AKA One Minute News."

23. "Treason: True to the Red, White & Blue," p. 27.

24. Richard H. Rovere, "Letter from Washington," *New Yorker,* February 26, 1949, pp. 80–81.

25. "'Axis Sally' Gets 10- to 30-Year Term," *New York Times,* March 26, 1949, p. 2. See also Lucas, "Axis Sally: The Americans behind That Alluring Voice," and Macías, "Gillars, Mildred Elizabeth."

26. Weyl, *Treason,* p. 377.

27. Ibid., p. 379.

CHAPTER 20. WHO'S THAT RAPPING ON MY FLOOR?—MAGGIE AND KATE FOX

1. Ruth Brandon, *The Spiritualists: The Passion for the Occult in the Nineteenth and Twentieth Centuries* (New York: Alfred A. Knopf, 1983), p. 1. See also Reuben Briggs Davenport, *The Death-Blow to Spiritualism* (New York: Arno Press, 1976, reprint of 1888 edition), pp. 81, 85–86; Nancy Rubin Stuart, *The Reluctant Spiritualist: The Life of Maggie Fox* (Orlando, FL: Harcourt, Inc., 2005), pp. 4–5; and Barbara Weisberg, *Talking to the Dead: Kate and Maggie Fox and the Rise of Spiritualism* (San Francisco: HarperSanFrancisco, 2005), pp. 1, 16–18, 43.

2. Brandon, *Spiritualists,* pp. 1–3. See also David Chapin, *Exploring Other Worlds: Margaret Fox, Elisha Kent Kane, and the Antebellum Culture of Curiosity* (Amherst, MA: University of Massachusetts Press, 2004), pp. 31–33; Davenport, *Death-Blow to Spiritualism,* p. 87; Stuart, *Reluctant Spiritualist,* pp. 5–7, 12; and Weisberg, *Talking to the Dead,* pp. 2, 18–20.

3. Brandon, *Spiritualists,* pp. 3–4. See also Chapin, *Exploring Other Worlds,* pp. 33–34; Davenport, *Death-Blow to Spiritualism,* pp. 88, 94–95; Stuart, *Reluctant Spiritualist,* pp. 7, 12–13; and Weisberg, *Talking to the Dead,* pp. 2, 19–21.

4. Chapin, *Exploring Other Worlds,* pp. 36–37, 89–90. See also Weisberg, *Talking to the Dead,* pp. 3, 28–29.

5. Ann Braude, *Radical Spirits: Spiritualism and Women's Rights in Nineteenth-Century America* (Bloomington, IN: Indiana University Press, 2001), p. 25. See also John H. Martin, "The Fox Sisters," from *Saints, Sinners, and Reformers,* reprinted in *Crooked Lake Review,* Fall 2005, http://www.crookedlakereview.com/books/saints_sinners/martin10.html (accessed October 5, 2011); James Randi, *An Encyclopedia of Claims, Frauds, and Hoaxes of the Occult and Supernatural* (New York: St. Martin's Press, 1995), p. 101; Stuart, *Reluctant Spiritualist,* p. 1; Weisberg, *Talking to the Dead,* pp. 3, 54, 260–61; and "Welcome," National Spiritualist Association of Churches, 2011, http://www.nsac.org (accessed October 26, 2011).

6. Braude, *Radical Spirits,* pp. xv, 27, 29, 58. See also Chapin, *Exploring Other Worlds,* pp. 40–43; Stuart, *Reluctant Spiritualist,* p. 37; and Weisberg, *Talking to the Dead,* p. 64.

7. Davenport, *Death-Blow to Spiritualism,* pp. 13–16. See also Martin, "Fox Sisters"; "Pranks the Spirits Play," *New York Sun,* October 22, 1888, p. 1; Randi, *Encyclopedia of Claims, Frauds, and Hoaxes,* pp. 101–102; "Spirit Mediums Outdone," *New York Daily Tribune,* October 22, 1888, p. 7; and Weisberg, *Talking to the Dead,* pp. 3–4.

8. Chapin, *Exploring Other Worlds,* p. 35. See also Martin, "Fox Sisters"; Stuart, *Reluctant Spiritualist,* p. 10; and Weisberg, *Talking to the Dead,* pp. 36–37, 63–64.

9. Brandon, *Spiritualists,* pp. 4–5, 40–41. See also Chapin, *Exploring Other Worlds,* pp. 38–40, 44–45; Davenport, *Death-Blow to Spiritualism,* pp. 102–103, 126–27; Martin, "Fox Sisters"; Stuart, *Reluctant Spiritualist,* pp. 27–28, 32–35, 40–41; and Weisberg, *Talking to the Dead,* pp. 7, 54.

10. Chapin, *Exploring Other Worlds,* pp. 44, 48–51. See also Davenport, *Death-Blow to Spiritualism,* p. 105; Martin, "Fox Sisters"; Randi, *Encyclopedia of Claims, Frauds, and Hoaxes,* p. 101; Stuart, *Reluctant Spiritualist,* pp. 39, 50–52; and Weisberg, *Talking to the Dead,* pp. 68, 76–80.

11. Chapin, *Exploring Other Worlds*, pp. 82, 85, 99. See also Davenport, *Death-Blow to Spiritualism*, pp. 16, 102–103; Randi, *Encyclopedia of Claims, Frauds, and Hoaxes*, p. 101; Stuart, *Reluctant Spiritualist*, p. 57; and Weisberg, *Talking to the Dead*, pp. 7, 144.

12. Braude, *Radical Spirits*, pp. 26–27. See also Martin, "Fox Sisters"; Stuart, *Reluctant Spiritualist*, pp. 96–97, 173; and Weisberg, *Talking to the Dead*, pp. 120–21, 144–46.

13. Brandon, *Spiritualists*, pp. 45–47, 101–102, 168. See also Martin, "Fox Sisters"; Stuart, *Reluctant Spiritualist*, pp. 171, 283; Troy Taylor, "The Davenport Brothers: Were They Mediums or Magicians?" Haunted Museum, 2003, http://www.prairieghosts.com/davenport.html (accessed October 25, 2011); Troy Taylor, "Spirit Cabinets: Communicating with the Spirits," Haunted Museum, 2003, http://www.prairieghosts.com/cabinets.html (accessed October 25, 2011); and Weisberg, *Talking to the Dead*, pp. 120–21, 144–46.

14. Chapin, *Exploring Other Worlds*, pp. 5–8. See also Stuart, *Reluctant Spiritualist*, p. 69, and Weisberg, *Talking to the Dead*, pp. 76, 89–91.

15. Chapin, *Exploring Other Worlds*, pp.75, 83. See also Davenport, *Death-Blow to Spiritualism*, p. 36; Stuart, *Reluctant Spiritualist*, pp. 70–72; and Weisberg, *Talking to the Dead*, pp. 86, 108, 110, 245–46.

16. Brandon, *Spiritualists*, p. 229. See also Chapin, *Exploring Other Worlds*, pp. 199, 212–13; Randi, *Encyclopedia of Claims, Frauds, and Hoaxes*, pp. 101–102; Stuart, *Reluctant Spiritualist*, pp. 190, 196–97, 218, 242, 282; and Weisberg, *Talking to the Dead*, pp. 102, 152, 170, 197, 212, 231, 235–36.

17. Brandon, *Spiritualists*, pp. 40–41, 228. See also Chapin, *Exploring Other Worlds*, pp. 212–15; Davenport, *Death-Blow to Spiritualism*, pp. 74–76; Martin, "Fox Sisters"; "Pranks the Spirits Play," p. 1; "Spirit Mediums Outdone," p. 7; Stuart, *Reluctant Spiritualist*, pp. 297–300; and Weisberg, *Talking to the Dead*, pp. 3, 7, 234–35, 241, 244–45.

18. Chapin, *Exploring Other Worlds*, pp. 31–32. See also Davenport, *Death-Blow to Spiritualism*, p. 84; Martin, "Fox Sisters"; "Pranks the Spirits Play," p. 1; Randi, *Encyclopedia of Claims, Frauds, and Hoaxes*, p. 101; "Spirit Mediums Outdone," p. 7; Stuart, *Reluctant Spiritualist*, p. 4; and Weisberg, *Talking to the Dead*, pp. 19, 242–43.

19. Brandon, *Spiritualists*, pp. 229, 235–36. See also Chapin, *Exploring Other Worlds*, pp. 215–16; Davenport, *Death-Blow to Spiritualism*, p. v; Martin, "Fox Sisters"; Randi, *Encyclopedia of Claims, Frauds, and Hoaxes*, pp. 101–102; and Weisberg, *Talking to the Dead*, p. 253.

20. Brandon, *Spiritualists*, pp. 229–30. See also Chapin, *Exploring Other Worlds*, pp. 215–16; Randi, *Encyclopedia of Claims, Frauds, and Hoaxes*, pp. 101–102; Stuart, *Reluctant Spiritualist*, pp. 303, 307–308, 310–13; and Weisberg, *Talking to the Dead*, pp. 3–4, 255–59.

21. Brandon, *Spiritualists*, pp. 166–68, 174–75. See also Houdini, *A Magician among the Spirits* (New York: Harper & Brothers, 1924), p. xix; Stuart, *Reluctant Spiritualist*, pp. 316–17; and Weisberg, *Talking to the Dead*, pp. 5, 264.

22. Martin, "Fox Sisters." See also Stuart, *Reluctant Spiritualist*, p. 315; Weisberg, *Talking to the Dead*, pp. 6, 260; "Welcome," Cassadaga Spiritualist Camp, http://www.cassadaga.org (accessed October 26, 2011); and "Welcome to Lily Dale," Lily Dale Assembly, 2011, http://www.lilydaleassembly.com (accessed October 26, 2011).

CHAPTER 21. THE WITCH OF WALL STREET—HETTY GREEN

1. Janet L. Coryell, "Green, Hetty," American National Biography Online, February 2000, http://www.anb.org/articles/10/10-00679.html (accessed August 1, 2011). See also Charles Slack, *Hetty: The Genius and Madness of America's First Female Tycoon* (New York: Ecco, 2004), p. ix, and Peter Wyckoff, "Queen Midas: Hetty Robinson Green," *New England Quarterly,* June 1950, pp. 147, 160.

2. Ladbroke Black, *Some Queer People* (London: Sampson Low, Marston & Co., 1931), p. 207. See also Coryell, "Green, Hetty," and Wyckoff, "Queen Midas," pp. 149, 170.

3. Black, *Some Queer People,* p. 209. See also Boyden Sparkes and Samuel Taylor Moore, *The Witch of Wall Street: Hetty Green* (Garden City, NY: Garden City Publishing, 1936), pp. 35, 40–41, 48, and Wyckoff, "Queen Midas," pp. 148–49.

4. Black, *Some Queer People,* pp. 209–10. See also Coryell, "Green, Hetty"; Sparkes and Moore, *Witch of Wall Street,* pp. 23–24; and Wyckoff, "Queen Midas," pp. 150–51.

5. Sparkes and Moore, *Witch of Wall Street,* p. 34. See also Wyckoff, "Queen Midas," p. 151.

6. Coryell, "Green, Hetty." See also Wyckoff, "Queen Midas," p. 151.

7. Black, *Some Queer People,* p. 211. See also Wyckoff, "Queen Midas," p. 151.

8. Black, *Some Queer People,* pp. 211–12. See also Coryell, "Green, Hetty"; Ishbel Ross, *Charmers and Cranks: Twelve Famous American Women Who Defied the Conventions* (New York: Harper & Row, 1965), p. 33; Sparkes and Moore, *Witch of Wall Street,* pp. 89–93; and Wyckoff, "Queen Midas," pp. 151–53.

9. Black, *Some Queer People,* pp. 212–14. See also Coryell, "Green, Hetty"; Ross, *Charmers and Cranks,* p. 33; Slack, *Hetty,* pp. 56, 62–63; and Sparkes and Moore, *Witch of Wall Street,* pp. 102, 104–105, 111–16.

10. Black, *Some Queer People,* p. 215. See also Coryell, "Green, Hetty"; Sparkes and Moore, *Witch of Wall Street,* p. 119; and Wyckoff, "Queen Midas," p. 154.

11. Ross, *Charmers and Cranks,* p. 34. See also Sparkes and Moore, *Witch of Wall Street,* p. 119.

12. Slack, *Hetty,* pp. 72–73. See also Wyckoff, "Queen Midas," p. 155.

13. Andrew Beattie, "Hetty Green: The Witch of Wall Street," Investopedia.com, June 30, 2009, http://www.investopedia.com/articles/financialcareers/09/hetty-green-witch-wall-street.asp#axzz1R3tAmZHM (accessed July 3, 2011). See also Coryell, "Green, Hetty."

14. Hetty Green, "Why Women Are Not Money Makers," *Harper's Bazaar,* March 10, 1900, p. 201.

15. Beattie, "Hetty Green." See also Ross, *Charmers and Cranks,* pp. 41–42; Sparkes and Moore, *Witch of Wall Street,* pp. 138–39; and Wyckoff, "Queen Midas," p. 153.

16. Coryell, "Green, Hetty." See also Slack, *Hetty,* pp. 86, 97; Sparkes and Moore, *Witch of Wall Street,* pp. 160–61; and Wyckoff, "Queen Midas," p. 157.

17. Black, *Some Queer People,* p. 216. See also Coryell, "Green, Hetty"; Slack, *Hetty,* p. 97; and Wyckoff, "Queen Midas," pp. 147–48, 158.

18. Coryell, "Green, Hetty." See also Slack, *Hetty,* pp. 134–35, and Wyckoff, "Queen Midas," pp. 161, 163.

19. Black, *Some Queer People,* p. 217. See also Coryell, "Green, Hetty"; "Hetty Green's Fortune," *New York Times,* July 9, 1916, p. E2; Ross, *Charmers and Cranks,* p. 45; Slack, *Hetty,* pp. 204–205; Sparkes and Moore, *Witch of Wall Street,* pp. 218–19; Jay Starkman, "Hetty Green: The Witch of Wall Street," *Current Accounts,* January/February 2009, p. 12; and Wyckoff, "Queen Midas," pp. 152, 160–61, 166.

20. Black, *Some Queer People,* p. 217. See also Sparkes and Moore, *Witch of Wall Street,* pp. 224–26, and Wyckoff, "Queen Midas," pp. 161–62.

21. Coryell, "Green, Hetty." See also Ross, *Charmers and Cranks,* p. 37; Slack, *Hetty,* pp. 84, 112–14; Sparkes and Moore, *Witch of Wall Street,* pp. 149–53; and Wyckoff, "Queen Midas," p. 156.

22. Black, *Some Queer People,* pp. 206–207. See also Ross, *Charmers and Cranks,* pp. 26, 57; Slack, *Hetty,* p. 107; and Wyckoff, "Queen Midas," pp. 166, 168.

23. Black, *Some Queer People,* p. 206. See also, Slack, *Hetty,* p. 217, and Starkman, "Hetty Green," p. 12.

24. Beattie, "Hetty Green." See also Coryell, "Green, Hetty"; "Hetty Green Dies, Worth $100,000,000," *New York Times,* July 4, 1916, p. 1; Slack, *Hetty,* p. 204; Sparkes and Moore, *Witch of Wall Street,* pp. 333, 337; and Wyckoff, "Queen Midas," pp. 147–48, 170.

25. Beattie, "Hetty Green." See also Coryell, "Green, Hetty"; "Hetty Green's Fortune," p. E2; and Starkman, "Hetty Green," p. 12.

26. "Jersey Seeks Green Tax," *New York Times,* July 9, 1916, p. 16. See also Slack, *Hetty,* pp. 204–206; Sparkes and Moore, *Witch of Wall Street,* pp. 337–38; and Wyckoff, "Queen Midas," p. 171.

27. Black, *Some Queer People,* pp. 217–18. See also, "Hetty Green's Fortune," p. E2, and Starkman, "Hetty Green," p. 12.

28. Beattie, "Hetty Green." See also Coryell, "Green, Hetty"; "Hetty Green's Fortune," p. E2; Slack, *Hetty,* pp. 205, 215–17, 223–26; Starkman, "Hetty Green," p. 12; and Wyckoff, "Queen Midas," p. 171.

CHAPTER 22. KING OF THE CANNIBAL ISLANDS—DAVID O'KEEFE

1. Francis X. Hezel, "The Man Who Was Reputed to Be King: David Dean O'Keefe," *Journal of Pacific History* 43, no. 2 (2008): 239–52, reprinted by Micronesian Seminar, http://www.micsem.org/pubs/articles/historical/frames/O'Keefefr.htm (accessed July 29, 2010).

2. Ibid.

3. Ibid.

4. Ibid. See also "O'Keefe and Yap," Pacific Worlds, http://www.pacificworlds.com/yap/visitors/okeefe.cfm (accessed July 29, 2010).

5. William Henry Furness, *The Island of Stone Money, Uap of the Carolines* (Philadelphia: J. B. Lippincott Co., 1910), pp. 92–96. See also Hezel, "Man Who Was Reputed to Be King"; "Land of Stone Money: State of Yap," Yap Visitors Center, Federated States of Micronesia, http://www.

visit-fsm.org/yap (accessed October 24, 2010); "O'Keefe and Yap"; and John Tharngan, "Stone Money," *Road to Riches,* BBC News, http://news.bbc.co.uk/hi/english/static/road_to_riches/prog2/tharngan.stm (accessed July 29, 2010).

   6. Furness, *Island of Stone Money,* pp. 101–102. See also Hezel, "Man Who Was Reputed to Be King"; "O'Keefe and Yap"; and Tharngan, "Stone Money."

   7. Hezel, "Man Who Was Reputed to Be King." See also "O'Keefe and Yap."

   8. Hezel, "Man Who Was Reputed to Be King." See also "O'Keefe and Yap."

   9. Francis X. Hezel, "A Yankee Trader in Yap: Crayton Philo Holcomb," *Journal of Pacific History* 10, no. 1 (1975): 3–19, reprinted by Micronesian Seminar, http://www.micsem.org/pubs/articles/historical/frames/yankeetradfr.htm (accessed July 29, 2010). See also Hezel, "Man Who Was Reputed to Be King."

   10. Jason Berg, "Yapese Culture," EMuseum, Minnesota State University, Mankato, http://www.mnsu.edu/emuseum/cultural/oldworld/asia/yapese_culture.html (accessed July 29, 2010). See also Hezel, "Yankee Trader in Yap"; Hezel, "Man Who Was Reputed to Be King"; and "Timeline of the Kingdom of Yap," Kingdom of Yap, http://www.kingdomofyap.org/timeline .html (accessed July 29, 2010).

   11. Hezel, "Man Who Was Reputed to Be King." See also "Timeline of the Kingdom of Yap."

   12. Hezel, "Man Who Was Reputed to Be King." See also "O'Keefe and Yap."

   13. Hezel, "Man Who Was Reputed to Be King."

   14. Joseph Conrad, *Lord Jim* (New York: Signet Classics, 2009), p. ix. See also, Hezel, "Man Who Was Reputed to Be King."

   15. Hezel, "Man Who Was Reputed to Be King." See also Lawrence Klingman and Gerald Green, *His Majesty O'Keefe* (New York: Charles Scribner's Sons, 1950), pp. vii, 276.

   16. Berg, "Yapese Culture." See also Hezel, "Man Who Was Reputed to Be King"; *His Majesty O'Keefe* [movie], Warner Brothers, 1954, rated at tcm.com, http://www.tcm.com/tcmdb/title/16812/His-Majesty-O-Keefe (accessed July 29, 2010); "O'Keefe and Yap"; Tharngan, "Stone Money"; and "Timeline of the Kingdom of Yap."

   17. Hezel, "Man Who Was Reputed to Be King."

   18. Ibid. See also "Land of Stone Money"; "O'Keefe and Yap"; "O'Keefe's Waterfront Inn," OkeefesYap.com, 2009, http://www.okeefesyap.com/history.htm (accessed July 29, 2010); and Tharngan, "Stone Money."

CHAPTER 23. MASTER SALESMAN OF A DUBIOUS LEGEND— HERBERT BRIDGMAN

   1. "Herbert Bridgman Dies at Sea at 80," *New York Times,* September 27, 1924, p. 15. See also Herbert L. Bridgman, "Ten Years of the Peary Arctic Club," *National Geographic,* September 1908, p. 668; "H. L. Bridgman's Body Here," *New York Times,* October 1, 1924, p. 19; Ann T. Keene, "Bridgman, Herbert Lawrence," American National Biography Online, February

2000, http://www.anb.org/articles/20/20-00109.html (accessed February 15, 2010); and Felix Riesenberg et al., *His Last Voyage: Herbert Lawrence Bridgman, 1844–1924* (Brooklyn, NY: *Brooklyn Standard Union,* 1924), p. 47.

2. "Herbert Bridgman Dies at Sea at 80," p. 15. See also "Cape York Meteorite," American Museum of Natural History, http://www.amnh.org/exhibitions/expeditions/treasure_fossil/ Treasures/Cape_York_Meteorite/capeyork.html?50 (accessed September 17, 2010); Helen Sawyer Hogg, "Out of Old Books," *Journal of the Royal Astronomical Society of Canada* 57, no. 1, pp. 41–48; and Keene, "Bridgman, Herbert Lawrence."

3. Russell W. Gibbons, "Cook, Frederick Albert," American National Biography Online, February 2000, http://www.anb.org/articles/20/20-00212.html (accessed February 15, 2010). See also Ted Heckathorn, "Dr. Frederick Cook's North Pole Claim," Frederick A. Cook Society, April 5, 2008, http://www.cookpolar.org/mckinley.htm (accessed December 11, 2011); Ted Heckathorn, "Peary, Robert Edwin," American National Biography Online, February 2000, http://www.anb.org/articles/20/20-00770.html (accessed February 15, 2010); Bruce Henderson, "Who Discovered the North Pole?" *Smithsonian Magazine,* April 2009, http://www.smithsonian mag.com/history-archaeology/Cook-vs-Peary.html?c=y&page=1 (accessed September 16, 2010); and Keene, "Bridgman, Herbert Lawrence."

4. "Herbert Bridgman Dies at Sea at 80," p. 15. See also Bridgman, "Ten Years of the Peary Arctic Club," pp. 661–68; Heckathorn, "Peary, Robert Edwin"; "His Last Voyage," *New York Times,* September 27, 1924, p. 14; "H. L. Bridgman's Body Here," p. 19; Keene, "Bridgman, Herbert Lawrence"; and Morgen Stevens-Garmon, "Finding Aid to the Archives of the Peary Arctic Club," Explorers Club, 2009, http://www.explorers.org/pdf/peary_arctic_club_finding _aid.pdf (accessed September 15, 2010).

5. "The Frederick A. Cook Society Collection," Byrd Polar Research Center Archival Program, 2010, http://library.osu.edu/sites/archives/polar/cook/cook.php (accessed September 21, 2010). See also Gibbons, "Cook, Frederick Albert"; Heckathorn, "Peary, Robert Edwin"; "Peary and the North Pole 100 Years Ago Today," *NatGeo News Watch,* April 6, 2009, http:// blogs.nationalgeographic.com/blogs/news/chiefeditor/2009/04/peary-and-the-north-pole .html (accessed August 31, 2010); and "Relief Expedition of Peary Arctic Club," *New York Times,* June 23, 1901.

6. Gibbons, "Cook, Frederick Albert." See also Heckathorn, "Peary, Robert Edwin"; Henderson, "Who Discovered the North Pole?"; and Wally Herbert, "Commander Robert E. Peary: Did He Reach the Pole?" *National Geographic,* September 1988, p. 392.

7. Heckathorn, "Peary, Robert Edwin." See also Henderson, "Who Discovered the North Pole?"; Herbert, "Commander Robert E. Peary," p. 412; and "Peary and the North Pole 100 Years Ago Today."

8. "Frederick A. Cook Society Collection." See also Gibbons, "Cook, Frederick Albert"; Heckathorn, "Dr. Frederick Cook's North Pole Claim"; Heckathorn, "Peary, Robert Edwin"; Henderson, "Who Discovered the North Pole?"; Herbert, "Commander Robert E. Peary," pp. 399–400, 412; "The North Pole Conspiracy [television program]," Smithsonian Channel, 2010, http://www.smithsonianchannel.com/sc/web/show/137272/the-north-pole-conspiracy

(accessed December 11, 2011); and Stevens-Garmon, "Finding Aid to the Archives of the Peary Arctic Club."

9. Herbert L. Bridgman, "Peary," reprinted from *Natural History* 20, no. 1 (1920): 11. See also Keene, "Bridgman, Herbert Lawrence"; Riesenberg et al., *His Last Voyage,* p. 47; and Stevens-Garmon, "Finding Aid to the Archives of the Peary Arctic Club."

10. Heckathorn, "Dr. Frederick Cook's North Pole Claim." See also Herbert, "Commander Robert E. Peary," p. 405; Keene, "Bridgman, Herbert Lawrence"; and "North Pole Conspiracy."

11. Helen Bartlett Bridgman, *Within My Horizon* (Boston: Small, Maynard & Co., 1920), p. 179.

12. Heckathorn, "Peary, Robert Edwin." See also Henderson, "Who Discovered the North Pole?"; Herbert, "Commander Robert E. Peary," pp. 388–89, 398, 411–13; and "Peary and the North Pole 100 Years Ago Today."

13. Herbert, "Commander Robert E. Peary," pp. 387, 404, 410. See also "Peary and the North Pole 100 Years Ago Today."

14. "Chronology of Frederick A. Cook and the Frederick A. Cook Society, 1865–1996," Byrd Polar Research Center Archival Program, 2010, http://library.osu.edu/sites/archives/polar/cook/cookchron.php (accessed September 21, 2010). See also Henderson, "Who Discovered the North Pole?"; Herbert, "Commander Robert E. Peary," p. 412; "North Pole Conspiracy"; and "Peary and the North Pole 100 Years Ago Today."

15. Bridgman, *Within My Horizon,* p. 184. See also Herbert, "Commander Robert E. Peary," pp. 387, 390–91, 413.

16. Bridgman, "Ten Years of the Peary Arctic Club," pp. 664–65. See also Gibbons, "Cook, Frederick Albert"; Heckathorn, "Peary, Robert Edwin"; and Herbert, "Commander Robert E. Peary," pp. 392, 397, 399.

17. "His Last Voyage," p. 14. See also "H. L. Bridgman's Body Here," p. 19; Riesenberg et al., *His Last Voyage,* p. 47; and Stevens-Garmon, "Finding Aid to the Archives of the Peary Arctic Club."

18. Bridgman, "Ten Years of the Peary Arctic Club," pp. 663, 667. See also Heckathorn, "Dr. Frederick Cook's North Pole Claim"; Heckathorn, "Peary, Robert Edwin"; Herbert, "Commander Robert E. Peary," pp. 390, 396, 399, 401, 412; and "North Pole Conspiracy."

19. Herbert, "Commander Robert E. Peary," pp. 388, 403.

20. Gibbons, "Cook, Frederick Albert."

CHAPTER 24. THE CONSUMMATE GOLD DIGGER—PEGGY HOPKINS JOYCE

1. Peggy Hopkins Joyce, *Men, Marriage, and Me* (New York: Macaulay Co., 1930), pp. 139–40, 145–49. See also Constance Rosenblum, *Gold Digger: The Outrageous Life and Times of Peggy Hopkins Joyce* (New York: Owl Books, 2001), pp. 89–90, 206, and "Says Peggy Hopkins Cost Him $1,398,316," *New York Times,* June 1, 1921, p. 13.

2. "Divorce for Joyce; $1,284,250 for Peggy," *New York Times,* November 9, 1921, p.

13. See also Eve Golden, "Peggy Hopkins Joyce: The Gentleman-Preferred Blonde," *Films of the Golden Age* 17 (Summer 1999): 28–32; "Peggy Hopkins Joyce Dies at 63; Showgirl of '20's Wed 6 Times," *New York Times*, June 13, 1957, p. 31; Hopkins Joyce, *Men, Marriage, and Me*, p. 125; and Rosenblum, *Gold Digger*, pp. 2–3, 80, 83–85, 104, 133.

3. Golden, "Peggy Hopkins Joyce," p. 30. See also "Peggy Hopkins Joyce Dies at 63," p. 31, and Rosenblum, *Gold Digger*, pp. 2, 4–7, 252–53.

4. Hopkins Joyce, *Men, Marriage, and Me*, p. 14. See also Rosenblum, *Gold Digger*, p. 21.

5. Hopkins Joyce, *Men, Marriage, and Me*, p. 12.

6. Rosenblum, *Gold Digger*, pp. 24–25.

7. Ibid., pp. 28–30.

8. Hopkins Joyce, *Men, Marriage, and Me*, pp. 38, 40. See also Rosenblum, *Gold Digger*, p. 31.

9. Rosenblum, *Gold Digger*, pp. 44–47.

10. Ibid., pp. 46–50, 52, 54, 58.

11. Ibid., pp. 61, 64–69.

12. Hopkins Joyce, *Men, Marriage, and Me*, pp. 116–19, 122, 124–25. See also Rosenblum, *Gold Digger*, pp. 77–80, 88.

13. Rosenblum, *Gold Digger*, pp. 92, 94–101.

14. "Divorce for Joyce," p. 13. See also "Peggy Hopkins Answers Joyce," *New York Times*, June 8, 1921, p. 27; Samuel Marx, *Wild Women of Broadway* (Girard, KS: Haldeman-Julius Publications, 1929), pp. 7–9; Rosenblum, *Gold Digger*, pp. 96–101, 106–107, 112–14; and "Says Peggy Hopkins Cost Him," p. 13.

15. Marx, *Wild Women of Broadway*, pp. 9–10. See also "Peggy Hopkins Joyce Dies at 63," p. 31; Rosenblum, *Gold Digger*, pp. 91, 111; and "Says Peggy Hopkins Cost Him," p. 13.

16. "Divorce for Joyce," p. 13. See also Hopkins Joyce, *Men, Marriage, and Me*, p. 170; Marx, *Wild Women of Broadway*, pp. 6–7; and Rosenblum, *Gold Digger*, pp. 88–89, 107, 115.

17. Hopkins Joyce, *Men, Marriage, and Me*, p. 202. See also Rosenblum, *Gold Digger*, pp. 131–36.

18. Hopkins Joyce, *Men, Marriage, and Me*, pp. 206–10. See also Marx, *Wild Women of Broadway*, p, 11; "Peggy Joyce Weds a Swedish Count," *New York Times*, June 4, 1924, p. 1; and "Sues Peggy Joyce to Void Marriage," *New York Times*, July 30, 1924, p. 1.

19. Golden, "Peggy Hopkins Joyce," pp. 30, 32. See also "Peggy Hopkins Joyce Dies at 63," p. 31, and Rosenblum, *Gold Digger*, pp. 6, 153–54, 211–16.

20. Hopkins Joyce, *Men, Marriage, and Me*, p. 132. See also Rosenblum, *Gold Digger*, p. 86.

21. Hopkins Joyce, *Men, Marriage, and Me*, p. 89.

22. Golden, "Peggy Hopkins Joyce," p. 30. See also Rosenblum, *Gold Digger*, pp. 3, 155–56, 191.

23. Hopkins Joyce, *Men, Marriage, and Me*, p. 148. See also "Joyce Will Is Filed," *New York Times*, November 9, 1957, p. 12, and Rosenblum, *Gold Digger*, pp. 242–43.

24. Hopkins Joyce, *Men, Marriage, and Me*, pp. 196–97. See also Marx, *Wild Women of Broadway*, p. 9; "Peggy Joyce Home again from Paris," *New York Times*, May 13, 1922, p. 24; Rosenblum, *Gold Digger*, p. 110; and "Says Peggy Hopkins Cost Him," p. 13.

CHAPTER 25. THE MAD, SAD POET OF GREENWICH VILLAGE— MAXWELL BODENHEIM

1. Jim Burns, "Maxwell Bodenheim," Penniless Press, http://www.pennilesspress.co.uk/ prose/bodenheim.htm (accessed February 13, 2010). See also Allen Churchill, *The Improper Bohemians: A Re-creation of Greenwich Village In Its Heyday* (New York: Dutton, 1959), pp. 179, 293, 309–10, 322, 334; Deborah Hatheway, "Bodenheim, Maxwell," American National Biography Online, February 2000, http://www.anb.org/articles/16/16-00140.html (accessed February 13, 2010); and Jack B. Moore, *Maxwell Bodenheim* (New York: Twayne Publishers, 1970), pp. 7, 168.

2. Alan Bisbort, "Mad Max: Death of a Bohemian King," Gadflyonline, April 22, 2001, http://www.gadflyonline.com/lastweek/bondenheimfeature.html (accessed February 13, 2010). See also "Bodenheim Asks Relief," *New York Times,* March 5, 1935, p. 17; Burns, "Maxwell Bodenheim"; Churchill, *Improper Bohemians,* pp. 309, 318; Hatheway, "Bodenheim, Maxwell"; Peter Miller, "Naked on Roller Skates," Freebird Books, February 2, 2010, http://www.free-birdbooks.com/2010/01/naked-on-roller-skates.html (accessed April 22, 2010); and Moore, *Maxwell Bodenheim,* pp. 14, 30–31.

3. Bisbort, "Mad Max." See also Hatheway, "Bodenheim, Maxwell," and Moore, *Maxwell Bodenheim,* pp. 13–16.

4. Bisbort, "Mad Max." See also Burns, "Maxwell Bodenheim"; Hatheway, "Bodenheim, Maxwell"; and Moore, *Maxwell Bodenheim,* pp. 16–17.

5. Moore, *Maxwell Bodenheim,* p. 20.

6. Ibid.

7. Bisbort, "Mad Max." See also Churchill, *Improper Bohemians,* p. 310; Ben Hecht, *A Child of the Century* (New York: Primus, 1985), p. 223; Miller, "Naked on Roller Skates"; and Moore, *Maxwell Bodenheim,* p. 20.

8. Bisbort, "Mad Max." See also Churchill, *Improper Bohemians,* p. 179, and Moore, *Maxwell Bodenheim,* pp. 18–19.

9. Hecht, *Child of the Century,* p. 331. See also Miller, "Naked on Roller Skates."

10. Burns, "Maxwell Bodenheim." See also Churchill, *Improper Bohemians,* p. 308; Miller, "Naked on Roller Skates"; and Moore, *Maxwell Bodenheim,* pp. 21, 30–31.

11. Churchill, *Improper Bohemians,* pp. 294, 298, 305–306.

12. "Bodenheim Cleared of Charges on Book," *New York Times,* March 21, 1928, p. 28. See also "Book Called Evil; Publisher Indicted," *New York Times,* July 1, 1925, p. 3; Churchill, *Improper Bohemians,* pp. 309–10; "Jury Frees Liveright in 'Jessica' Case," *New York Times,* March 24, 1928, p. 30; and "T. R. Smith Is Cleared in 'Jessica' Trial," *New York Times,* March 23, 1928, p. 14.

13. Bisbort, "Mad Max." See also Burns, "Maxwell Bodenheim"; Churchill, *Improper Bohemians,* p. 311; "Keeps Missing Girl from Bodenheim," *New York Times,* July 22, 1928, pp. 1, 9; and Moore, *Maxwell Bodenheim,* p. 109.

14. Bisbort, "Mad Max." See also "Bodenheim Vanishes as Girl Takes Life," *New York*

Times, July 21, 1928, pp. 1, 7; Burns, "Maxwell Bodenheim"; Churchill, *Improper Bohemians,* pp. 311–13; and Moore, *Maxwell Bodenheim,* p. 109.

15. Bisbort, "Mad Max." See also Burns, "Maxwell Bodenheim"; Churchill, *Improper Bohemians,* p. 317; and Moore, *Maxwell Bodenheim,* p. 109.

16. Bisbort, "Mad Max." See also Burns, "Maxwell Bodenheim"; Churchill, *Improper Bohemians,* p. 317; and Moore, *Maxwell Bodenheim,* p. 109.

17. "Bodenheim Dropped in WPA Red Inquiry," *New York Times,* August 2, 1940, p. 2. See also Burns, "Maxwell Bodenheim"; Hatheway, "Bodenheim, Maxwell"; Hecht, *Child of the Century,* p. 217; Roseann Reinemuth Hogan and Derek Agard, "WPA Telling Living History," *Ancestry Magazine,* July/August 2005, http://www.ancestry.com/learn/library/article .aspx?article=11101 (accessed February 13, 2010); and Moore, *Maxwell Bodenheim,* p. 158.

18. Hatheway, "Bodenheim, Maxwell." See also Hecht, *Child of the Century,* p. 218.

19. Bisbort, "Mad Max." See also Burns, "Maxwell Bodenheim"; Hatheway, "Bodenheim, Maxwell"; and Moore, *Maxwell Bodenheim,* pp. 169–70.

20. Bisbort, "Mad Max." See also "Bodenheim Case Closed," *New York Times,* April 8, 1954, p. 24; Burns, "Maxwell Bodenheim"; Churchill, *Improper Bohemians,* pp. 335–36; Miller, "Naked on Roller Skates"; Moore, *Maxwell Bodenheim,* pp. 172–73; Emanuel Perlmutter, "Confession Cited in Poet's Murder," *New York Times,* February 11, 1954, p. 43; and Wayne Phillips, "Maxwell Bodenheim, Wife Slain in the Poet's Dingy Bowery Room," *New York Times,* February 8, 1954, p. 1.

21. Bisbort, "Mad Max." See also Burns, "Maxwell Bodenheim"; Churchill, *Improper Bohemians,* pp. 180, 307, 309; Hatheway, "Bodenheim, Maxwell"; Miller, "Naked on Roller Skates"; and Moore, *Maxwell Bodenheim,* pp. 15, 30–31.

22. Bisbort, "Mad Max." See also Burns, "Maxwell Bodenheim"; Miller, "Naked on Roller Skates"; and Moore, *Maxwell Bodenheim,* p. 33.

23. Maxwell Bodenheim, *Minna and Myself* (New York: Pagan Publishing Co., 1918), p. 42.

24. "Ben Hecht to Pay for Poet's Burial," *New York Times,* February 9, 1954, p. 13. See also Bisbort, "Mad Max"; Burns, "Maxwell Bodenheim"; and Moore, *Maxwell Bodenheim,* p. 173.

CHAPTER 26. THE BIFURCATED CONGRESSMAN—SAMUEL DICKSTEIN

1. Mark I. Gelfand, "McCormack, John," American National Biography Online, February 2000, http://www.anb.org/articles/07/07-00343.html (accessed April 7, 2010). See also Walter Goodman, *The Committee: The Extraordinary Career of the House Committee on Un-American Activities* (New York: Farrar, Straus and Giroux, 1968), pp. 3, 10; "Justice Dickstein Dies at Age of 69," *New York Times,* April 23, 1954, p. 27; "Records of the Select Committees of the House of Representatives," National Archives, http://www.archives.gov/legislative/guide/house/chapter-22-select-propaganda.html (accessed May 4, 2010); and Allen Weinstein and Alexander Vassiliev, *The Haunted Wood: Soviet Espionage in America—the Stalin Era* (New York: Random House, 1999), pp. 141, 148–49.

2. "Dickstein Questions Nazi Camp Leaders," *New York Times,* August 24, 1934, p. 6. See

also Goodman, *Committee*, pp. 11–12; "Justice Dickstein Dies at Age of 69," p. 27; and "Records of the Select Committees of the House of Representatives."

3. "Vast Nazi Campaign in U.S. Is Charged," *New York Times*, May 4, 1936, p. 11.

4. Goodman, *Committee*, pp. 10–12. See also "Justice Dickstein Dies at Age of 69," p. 27; "Records of the Select Committees of the House of Representatives"; "Vast Nazi Campaign in U.S. Is Charged," p. 11; and Weinstein and Vassiliev, *Haunted Wood*, p. 141.

5. Goodman, *Committee*, pp. 25–26, 36. See also Benedict Nightingale, "Mr. Euripides Goes to Washington," *New York Times*, September 18, 1988, www.nytimes.com/1988/09/18/books/mr-euripides-goes-to-washington.html?sec=&spon=&pagewanted=2 (accessed May 10, 2010), and Kenneth O'Reilly, "Dies, Martin," American National Biography Online, February 2000, http://www.anb.org/articles/07/07-00076.html (accessed February 13, 2010).

6. "Justice Dickstein Dies at Age of 69," p. 27. See also Weinstein and Vassiliev, *Haunted Wood*, p. 141.

7. Weinstein and Vassiliev, *Haunted Wood*, pp. 140, 144, 147, 149.

8. Ibid., pp. 141–43.

9. Ibid., pp. 142–43.

10. Ibid., p. 147.

11. Ibid., pp. 148–49.

12. Ibid., pp. 144, 146, 149.

13. "House Un-American Activities Committee," Eleanor Roosevelt National Historic Site, 2003, www.nps.gov/archive/elro/glossary/huac.htm (accessed May 5, 2010). See also Michael Mills, "Blacklist: A Different Look at the 1947 HUAC Hearings," ModernTimes.com, http://moderntimes.com/blacklist (May 5, 2010), and Charlotte Pomerantz, ed., *A Quarter-Century of Un-Americana, 1938–1963: A Tragico-Comical Memorabilia of HUAC, House Un-American Activities Committee* (Chicago: Chicago Center, 1997), p. 5, 15–16.

14. Athan G. Theoharis and John Stuart Cox, *The Boss: J. Edgar Hoover and the Great American Inquisition* (Philadelphia: Temple University Press, 1988), p. 312. See also "House Un-American Activities Committee."

15. Committee on Un-American Activities, *This Is YOUR House Committee on Un-American Activities* (Washington, DC: US House of Representatives, 1954), p. 1.

16. Patricia Donovan, "Real to Reel," *UB Reporter*, August 23, 2012, http://www.buffalo.edu/ubreporter/archive/2012_08_23/real_to_reel.html (accessed June 4, 2013). See also Mills, "Blacklist."

17. Pomerantz, *Quarter-Century of Un-Americana*, p. 127.

18. Goodman, *Committee*, p. 3.

19. Ibid., p. 22. See also Pomerantz, *Quarter-Century of Un-Americana*, p. 15.

20. "Dickstein Left $2,500 Estate," *New York Times*, May 12, 1954, p. 25. See also Goodman, *Committee*, p. 11, and "Justice Dickstein Dies at Age of 69," p. 27.

21. "Dickstein Memorial Service," *New York Times*, April 28, 1954, p. 54. See also "Justice Dickstein Dies at Age of 69," p. 27.

22. Weinstein and Vassiliev, *Haunted Wood*, p. 149.

CHAPTER 27. THE FRUGAL COUNTERFEITER—EMERICH JUETTNER

1. St. Clair McKelway, "Old Eight Eighty," part 1, *New Yorker,* August 27, 1949, p. 36. See also St. Clair McKelway, "Old Eight Eighty," part 2, *New Yorker,* September 3, 1949, pp. 30, 33; St. Clair McKelway, "Old Eight Eighty," part 3, *New Yorker,* September 10, 1949, p. 84; Joseph McNamara, ed., *The Justice Story: True Tales of Murder, Mystery, Mayhem* (New York: Bannon Multimedia Group, 2000), pp. 206–208; and "Snow, Fire Turn Up Elusive Suspect in 15-Year Crop of Bogus $1 Bills," *New York Times,* January 15, 1948, pp. 1, 48.

2. William Bryk, "Little Old Moneymaker," *New York Sun,* February 16, 2005, http://www.nysun.com/on-the-town/little-old-moneymaker/9282 (accessed July 3, 2011). See also George Hagenauer et al., *The Big Book of Little Criminals: 63 True Tales of the World's Most Incompetent Jailbirds!* (New York: Paradox Press, 1996), p. 86.

3. Bryk, "Little Old Moneymaker." See also McKelway, "Old Eight Eighty," part 1, p. 36; St. Clair McKelway, *True Tales from the Annals of Crime and Rascality* (New York: Random House, 1951), pp. 215–16, 220, 234; McNamara, *The Justice Story,* pp. 206, 208; Philip H. Melanson with Peter F. Stevens, *The Secret Service: The Hidden History of an Enigmatic Agency* (New York: Carroll & Graf Publishers, 2005), pp. 54–55; and "Snow, Fire Turn Up Elusive Suspect," pp. 1, 48.

4. Mara Bovsun, "Finding 'Mr. 880': The Case of the $1 Counterfeit," NYDailyNews.com, April 3, 2011, http://articles.nydailynews.com/2011-04-03/news/29395968_1_secret-service-bill-apartment-building (accessed July 3, 2011). See also, Bryk, "Little Old Moneymaker"; McKelway, "Old Eight Eighty," part 1, p. 36; McKelway, "Old Eight Eighty," part 2, p. 33; McKelway, *True Tales,* pp. 216, 220, 228, 234; McNamara, *Justice Story,* p. 208; and "Snow, Fire Turn Up Elusive Suspect," p. 48.

5. Bovsun, "Finding 'Mr. 880.'" See also Bryk, "Little Old Moneymaker"; McKelway, "Old Eight Eighty," part 1, p. 32; McKelway, "Old Eight Eighty," part 2, pp. 30, 33; McKelway, *True Tales,* pp. 215–20, 230–32, 252–53; McNamara, *Justice Story,* pp. 204, 207; and "Snow, Fire Turn Up Elusive Suspect," p. 48.

6. Bovsun, "Finding 'Mr. 880.'" See also Bryk, "Little Old Moneymaker"; McKelway, "Old Eight Eighty," part 1, p. 36; McKelway, *True Tales,* pp. 215–20, 231–33, 236, 252; McNamara, *Justice Story,* p. 205; and "Snow, Fire Turn Up Elusive Suspect," p. 48.

7. Bovsun, "Finding 'Mr. 880.'" See also, Bryk, "Little Old Moneymaker"; McKelway, "Old Eight Eighty," part 1, pp. 32, 34, 36; McKelway, "Old Eight Eighty," part 2, p. 30; McKelway, "Old Eight Eighty," part 3, p. 88; McKelway, *True Tales,* pp. 228, 232, 237–38, 250–51, 256; Melanson with Stevens, *Secret Service,* p. 55; and "Snow, Fire Turn Up Elusive Suspect," pp. 1, 48.

8. Bovsun, "Finding 'Mr. 880.'" See also Bryk, "Little Old Moneymaker"; McKelway, "Old Eight Eighty," part 1, p. 32; McKelway, "Old Eight Eighty," part 2, p. 30; McKelway, "Old Eight Eighty," part 3, p. 88; McKelway, *True Tales,* pp. 228–29, 232, 234, 237, 239, 250–51; McNamara, *Justice Story,* pp. 203–204; and Melanson with Stevens, *Secret Service,* p. 54.

9. Bovsun, "Finding 'Mr. 880.'" See also Bryk, "Little Old Moneymaker"; McKelway, "Old Eight Eighty," part 1, pp. 32, 34; McKelway, "Old Eight Eighty," part 3, p. 82; McKelway, *True*

Tales, pp. 216–17, 220–29, 232–38, 243, 256; McNamara, *Justice Story,* p. 208; and "Snow, Fire Turn Up Elusive Suspect," p. 48.

10. Bryk, "Little Old Moneymaker." See also McKelway, *True Tales,* pp. 216–17, 220–29, 232–38, and McNamara, *Justice Story,* p. 205.

11. Edwin P. Hoyt, *Coins, Collectors, and Counterfeiters* (Nashville: Thomas Nelson, 1977), pp. 106, 111–12. See also McKelway, "Old Eight Eighty," part 1, pp. 30–32, and McKelway, *True Tales,* pp. 220–21, 230, 233, 259.

12. Hoyt, *Coins, Collectors, and Counterfeiters,* p. 97. See also McKelway, "Old Eight Eighty," part 1, pp. 30, 33; McKelway, *True Tales,* pp. 220–21, 230, 233, 259; and Ben Tarnoff, *Moneymakers: The Wicked Lives and Surprising Adventures of Three Notorious Counterfeiters* (New York: Penguin Press, 2011), pp. 2, 5, 255–56.

13. Hoyt, *Coins, Collectors, and Counterfeiters,* pp. 124–28. See also McKelway, "Old Eight Eighty," part 1, p. 32, and Tarnoff, *Moneymakers,* pp. 4, 255.

14. Bovsun, "Finding 'Mr. 880.'" See also Bryk, "Little Old Moneymaker"; McKelway, "Old Eight Eighty," part 3, pp. 84–87; McKelway, *True Tales,* pp. 243, 246–50; McNamara, *Justice Story,* pp. 206–207; Melanson with Stevens, *Secret Service,* pp. 54–55; "Snow, Fire Turn Up Elusive Suspect," p. 1; and "Suspect Is Released: Man Seized in Bogus Bill Case Awaits Grand Jury Action," *New York Times,* January 16, 1948, p. 16.

15. Bovsun, "Finding 'Mr. 880.'" See also Bryk, "Little Old Moneymaker"; McKelway, "Old Eight Eighty," part 1, p. 36; McKelway, "Old Eight Eighty," part 3, pp. 85–88; McKelway, *True Tales,* pp. 243, 246–49; McNamara, *Justice Story,* pp. 206–207; Melanson with Stevens, *Secret Service,* pp. 54–55; "Snow, Fire Turn Up Elusive Suspect," p. 1; and "Suspect Is Released," p. 16.

16. Melanson with Stevens, *Secret Service,* pp. 54–55. See also "Snow, Fire Turn Up Elusive Suspect," p. 1.

17. Bovsun, "Finding 'Mr. 880.'" See also Bryk, "Little Old Moneymaker"; McKelway, "Old Eight Eighty," part 3, pp. 82, 88–89, 91; McKelway, *True Tales,* pp. 216, 220, 243–44, 252–53; "Snow, Fire Turn Up Elusive Suspect," p. 48; and "Suspect Is Released," p. 16.

18. Bovsun, "Finding 'Mr. 880.'" See also Bryk, "Little Old Moneymaker"; McKelway, "Old Eight Eighty," part 3, pp. 89–94; and McKelway, *True Tales,* pp. 219, 243–44, 253–61.

19. Bryk, "Little Old Moneymaker."

20. Bovsun, "Finding 'Mr. 880.'" See also McKelway, *True Tales,* pp. 217, 219, 256, 261, and "Miscellany," *Time,* July 12, 1948, www.time.com/time/printout/0,8816,804707,00.html (accessed August 30, 2011).

CHAPTER 28. IMPERFECT PITCH—DON LAPRE

1. "Don Lapre Sells Tiny Classified Ads," YouTube, http://www.youtube.com/watch?v =mubCkCAEiDQ&feature (accessed December 21, 2011).

2. Leigh Farr, "Don Wan," *Phoenix New Times,* January 13, 2000, http://www.phoenix newtimes.com/issues/2000-01-13/feature.html/page1.html (accessed December 21, 2011).

3. Farr, "Don Wan." See also "Obituary: Donald Lapre," azcentral.com, 2011, http://www
.legacy.com/obituaries/azcentral/obituary.aspx?n=donald-lapre&pid=154000937 (accessed
December 21, 2011).

4. Kevin Maynard, "Television; They Pitch, and We Catch; Infomercials Get No Respect,
but They Fuel Sales in the Billions. No Wonder They're Multiplying," *Los Angeles Times*,
November 17, 2002, p. E29.

5. "Billy Remembered as Natural Seller," Discovery Communications, 2011, http://dsc
.discovery.com/tv/pitchmen/billy-mays/sympathy.html (accessed December 21, 2011). See also
"Pitchmen: Snake Oil Salesmen or Genius?" Lachapelle Communications, June 3, 2009, http://
lachapellecommunications.com/index.php/2009/06/03/pitchmen (accessed December 21,
2011).

6. Ann Anderson, *Snake Oil, Hustlers, and Hambones: The American Medicine Show*
(Jefferson, NC: McFarland & Co., 2000), pp. 1–2, 31–35, 62–63, 112–14. See also Mary
Calhoun, *Medicine Show: Conning People and Making Them Like It* (New York: Harper & Row,
1976), pp. 1–3, 30, 35, 43, 50–51, 54–56, 61–62.

7. Farr, "Don Wan." See also Timothy Quill and Stephen Barrett, "The Rise and Fall of
Don Lapre, Doug Grant, and 'The Greatest Vitamin in the World,'" Quackwatch, October 7,
2011, http://www.quackwatch.org/11Ind/lapre.html (accessed December 21, 2011).

8. Farr, "Don Wan." See also Don Lapre, *Small Ads, Big Profits: How You Could Turn $30
into a Fortune* (Phoenix: New Strategies, 2000), pp. 2–3, and Quill and Barrett, "Rise and Fall of
Don Lapre."

9. Farr, "Don Wan." See also Lapre, *Small Ads, Big Profits,* p. 17, and Quill and Barrett,
"Rise and Fall of Don Lapre."

10. Farr, "Don Wan." See also Baldomero Garcia, "Don Lapre: The Money Making
Package," *Direct Marketing Review,* 2003, http://www.klausdahl.com/Don_Lapre_The_Money
_Making_Package_review.htm (accessed January 17, 2012); "900 Numbers," 900Numbers.com,
2011, http://900numbers.com (accessed January 22, 2012); and Quill and Barrett, "Rise and Fall
of Don Lapre."

11. Farr, "Don Wan." See also Garcia, "Don Lapre: The Money Making Package"; Lapre,
Small Ads, Big Profits, pp. 74–75; and Quill and Barrett, "Rise and Fall of Don Lapre."

12. Timothy R. Dougherty, "Don LaPre's Pitch Draws Complaints," *Newsday,* November
14, 1993, p. 87. See also Farr, "Don Wan," and Quill and Barrett, "Rise and Fall of Don Lapre."

13. Farr, "Don Wan." See also Quill and Barrett, "Rise and Fall of Don Lapre."

14. Quill and Barrett, "Rise and Fall of Don Lapre."

15. Ibid. See also *United States of America, Plaintiff v. Don Lapre, Defendant*, United
States District Court, District of Arizona, June 8, 2011, http://www.casewatch.org/doj/lapre/
indictment.pdf (accessed December 21, 2011).

16. "Cyber Letters 2006," Department of Health and Human Services, April 2006, http://
www.fda.gov/Drugs/GuidanceComplianceRegulatoryInformation/EnforcementActivitiesby
FDA/CyberLetters/ucm054691.htm (accessed December 21, 2011). See also Quill and Barrett,
"Rise and Fall of Don Lapre."

17. Quill and Barrett, "Rise and Fall of Don Lapre." See also "TV Pitchman Accused of Bilking 220,000 out of $52m," MyFoxPhoenix.com, June 15, 2011, http://www.myfoxphoenix .com/dpp/news/justice/tv-pitchman-accused-of-bilking-220k-out-of-52m-apx-06152011 (accessed December 21, 2011), and *United States of America, Plaintiff v. Don Lapre, Defendant.*

18. "Embattled 'King of Infomercials' Don Lapre 'Slit His Own Throat with a Razor' in Arizona Jail Cell," *Mail Online,* October 5, 2011, http://www.dailymail.co.uk/news/article -2045809/King-Infomercials-Don-Lapre-slit-throat-razor.html (accessed December 21, 2011). See also Quill and Barrett, "Rise and Fall of Don Lapre."

19. Farr, "Don Wan."

20. Ibid.

BIBLIOGRAPHY

Sources used in addition to those cited in Notes.

CHAPTER 1. MERCHANT OF MISERY—JAMES DEWOLF

Curtin, Philip D. *The Atlantic Slave Trade: A Census.* Madison, WI: University of Wisconsin Press, 1969.

"De Wolf, James, (1764–1837)." *Biographical Directory of the United States Congress.* http://bioguide.congress.gov/scripts/biodisplay.pl?index=D000295 (accessed November 23, 2011).

Greene, Lorenzo Johnston. *The Negro in Colonial New England, 1620–1776.* New York: Columbia University Press, 1942.

Klein, Herbert S. *The Atlantic Slave Trade.* Cambridge, England: Cambridge University Press, 1999.

Munro, W. H. *The History of Bristol: The Story of the Mount Hope Lands.* Providence, RI: J. A. & R. A. Reid, 1880.

Northrup, David, ed. *The Atlantic Slave Trade.* Lexington, MA: D. C. Heath, 1994.

Pope-Hennessy, James. *Sins of the Fathers: A Study of the Atlantic Slave Traders, 1441–1807.* New York: Alfred A. Knopf, 1968.

Thomas, Hugh. *The Slave Trade: The Story of the Atlantic Slave Trade, 1440–1870.* New York: Simon & Schuster, 1997.

CHAPTER 2. THE CUTTHROAT CAPTAIN OF CAVE-IN-ROCK—SAMUEL MASON

Allen, John W. *Legends & Lore of Southern Illinois.* Carbondale, IL: Southern Illinois University Press, 1963.

Bell, Raymond Martin. *Captain Samuel Mason: Ohio County (West) Virginia, Washington County, Pennsylvania.* Washington, PA: R. M. Bell, 1992.

———. *Samuel Mason, 1739–1803: Captain in Virginia, Judge in Pennsylvania, River Pirate in Kentucky, Desperado in Mississippi.* Washington, PA: R. M. Bell, 1985.

Botkin, B. A., ed. *A Treasury of Mississippi River Folklore: Stories, Ballads, Traditions and Folkways of the Mid-American River Country.* New York: Crown Publishers, 1955.

"Cave-In-Rock State Park." Illinois Department of Natural Resources, 2011. http://www.dnr
.state.il.us/lands/Landmgt/PARKS/R5/CAVEROCK.htm (accessed December 20, 2011).

How the West Was Won [motion picture]. Metro-Goldwyn-Mayer and Cinerama, 1962.

"Samuel Mason Survives Indian Attack." This Day In History, History.com, August 31, 2011.
http://www.history.com/this-day-in-history/sam-mason-survives-indian-attack (accessed
December 20, 2011).

Starling, Edmund L. "Captain Young and the Exterminators." *History of Henderson County, Kentucky,* 1887. Reprinted by Jon's Southern Illinois History Page, 2000. http://www.illinois
history.com/captyoung.html (accessed January 3, 2012).

"Two Centuries on the Ohio River." Tall Stacks '99, Cincinnati.com. http://www.cincinnati.
com/tallstacks/history_2centuries.html (accessed December 30, 2011).

CHAPTER 3. ARCHITECT OF A TRAGEDY—JOHN CHIVINGTON

Cahill, Kevin. "Silas Soule." KcLonewolf.com, 2006. http://www.kclonewolf.com/History/
SandCreek/Bio/silas-soule-biography.html (accessed March 13, 2011).

"Capt. Soule's Funeral." *Weekly Rocky Mountain News,* May 3, 1865: 1.

Cummins, Joseph. *The World's Bloodiest History: Massacre, Genocide, and the Scars They Left on
Civilization.* Beverly, MA: Fair Winds Press, 2010.

"500 Indians Killed." *Weekly Rocky Mountain News,* December 14, 1864: 1.

Gesell, Laurence E. *Saddle the Wild Wind: The Saga of Squirrel Tooth Alice and Texas Billy
Thompson.* Chandler, AZ: Coast Aire Publications, 2001.

Greene, Jerome A., and Douglas D. Scott. *Finding Sand Creek: History, Archeology, and the 1864
Massacre Site.* Norman, OK: University of Oklahoma Press, 2004.

"The Homicide Last Night." *Weekly Rocky Mountain News,* April 26, 1865: 2.

Prentice, C. A. "Captain Silas S. Soule, a Pioneer Martyr." *Colorado Magazine,* May 1927. http://
www.kclonewolf.com/History/SandCreek/sc-documents/soule-pioneer-martyr.html
(accessed March 24, 2011).

"Silas S. Soule—Two Letters Regarding the Sand Creek Massacre [December 18, 1864; January
8, 1865]." KcLonewolf.com, 2005. http://www.kclonewolf.com/History/SandCreek/sc-
documents/sc-soule-letters.html (accessed March 13, 2011).

CHAPTER 4. THE LATE, UNLAMENTED LITTLE PETE—FONG CHING

"Asian Street Gangs and Organized Crime in Focus: A Rising Threat From the Far East." IPSN,
2006. http://www.ipsn.org/asg08107.html (accessed October 12, 2011).

"Chinese Secret Societies/Freemasons." Chinese in Northwest America Research Committee,
2008. http://www.cinarc.org/Freemasons.html (accessed October 2, 2011).

"Highbinder War in Chinatown." *San Francisco Call,* April 30, 1899: 19.

"A History of Chinese Americans in California." National Park Service, November 17, 2004. http://www.cr.nps.gov/history/online_books/5views/5views3a.htm (accessed October 5, 2011).

"History of the Highbinder's War." *San Francisco Call* Sunday Magazine Section, January 7, 1900: 1, 11.

"The Last of the Highbinders." *Washington Herald* Feature Section, October 31, 1915.

"'Little Pete' Is Avenged." *San Francisco Chronicle,* April 4, 1898: 10.

"'Little Pete' Murdered by His Enemies." *San Francisco Call,* January 24, 1897: 1, 8.

"Little Pete's Career." *San Francisco Chronicle,* May 25, 1896: 6.

"Little Pete Shot in Chinatown." *San Francisco Chronicle,* January 24, 1897: 27.

Masters, Frederic J. "Among the Highbinders: An Account of Chinese Secret Societies." *Californian Illustrated Magazine,* January 1892: 62–74.

"Reward for the Chinese Murderers." *San Francisco Chronicle,* January 29, 1897: 14.

"Three Bullets in Little Pete." *San Francisco Chronicle,* January 25, 1897: 12.

CHAPTER 5.   THE KILLER THEY CALLED HELL'S BELLE— BELLE SORENSEN GUNNESS

"Aid to Mrs. Gunness." *Washington Herald,* May 26, 1908: 3.

Duke, Thomas S. *Celebrated Criminal Cases of America.* San Francisco: James H. Barry Co., 1910.

"100-Year Mystery: Did 'Lady Bluebeard' Get Away with Murder?" Associated Press, April 27, 2008. http://www.foxnews.com/story/0,2933,352784,00.html (accessed September 24, 2010).

Lorenzi, Rossella. "Legendary Murderess Mystery: Case Closed?" Discovery Channel, January 14, 2008. http://dsc.discovery.com/news/2008/01/14/belle-gunness.html (accessed September 30, 2010).

Lovoll, Odd S. "Norwegians." *A Century of Urban Life: The Norwegians in Chicago before 1930,* 1988. Reprinted by Chicago Historical Society, 2005. http://encyclopedia.chicagohistory.org/pages/911.html (accessed October 13, 2010).

"Mrs. Gunness Dead." *New York Tribune,* May 20, 1908: 8.

Sifakis, Carl. *The Encyclopedia of American Crime,* vol. 1. New York: Facts On File, 2001.

CHAPTER 6.   PARTNERS IN PERFIDY—ISAAC HARRIS AND MAX BLANCK

"Blame Shifted on All Sides for Fire Horror." *New York Times,* March 28, 1911: 1.

"Deny Locked Doors, but Girls Insist." *New York Times,* December 19, 1911: 8.

"Door Was Locked at Factory Fire." *New York Times,* December 9, 1911: 3.

"Enraged Women Mob Triangle Waist Men." *New York Times,* December 6, 1911: 24.

"Exhibit Shot Bolt at Triangle Fire." *New York Times,* December 15, 1911: 5.

"Exits Shut Tight at Triangle Fire." *New York Times,* December 14, 1911: 3.

"Girls Fought Vainly at Triangle Doors." *New York Times,* December 12, 1911: 4.

"Indict Owners of Burned Factory." *New York Times,* April 12, 1911: 1.

"Locked in Factory, the Survivors Say, When Fire Started That Cost 141 Lives." *New York Times,* March 27, 1911: 1.

McFarlane, Arthur E. "Fire and the Skyscraper." *McClure's Magazine,* September 1911: 466–83.

"Quick Grand Jury Fire Investigation." *New York Times,* March 26, 1911: 5.

"Triangle Owners Acquitted by Jury." *New York Times,* December 28, 1911: 1.

CHAPTER 7. CHICAGO'S FLORIST-MOBSTER—DEAN O'BANION

"Bury O'Banion without Benefit of Clergy Today." *Chicago Tribune,* November 14, 1924: 2.

"Call O'Banion Hard Boiled or Kind, as One Found Him." *Chicago Tribune,* November 11, 1924: 2.

"Coroner's Jury Unable to Name O'Banion Killers." *Chicago Tribune,* April 22, 1925: 5.

Helmer, William J., and Arthur J. Bilek. *The St. Valentine's Day Massacre: The Untold Story of the Gangland Bloodbath That Brought Down Al Capone.* Nashville, TN: Cumberland House, 2004.

O'Brien, John. "February 14, 1929: The St. Valentine's Day Massacre." *Chicago Tribune,* 2012. http://www.chicagotribune.com/news/politics/chi-chicagodays-valentinesmassacre-story,0,1233196.story (accessed March 15, 2012).

CHAPTER 8. A HUCKSTER'S RISE AND FALL—JOHN BRINKLEY

"About the Bureau of Consumer Protection." Federal Trade Commission, June 16, 2009. http://www.ftc.gov/bcp/about.shtm (accessed October 20, 2009).

"AMA's Bureau of Investigation Exposed Fraud." *Journal of the American Medical Association,* October 18, 1985. http://jama.amaassn.org/cgi/content/summary/254/15/2043 (accessed October 20, 2009).

Cannon, Bill. *Texas: Land of Legend and Lore.* Lanham, MD: Republic of Texas Press, 2004.

"The Goat Gland Doctor [video]." PBS Station KTWU. http://store01.prostores.com/servlet/ktwuwebstore/Detail?no=1 (accessed October 19, 2009).

"Medicine: Goat Glands & Sunshine." *Time,* November 16, 1931. http://www.time.com/time/magazine/article/0,9171,742618,00.html (accessed October 19, 2009).

O'Neal, James E. "Goat Gland Man Has Enduring Appeal." *Radio World,* December 10, 2008. http://www.rwonline.com/article/71102 (accessed October 19, 2009).

Rudel, Anthony. *Hello Everybody! The Dawn of American Radio.* New York: Houghton Mifflin Harcourt Publishing, 2008.

CHAPTER 9. HITCHCOCK'S HIDEOUS INSPIRATION—ED GEIN

Bliss, George. "Identify Head of 2nd Woman on Farm." *Chicago Tribune,* November 20, 1957: 1.

"Decide to Open Graves in Gein Murder Probe." *Chicago Tribune,* November 23, 1957: 3.

Douglas, John, and Mark Olshaker. *Obsession: The FBI's Legendary Profiler Probes the Psyches of Killers, Rapists, and Stalkers and Their Victims and Tells How to Fight Back.* New York: Scribner, 1998.

"Ed Gein, 77; Inspired Hitchcock's 'Psycho.'" *Chicago Tribune,* July 27, 1984: A6.

"Gein to Get Sanity Hearing; Rule He Can't Stand Trial." *Chicago Tribune,* December 24, 1957: 6.

Holmes, Paul. "15 Horror Victims Found." *Chicago Tribune,* November 20, 1957: 1.

———. "Hint Killer Is Cannibal!" *Chicago Tribune,* November 19, 1957: 1.

Schechter, Harold. *The Serial Killer Files: The Who, What, Where, How, and Why of the World's Most Terrifying Murderers.* New York: Ballantine Books, 2004.

Stokes, Bill. "A Grim Anniversary Stirs Uneasy Memories." *Chicago Tribune,* November 14, 1982: F8.

"Wisconsin Killer Gein Ruled Guilty, Insane; Recommitted." *Chicago Tribune,* November 15, 1968: 12.

CHAPTER 10. SALEM'S RABID WITCH-HUNTER—WILLIAM STOUGHTON

"Chronology of Events Relating to the Salem Witchcraft Trials." University of Missouri-Kansas City School of Law, September 2009. http://law2.umkc.edu/faculty/projects/ftrials/salem/ASAL_CH.HTM (accessed February 15, 2012).

"Famous American Trials: Salem Witchcraft Trials 1692." University of Missouri-Kansas City School of Law, September 2009. http://law2.umkc.edu/faculty/projects/ftrials/salem/SALEM.HTM (accessed October 27, 2011).

"The Salem Witchcraft Site." Tulane University. http://www.tulane.edu/~salem/index.html (accessed February 5, 2012).

"Salem Witch Trials." University of Virginia, 2002. http://salem.lib.virginia.edu/home.html (accessed February 16, 2012).

"Understanding the Salem Witch Trials." Edsitement, National Endowment for the Humanities. http://edsitement.neh.gov/lesson-plan/understanding-salem-witch-trials#sect-background (accessed February 9, 2012).

Upham, Caroline E. *Salem Witchcraft in Outline: The Story without the Tedious Detail.* Salem, MA: Eben Putnam, 1895.

Woodward, W. Elliot, ed. *Records of Salem Witchcraft, Copied from the Original Documents.* New York: Da Capo Press, 1969 (reprint of 1864–65 editions).

CHAPTER 13. LINCOLN'S MISSING BODYGUARD—JOHN PARKER

"Ford's Theatre and the House Where Lincoln Died." National Park Service, 1987.
Good, Timothy Sean. *We Saw Lincoln Shot.* Jackson, MS: University Press of Mississippi, 1995.
Pace, Gina. "What If Lincoln Lived?" CBS News, May 18, 2007. http://www.cbsnews.com/stories/2007/05/18/national/main2825645.shtml (accessed July 6, 2009).

CHAPTER 14. SQUIRREL TOOTH ALICE—LIBBY THOMPSON

Agnew, Jeremy. *Brides of the Multitude: Prostitution in the Old West.* Lake City, CO: Western Reflections Publishing, 2008.
Butler, Anne M. *Daughters of Joy, Sisters of Misery: Prostitutes in the American West, 1865–90.* Urbana, IL: University of Illinois Press, 1985.
"The Rail Heads of the Great Texas Cattle Trails." KansasCattleTowns.org. http://www.kansas cattletowns.org/index.html (accessed August 7, 2011).

CHAPTER 16. THE VERY MELLOW YELLOW KID—JOSEPH WEIL

Maurer, David W. *The Big Con: The Story of the Confidence Man.* New York: Anchor Books, 1999. Reprint of 1940 edition.
Nash, Jay Robert. *Bloodletters and Badmen: A Narrative Encyclopedia of American Criminals from the Pilgrims to the Present.* New York: M. Evans and Co., 1995.
———. *Hustlers and Con Men: An Anecdotal History of the Confidence Man and His Games.* New York: M. Evans and Co., 1976.
"Yellow Kid, 82, Hospitalized; Charity Case." *Chicago Tribune,* June 29, 1957: 21.
"'Yellow Kid,' Still Dapper, Hale, Nears 86." *Chicago Tribune,* June 26, 1961: B2.

CHAPTER 17. YOU BET YOUR LIFE—ALVIN THOMAS

Bradshaw, Jon. *Fast Company.* New York: Vintage Books, 1987.
Kaplan, Michael. "All Bets Are On." *Cigar Aficionado,* August 1, 2002. http://www.cigar aficionado.com/webfeatures/show/id/All-Bets-Are-On_7140 (accessed February 25, 2012).

Minnesota Fats, with Tom Fox. *The Bank Shot and Other Great Robberies*. Cleveland: World Publishing Co., 1966.

"Rothstein Evidence Ample, Says Banton." *New York Times,* December 2, 1928: 1.

"'Titanic' Thompson Recovering Rapidly." *New York Times,* November 15, 1929: 23.

CHAPTER 19. THE SILKEN VOICE OF TREACHERY—MILDRED GILLARS

"'Axis Sally' Is Found Guilty; Sentence on Treason Delayed." *New York Times,* March 11, 1949: 1.

"Axis Sally Is Freed From Federal Prison on Parole." *New York Times,* July 11, 1961: 14.

"'Axis Sally' Jurors Hear Last Witness." *New York Times,* March 5, 1949: 4.

Edwards, John Carver. *Berlin Calling: American Broadcasters in Service to the Third Reich*. New York: Praeger Publishers, 1991.

CHAPTER 21. THE WITCH OF WALL STREET—HETTY GREEN

"Hetty Green's Son and Heir Trained by Her." *New York Times,* July 9, 1916: SM5.

Jepson, Jill. *Women's Concerns: Twelve Women Entrepreneurs of the Eighteenth and Nineteenth Centuries*. New York: Peter Lang, 2009.

Lewis, Arthur H. *The Day They Shook the Plum Tree*. New York: Harcourt, Brace & World, 1963.

"Seventy Years Rest Lightly on Mrs. Hetty Green." *New York Times,* November 5, 1905.

CHAPTER 22. KING OF THE CANNIBAL ISLANDS—DAVID O'KEEFE

Hezel, Francis X. *Strangers in Their Own Land: A Century of Colonial Rule in the Caroline and Marshall Islands*. Honolulu: University of Hawaii Press, 1995.

Hezel, Francis X. *The First Taint of Civilization: A History of the Caroline and Marshall Islands in Pre-colonial Days, 1521–1885*. Honolulu: University of Hawaii Press, 1983.

CHAPTER 23. MASTER SALESMAN OF A DUBIOUS LEGEND— HERBERT BRIDGMAN

Babst, Earl D. "In Memory of Herbert L. Bridgman." *Diamond of Psi Upsilon,* November 24, 1924: 3–10.

"Baffin Bay & Davis Strait." PEW Environment Group, 2010. http://www.oceansnorth.org/baffin-bay-davis-strait (accessed September 16, 2010).

Brendle, Anna. "Profile: African-American North Pole Explorer Matthew Henson."

National Geographic News, January 15, 2003. http://news.nationalgeographic.com/news/2003/01/0110_030113_henson.html (accessed August 31, 2010).

"Peary Discovers the North Pole after Eight Trials in 23 Years." *New York Times,* September 7, 1909: 1. http://www.nytimes.com/learning/general/onthisday/big/0406.html (accessed September 17, 2010).

CHAPTER 24. THE CONSUMMATE GOLD DIGGER—PEGGY HOPKINS JOYCE

Joyce, Peggy Hopkins. *Transatlantic Wife.* New York: Macaulay Co., 1933.

"Peggy Hopkins Joyce." Internet Broadway Database, 2011. http://www.ibdb.com/person.php?id=47282 (accessed November 22, 2011).

"Peggy Hopkins Joyce (1893–1957)." Internet Movie Database, 2011. http://www.imdb.com/name/nm0431591 (accessed November 22, 2011).

"Peggy Hopkins Joyce Re-Wed." *New York Times,* May 31, 1956: 13.

"Sues Peggy Hopkins for His Freedom." *New York Times,* April 12, 1921: 8.

CHAPTER 25. THE MAD, SAD POET OF GREENWICH VILLAGE— MAXWELL BODENHEIM

"Anti-Red Writers Barred from WPA, Witness Declares." *New York Times,* September 16, 1938: 1.

Bodenheim, Maxwell. *Replenishing Jessica.* New York: Boni & Liveright, 1925.

Bodenheim, Maxwell. *Selected Poems of Maxwell Bodenheim, 1914–1944.* New York: Beechhurst Press, 1946.

"Bodenheim Service Will Be Held Today." *New York Times,* February 10, 1954: 26.

Day, Dorothy. *Loaves and Fishes.* New York: Harper & Row, 1963.

"Defends Writings of WPA Authors." *New York Times,* July 22, 1937: 9.

"Mental Tests Set for Poet's Slayer." *New York Times,* February 12, 1954: 33.

Rotella, Carlo. "Chicago Literary Renaissance." *Encyclopedia of Chicago,* 2005. http://www.encyclopedia.chicagohistory.org/pages/257.html (accessed April 23, 2010).

Solotaroff, Ted, ed. *A Discourse on Hip: Selected Writings of Milton Klonsky.* Detroit: Wayne State University Press, 1991.

CHAPTER 26. THE BIFURCATED CONGRESSMAN—SAMUEL DICKSTEIN

Berlet, Chip, and Matthew N. Lyons. *Right-Wing Populism in America: Too Close for Comfort.* New York: Guilford Press, 2000.

"Dickstein Assails 'Isms.'" *New York Times,* May 24, 1936: 6.

"Dickstein, Samuel, (1885–1954)." *Biographical Directory of the United States Congress,* 2010. http:// bioguide.congress.gov/scripts/biodisplay.pl?index=D000335 (accessed April 28, 2010).

Morrison, David. *Heroes, Antiheroes, and the Holocaust: American Jewry and Historical Choices.* Jerusalem: Gefen Publishing House, 1999.

Ogden, August Raymond. *The Dies Committee: A Study of the Special House Committee for the Investigation of Un-American Activities, 1938–1944.* Westport, CT: Greenwood Press, 1984.

CHAPTER 27. THE FRUGAL COUNTERFEITER—EMERICH JUETTNER

Bloom, Murray Teigh. *Money of Their Own: The Great Counterfeiters.* New York: Charles Scribner's Sons, 1957.

Mister 880 [movie]. Twentieth Century Fox, 1950. Rated at tcm.com, http://www.tcm.com/ tcmdb/title/83700/Mister-880 (accessed August 29, 2011).

"Secret Service History." United States Secret Service, 2010. http://www.secretservice.gov/ history.shtml (accessed September 8, 2011).

CHAPTER 28. IMPERFECT PITCH—DON LAPRE

Duell, Mark. "Top TV Pitchman Don Lapre 'Commits Suicide' in Prison Just Two Days Before $52m Fraud Trial." *Mail Online,* October 3, 2011. http://www.dailymail.co.uk/news/ article-2044687/Don-Lapre-dead-Arizona-TV-pitchman-commits-suicide-cell-52m-fraud-trial.html (accessed December 21, 2011).

"Indicted Donald Lapre Captured in Tempe." MyFoxPhoenix.com, June 23, 2011.

http://www.myfoxphoenix.com/dpp/news/crime/indicted-donald-lapre-captured-in-tempe-6-23-2011 (accessed December 21, 2011).

Lapre, Don. *Profit Per Minute: How to Get into the 900 Number Business.* Phoenix: New Strategies, 1993.

Mr. Pigeon. "Get Rich Quick! Mr. Pigeon Pays $79.95 for the Secrets of Wealth." *Minneapolis Star Tribune,* April 3, 1994: 01D.

Mr. Pigeon. "Secret of Success: Mr. Pigeon Is 11 Steps Closer to Big Bucks." *Minneapolis Star Tribune,* May 1, 1994: 01D.

"Phoenix TV Pitchman to Remain in Custody." MyFoxPhoenix.com, July 29, 2011.

http://www.myfoxphoenix.com/dpp/news/crime/apx-AZPitchman-Charged_63768879-07292011 (accessed December 21, 2011).

"Ron Popeil." *Biography,* A&E Television Networks, 2012. http://www.biography.com/people/ ron-popeil-177863 (accessed January 22, 2012).

"TV Pitchman a No Show at Federal Arraignment." MyFoxPhoenix.com, June 23, 2011.

http://www.myfoxphoenix.com/dpp/news/justice/tv-pitchman-a-no-show-at-federal-arraignment -apx-06232011 (accessed December 21, 2011).

ILLUSTRATION CREDITS

James DeWolf, page 15: Courtesy of US Senate Historical Office.

Samuel Mason, page 23: Oil painting by J. Bernhard Alberts, 1916.

John Chivington, page 29: Used with permission from the Denver Public Library, Western History Collection, Z-128.

Fong Ching, page 37: Photographic print. Used with permission from the San Francisco History Center, San Francisco Public Library.

Belle Sorensen Gunness, page 45: Courtesy La Porte County Historical Society Museum.

Isaac Harris and Max Blanck, page 53: Photograph by Brown Brothers, ca. early 1900s, used with permission from Kheel Center for Labor-Management Documentation and Archives, Cornell University, http://www.ilr.cornell .edu/trianglefire/.

Dean O'Banion, page 61: © Bettmann/CORBIS.

John Brinkley, page 69: Photographic print, 1920, Library of Congress, Prints and Photographs Division, LC-USZ62-107748.

Ed Gein, page 77: Photographic print, 1957, United Press International telephoto, New York World Telegram & Sun Newspaper Photograph Collection, Library of Congress, Prints and Photographs Division, LC-USZ62-128628.

William Stoughton, page 85: Harvard Art Museums/Fogg Museum, Harvard University Portrait Collection, Gift of John Cooper to Harvard College, 1810, H37.

Daniel Drew, page 93: Wood engraving from photograph by Mathew B. Brady, 1867, Library of Congress, Prints and Photographs Division, LC-USZ62-138440.

James Lane, page 101: Glass, wet collodian, ca. 1855–1865, Brady-Hand Photograph Collection, Library of Congress, Prints and Photographs Division, LC-DIG-cwpbh-01175.

John Parker, page 107: Albumen print, 1865, Civil War Photograph Collection, Library of Congress, Prints and Photographs Division, LC-DIG-ppmsca-23872.

Libby Thompson, page 113: Used with permission from Kansas State Historical Society.

Burt Alvord, page 121: Used with permission from Arizona Historical Society, PC 1000, Portraits–Alvord, Burt, # 29897.

Joseph Weil, page 129: Front cover of *"Yellow Kid" Weil: The Autobiography of America's Master Swindler* by J. R. "Yellow Kid" Weil and W. T. Brannon, reprinted 2011 by Nabat/AK Press.

Alvin Thomas, page 137: Associated Press.

Charles Davenport, page 143: Courtesy of Cold Spring Harbor Laboratory Archives.

Mildred Gillars, page 153: Associated Press photograph, 1946, New York World Telegram & Sun Newspaper Photograph Collection, Library of Congress, Prints and Photographs Division, LC-USZ62-117758.

Maggie and Kate Fox, page 163: Photo by Thomas M. Easterly, 1852. Courtesy of the Missouri History Museum, St. Louis.

Hetty Green, page 171: Photographic print, ca. 1897, Library of Congress, Prints and Photographs Division, LC-USZ62-42657.

David O'Keefe, page 179: Courtesy of Don Evans, O'Keefe's Waterfront Inn, Yap, Micronesia.

Herbert Bridgman, page 187: Photo by Gessford, from *His Last Voyage: Herbert Lawrence Bridgman, 1844–1924,* published 1924 by *Brooklyn Standard Union.*

Peggy Hopkins Joyce, page 195: Used with permission from Wisconsin Center for Film and Theater Research, Image ID: 100887.

Maxwell Bodenheim, page 203: Photographic print, 1919, New York World Telegram & Sun Newspaper Photograph Collection, Library of Congress, Prints and Photographs Division, LC-USZ62-112040.

Samuel Dickstein, page 211: Photo by Harris and Ewing, ca. 1937, Harris & Ewing Collection, Library of Congress, Prints and Photographs Division, LC-DIG-hec-22296.

Emerich Juettner, page 219: Photo by Nick Peterson/*New York Daily News* via Getty Images.

Don Lapre, page 227: Front cover of *Small Ads, Big Profits: How You Could Turn $30 into a Fortune* by Don Lapre, published 2000 by New Strategies.

INDEX

Aberdeen, SD, 49
Abilene, KS, 115, 116
abolitionism, 17, 20, 31, 32, 102, 165, 166
advertising, Don Lapre's use of, 227–33
Aiken, Conrad, 206
Alvord, Albert "Burt," 121–28
Alvord, Charles E., 123, 125, 127
Alvord, Lola, 124, 126
Alvord, Lucinda, 123, 125
Alvord, Mary, 127
American Civil Liberties Union, 213
American Communist Party, 208, 213, 214, 215–16
American Eugenics Society, 147, 150
American Medical Association, 73, 74
American Mercury (magazine), 207
American Museum of Natural History, 188
American Newspaper Publishers Association, 189
Amherst, MA, 189
Amherst College, 189
Amundsen, Roald, 190
Anderson, George, 49
Anderson, Margaret, 205
Anderson, Sherwood, 206
Anna Sims (schooner), 180
Antarctica, 190, 192
anti-Semitism, 149, 154, 156, 157, 205, 212, 213, 214
Apache Indians, 114
Appomattox Court House, 107
Arapaho Indians, 29–30, 33, 34
Archibald, Everett, Jr., 197
Arctic exploration, 187–93
Argus (newspaper), 102

Arizona
    Alvin Thomas in, 139
    Burt Alvord in, 122, 123, 124, 126, 127
    Don Lapre in, 228, 230, 231, 232
Arizona Historical Society, 127
Arizona Rangers, 126
Arkansas
    Alvin Thomas in, 138, 139
    John Brinkley in, 71
Arnold, Eddie, 73
arsenic poisoning, 50
arson, 46, 50, 51, 81
Asch Building, 54, 55, 56, 58
Astor, John Jacob, 94
Atlanta federal penitentiary, 130, 134
Autry, Gene, 73
Axis Sally. *See* Gillars, Mildred "Axis Sally"

Baffin Bay, 187
Baldwin, James, 217
Barnum, P. T., 168
Bates, Norman (fictional character), 82
Battle of Dry Wood Creek, 103
"beer wars," 62
Bell, Alexander Graham, 147, 192
Bell, John, 165
Bellows Fall, VT, 175
Belvidere (merchant ship), 180
Bennett Medical College, 71
Berlin, Germany, 155–56, 157
Berry, George, 48
Better Business Bureau, 230
betting scams, 132, 133, 141–42
Beverley Hillbillies, The (TV show), 94
Bibliographies and Indices Project, 208

Big Nose Kate, 117
Bisbee gang, 123
Bishop, Bridget, 86, 89
Black, Ladbroke, 177
Black, Starr & Frost (jewelry store), 196
Black Fonso (race horse), 132
Black Kettle (chief), 29–30, 31, 32, 33, 34
Blanck, Max, 53–60
Blaylock, Mattie, 117
Blaze Ball (artists' soiree), 207
Blazing Saddles (movie), 122
Bloch, Robert, 82
"Bloodless Third." *See* Third Colorado
  Cavalry
Bloody Market Streeters (gang), 63
Bodenheim, Maxwell "Bogie," 203–210
Bodenheimer, Caroline, 205
Bodenheimer, Solomon, 205
boo how doy ("highbinders"), 40–41, 42
Booth, John Wilkes, 12, 110, 111
Bo Sin Seer Tong, 41
Bostwick, Charles, 57
Bradford, William, 19
Brazos River, 114
Brennan, Walter, 24
Bridgman, Helen Bartlett, 191, 192
Bridgman, Herbert, 187–93
Brinkley, John, 69–75
Brinkley, Johnny Boy, 74
Brinkley, Minnie. *See* Jones, Minnie
Brinkley, Sally. *See* Wike, Sally
Brinkley Goats (baseball team), 72
Brinkley-Jones Hospital, 72
Bristol, RI, 15–16, 17, 20, 21, 22
Brooklyn Institute of Arts and Sciences, 189
Brooklyn Polytechnic Institute, 145
Brooklyn Standard Union (newspaper), 189
Brother Jonathan (a pitch artist), 229
Brown, John, 19
Browne, Katrina, 21
Brown University, 19
Bryan, William Jennings, 178
Bryant, William Cullen, 168
Buck, Carrie, 143–45

Budsberg, Ole, 48, 50
Buffalo Bill (fictional serial killer), 82
Buffett, Warren, 94
Bunker, Archie (fictional character), 94
Burned-Over District in New York State,
  166
Burns & Allen, 200
Burnt District, 105
Burroughs, George, 89
Burts, Matt, 125
business cons. *See* hucksters, swindlers, and
  cons
businessmen and women
    Daniel Drew (speculator), 93–99
    David O'Keefe (South Pacific trader),
      179–85
    Don Lapre (pitchman and huckster),
      227–33
    Hetty Green (Wall Street investor/
      miser), 171–78
    Isaac Harris and Max Blanck (Triangle
      Shirtwaist Factory), 53–60
    James DeWolf (slave trade), 15–22
    John Brinkley (medical malpractice),
      69–75

Cagney, James, 62
Cairo, IL, 24
California, 69–75
    Burt Alvord in, 123
    Chinese gangs in, 37–43
    Hetty Green in, 176
    involuntary sterilizations in, 148
    John Brinkley in, 72
    Libby Thompson in, 119
California State Board of Charities and Cor-
  rections, 148
Cannon, James, 34
Canton, China, 39
Cape York meteorites, 188
Capone, Al, 62, 64, 65, 66, 138
Carlson, Ester, 51
Carmel, NY, 94, 99
Carnegie, Andrew, 94, 177

Carnegie Institution for Science, 147
Caroline Islands, 180, 181–82, 183, 184, 185
Carroll, Earl, 200
Carson, Rachel, 209
case number 880, 222, 223, 224–25
Cassadaga, FL, 169
Cassidy, Butch, 126
Catholic Encyclopedia, 135
Catholicism, 159
cattle business, 93–95, 97
Cave-in-Rock, OH, 24, 25–26, 28
Chacon, Augustine "The Hairy One," 124, 126
Chandler, Harry, 72
Chaplin, Charlie, 196
charlatanism. *See* hucksters, swindlers, and cons
Charleston, SC, 16, 17
Charles Town, WV, 25
Chase, Bert, 48–49
cheapskate, Hetty Green as a, 174, 176–77
Chee Kung Tong, 40
Chemical National Bank, 176
Chevy Chase College, 197
Cheyenne Indians, 29–30, 32, 33, 34
Chia Pets, 229
Chicago, IL
    Belle Sorensen Gunnes in, 45–46, 47, 48, 51, 52
    Charles Davenport in, 146
    Chicago Renaissance, 205
    Dean O'Banion in, 61–67
    Hetty Green in, 176
    John Brinkley in, 70, 72
    Joseph "Yellow Kid" Weil in, 129–30, 131–32, 135
    Maxwell Bodenheim in, 205–206
    Peggy Hopkins Joyce in, 195, 198, 199
Chicago Tribune (newspaper), 66, 81, 130, 134, 135
Chinese Exclusion Act of 1882, 39
Chinese gangs, 37–43
Ching, Fong. *See* Fong Ching
Chisholm Trail, 116, 117

Chivington, John, 29–35
Chrysler, Walter, 196
circus, 95, 135
City College of New York, 212
Civil War, 12, 30, 31, 97, 99, 102, 107, 114, 166, 223
Clairmont, Robert, 207
Clanton, Billy, 122
Clanton, Ike, 122
Clark, Snow, 139
Cleaver, Ward and June (fictional characters), 145
Cochise County, AZ, 123, 124, 125, 126, 127
Cold Springs Harbor, NY, 146, 150
Cold War, 215
Collins, Charles, 20
Colorado
    Libby Thompson in, 117
    Sand Creek massacre, 29–35
Comanche Indians capture of Libby Thompson, 114
Communist Party. *See* American Communist Party
Congress. *See* House of Representatives; Senate
Congressman, Samuel Dickstein as, 211–18
con men. *See* hucksters, swindlers, and cons
Conrad, Joseph, 184
Cook, Frederick A., 188, 189–90, 191, 192
Cooper, James Fenimore, 168
Copper Queen mine, 133
copra, 181, 182, 183, 184
Corey, Giles, 89–90
Corinthian Hall, 167
Cortez, Aimee, 208
Cotton Tail, 117
Coughlin, "Bathhouse John," 131
counterfeiter, Emerich Jeuttner as, 219–25
courtesan, Peggy Hopkins Joyce as, 195–201
Court of Oyer and Terminer, 88, 90
Coward, Noel, 196
Crain, Thomas, 58
Cramer, Joseph, 31, 32, 33

Crawford, James, 71, 74
Crime Does Not Pay—Enough (Weil), 135
Croker, Edward, 57, 60
"Crook." *See* Dickstein, Samuel
Crook, William H., 110
Cuba, slaves in, 19, 20
Curtis, Samuel, 31, 32
Custer, George Armstrong, 34

dance hall girl, 115, 116–17
Darwin, Charles, 146, 166
Davenport, Charles Benedict, 143–51
Davenport Brothers (spiritualists), 168
Dear, Dorothy, 208
"Death" (poem by Bodenheim), 210
Del Rio, TX, 73, 74
Denver, CO, and the Sand Creek massacre,
    29, 30, 31, 33, 34
Dewey, C. (dog), 177
DeWolf, Charles, 18
DeWolf, George, 18, 20
DeWolf, James, 15–22
DeWolf, John, 18
DeWolf, Levi, 18, 19
DeWolf, Mark Anthony, 18
DeWolf, Nancy (Bradford), 16
DeWolf, Thomas Norman, 21
DeWolf, William, 18
"Diamonds Are a Girl's Best Friend" (song),
    201
Dickstein, Samuel, 211–18
Dickstein Resolution, 212
"Dickstein's Monster." *See* House of Repre-
    sentatives, House Un-American Activities
    Committee
Dies, Martin, 213
Dies Committee, 213–14, 215
dietary supplements, 231–32, 233
Dimples (silent film), 198
direct-response advertising on TV, 229
District Court in Arizona, 232
District Court in Washington, DC, 157–58
Dr. Strangelove (movie), 148
Dodge City, KS, 117, 118

dollar bills, counterfeiting of. *See* Juettner,
    Emerich
Downing, Bill, 125
Doyle, Arthur Conan, 165
Dreiser, Theodore, 206
Drew, Daniel, 93–99
Drew, Robinson & Company, 97
Drew, Virginia, 207–208
Drew Female Seminary, 99
Drucci, Vincent "Schemer," 64, 66
Duffy, John, 66
Dugan, Mickey (fictional character), 131
Dunlap, "Three-Fingered Jack," 124, 125
Durcal, Duke of, 199
Durocher, Leo, 48
Dutch Jake, 117

Earp, Morgan, 122
Earp, Virgil, 122
Earp, Wyatt, 114, 117, 122
earthquake in New Madrid, MO, 26–27
Easton, Anthony, 200
Eastwood, Clint, 11
Eclectic Medical University, 71
880, case number, 222, 223, 224–25
Elbow Lake, MN, 48
"Electro Medic Doctors," 71
Eliot, T. S., 207
Ellesmere Island, 187
Ellsworth, KS, 117
ergot causing hallucinations, 90–91
Ermond, Charles, 49
eugenics and Charles Davenport, 143–51
Eugenics Record Office, 146, 149, 150
Euless, TX, 142
Evans, John, 34
Ewing, Thomas, 104–106
Examination of a Witch (Matteson), 89
Explorers Club, 189, 190

Fagan, Ruth, 209
Fairbank, AZ, 125
Falcon (steamer), 187–88
Farewell to Arms, A (screenplay), 206

FBI, 215, 216
F. C. Peters & Company, 39
Federal Radio Commission, 73
Federal Reformatory for Women, 159
Federal Theatre Project, 214
Federal Trade Commission, 74
Federal Writers' Project, 208, 214
Fields, W. C., 200
"Fighting Parson." *See* Chivington, John
Finan, Grace, 209
First Colorado Cavalry, 30, 31
Fishbein, Morris, 73, 74
Fish Committee, 213
Fisk, James, 97, 98
Fitzgerald, F. Scott, 210
Flanagan, Hallie, 214
flimflam. *See* hucksters, swindlers, and cons
Folsom State Prison, 41
Fong Ching, 37–43
Food and Drug Administration, 231–32
Fordham University, 176
Ford's Theatre, 12, 108, 109–110
forgery, Emerich Juettner as a counterfeiter, 219–25
Fort Henry, 25
Fort Leavenworth, 205
Fort Lyon, 29–30, 31
Fort Riley, 32
Fort Worth, TX, 114
Fox, John, 163
Fox, Kate, 163–70
Fox, Leah, 166, 169
Fox, Maggie, 163–70
Fox, Margaret, 163
Frances, Madame, 197–98
Frank Leslie's Illustrated Newspaper, 189
Frederick County, VA, 25, 109
French, Barton, 199
Friends of New Germany, 213
Front Page, The (screenplay), 206

Galton, Francis, 146
gambler, Alvin Thomas as a, 137–42
gangs, 23–28, 37–43, 61–67, 104–106, 123

Gein, Augusta, 78, 79
Gein, Edward Theodore "Ed," 11, 77–82
Gein, Henry, 78, 79
Genna brothers, 65, 66
Gentlemen Prefer Blondes (Loos), 201
Georgia, David O'Keefe in, 179
Georgie May (Bodenheim), 208
Germany
    desire for the Caroline Islands, 183
    See also Nazi Germany
Gesell, Laurence E., 119
Gibson Girl look, 54
Gilded Age, 99
Gillars, Mildred "Axis Sally," 11, 153–59
Gi Sin Seer Tong, 40
Glenwood Cemetery, 111
goat glands, 70, 72–73, 74
gold digger, Peggy Hopkins Joyce as, 195–201
Golden Globe Award, 225
golf course scams, 141–42
Gollmar, Robert H., 82
Gone with the Wind (screenplay), 206
Good, Dorcas, 88
Good, Sarah, 87, 88, 90
Goodman, Walter, 217
Gould, Jay, 97, 98
Grant, Doug, 231
Grant, Madison, 149
Grant, Ulysses S., 107, 108
Grapes of Wrath, The (Steinbeck), 210
Great Depression, 70, 200, 204, 208, 210
Greatest Vitamin in the World, 231–32, 233
Great Gatsby, The (Scott), 210
greed, 12, 52, 59, 74, 94, 130, 134, 159, 173, 215, 217
    lack of greed, 222
Greeley, Horace, 168
Green, Edward, 175, 176, 177
Green, Gerald, 184
Green, Hetty, 171–78
Green, Ned, 175, 176, 177, 178
Green, Sylvia, 175, 178
Greenland, 187, 192

Greenville, SC, 71
Greenwich Village, poet of, 203–210
Greta Garbo Social Club, 207
grifters. *See* hucksters, swindlers, and cons
Grim Chieftain. *See* Lane, James H.
Gunness, Belle Sorensen, 45–52
Gunness, Peter, 47, 48, 52
Gunness, Philip, 48, 50
Gunsmoke (TV show), 115
Gurholdt, Henry, 48, 50
Guys and Dolls (musical), 138
Gwenn, Edmund, 225

Haley, James, 114, 115
Haley, Mary Elizabeth. *See* Thompson, Libby
Hamlin's Wizard Oil, 229
Han Chinese, 38
Hardin County, OH, 24
Hardy, Oliver, 57
Harpe, Micajah, "Big Harpe," 26, 27
Harpe, Wiley, "Little Harpe," 26, 27–28
Harriman, Mary, 147
Harris, Clara, 108
Harris, Ira, 108
Harris, Isaac, 53–60
Harvard College/University, 88, 90, 91, 146, 147
Haskell, Eddie (fictional character), 228
hatchet men. *See* "highbinders" (*boo how ody*)
Haunted Wood: Soviet Espionage in America—the Stalin Era, The (Weinstein and Vassiliev), 215
Hawkins, Jeb (fictional character), 24
Hecht, Ben, 206, 209, 210
Helgelein, Andrew, 49, 50
Helgelein, Asle, 49, 50
"Hell's Belle." *See* Gunness, Belle Sorensen
Henderson, KY, 25
Henson, Matthew, 192
Herbert, Wally, 191
Heredity in Relation to Eugenics (Davenport), 147, 149
Hermanville, MS, 204
Hezel, Francis X., 184

Hickok, Wild Bill, 116
"highbinders" (*boo how ody*), 40–41, 42, 43
highwaymen, 23–28
hijackings, 64
Hirsch, Michael, 56
His Majesty O'Keefe (Klingman and Green), 184
Hiss, Alger, 215
Hitchcock, Alfred, 77–82
Hitler, Adolf, 149, 150, 154, 211, 213, 214, 217
Hoffman, Abbie, 216
Hogan, Ben, 142
Hogan, Frank, 131
Hogan, Mary, 80
"Hogan's Alley" (comic strip), 131
Holcomb, Crayton Philo, 182–83
Holliday, Doc, 114, 117, 122
Holmes, Oliver Wendell, Jr., 145
Holmes, Sherlock (fictional character), 165
Holy Name Cathedral, 66, 67
Holy Name Parochial School, 63
Homeland Security, 222
"Home Sweet Home" (Nazi radio show), 156
Hong Kong, 180
Hood County, TX, 114
Hoover, J. Edgar, 216
Hopkins, Sherburne P., 197–98
horse racing scams, 132, 141
horseshoes, 141
Houdini, Harry, 138, 169
House of Representatives
    House Un-American Activities Committee (HUAC), 212, 213–14, 215
    Samuel Dickstein in, 211–18
Howland, Gideon, 172, 173
Howland, Sylvia, 172, 173, 174
How the West Was Won (movie), 24, 26
HUAC. *See* House of Representatives, House Un-American Activities Committee
hucksters, swindlers, and cons
    Alvin Thomas (gambler), 138

Daniel Drew (speculator), 93–99
Don Lapre (pitchman and huckster),
    227–33
John Brinkley (medical huckster),
    69–75
Joseph Weil (con man), 129–35
Maggie and Kate Fox (Spiritualism),
    163–70
Hudson, Ernest, 199
Hunter College, 156
Hurley, Elizabeth, 51
hustlers. *See* hucksters, swindlers, and cons
Hydesville, NY, 163, 166, 168

Illinois
    Dean O'Banion in, 63
    Mary Todd Lincoln returning to, 111
    Samuel Mason in, 23, 24, 26
    See also Chicago, IL
Indiana
    Belle Sorensen Gunnes in, 46, 47, 48,
        50, 52
    involuntary sterilizations in, 148
    James Lane in, 102
Indian John (slave), 87
infomercials of Don Lapre, 227–33
*Inheriting the Trade: A Northern Family
    Confronts Its Legacy as the Largest
    Slave-Trading Dynasty in U.S. History*
    (DeWolf), 21
insanity
    Ed Gein found criminally insane, 81, 82
    See also psychopaths
insurance claims
    collected by Belle Sorensen Gunness,
        46, 47
    for Triangle Shirtwaist Factory fire, 58
Internal Revenue Service, 74, 231
International House (movie), 200
Inuits, 188, 192
involuntary sterilization. *See* eugenics and
    Charles Davenport
Irish Queen, 117

Jackson, Frank, 141
James, Edgar, 199
James, Frank, 104, 105, 106
James, Jesse, 105
James-Younger gang, 104–106, 125
Japan, 184
Jayhawkers, 102, 103, 104, 105
Jazz Age, 197, 200, 203–204, 207, 208, 210
Jersey City, NJ, 98
John J. Cisco and Son, 175–76
Johnson, Esther, 51
Johnson, Jim, 139
Joliet prison, 134
Jones, Minnie, 71, 72
Journal of the American Medical Association,
    73, 74
Joyce, James Stanley, 195–96, 198–200, 201
Joyce, Peggy Hopkins, 195–201
Joyce, Stanley, 195–96
Joyce, William, 156
Juettner, Emerich, 219–25
June, Titus, Angevine & Crane Circus, 95

Kaiser Wilhelm Institute for Psychiatry, 150
Kansas
    James Lane in, 101–106
    John Brinkley in, 69, 70, 71, 72, 73
    John Chivington in, 31
Kansas Brigade, 102
    See also Jayhawkers
Kansas City, KS, John Brinkley in, 70, 71, 73
Kansas City Star (newspaper), 73
"Kansas First, Kansas Best." *See* KFKB radio
    station
Kansas Medical Board, 73
Keckley, Elizabeth, 111
Kellogg, John, 147
Kentucky, Samuel Mason in, 25, 26, 27
KFKB radio station, 72–73
KHJ radio station, 72
Kickapoo Indian Sagwa, 229
King, Wong Doo, 43
"King of Chinatown." *See* Fong Ching
Kiowa Indians, 30, 114

Klingman, Lawrence, 184
Koischwitz, Max Otto, 156–57, 158
Konitzberg, Herman, 48
Kreymborg, Alfred, 206
Ku Klux Klan, 214
Kutter, H. L., 130, 134

labor disputes at Triangle Shirtwaist Factory,
    54
La Crosse, WI, 78
"Lady Bluebeard." *See* Gunness, Belle
    Sorensen
Lady of the Orchids, The (play), 200
Lake Selbusjoen, Norway, 46
Lamarr, Hedley (fictional character), 122
Lamphere, Ray, 49, 50, 51, 52
Lancaster, Burt, 184
Lane, James H., 101–106
La Porte, IN, 47, 48
Lapre, Don, 11, 227–33
Laurel, Stan, 57
Lawrence, KS, massacre, 104–105
Leatherface (fictional character), 82
Leavenworth prison, 134
Lee, Lorelei (fictional character), 201
Lee, Robert E., 107, 108
Leech, Margaret, 108
Lee Chuck, 41
Lem Sier, 42
Leo XIII (pope), 183
Letellier, Henri, 199
Lewis, Del, 126
Lewis, Mercy, 89
Lily Dale, NY, 169
Lincoln, Mary (Todd), 108, 111, 165
Lincoln, Abraham and the missing body-
    guard, 107–112
Linden Place (mansion), 20
Little Hellions (street gang), 63
"Little Pete." *See* Fong Ching
Little Review, The (magazine), 205
Liveright, Horace B., 203–204
Loeb, Gladys, 207
London, England, 174–75

Long Branch saloon, 117
"long cons," 131, 133
Loos, Anita, 201
Lord Haw Haw. *See* Joyce, William
Lord Jim (Conrad), 184
Lord's Prayer, 89
Los Angeles, CA, 113–14, 127
Los Angeles Times, 72
Louisiana Territory, 26, 27, 28
Lynchburg, VA, 144

"Making Money" (self-help package sold by
    Lapre), 228, 230
malpractice and John Brinkley, 69–75
manslaughter, Harris and Blanck charged
    with, 57
Mapia (island), 184
Marble Heart, The (play), 110
Marlowe, Christopher, 214
Marona, IL, 62–63
Marshall Islands, 184
Mason, Samuel, 23–28
Massachusetts
    Herbert Bridgman in, 189
    Hetty Green in, 172
    politicians from, 212
    Salem witch trials, 85–92
massacres
    James Lane causing Lawrence massacre,
        101–106
    John Chivington and Sand Creek mas-
        sacre, 29–35
    St. Valentine's Day massacre, 62, 66
Masters, Catherine. *See* O'Keefe, Catherine
Masters, Edgar Lee, 206
Masterson, Bat, 114, 118
Masterson, Sky (fictional character), 138
Mather, Cotton, 88, 90
Mather, Increase, 90
Matteson, T. H., 89
Maus, Mary America, 109
Maverick, Maury, 217
Maxson, Joe, 50
May, James, 27–28

Mays, Billy, 229
McCarthy, Joseph, 216, 217
McCormack, John, 212
McCormack-Dickstein Committee. *See*
  House of Representatives, House Un-
  American Activities Committee
McGovern's bar and brothel, 63
McKelway, St. Clair, 224
McLaury, Frank, 122
McLaury, Tom, 122
McManus, George, 140–41
media manipulation, 187–93
medical malpractice of John Brinkley, 69–75
medical treatment, Hetty Green trying to
  obtain free, 172, 177
mediums. *See* spiritualism and the Fox sisters
Memphis, TN, 71, 205
Men, Marriage, and Me (Joyce), 196
Mendel, Gregor, 146
Meriwether, Doc, 131
Merlo, Mike, 65
Method (movie), 51
Methodist church, 94, 99
Metropolitan Police Force, 108, 109, 111
Mexican-American War, 102
Mexican Rurales, 126
Meyer, Andrew, 200–201
"Midge at the Mike" (Nazi radio show), 156
Milford, KS, 69, 70, 72, 118
Milton, John, 12, 30
mind-reading scam, 133
Minna and Myself (Bodenheim), 206–207, 210
Minnesota, 48, 105
Minnesota Fats, 138
Miracle on 34th Street (movie), 225
Miranda (ship), 190
miser, Hetty Green as a, 174, 176–77
Mishawaka, IN, 49
Miss 1917 (musical revue), 198
Mississippi
  Maxwell Bodenheim in, 204
  Samuel Mason in, 26, 27
Mississippi River, 23, 24, 26, 28
Miss Kitty (fictional character), 115

Missouri
  Alvin Thomas in, 139, 140
  James Lane in, 101–106
  Samuel Mason in, 26
Missouri-Kansas border war, 102, 104–105
  attack on Lawrence, KS, 103–104
Missouri State Guard, 103
Mister 880 (movie), 225
Mob and Dean O'Banion, 61–67
Mobeetie, TX, 118
Monroe, Harriet, 205
Monroe, Marilyn, 201
Moo, John, 48, 50
Moran, George "Bugs," 64, 66
Morgan, J. P., 94, 133, 177
Mormonism, 166
Morner, Gosta, 200
Mount, The (DeWolf mansion), 16
Mountain View, OK, 118
Mount Carmel Cemetery, 62
Mount McKinley (Denali), 190
Mouvet, Maurice, 199
Mueller, Edward. *See* Juettner, Emerich
Munro, Wilfred H., 22
Murray, Ed, 38
Mutiny on the Bounty (screenplay), 206

Naked on Roller Skates (Bodenheim), 208
Natchez Trace, 24, 27
National Archives, 191
National Geographic (magazine), 191
National Geographic Society, 190, 192
National Historic Landmark, 60
Native Americans
  capture of Libby Thompson, 114
  massacre of, 29–35
Natural History (magazine), 191
Nazi Germany
  and eugenics, 145, 149, 150
  Mildred Gillars as propagandist for,
    153–59
  US Congress reaction to, 212, 213–14,
    217
Nelson, Byron, 138, 142

New Bedford, MA, 173
New Castle, PA, 49
New Deal, 208
New Jersey
    Daniel Drew in, 210
    and Hetty Green, 176, 178
    Maxwell Bodenheim in, 210
New Madrid, MO, 26, 27
Newman, Paul, 131
New Mexico, John Chivington in, 30, 31, 33, 34
Newport, RI, 17
New Republic (magazine), 207
New Rochelle, NY, 203–204
newspaper classifieds, 230
New Strategies (company), 230
New York & Erie Railroad, 97–98
New York City, 95, 97
    Alvin Thomas in, 140
    Daniel Drew in, 95, 97
    Emerich Juettner in, 219–25
    Hetty Green in, 171–78
    Isaac Harris and Max Blanck in, 53–60
    Maggie and Kate Fox in, 168–69
    Maxwell Bodenheim in, 206, 208, 209
    Mildred Gillars in, 155
    Peggy Hopkins Joyce in, 195–96, 198, 199
    Samuel Dickstein in, 212
New York Daily Tribune (newspaper), 184
New Yorker (magazine), 158–59, 207, 224
New York Evening Post (newspaper), 200
New York Law School, 212
New York State
    Charles Davenport in, 143–51
    Daniel Drew in, 93–99
    estate taxes for Hetty Green, 178
    Herbert Bridgman in, 189
    Maggie and Kate Fox in, 163–70
    Maxwell Bodenheim in, 203
    Samuel Dickstein in, 211–18
New York State Supreme Court, 215, 217
New York Times (newspaper), 175, 178, 192, 208, 217, 224
New York Tribune (newspaper), 51, 189
New York University, 60

900 telephone lines, 230, 231
Nogales, AZ, 124, 126
Norfolk, VA, 25, 197
Norfolk Street Synagogue, 212
Norris, Frank, 42
North Korea and counterfeit American currency, 223
North Pole, discovery of, 188–89, 190, 191–92, 193
North Side Gang, 62, 64, 65, 66
North State Street flower shop, 64
Notorious (screenplay), 206
Noureddin Vlora (prince of Albania), 199

O'Banion, Charles "Dean," 61–67
O'Banion, Viola, 61, 64
Ohio
    John Chivington in, 30
    Mildred Gillars in, 155, 159
    Samuel Mason in, 23–28
Ohio River, 23–24, 26, 28
Ohio Wesleyan University, 155, 159
O. K. Corral, 122–23
O'Keefe, Catherine, 180, 182, 184
O'Keefe, Charlotte, 182, 183
O'Keefe, David, 179–85
O'Keefe, Dolibu, 182, 183, 184
O'Keefe, Louisa "Lulu," 180, 182, 184
O'Keefe's Kanteen, 185
O'Keefe's Waterfront Inn, 185
"Old Mr. 880." *See* Juettner, Emerich
Old West, the
    Burt Alvord (outlaw), 121–28
    James-Younger gang, 104–106, 125
    Libby Thompson (madam in the Old West), 113–19
Olsen, Jennie, 47, 50
O'Neill, Eugene, 206
On the Origin of Species (Darwin), 166
Oradell, NJ, 210
Orange Glo, 229
Order No. 11, 104–105
O'Reilly, Mae, 51
Osage River, 101

Osborn, Sarah, 87
Oscar nomination for Edmund Gwenn, 225
Osceola, MO, sacking of, 103, 105, 106
Others (magazine), 206
Ouijah board, 168
Our American Cousin (play), 108
outlaws
    Burt Alvord, 121–28
    James-Younger gang, 104–106
    Samuel Mason, 23–28
Overman Committee, 213
Oxford University, 88
OxiClean, 229

Pacific region, David O'Keefe in, 179–85
Page, Patti, 114
Palace Theatre, 198
Palau (island), 181
Palm Beach, FL, 199
Palo Pinto, TX, 118
Pani, Joe, 199
panics of 1893 and 1897, 176
Paris, France
    Mildred Gillars in, 155
    Peggy Hopkins Joyce in, 196, 199
Parker, John Frederick, 12, 107–112
Parris, Betty, 86, 87, 90
Parris, Samuel and Elizabeth, 86–87
*Passing of the Great Race, or The Racial Basis
    of European History, The* (Grant), 149
PBS, 21
Pearce, AZ, 124
Pearl Harbor, 156
Peary, Josephine, 188
Peary, Marie, 188
Peary, Robert E., 12, 187–93
Peary Arctic Club, 189, 192
Peg Leg Annie, 117
People's Line, 96
Perkins, Frances, 59
Phips, William, 88, 90
Phoenix, AZ, 229
photoengraving counterfeit money. *See*
    Juettner, Emerich

pirate, Samuel Mason as, 23–28
pitchman, Don Lapre as, 227–33
Plainfield, WI, 77–78, 79, 80, 81
Pocket Fisherman, 229
poet of Greenwich Village, Maxwell Boden-
    heim as, 203–210
Poetry (magazine), 205
Poland, German invasion of, 155
Polly (ship), 19
Ponzi schemes, 133
Popeil, Ron, 229
Portland, ME, 155
Portuguese Diamond, 201
Postal Service, 74
Powers, Tom (fictional character), 62
prairie dogs, Libby Thompson keeping as
    pet, 116
Prescott, Zebulon, 24
Price, Sterling, 103
Princess Lotus Blossom (a pitch artist), 229
privateers, 19
*Profit Per Minute: How to Get into the 900
    Number Business* (Lapre), 230
Prohibition, 62, 64, 66, 140, 197, 207
propagandist
    Herbert Bridgman selling the Robert
        Peary story, 187–93
    Mildred Gillars "Axis Sally" for Nazi
        Germany, 153–59
prostitution, 115, 116, 117, 118–19
Providence, RI, 229
psychic phenomena. *See* spiritualism and the
    Fox sisters
Psycho (movie/book), Ed Gein as inspiration
    for, 11, 77–82
psychopaths
    Adolf Hitler as, 154
    Belle Sorensen Gunnes as, 52
    Micajah and Wiley Harpe as, 26
Public Enemy, The (movie), 62
Putnam, Ann, 90
Putnam family, 89
pyromania, 46

Qing Dynasty, 38
Quakers, 166, 172
Quantrill, William, 104

Race Betterment Foundation, 147
Race Crossing in Jamaica (Davenport), 148–49
racial purity. *See* eugenics and Charles
    Davenport
radio, use of, 72–73, 74
rai (Yap currency), 181, 185
railroads, 39, 97, 147, 175, 176, 179
    train robberies, 124–25
Rathbone, Henry, 108
Rawling, Linus, 24
Reconstruction, 111–12
Red Banks, KY, 25
Redfield, Mary, 164
Redford, Robert, 131
Red Menace, 215
Replenishing Jessica (Bodenheim), 204, 207
Revolutionary War, 19, 25
Rhode Island
    Don Lapre in, 229
    James DeWolf in, 16, 17, 18, 19, 20
Rhode Island College (Brown University), 19
Richmond, VA, 197
Ripper, Jack D. (fictional character), 148
river pirate, Samuel Mason as, 23–28
Roaring Twenties, 70, 140, 196–97, 204,
    207, 210
Robinson, Abby Howland, 172, 173
Robinson, Edward Mott, 172, 173–74
Robinson, Henrietta Howland. *See* Green,
    Hetty
Rochester, NY, 166, 167
Rockefeller, John D., 94, 177
Rockefeller Foundation, 147
Rocky Mountain News (newspaper), 33
Rogers, AR, 138–39
rogues, definition of, 11
Roman Empire treatment of forgers, 223
Roosevelt, Franklin D., 59, 154, 208
Roosevelt, Theodore "Teddy," 147
Rosenberg, Julius and Ethel, 215

Rothstein, Arnold, 140–41
Rovere, Richard H., 158–59
Royal Geographical Society of Denmark, 190
RRG (German state radio system), 154, 155,
    156, 158
Rubin, Jerry, 216
Rüdin, Ernst, 150
Runyan, Paul, 138
Runyon, Damon, 138
Russian Revolution, 213

safecracking, 63
St. David's Island, 181–82
St. Joseph, MO, 140
St. Louis, MO, 140
St. Paul's Methodist Episcopal Church, 99
St. Regis Hotel, 195
St. Valentine's Day Massacre, 62, 66
Salem witch trials, 12, 85–92
Sam Yup Company, 40
Sandburg, Carl, 111, 206
Sand Creek massacre, 29–35
San Francisco, CA
    Alvin Thomas in, 138, 140
    Fong Ching in, 37–43
San Francisco Chronicle (newspaper), 42
Santa Cruz (schooner), 184
Saracino, Sara and Tessie, 54, 56, 59
Saturday Night Live (TV show), 228
Savannah, GA, 180, 183
Sbarbaro funeral home, 61
scalps, collecting of, 25
Scandinavia, WI, 48
Schein, Minna, 206–207, 209, 210
Schofield Company, 64
scientific racism, 148
Scott, Cora L. V., 167–68
scoundrels, definition of, 11
Sea Around Us, The (Carson), 209
séances. *See* spiritualism and the Fox sisters
*Secret Heroes: Everyday Americans Who
    Shaped Our World* (Martin), 11, 12
Secret Service and Emerich Juettner, 222,
    223, 224

selective breeding. *See* eugenics and Charles Davenport
Seminarius (merchantman ship), 16–17
Senate, 20, 216
Seneca Falls, NY, 166
serial killers
    Belle Sorensen Gunness, 45–52
    Ed Gein, 77–82
    John Brinkley, 75
Sewall, Samuel, 90
Shakers, 166
shell game, 131
Shepherd, William, 55–56
"Shirtwaist Kings." *See* Blanck, Max; Harris, Isaac
"short cons," 131
Shubert, Lee, 196
Sibley, John Langdon, 91
Sibley Warehouse, 64
Sicilian Union, 65
Silence of the Lambs, The (movie), 82
Silk Hat Harry (a pitch artist), 229
Silver Shirts of America, 213
Sioux Indians, 30, 33
Six Companies (Chinese benevolent associations), 40
Slaughter, John, 123–24
slavery
    issue of in Kansas Territory, 102
    James DeWolf as slave trader, 15–22
Slave Trade Act (1794), 19
Sleepless Night, A (play), 198
Slocum, Charles, 17
Slow Vision (Bodenheim), 208
Small Ads, Big Profits: How You Could Turn $30 into a Fortune (Lapre), 230
Smith, Joseph, 166
Smithsonian National Gem Collection, 201
Smokeless Ashtray, 229
Smoky Hill River, 32
Snead, Sam, 142
Some Like It Hot (screenplay), 206
Sonsorol (island), 184
Sorensen, Axel, 47

Sorensen, Belle. *See* Gunness, Belle Sorensen
Sorensen, Caroline, 47
Sorensen, Lucy, 47, 48, 50
Sorensen, Mads, 46–47
Sorensen, Myrtle, 47, 48, 50
Soule, Silas, 31, 32–33, 34
South Pacific, David O'Keefe in, 179–85
South Pole, 190
South Side gang, 64, 65
Soviet Union, Samuel Dickstein spying for, 212, 214–15
Spain, desire for the Caroline Islands, 183
Spanish-American War, 183
Sparrow, Jack (fictional character), 28
Spaulding, Evan, 199
Special Committee on Un-American Activities Authorized to Investigate Nazi Propaganda and Certain Other Propaganda Activities (HUAC). *See* House of Representatives, House Un-American Activities Committee
spiritualism and the Fox sisters, 163–70
Sports Illustrated (magazine), 142
Springfield Republican (newspaper), 189
spy, Samuel Dickstein as, 212, 214–15
Squires, Charles, 34
Squirrel Tooth Alice. *See* Thompson, Libby
Stagecoach (screenplay), 206
Stalin, Joseph, 214
Stanford University, 148
Stanton, Edwin, 108
Starnes, Jo, 214
Star Saloon, 110
State University of New York, 189
Station for Experimental Evolution, 146, 150
steamboat business, 95–97
Steinbeck, John, 210
sterilization, involuntary. *See* eugenics and Charles Davenport
Steuer, Max, 57, 58
Stiles, Billy, 125–26
Sting, The (movie), 131
Stittsworth, William, 70, 72
stock manipulation/swindles, 97, 132

Storset, Brynhild Paulsdatter. *See* Gunness, Belle Sorensen

Stoughton, William, 85–92

striking workers at the Triangle Shirtwaist Factory, 54

strychnine poisoning, 47, 50

"Style Show" (vaudeville revue), 198

Sudan: Africa from Sea to Center, The (Bridgman), 189

suicides
    Don Lapre committing, 228, 232, 233
    women killing selves for Bodenheim, 207–208

Sunbeam Rest Home, 113–14

Sundance Kid, 126

Superman (TV show), 114

Supreme Court, 144–45, 149

Sweetwater, TX, 118

Swift meatpacking company, 70

swindlers. *See* hucksters, swindlers, and cons

Tarang (island), 182

Tarkio, MO, 49

tax avoidance/evasion, 178

Taylor's Hotel, 98

Tempe, AZ, 232

Tennessee
    John Brinkley in, 71
    Maxwell Bodenheim in, 205

Texas
    Alvin Thomas in, 138, 140, 142
    Hetty Green and, 172, 176
    John Brinkley in, 73, 74
    Joseph Weil and, 133
    Libby Thompson in, 114, 115, 116, 117, 118
    politicians from, 213, 217

Texas Chainsaw Massacre, The (movie), 82

Texas Rangers, 118, 123

Thalberg, Irving, 196

Third Colorado Cavalry, 30, 31

Third Reich. *See* Nazi Germany

This Is YOUR House Committee on Un-American Activities (HUAC pamphlet), 216

Thomas, Alvin Clarence (aka Titanic Thompson), 137–42

Thomas, Jeannette, 142

Thomas "Slim." *See* Thomas, Alvin Clarence (aka Titanic Thompson)

Thompson, Ben, 117

Thompson, Libby, 113–19

Thompson, Rance, 117

Thompson, "Texas Billy," 115–16, 117, 118

Thompson, Titanic. *See* Thomas, Alvin Clarence (aka Titanic Thompson)

three-card monte, 131

Timberline, 117

Time (magazine), 157, 158

Titanic (ship), 139

Tituba (slave), 87

Tobias, J. J., 72

Toguri, Iva (aka Tokyo Rose), 159

Tombstone, AZ, Burt Alvord in, 121–28

tongs. *See* Chinese gangs

Torrio, Johnny, 64, 65, 66

Traces of the Trade: A Story from the Deep North (documentary film), 21

Transatlantic Wife (Joyce), 200

treason, Mildred Gillars charged with, 154, 157, 158, 159

Treasury Department, 222

Triangle Shirtwaist Factory, 53–60

Triangle Trade, 17–18

Truman, Harry, 216

Truth about Belle Gunness, The (Gold Medal Books), 51

Turmoil, The (silent film), 198

Tuscola, IL, 48

Tweed, Boss, 97

Twentieth Century Fox, 225

tycoons, 94, 99, 147
    See also businessmen and women; hucksters, swindlers, and cons

un-American activities. *See* House of Representatives, House Un-American Activities Committee

Uncle Daniel. *See* Drew, Daniel

University of California Board of Regents, 148

University of Chicago, 146
    University of Chicago Law School, 72

University of Kansas, 106

University of Missouri, 106

Upton, Peggy. *See* Joyce, Peggy Hopkins

Vallee, Rudy, 200

Vanderbilt, Cornelius, 94, 96, 97, 98, 177

Vanities (theatrical revue), 200

Vassiliev, Alexander, 215

Verde-Grande Copper Mining Company, 133

Vermont and estate taxes for Hetty Green, 178

Vernon County, MO, 103

Villa, Pancho, 205

villains, definition of, 11

Vilnius, Lithuania, 211

Virginia
    Army of Northern Virginia, 107
    involuntary sterilizations in, 143–45, 148
    John Parker in, 109
    Samuel Mason in, 25

Virginia Colony for the Epileptic and Feebleminded, 144

Virtuous Girl, A (Bodenheim), 208

Vision of Invasion (radio play), 157, 158, 159

Wallace, Alfred Russel, 165

Wall Street, 12
    Daniel Drew, 94, 97, 99
    Hetty Green, 171–78

Wanderone, Rudolf. *See* Minnesota Fats

Warrington, James R., 129–30

Washburn, Emory, 91

Washington, DC
    Lincoln's missing bodyguard, 107–112
    Peggy Hopkins Joyce in, 197–98

Washington, George (misspelling of name on dollar bills), 221

Washington County, PA, 25

Washita River, 34

waterlogged cattle, 94

Water Witch (steamboat), 95–96

Watkins, Adeline, 81

Weil, Joseph "Yellow Kid," 129–35

Weinberg, Harold, 209

Weinstein, Allen, 215

Weiss, Earl "Hymie," 64, 66

Wellesley College, 177

Wesleyan University, 99

Western Union, 70

Weston, MO, 102

West Side Story (movie and play), 40

West Virginia
    Mildred Gillars in, 159
    Peggy Hopkins Joyce in, 197
    Samuel Mason in, 25

Weyl, Nathaniel, 159

whaling, 172–73

Wheeling, WV, 25

White, Scott, 124, 125

White, William Allen, 74–75

Whitney, Chauncey, 117

Wike, Sally, 70, 71

Willcox, AZ, 124, 125

Williams, Abigail, 87, 90

Williams, Hank, 73

Williams, William Carlos, 206

"Wilson's Liquor Vault and House for Entertainment," 26

Wisconsin, Ed Gein in, 77–78, 79, 80, 81

witch hunting, 85–92

Within My Horizon (Bridgman), 191

witness bribery, 58

Wolf Island, 26

Wolfman Jack, 73

Wong Chung, 38, 41

Worden, Bernice, 80, 81, 82

Worden, Frank, 80

Works Progress Administration, 208, 214

World Series, fixing of in 1919, 140

World War II, Mildred Gillars as propagandist for the Nazis, 153–59

WPA. *See* Works Progress Administration

Wyandot Indians, 31
Wynkoop, Edward, 30, 32, 33

XER radio station, 73–74

Yankee (brig), 19
Yap (island), 181–85
"Yellow Kid." *See* Weil, Joseph "Yellow Kid"
*"Yellow Kid" Weil: The Autobiography of
   America's Master Swindler* (Weil), 135
Yen Yuen, 41

Yoas, "Bravo Jaun," 125, 126
Younger, Bob, 105
Younger, Cole, 104, 105, 106
Younger, Jim, 105
YouTube, 232
Yuma Territorial Prison, 126–27

Ziegfeld Follies (musical revue), 198
Zito, Joseph, 56
Zucca, Rita, 158